D1611602

© 2002 by Northern Illinois University Press

Published by the Northern Illinois University Press, DeKalb, Illinois   60115

Manufactured in the United States using acid-free paper

All Rights Reserved

Library of Congress Cataloging-in-Publication Data

Marlett, Jeffrey D.

   Saving the heartland : Catholic missionaries in rural America / Jeffrey D. Marlett.

     p. cm.

   Includes bibliographical references and index.

   ISBN 0–87580–291–5 (alk. paper)

     1. Catholic Church—Missions—United States—History—20th century. 2.

   United States—Church history—20th century. I. Title.

   BV2766.C5 M37 2002

    266'.273—dc21   2001052156

Frontispiece photograph: Bishop Thomas Toolen raising the Blessed Sacrament on the St. Theresa motor chapel; Father Arthur Terminiello kneeling behind him inside the trailer, Montgomery, Alabama. (Courtesy Loyola University, Chicago Archives)

Contents

Acknowledgments

The legions helped me complete this book. It seems awkward to cram the names of so many people into such a short space, but every one of them helped in some way or another. I alone bear responsibility for any remaining errors or mistakes.

The first and most belated thanks go to my parents, James and Carol, and my sister, Jennifer, for all their good-humored support. The same gratitude extends to the Marlett family in Indiana. The rootedness of all these people has blessed me with a perspective that I hope will receive the respect and attention it has long deserved.

Martin Johnson and the editors at Northern Illinois University Press pursued this project with patient interest. Parts of chapters 1 and 2 appeared previously in *U.S. Catholic Historian* (fall 1998), *Ecotheology* (January/June 1999), and the anthology of papers read at the Dorothy Day/Catholic Worker Centenary and published by Marquette University Press. I appreciate the permission for republication granted by, respectively, Christopher Kauffman, Mary Grey, and William Thorn.

A significant group of archivists graciously allowed me access to their holdings: Phil Runkel at Marquette University; Don Buske, the archivist for the Glenmary Home Missioners in Cincinnati; Father Louis M. Derbes, C.M., the archivist at St. Mary of the Barrens Seminary in Perryville, Missouri; Father John Miller, C.S.C., and the staff of the Catholic Central Union of America in St. Louis; and Brother Michael Grace, S.J., the archivist for Loyola University, Chicago. Phil Runkel merits special mention for his gracious and patient guidance.

The following diocesan archives facilitated what became chapter 4 by answering my first inquiries concerning motor missions: Denver, Colorado; Lincoln, Nebraska; Mobile, Alabama; Nashville, Tennessee; and Wichita, Kansas. John Waide, director of the Saint Louis University archives, always gave encouragement and advice. One floor below John in the Pius XII Memorial Library, Ellen Aufenthie and Ron Crown answered my queries about reference and interlibrary loan matters. During my one year at Lyon

College, Cathy Whittenton, Karen Austin, and Karl Kemp supplied crucial assistance with interlibrary loan and computer matters. This support continued at Saint Rose, thanks to Pete Koonz, Kate Moss, and the Neil Hellmann Library staff.

Natalie Villmer and the Rural Parish Workers of Christ the King provided me with a great lunch as well as telling me their marvelous story. Julian Pleasants kindly sent me a wonderful letter and several articles on rural issues. Timothy Miller, Christy Cousino, and Sarah McFarland Taylor supplied some important insights concerning biodynamic farming and contemporary Catholic literature. Meeting Craig Prentiss brought friendship as well as the benefit of some solid scholarship. It has been a pleasure getting to know Andrew Moore and his work concerning Catholics in Alabama.

Like many others, I have been blessed by studying with some great teachers, such as Sandy Newcomer, Marion Falmer, and, at Vanderbilt Divinity School, Jack Forstman. Three from Wabash College—David Blix, John Fischer, and Bill Placher—have continued to mentor and advise me. It is an honor to thank them for all their help and friendship. Bill especially has shaped my personal and professional goals; his influence extends far beyond the work at hand. At Saint Louis University, James T. Fisher started it all by insisting on what became my dissertation subject. His buoyant sense of irreverent humor and incisive comments made sure the work stayed lively. Intercessory assistance also came from Belden Lane, Kenneth Parker, and Richard Valantasis.

After Saint Louis University, I went from working for outstanding teachers to working with a group of them at Lyon College. Brad Gitz, Bob Gregerson, Ed Tenace, Helen Robbins, and David Stricklin all provided support and friendship throughout my first full year in college teaching. Lyon also supplied travel funds, for which I am especially grateful. In 1998 I moved to The College of Saint Rose in Albany, New York. Mary Daly credits the college as the place where her Be-dazzling journey began; for me, it has become the harbor in which this book's journey concludes. Saint Rose provided the time and professional-development funding necessary for me to complete the manuscript and attend conferences to discuss it. My colleagues Laura Weed, Ben Clansy, Melissa Clarke, and Bruce Johnston have probably come to learn more about American Catholicism's green underside than they ever imagined possible. Students Michelle D'Onofrio, Stacie Leininger, Regina Vertone, Anthony Wilson, and Kevin Wood all hunted down many final details. Saint Rose, moreover, has given me the opportunity to live a little. Few deserve more thanks for that than Matt Amico, Ken Scott, and the rest of the noontime basketball league.

Good friends do make the long, strange trip of research and writing all the easier: back at home, Matt Ticknor, Mike McGaha, Deanna Cole McElveen, and Erick Stirewalt Lourraine; at Saint Louis University, Laura Hobgood-Oster, Kevin O'Connor, David Vila, Lori Hunt, Trey Hammond,

Saving the Heartland

Catholic Rural Life?

> Behold the sower went forth to sow. . . . And others fell
> upon good ground and they brought forth fruit, some a
> hundredfold, some sixtyfold, and some thirtyfold. He that
> hath ears to hear, let him hear.
>
> —Matthew 13:3–9[1]

The Catholic rural life movement, more than any other group within the American Catholic Church, combined its faith with everyday American life. The results often took some unusual forms. One night in 1938, a group of Vincentian priests readied their "trailer chapel" for a street-preaching service in Fremont, Missouri. However, no one showed up. The priests realized that everyone in the tiny Ozark town had stayed home listening to the Joe Louis–Max Schmeling heavyweight boxing match. So they hooked their own radio up to the speakers on their trailer and, using their portable power generator, turned up the volume. They succeeded in drawing a crowd, and the self-styled "Catholic revival" began soon after the fight ended. Another group of Vincentian clergy in Fremont, Nebraska, used the same tactic and enjoyed a crowd "extraordinarily large that night."[2]

Such innovation was commonplace among the various groups making up the Catholic rural life movement. However, appreciation from American Catholics was not forthcoming then, nor has it been since from scholars of American Catholic history. "Every cause," wrote Walter Ong, S.J., "must be dead at least once to appeal to the American Catholic soul." A widely respected linguistic philosopher, Ong applied this remark to the declining Catholic interest in scholasticism. It was a philosophical system, Ong thought, that had seen its day come and go more than once. At the time his words seemed prophetic.[3] The Catholic Revival indeed appeared, as one historian has described it recently, as "a world about to fall."[4] Between the world wars the intellectual program that fused committed faith with objective reason had won support from both Catholic and non-Catholic critics. By 1957, when Ong made his remark, the Catholic Revival simply seemed creaky and old-fashioned. Within five years a new pontificate and the Second

Vatican Council (1962–65) had solidified that belief. A new day had indeed dawned in Roman Catholicism, and the old way of doing things would no longer suffice. Much as the Church had earlier distanced itself from its own Jewish heritage, Catholics inspired by the Council now viewed the Catholic Revival as a mind-numbing, legalistic, authoritarian, and inauthentic vision of the faith. New wine indeed demanded new wineskins, and since the Catholic Revival, after all, retrieved and celebrated the Church's medieval days, it certainly had to go.

Lost in the rush was a particular vision of social and environmental stewardship that had flourished in the middle decades of the century known as Catholic agrarianism, or the Catholic rural life movement. Built upon the Catholic Revival's neo-Scholastic edifice, it was given to occasional bouts of good old-fashioned Catholic triumphalism. However, Catholic agrarians also shared a deep concern for the trajectory that America's industrial heritage forecast for the nation. In attempting to solve a variety of dilemmas facing rural America and especially rural Catholics, Catholic agrarianism became quite well known in the period before the Second Vatican Council. If Peter Huff's study of the converted Southern Agrarian poet Allen Tate tells the story correctly, it was Catholic agrarianism that attracted much of the non-Catholic attention to the Catholic Revival. It is ironic that the overwhelmingly urban (and intellectually stodgy, if some critics are to be believed) Roman Catholic Church in America began its embrace of modern life in rural America, precisely where the Church was least well represented.[5]

At first glance this should not seem so surprising; the Christian tradition provided ample material for such a movement. Scripture itself radiates rural and agricultural images, such as Israel's land of milk and honey and Amos's restorative vision of the plow overtaking the reaper. These culminate in Jesus' Gospel parables of the Good Shepherd, the Sower, and the lilies of the field. Within the Catholic tradition itself, Benedictine monasticism has usually interpreted its exhortation "ora et labora" as applying first to farming. Yet the story of American Catholicism is centered in the city, and with good reason. The 1910 census indicated that approximately 80 percent of all American Catholics lived in urban areas. So it stood to reason that farming was an occupation with few Catholic practitioners.

By offering a Catholic perspective on how agriculture might reform itself, however, the Catholic rural life movement found a willing non-Catholic audience. Along with just about every other aspect of modern life, agriculture has been transformed repeatedly during the twentieth century. At times only a small group of environmentalists and farm-reform advocates seemed to notice. Many of the leading farm-reform advocates saw the rural church as part of the problem as well as part of the solution. Rural churches needed help preaching the message of reform, either of farming or of religion itself. The Catholic agrarians joined this reform group and assumed the same attitudes toward rural Catholics. They insisted that Catholicism integrated Christian faith and rural life far more completely than any other response to agricultural and ecological crises. A better life for everybody lay in listening to, and then applying, Church teachings.

> Souls are not soils but the soil of the country church has a great bearing on the souls of the parish. The deterioration of many a rural church may be placed to the deterioration of the soil; the erosion of the soil terminating in the souls or people of a country church. To hold the people on the land and in rural churches there must be the opportunity to be able to live on and off of the land. The good earth becomes common ground, the foundation of the prosperity and the continuance of the rural group and their church.[6]

George Hildner, the Missouri priest who wrote these words, and the rest of the Catholic rural life movement suggested that the entire Church in the United States would benefit from a similar "pegging" in rural America. The relationship between "the land" and the Church came to serve as a basis from which a certain group of American Catholics prescribed a social and spiritual program for all Americans.

Besides its plan, its setting made Catholic agrarianism revolutionary. "Rural" simply does not appear in the Catholic lexicon. The Catholic agrarians sought to change that through some familiar channels. Intellectually, they took their cue from the Catholic Revival. On the popular level, "Catholic Action" became a shorthand term for the movement monitoring how all the intellectual work trickled down to parishioners filling the pews. In the United States, Catholic Action held a vision of completely "Catholicizing" all aspects of American life. The members of this grassroots movement strove, with clerical assistance, to make their Catholic faith noticeable and applicable in the realms they knew best—the world of work and family. Professional societies figured prominently; Catholic psychologists, lawyers, doctors, and educators all formed their own groups to promote their distinctness from their non-Catholic colleagues in the same profession. At a more personal level, numerous devotional organizations—the Legion of Mary, the Holy Name society, sodalities, the Sacred Heart—and a host of saints connected with various ethnic constituencies offered to make the faith real in every Catholic's life, no matter where they worked. Through one organization, the National Catholic Rural Life Conference (NCRLC), Catholic agrarians pursued the same goals for American farmers.[7]

From this perspective, the Catholic rural life movement offered a familiar program in an unfamiliar (rural) location. The result was a melding of city and country, Catholics and non-Catholics, agrarianism and urbanization, tradition and innovation. Throughout the twentieth century, the nation's rural denizens have usually been viewed at least somewhat negatively. They have been the object of condescension (such as the barbed wit of H. L. Mencken or the current reaction against country music's resurgence) or syrupy sentimentalism that praises the simple moral virtues of rural life but does not acknowledge any of its complexities.

Antiruralism has held particular, albeit unnoticed, importance for American Catholics. Since the 1970s, the historiography of American Catholicism has rightly emphasized how Catholic immigrant communities, by insisting on protecting their own ethnic identities, helped create the modern American urban area. This increased the distance between Catholics and the nation's rural heritage. Robert Orsi has shown that because Italians in New York understandably wanted to preserve something of their ethnic heritage, they took steps to avoid "lapsing" into becoming "merely" Americans. Even after World War II, when American Catholics strode into the suburbs, they did so in their own style. Of course Catholics were Americans; hadn't they helped win the war? Wasn't their growing presence in the suburbs proof that "even a Catholic" could pursue the American dream? The hard, smelly realities of farm life seemed far removed from all the confidence, then as well as today. This continued ignorance at both popular and scholarly levels of rural American Catholicism was precisely what Catholic agrarians had struggled to bring to an end.[8]

This book explores the Catholic agrarian agenda and the theological vision that motivated it. Some of the usual suspects of twentieth-century American Catholic life will be covered: the radio priest Charles Coughlin, converts Dorothy Day and Thomas Merton, the European Catholic apologists G. K. Chesterton and Hilaire Belloc, and popes Pius X, XI, and XII. After that, names and locations rapidly lose familiarity. What about the Company of St. Isidore, a rural Catholic devotional league that once enjoyed ten thousand paying members? What about Catholic street-preaching in small towns across the Midwest and South, where priests conducted the Mass in English while facing the people (twenty or thirty years before this became standard practice) and where the Bible translation of choice was the King James Version? What about Catholic attempts at rural communal living, decades before the well-documented countercultural efforts of the 1960s? What about the theological presumption beneath much of this, which connected Christ's promise of eternal life to farming the land—a vocation in a location removed from the experience of most American Catholics? All these expressions of Catholic agrarianism emerged in the great beyond that was rural America. The field of American Catholic studies has widened considerably beyond narratives of bishops, missionary priests, and hardworking nuns (although the latter still deserve far more attention than they receive). This book contributes to the newer narratives by focusing on Catholic agrarianism's interaction with rural America.

In doing so, it also contributes to the ongoing discussion of pre–Vatican II Catholicism. Philip Gleason has noted two trends within postconciliar historiography: one that rejects the immediate preconciliar past in search of a "usable" past, and another that attempts to understand how the postconciliar Church emerged from the time just before the Council. This study follows the continuities, not the sudden differences, though this choice stems less from any ideological agenda than from the rather surprising nature of the subject matter. Much of what American Catholicism has become preserves some link to the Catholic agrarian past. This holds true for certain strands in American cultural and intellectual life, too. After all, the countercultural farm communes started by Catholics and those started later, in the 1960s, have more in common than just dirt.[9]

Similarly, the Liturgical Movement's pursuit of a more "natural" celebration of the Christian mysteries sprang partially from its embrace of Catholic agrarianism; it also sought to connect with the passion lurking in American culture for simplicity and "down-home" authenticity. Much of what the Catholic agrarians said about nature could—shorn of its Catholic identity—be mistaken for contemporary environmentalism, including even deep ecology. Long before multiculturalism became part of the American cultural dialogue, the Catholic agrarians realized that rural Catholics, just like any other group, needed their own devotions, celebrations, and publications. Essentially a subculture all their own, rural Catholics could thereby maintain their identity in the face of an equally vibrant thread of American life—the pressure to conform.

This much was certain: the Catholic agrarians were Americans concerned about farming. To them, agriculture, much like the Mass, created a channel of saving grace for the entire nation when performed properly. Many other Americans felt exactly the same way, minus the Catholic emphasis, of course. Catholic agrarians joined a whole host of other groups concerned with improving how American farmers farmed. At the same time, the Catholic rural life movement joined another movement (not at all mutually exclusive with the farm-reform efforts) that attempted to create what might best be called a "resettlement," or repopulation, of rural America: because rural life was so beneficial, the demographic shift toward the city had to be reversed.

These affiliations placed Catholic agrarians in contact with secular agrarians (such as Ralph Borsodi and the preconversion Allen Tate), as well as other religiously based rural interest groups (such as the American Country Life Association and the Jewish Agricultural Society). They also placed the Catholic agrarians in an awkward relationship with the very people the Catholic rural life movement sought to help: rural Catholics. Similar to the Catholic community in Latin America today, indigenous practice and official institutions often stood at odds. There were Catholics living in rural Maine, Wisconsin, and New Mexico, but their religious affiliation might have been all they had in common. The Catholic agrarians had fewer geographical limitations. They were not the first to notice the various traditions of rural Catholicism (although they saw only one legitimate tradition), but they were the first to elevate rural life as something meaningful for all American Catholics. They made assumptions about rural life in America that eventually did not match the realities. As will be seen, the experiences of rural Catholics occasionally closely resembled those of their non-Catholic neighbors. Sometimes that was the problem: rural Catholics seemed to blend in too well. This created a dilemma for Catholic agrarians. The very group they extolled as both preeminently American and Catholic could at times be *too* American, and that meant "too Protestant." When the terms of this dialectic changed in the 1950s, these assumptions and concerns about rural America became the Catholic agrarians' undoing.[10]

This incongruity between message and reality reveals that studying rural Catholicism introduces people, themes, texts, and locations far different from the standard urban narratives.[11] What defines "American Catholicism" becomes even broader, because now it must include some of the most traditionally American images and values, ones that are intrinsically rural. This is not to suggest that rural American Catholicism stands completely separate from urban Catholicism, but it is certainly different enough that one risks misstatement to speak of American Catholicism and have in mind only images of urban and suburban parishes in Boston, New York, Philadelphia, or Chicago. It is important to remember James Davidson's admonition in the preface to his eloquent study of classical Athens and its people: "[It is dangerous] to think of them as our cousins and to interpret everything in our own terms." And yet the Catholic agrarians, much like the Greeks, will at times seem quite familiar. Nevertheless,"they are not our cousins, but neither are they our opposites. They are just different, just trying to be themselves."[12] In its marriage of American culture and Catholicism, the Catholic rural life movement requires us to distinguish between the familiar and the foreign.[13]

Why these links between past and present have remained relatively undiscussed cuts to the heart of a greater assumption about American life. Even though Thomas Jefferson made citizen-farmers the foundation of his American vision, rural America has stood as the mysterious "Other" against which "sophisticated" identities have been constructed. Jim Goad calls this opposition an "ideological *Anschluss* against white trash." Following Edward Said's argument in *Orientalism,* what is considered "rural" in the nation usually has more to do with the way urban Americans perceive rurality than with its reality. The Catholic rural life movement, peopled with Catholics fleeing urban areas, certainly experienced this prejudice. It extends beyond scholarship to popular culture, in movies such as *Deliverance* and *Ma and Pa Kettle* and in the once-thriving interest in frontiersmen such as Davy Crockett or rogues such as the Missouri bandit Jesse James.[14]

The enshrinement of the rural "Other" runs deep in the American mind. The current discussions of multiculturalism and globalism only reinforce this otherness when rural voices are presented merely as opponents to such perspectives. Contemporary criticisms of the damaging environmental impact of modern agribusiness occasionally extend to the few remaining American farmers, who are now "not much more than . . . tractor driver[s] and poison sprayer[s]." Rural America is now often construed, in the words of Kevin Flynn and Gary Gerhardt, as "the new 'red, white, and blue'—red neck, white skin, and blue collar." As Said suggests, what these extrarural discussions do is silence, or at least ignore, rural voices themselves. The silence, though, broods with rebellion. J. W. Williamson warns that "buried within that reassurance for an urban audience is an appalling ambiguity: the sense that these [rural] people survive and even thrive despite our low opinion of their worth."[15]

These issues will appear in the following examination of Catholic agrarianism, its followers, and its discontents. This study will, at times, recall Michel Foucault's wish to pursue a discourse in a labyrinth "forcing it to go far from itself, finding overhangs that reduce and deform its itinerary."[16] The rural Midwest enjoys most of the attention, followed by the South. The Latino/a Catholic experience in the United States admittedly receives scant treatment. Chapter 1 examines the emergence of Catholic agrarianism's antiurban theology and the organizations that fostered it. Chapter 2 studies Catholics' rural colonization efforts, the culmination of Catholic agrarianism's utopian endeavors. This trend in American Catholic life actually surfaced much earlier and contributed to the thin but unbroken line of communitarianism in American religious history. Chapter 3 turns to the human material the Catholic agrarians hoped to improve and defend: rural Catholics themselves. Often, though, the laity itself determined the extent to which the official programs were followed. Catholics had arrived in rural America long before the Catholic rural life movement considered moving them there. The alienation of some rural Catholics from Catholic agrarianism's policies and adherents stemmed from certain rural realities that the agrarian ideologues frequently brushed aside. This disparity, far from being merely a reaction to the clerical heavy hand, follows a thread beginning with the original settlement of rural Catholic America. Chapter 4 examines an instance where the Catholic rural life movement did manage a unique and successful interaction with rural America—the "motor missions" that became street-preaching events. As they gained favor among Catholic agrarians and rural America, these missions blended Catholic and evangelical Protestant elements almost seamlessly.

Those within the Catholic rural life movement ultimately sought to fulfill a basic pastoral goal: improving the spiritual lives of their rural congregations. The myriad ways in which they pursued that goal belied Walter Ong's remark that only dead causes appeal to the Catholic soul. For a while, at least, the Catholic agrarians and their friends outside the Church did not need to resuscitate the rural American ideal. The cause was not yet lost, and green fields shone on the horizon.

Fertile Land and Fertile Souls

The Catholic Rural Life Movement and Its Antiurban Theology

> For we have not here a lasting city,
>
> but we seek one that is to come.
>
> —Hebrews 13:14

The Catholic rural life movement in the United States enjoyed its greatest activity in the mid-twentieth century. It took inspiration equally from secular sources, such as Jefferson's agrarianism and the budding environmentalist movement, and the neo-Scholastic Catholic Revival, whose principles it shared with other Catholic organizations. Committed to an antiurban vision of small subsistence farms, a minimum of centralized industry, and homogenous religious communities, the adherents of the Catholic rural life movement inaugurated a vigorous program to instill this agrarian model of the Church among parish priests, women religious, and the laity of rural America. These projects were supported by a theological worldview in which farming sacramentally represented the soul's relationship with God. According to Catholic agrarians, farming sustained what God had begun in creation and had completed with the Incarnation in Jesus Christ: it was divinely appointed care for God's own world.

Catholic agrarianism emerged in large part as a response to the crises plaguing rural America in the 1920s. The "Catholic rural problem," as it came to be called, arose from the Church's complete reliance on urban areas, not the countryside. Father Edwin V. O'Hara, raised on a Minnesota farm and trained as a sociologist, understood the importance of the social networks of rural communities and their parishes and was one of the first to perceive a relationship between the small-town Catholic parish and the more numerous ones in America's cities:

> Population flows from the country to the city. Just as the city protects the source of its water supply to keep it wholesome and abundant, city Catholic parishes have a religious interest in maintaining strong rural parishes where a well-

instructed and abundant Catholic population may flow each generation. The decline of the country parish will mark the decline of the Church in America.[1]

O'Hara wrote that in 1927. This unknown priest declared, one year before New York Catholic Alfred E. "Al" Smith lost a presidential election largely because he could not convince Protestant voters of his political virtues, that the rural Catholic neighbors of these same Protestants stood as the Church's future. Seemingly brash in its conclusion, this view of Catholic rural America would remain a fixture of American Catholicism until the Second Vatican Council.

The paradoxical belief that the future of urban Catholic America depended upon the spiritual and physical fertility of rural Catholics rested on the desire to cure what O'Hara had labeled the "Catholic rural problem." With his sociology background, he had uncovered in the 1910 census records a disturbing fact: urban birthrates had fallen, while those in rural areas had increased. O'Hara's fear stemmed from his knowledge that, since the middle of the previous century, the majority of American Catholics had lived in cities—approximately 80 percent by 1910. (The census also reported that, for the first time, a majority of the U.S. population lived in urban areas.) Declining urban birthrates and the Catholic Church's urban character laid the basis for the "Catholic rural problem": O'Hara concluded that if the Church wanted a supply of future members, it must ensure that rural Catholics remained on the land and continued to produce future generations; otherwise, the Church would essentially breed itself out of existence by 1960, or at the latest 1980. Compounding this frightening prospect was the poor understanding most rural Catholics had of their own faith. Even if they moved to the city and compensated for lower urban birthrates, this would not necessarily raise the level of Catholic awareness and influence. O'Hara looked at all this and saw a disaster brewing for the not-too-distant future.[2]

Nevertheless, he also saw a great opportunity to organize American Catholic rural life, and his efforts to do so in the 1920s quickly blossomed into the Catholic rural life movement. A loosely affiliated group of Catholics with agrarian leanings, the movement took its direction from the National Catholic Rural Life Conference (NCRLC), which O'Hara organized in St. Louis, Missouri, in 1923. From that meeting until the late 1950s, Catholic agrarians (a term they often applied to themselves) sought to solve the "Catholic rural problem," and in doing so to solve some of the nation's rural problems as well. This group, composed of priests, bishops, women religious, and laypeople, urged the creation of rural life organizations at the diocesan level to better address particular rural needs. A host of publications, such as *St. Isidore's Plow* (named after the saint who would be chosen as the NCRLC's patron), *Landward, Land and Home,* and *The Christian Farmer,* disseminated the movement's ideas. Important books included *Manifesto on Rural Life,* published in 1939 by the NCRLC, and *Rural Roads to Security:*

America's Third Struggle for Freedom, published in 1940 by Midwestern priests Luigi Ligutti and John C. Rawe, S.J.

Reforming Rural America

The foundations upon which Catholic agrarianism grew have often escaped notice. The NCRLC perceived itself as the first national attempt by Catholics to do anything about the "Catholic rural problem." However, the movement had not emerged in a vacuum. In 1905 Francis C. Kelley had established the Catholic Church Extension Society to support the construction of Catholic parishes in remote areas. At roughly the same time, the Country Life Movement, a Protestant-oriented group of agriculturists, rural sociologists, college professors, and ministers, sought to improve and modernize rural life for the new century. The NCRLC utilized developments from both of these organizations to counter the "Catholic rural problem" with stronger parishes and general rural uplift. Therefore, understanding mid-twentieth-century Catholic agrarianism requires starting at the century's beginning, and not necessarily with Catholics.[3]

By 1920 American agriculture had experienced two traumatic decades. In that period the majority of the nation's population shifted from rural to urban residence. More and more Americans left the farm for the factory, seeking better prospects. Farm prices climbed briefly to unprecedented levels but plummeted during a postwar depression, which preceded the Great Depression by a decade. Amid all the despair stood the American Country Life Association (ACLA), offering a way for rural America to reform itself. The ACLA, founded in 1919 and made up mostly of mainstream Protestants, developed out of the Country Life Movement, which had received its impetus from Theodore Roosevelt's 1908 National Commission on Country Life. A devotee of Thomas Jefferson's agrarianism, Roosevelt wanted an assessment of American agriculture for the new century. Although they differed among themselves over whether rural life was inherently good or bad, the leading agrarians making up the commission, such as Kenyon Butterfield, Henry A. Wallace Sr., and Liberty Hyde Bailey, agreed that rural life was too wasteful for the new century and was in need of "modernization." Affiliated with state agricultural colleges, Butterfield, Charles Galpin, and others later created rural sociology as a specific discipline. The Country Life adherents shared a predilection for Walter Rauschenbusch's Social Gospel, which had proved effective in reforming urban slums. They saw the need for a rural equivalent of the Social Gospel and believed that sociological methods would reveal an unquestionably sound approach.[4]

The Country Life Movement formulated numerous plans for "improving" rural life. Roads were to be paved, new farm equipment purchased, kitchens—perceived as the distinct realm of farm women—modernized, and Prohibition observed. All these improvements centered around "community-building." The underlying problem with country life was seen to be the lack of a viable, unified community structure to help farmers and ease the diffi-culties of rural isolation.[5]

Two institutions, the rural church and the rural school, contributed the most to the community, so they drew the reformers' attention first. Clearly, both needed improvement. The sheer numbers of each indicated to the Coun-try Life adherents that something was seriously amiss. The prevailing one-room schoolhouse was seen as irredeemably outdated. A 1911 survey of three Indiana counties by the Presbyterian Church in the United States discovered a great excess of churches of various denominations—in one case, three located within a quarter mile. Every Sunday these churches competed for the atten-dance of the rural populace, which itself was dwindling. Since the brightest young people often left the farm for the city, the churches fought for the pre-sumably less ambitious leftovers. The Country Life reformers thought they saw proof of this problem in the countryside's growing number of "sectarian" churches such as the Assemblies of God and the Church of the Nazarene. Even national figures contributed to the dire situation. William Jennings Bryan once admitted to never having studied, nor particularly caring about, the differences between the Baptist, Methodist, and Presbyterian churches.[6]

The Country Life Movement's utopian outlook coupled idealism with condescension. David Danbom has shown that in an era when all things were believed to be improving, the Country Life Movement thought it knew how to improve American agriculture. "In agriculture the drive for or-ganization and efficiency came not from the group to be organized and made efficient—in other words, the farmers—but from predominantly ur-ban people who were not part of the rural community." The urban roots of the Country Life movement revealed its ultimate concern with respect to American rural life: support for cities. "For the Country Lifers, efficiency in the countryside was less an end in itself than the means to national ends which transcended the rural community."[7]

The county extension agents served as the primary messengers of effi-ciency. As graduates of the state agricultural colleges, where many of the Country Life reformers held teaching positions, the extension agents intro-duced new techniques for farming and home economics. The authoritarian manner with which the Country Lifers attempted to impose their solutions guaranteed resistance from the very people who were supposed to benefit from them.[8] Rural Americans ignored many of the reformers' most prized suggestions, especially plans for church mergers. Salvation, not improved so-cial services, attracted church members. The ACLA satisfied the Country Life Movement's desire for a national organization to address rural problems. It seemed, though, to teeter perpetually on the brink of evaporation. Very little ever materialized from programs begun with great hopes, especially those designed in general terms to "unify" the rural community. The subjects of these programs—rural Americans themselves—remained unconvinced.[9]

Catholics interested in rural life issues, however, thought the ACLA offered enormous possibilities. The enthusiasm with which rural Catholic leaders embraced the Country Life perspective stemmed more from the Catholic Action impetus to unite the secular, non-Catholic world through a revival of the Thomistic synthesis than from a desire to assimilate into American life. Instead of separating the Church from the world, as was the case in the urban "Catholic ghetto" areas of the East, the predominantly Midwestern Catholic rural life movement engaged other agrarians in a critique of American culture that included both positive and negative evaluations. Instead of condemning American life from the smugly secure confines of a revitalized Thomism, Catholic agrarians used this intellectual foundation to retain and yet transform rural Catholics. They thus became active participants in the vigorous debate concerning the direction of American agriculture.

Serving parishes in Oregon, still considered a missionary territory, Edwin O'Hara realized the need to address the rural Catholics' often abysmal knowledge of their faith. His report to the National Catholic Education Association in 1920 concluded with a call for a national Catholic program centered around rural religious leaders that would make rural life and religion attractive once more by improving efforts such as publications and educational services in rural areas. Benedictine monks had accomplished this once already in medieval Europe, and "American rural life cries out for a modern Benedict of Nursia."[10] The Bishops' Program for Social Benefit (authored by O'Hara's sociology professor, Minnesota priest John A. Ryan) had just been released by the National Catholic Welfare Conference (NCWC). O'Hara's rural program appeared to fit well with the Church's new perspective on American life. A year after establishing the Catholic Church's Rural Life Bureau in 1920, O'Hara joined the ACLA, becoming one of only a handful of Catholic members. He nevertheless corresponded frequently with many of the ACLA's constituencies: county farm extension agents, the Farm Bureau, a rural insurance cooperative, and professors at state agricultural colleges. He discovered, much to his surprise, that the Jewish Agricultural Society was carrying out a similar agenda for the nation's small but increasing number of Jewish farmers.[11]

The pages of *St. Isidore's Plow,* the monthly newspaper "dedicated to the promotion of rural welfare" that O'Hara produced for the Rural Life Bureau, reflected its close affiliation with these non-Catholic groups. The first page of the inaugural issue of October 1922 featured a letter from O'Hara to J. P. Howard of the American Farm Bureau Federation. O'Hara praised the Farm Bureau for effectively promoting "the diffusion of scientific methods of agriculture, which is the indispensable basis of better agriculture." Bernard Baruch, who later became Franklin Roosevelt's treasury secretary, contributed an article that insisted upon the continual expansion of farm markets through better farming methods. "No matter what transportation and what distributive agencies you may have there must be a market; and that market, as in any other business you must continually endeavor to widen." A priest from Pullman, Washington, home of the state's agricultural college, linked better farming with the solution to O'Hara's "Catholic rural problem": "If knowledge of the best farming practices as advocated by agricultural colleges helps to increase the farmers' income at all, then agricultural education will tend to keep the Catholic population on the land."[12]

The Rural Life Bureau operated on a shoestring budget, consisting solely of O'Hara's finding spare time to print *St. Isidore's Plow*. When powerful bishops such as Boston's Cardinal William O'Connell denounced the NCWC, for its possible threat to episcopal authority as well as for its social welfare programs, O'Hara realized he needed an organization free of episcopal control. He saw his opportunity in 1923 when he was asked to serve as the Catholic representative to the ACLA convention in St. Louis. Given permission by the NCWC and St. Louis archbishop John J. Glennon, O'Hara set about organizing a Catholic convention on rural life to run parallel to the ACLA meeting. Frederick Kenkel, director of the St. Louis–based Central Bureau of the Central Verein (an umbrella organization of German Catholic societies), managed the scheduling details, inviting local priests and sisters involved with rural issues—such as Father George Hildner, known for his prize-winning chickens at the Missouri state fair. O'Hara and Kenkel decided that the fledgling Catholic group would alternate its meetings with those of the ACLA, so that members could attend all sessions. The ACLA had designated Sunday, November 11, as Rural Life Day at the convention and had secured St. Louis–area pulpits for ordained Country Life members to preach. When ACLA president Henry Israel asked O'Hara to preach as well, O'Hara sent notice to all priests in the United States asking them to include rural topics in that Sunday's sermon. To help, he published encouraging notes in *St. Isidore's Plow*. The *Plow* had already stated that the "rural problem is chiefly a social problem, and the Church is a social agent." Sessions at the convention addressed precisely how that agency could solve the "Catholic rural problem." The ACLA and its new Catholic counterpart—the National Catholic Rural Life Conference—considered the St. Louis meeting a success.[13]

Buoyed by the encouraging start, the NCRLC maintained its relationship with the ACLA by meeting jointly with it throughout the 1920s. After the 1927 conventions in Lansing, Michigan, the NCRLC began to draw even more attendees than the ACLA. Decimated numerically, the ACLA faltered as its "community-first" approach to solving rural problems became irrelevant to others interested in the same issues. Groups with more specific concerns, such as rural sociologists, began forming their own independent, specialized societies. Mainline Protestant denominations had begun curtailing rural mission work as early as 1915, and this trend continued in the 1920s. By 1941 the ACLA needed a loan from the NCRLC to meet operating expenses. To that extent, Catholic agrarians could allow themselves a little arrogance in comparison to their Protestant counterparts.[14]

Even before they shared finances, the two groups held remarkably similar visions of the future rural church. The ACLA sought rural Protestant unity through sociological research and the Social Gospel. By worshiping in one church and studying an updated curriculum in a consolidated school, rural Americans would be better equipped intellectually and spiritually to accommodate the modernization process that was believed to be inevitable.[15] Catholic agrarians followed their Protestant predecessors in these assumptions. The May 1925 issue of *Catholic Rural Life* hinted at how the Catholic agrarian perspective would develop:

> [The rural priest] shall see Christ among the farmers; he shall see His spirit in truly cooperative enterprises which provide a Christian organization of industry. He shall understand how the farm supports the fabric of the Christian family; how it gives the opportunity for realizing the Catholic ideal of private ownership of productive property.[16]

Claiming a Catholic stake in one of the nation's most stalwart self-images, that of the Jeffersonian farmer, the NCRLC combined "American" and "Catholic" identities in a way that few other Catholic organizations managed before John F. Kennedy's election in 1960. The NCRLC, for example, shared the Country Life Movement's assumption that agriculture must be better organized in order to serve the needs of a growing industrial nation. For the NCRLC, just as much as for the Country Lifers, farming was a way of life to support the needs and solve the problems of industrial America.

Besides the Country Life Movement and the ACLA, the NCRLC also had Catholic antecedents. The Catholic Church Extension Society, started by Francis Clement Kelley, sought, as its name indicated, to extend the Catholic Church's presence into new areas. The roots of Extension date to 1893, when the Canadian-born Kelley received an assignment to Immaculate Conception parish in Lapeer, Michigan. The young priest arrived in the state's "thumb" to face a small, dilapidated church, two tiny missions in Imlay City and Richfield, and a disastrous relationship with the parish's first priest, who apparently had lost his faith and still lived in the area. The parishioners, while nice enough, did not seem too concerned with the situation or inclined to improve it. When Lapeer's Methodists began building a notably robust stone structure, Kelley wondered how they were able to afford such expenditures. He then learned that a denominational "extension society" had provided the necessary starting funds for the Methodists.[17]

Not finding a similar Catholic organization, Kelley raised funds for his Michigan church by joining a lecture circuit with tales of his experiences as a chaplain in the Spanish-American War. While speaking in the South and Midwest, Kelley discovered that other priests shared his financial difficulties. With the support of Chicago archbishop James Quigley, he established the Extension Society in 1905. Together with its popular magazine, *Extension* (founded the following year), the society aimed to strengthen the Catholic Church in areas where it had only a nominal presence, helping to build churches and ship sacramental items such as monstrances and servable vestments to needy parishes.[18]

Kelley and the Extension Society felt it necessary to focus on areas where Catholics lacked what was deemed to be a sufficient presence, despite the visibility of rural Catholics in certain regions of the United States, as well as a tradition of support from foreign mission societies. Kelley's overlooking of preexistent rural Catholic communities established a pattern for much of the twentieth century. Pope Pius X's removal of the United States from the Propaganda Fide lists of missionary territories in 1908 only heightened the sense of urgency with which Extension conducted its business. If America was no longer a missionary country, then what was to be done with the areas where no Catholic church existed? Perhaps better known for his 1907 encyclical *Pascendi Dominici Gregis,* which condemned modernism, Pius X expressed what was for Kelley and his cohorts a more relevant order in his pontifical motto: *instauare omnia in Christo* (to restore all things in Christ). For the Extension Society, accomplishing this meant replicating urban Catholic success where it previously had not existed. Kelley wrote, "The Society really had begun the education of the Catholic East to a knowledge of its own greatness; for the Catholic West is the child of the Catholic East. . . . It is an Eastern seedling, transplanted to Western soil, growing to the glory of East and West."[19]

Both the Catholic Church Extension Society and the Country Life Movement depicted rural America as a place in social, cultural, economic, and religious peril. Rural residents would be rescued from this impending catastrophe by the reformers' efforts. Though mutually exclusive in terms of membership, the two groups shared a certain interest in reorganizing rural life, especially around a new church. Country Lifers went forth to convince farmers and their families that consolidated schools and churches were in their best interests, socially and financially; the Extension Society sent money for the scattered parishioners to consolidate themselves around a newly built or refurbished mission chapel. Both organizations increasingly wished to remake rural America in the image of urban America. The nation's cities had for years been the economic centers; now they wished to bring the countryside to their level in all things, rejecting the presumed moral and cultural superiority that agrarians treasured so highly.

However, the Extension Society and the neophyte NCRLC rarely communicated clearly with each other. Part of the reason was O'Hara's wish to remain independent of Kelley's plans. The influence of Kelley was evident at the first NCRLC meeting in St. Louis when his Lapeer successor, Thomas Carey, was elected president. Kelley also smoothed the waters with visiting ACLA members who exhibited some displeasure at being served fish on a Friday; he sided with them, declaring, "Gentlemen, I have a Protestant stomach." Nevertheless, O'Hara and the Extension Society did not share much—in the way of ideas, funding, or people—after the NCRLC came to life. However, the NCRLC's broader agenda changed emphasis according to who was leading the organization and who was implementing its plans. Former Catholic agrarian diehards occasionally returned to rekindle their relationship with Extension. William Howard Bishop served as the NCRLC's president from 1928 to 1934, publishing *Landward* from his rural rectory in Maryland; he then left to found the Glenmary Home Missioners in Cincinnati, which reestablished his contact with Extension. By the mid-1940s, O'Hara, now the bishop of Kansas City, Missouri, was utilizing the Extension Society, not the NCRLC, to establish ten small-town parishes in southwest Missouri.[20]

Consequently, the NCRLC "for many years . . . was of necessity only a discussion group . . . for the purpose of exchanging ideas and furthering its existence as a propaganda agency."[21] Through the 1920s, Catholic rural reforms were carried out piecemeal by individual conference members. George Hildner, who served as the NCRLC's first recording secretary, provided a laudatory and oft-cited example. His first parish, in Claryville, Missouri, lay in the Mississippi River floodplain, and after a particularly disastrous flood the priest worked with the Army Corps of Engineers to construct a levee system. He acquired his acclaimed poultry-raising skills, with the help of the county agent's suggestions, when local farmers were confounded by a virulent disease infecting their flocks. Bishop likewise demonstrated what an individual priest could accomplish. The Harvard-educated cleric spent all but two years of his career in rural parishes. When his parish in Clarksville, Maryland, lacked the funds to construct a school, Bishop organized the League of the Little Flower, the prototypical diocesan rural life bureau. Named after St. Thérèse of Lisieux, the nineteenth-century French nun known for her simple yet profound faith, the league consisted of those who donated money to support rural parishes outside of Washington, D.C. Facing a far more expansive diocese, Victor Day of Helena, Montana, established a correspondence course on the Baltimore Catechism, which O'Hara, Kelley, and the NCRLC all praised. While Hildner improved rural Catholics' agricultural skills and Bishop constructed schools for them where none previously existed, Day sought to strengthen their faith by instructing them in the basic points of Catholic doctrinal and moral teaching.[22]

While Extension pursued its own rural agenda, other Catholic groups, mostly made up of laypeople, found the NCRLC's agrarianism to be in accord with their own interests. Efforts to address the "Catholic rural problem" found a ready audience among German American Catholics. Many already lived in rural areas, especially in the Midwest. The Central Verein and its director, Frederick Kenkel, had done much of the background work for the 1923 St. Louis convention. Its assistance to O'Hara did not end there. Connected to diocesan and parish organizations around the country, the Central Verein provided the NCRLC with its first local-level network. Kenkel himself attended every national convention of the conference for its first twenty-five years. Immovably committed to the spiritual benefits of farming, he saw the NCRLC's work as part of the conservative reforms he had already been advocating for two decades in the Central Verein. In the pages of *Central Blatt and Social Justice,* Kenkel promoted a school of thought known as corporatism or solidarism. It envisioned an organic and orderly society as the product of people grouped together in vocational bodies. Together these bodies amounted to one "corporate" culture, which functioned smoothly as long as each group pursued its assigned task. Not surprisingly, farming was one such vocation.[23]

In 1925 Kenkel was joined in his support for the NCRLC by Joseph Matt, publisher of the German Catholic weekly *Der Wanderer* (St. Paul). Matt shared Kenkel's interests in social reform and agrarianism. The NCRLC now had the backing of two prominent German Catholic weeklies—*Der Wanderer* and Kenkel's St. Louis–based *Amerika*—and the publications of the Central Verein. The 1928 NCRLC convention in Atchison, Kansas, introduced Benedictine priest Edgar Schmiedeler. A native of Kansas City, Kansas, Schmiedeler had earned a doctorate in rural sociology from Kansas State Agricultural College. His training was evident in the numerous rural life items that he published. Schmiedeler, though, was one of the last of the prominent German-Americans active in the Catholic rural life movement. The Central Verein, while its agrarianism never faltered, became less of a force as its membership dwindled in the mid–twentieth century. As fewer German Catholics emigrated to the United States, the pool of potential new members shrank as well.[24]

Other groups of laypeople followed, bubbling with a new romantic vision of Catholicism's power to change American life. Dorothy Day, a convert, founded (in May 1933) and edited the monthly newspaper *The Catholic Worker*. The paper brought together her interests in social radicalism and religion with those of Peter Maurin, a transplanted French peasant who called himself "a radical of the right." *The Catholic Worker* repeatedly has received praise for its social justice commitments. Nevertheless, one recent study notes that even while the paper was enjoying its greatest popularity in the mid-1930s, most American Catholics had not even heard of Dorothy Day, and if they had, they regarded her as "at best a deluded, unpatriotic crank." Another study has suggested that Day, Maurin, and the other Catholic Workers fed off precisely that sort of opposition.[25] It certainly did not diminish their interest in realizing an agrarian vision of the Catholic Church. Although *The Catholic Worker* was based in New York, it covered agricultural matters from its first issue. For example, the fourth issue (September 1933) featured a report on a strike by dairy farmers in upstate New York. Maurin's "Easy Essays," a genre of his own making, described the "Green Revolution" of "cult, culture, and cultivation." The paper's coverage closely resembled the notion in the NCRLC's many publications that a particularly Catholic perspective on agriculture aided everyone, Catholic or not. The Catholic Workers also encouraged the practice of the corporal works of mercy, which included charity for the poor. To this end, they set up a number of urban "Houses of Hospitality" and rural "farm communes" across the nation to aid the homeless and unemployed.[26]

The Grail organization of Loveland, Ohio, started another apostolate, this one specifically for women. Founded in 1942 by Dutch Catholics and inspired by the social-justice vision of the European JOC (Jeunesse Ouvrière Chrétienne, or Young Christian Workers), the Grail sought to "convert like with like." In Europe this meant organizing Catholic factory employees to convert their co-workers. In the United States the same outlook translated into organizing rural Catholic women to lead their neighbors and friends in the Catholic plan for "social reconstruction." Life in the Grail's summer leadership schools was characterized by a strict regimen of prayer, farm work, and the study of Catholic Revival authors. Grail members sought to "restore the sacred" to aspects of everyday life, including "women's work" with the house and family.[27]

Part of the NCRLC's appeal, to its members and its outside supporters, lay in its location in the Midwest, the region that was quickly replacing the South as the quintessential rural America. The conference's geographical boundaries expanded in the late 1930s. The first non-Midwestern convention took place in 1935 in Rochester, New York, and in 1937 it met in Richmond, Virginia—the first meeting in the South. The NCRLC completed its national expansion two years later when it convened in Spokane, Washington. Nevertheless, the Midwest remained the heartland of the conference, as well as of the nation. After becoming the NCRLC's executive secretary in 1940, Luigi M. Ligutti moved its headquarters, but only from St. Paul to Des Moines. During the war years, conventions were confined to Missouri, Illinois, Ohio, Iowa, and Wisconsin—states that held a majority of the conference's clerical and lay members. The Midwestern character of the conference showed clearly in 1946 when *Land and Home* announced the upcoming "Victory" convention with the headline "All Roads Lead to Green Bay." An accompanying map of the Upper Midwest with Green Bay prominently located included such cities as St. Louis, Detroit, Omaha, Kansas City, and Toledo. Cairo as well as Chicago appeared in Illinois. Although the map showed the New England and Mid-Atlantic regions, the easternmost city marked was Buffalo, New York. The conventions with the largest attendance met at St. Cloud, Minnesota, in 1940 and La Crosse, Wisconsin, in 1948.[28]

Underlying these transitions—of membership and leadership, from discussion group to national organization—was the basic intellectual framework of Catholic agrarianism. Although the Catholic rural life movement took its lead from the ACLA, it quickly developed its own Catholic agrarian agenda. An antiurban theology dominated this vision. Environmental disasters such as the Dust Bowl were seen as proving that urban America's corruption could extend even to agriculture itself. However, a truly Catholic appreciation of rural life would recover the early pioneering freedom the nation had seemingly discarded. Utilizing this freedom properly would help solve the "Catholic rural problem," since rural America was inherently fertile, spiritually as well as physically. Thomas Jefferson's ideal of citizen-farmers received noticeable support. The family farm was, according to the Catholic agrarians, the wellspring of rural fertility. Bio-dynamic farming, a particular method of organic, small-scale agriculture, was the way by which Catholic agrarian family farms would save the nation's soul and soil while feeding its mouths.

Antiurbanism among Catholic Agrarians

The "Catholic rural problem" as O'Hara formulated it stemmed from a number of demographic and devotional difficulties. These began with the city and its declining birthrate. Cities grew only because of foreign immigration; most young people were leaving the farms for urban areas. This did not bode well for the continued growth of a church that was already 80 percent urban. If something was not done to keep rural Catholics rural, the Church's source of replenishment to compensate for the low urban birthrate would disappear, and with it, O'Hara concluded, the Church itself.

> In the country . . . is found the fertile and prolific population, and any influence set to work there grows with the passage of time like the tiny mountain stream which swells into a mighty river as it is joined by the waters from other springs in its course through the plains below. A religious center in the country, consequently, is a fountain bubbling up like Jacob's well[,] a blessing for future generations.[29]

The rural problem therefore possessed a religious element as well as a demographic one. Fighting rural isolation and boredom served the best interests of all Catholics. Under the circumstances, it was no longer enough for the Church to simply "extend" itself into the country. The perilous situation required an entire socioreligious agenda, and the agrarian-minded NCRLC and its followers could certainly provide that. The "Catholic rural problem," which urban Catholics previously could have ignored, had become an issue with which the entire Church—in both country and city—should be concerned.

Many formulators of the Catholic antiurban tradition were themselves city dwellers. *The Catholic Worker* and John La Farge, S.J. (who wrote on rural issues as well as interracial ones), were both based in New York City, and many of the NCRLC's leaders hailed from or lived in the larger Midwestern cities. Frederick Kenkel and Archbishop John Glennon, a notable early NCRLC supporter, lived in St. Louis. This, though, did not seem incongruous. The increasing popularity of the Mystical Body of Christ ecclesiology helped soften the apparent contradiction. Rudolf Schuler, the priest directing the St. Louis archdiocese's program wrote: "Both the city and the Church in the city are destined to profit from the Rural Life program. Unmistakable evidence points to a more sympathetic, and more Catholic, attitude of the city Catholic toward his country brother, of the urban member of Christ's Mystical Body towards the rural counterpart." While rural Catholics supplied urban parishes with fresh members, St. Louis Catholics offered spiritual and financial support for "their adopted 'rural babies.'"[30] Leo Steck, Schuler's successor, provided a rural Missouri mission staffed by Catholic laywomen with a 1929 Model A Ford to distribute donated clothing from the city.[31]

Therefore, Catholic antiurbanism was concerned with people as well as the land itself. Unnerved by the declining urban birthrate and its implications for the Church, O'Hara and others insisted that rural Catholics must provide the Church's future membership. O'Hara stated bluntly, "Cities are relatively sterile, and the country relatively fertile." Preaching in St. Paul for the 1925 NCRLC convention, Thomas Carey warned that "immigration has now been reduced to a minimum, and the city parish henceforth must draw its recruits from the country. Unless the Catholics who come from the country are well instructed and well grounded in their faith, it will be the Church's loss and the loss, in all probability, will be irrevocable."[32]

A 1940 *Commonweal* article published by Ligutti on the continued decline of birthrates bore the blunt title "Cities Kill." The article echoed O'Hara's forecast of a decline for the American Catholic Church. Writing from his parish in Iowa, Ligutti made sure his readers realized the apocalyptic implications: "It is a fine thing for us to spend money and use manpower in the interests of higher education, but it would seem from the figures that it is the children of the Okies, the children of the Grapes of Wrath, and not the children of professional and business men who will populate tomorrow's America." For Ligutti, the land retained an inherent stability even in the face of one of the nation's most pressing problems, the Depression-induced migration of white tenant farmers. Whether the people who lived on the land posed a threat or an opportunity for Catholic reform, nature's fertility offered a kind of divine strength that no city could equal.[33]

Catholic agrarians saw more wrong with the city than merely their Church's possibly bleak future. The modern industrial city was characterized by everything that was artificial and dangerously inauthentic about America. In 1933 W. Howard Bishop fumed about the havoc that the current economic system had wrought for farmers as well as the nation:

> Why, I ask, must fewer men aspire to be farmers? . . . We must revive the almost forgotten Christian-Democratic ideal of the greatest good for the greatest number. Then and then only we shall have true efficiency in farming when we learn to use machinery as a servant and not serve it as a god, and when Christian ideals that consider the ultimate good of mankind and not profits as the highest achievement of society have gained the respect that is due them.[34]

Charles Morrow Wilson had arrived at the same conclusion in an article for *Commonweal:* "We have become overcitied, overindustrialized, overtechnical. Our church and public charities cannot give indefinite support to misplaced flotsam of cities. Therefore the nation is again seeking rural refuge, more well-anchored peasants in place of the millions of disillusioned city drifters."[35]

Across the country, those suspicious of modern cultural trends like centralization and homogenization likewise decried the cultural evils of urban pleasure-seeking. No longer were people satisfied with making their own way and their own fun. Reacting to the Jazz Age, many felt that life had become too cluttered and superficial to be enjoyed. Catholic agrarians added their own version of the criticism: "But here again we ask, is all this valuation of comfort a Christian thing? Where is the Christian ascetic teaching of denying self, of giving up, of enduring hardness?"[36] Life on the land precluded the need to seek superfluous pleasures, since farm work held its own attractions. Even if the work itself did not satisfy recreational needs, groups such as the Grail had demonstrated that rural life had its own enjoyments, such as the folk dances and artistic styles that Grail members strove to preserve.[37]

In this war against the hated city, country simplicity became a badge of honor. Catholic agrarians rebuked the suburbanite abhorrence of rural life's inherent earthiness. "What business have our Catholic colleges in making their buildings and their furniture so fine that they make young people so dissatisfied with the simple living of the farm?" wrote Willis D. Nutting in 1938. "One might say that the confidence with which a person walks through a barnyard varies inversely with the number of years that person has spent in college." Even as late as the 1950s, when American agriculture had almost completed its transformation into agribusiness, a romantic agrarian affiliated with *The Catholic Worker* could write that "[t]his is a time for working with dung and urine . . . [instead of] the hermetically-sealed and therapeutic world of Bernardsville, New Jersey." The Catholic Worker farm outside of Easton, Pennsylvania, hoped to plant an acre of flax once every three years. Then, one Worker prophesied, "we will have to learn the pride of wearing this homespun and hand-woven linen."[38]

The renewed emphasis on rural Christian simplicity grew out of Catholic historical precedents. According to Ignatius Esser, O.S.B., St. Benedict's emphasis on labor and his requirement of a vow of stability provided the key to true rural success: "The future Archbishops of Canterbury, St. Thomas à Becket, St. Anselm, and Lanfranc, had in their earlier days worked in the harvest fields and in the monastery barns, earning their daily bread in the sweat of their brow."[39] Pope Pius X emerged as the pontiff with whom rural American Catholics could best identify. His canonization in 1954 occurred in part through strong American support organized by Edwin O'Hara. According to Steven Avella, O'Hara accomplished this by peddling Catholic ultramontanism in a specifically American idiom. The results of this strategy certainly emerged in the Catholic agrarian appreciation of Pius.[40] Born in a Venetian farming village, the future pope had walked barefoot to school in order to preserve his one pair of shoes. A column in *Land and Home* compared his story with that of Horatio Alger. However, that comparison concluded, "It was the glory of Pius X that he had no worldly ambitions, no desire for gain. From priesthood to Papacy he remained in essence a country boy."[41] According to Catholic agrarians, true farm work needed to respect the spiritual and physical fertility of the land while not separating family, land, and church, as did industry and, in the past, American agriculture as well—including rural Catholics. The Catholic agrarians saw "the need of a change in 'personal attitudes' from those which were practicable in pioneer days, if agriculture is to survive and create opportunity for all."[42]

Saving the Land

The Catholic rural life movement's antiurban spirit amounted to a Catholic theology of nature, characterized by a dualism of urban sterility and rural fertility. Catholic agrarians maintained that rural life provided the nation's most stable populace. This belief was in accord with neo-Scholasticism as well as the Jeffersonian and decentralist traditions. The rural life movement held what contemporary environmentalism calls an androcentric—human-centered—view of nature, in which nature's importance stems from its availability for human usage. Such a perspective withers today under radical ecology's criticism that it oppresses nature. Even during the period of greatest Catholic agrarian activity, there were voices that prophesied today's common assumption that environmentalism and traditional Christianity are incompatible. Introducing his *Sand County Almanac* of 1949, Aldo Leopold remarked that "conservation is getting nowhere because it is incompatible with our Abrahamic concept of land. We abuse land because we regard it as a commodity belonging to us." As will be seen, the Catholic agrarians would have hesitated to decenter humanity so completely. They were certain, though, that human arrogance and agricultural ineptitude caused the environmental disasters that were destroying American agriculture in the first half of the century. In this concern they shared a great deal with environmentalists such as Leopold.[43]

At the 1923 NCRLC convention, Vincent Wehrle the bishop of Bismarck, North Dakota, remarked that "there is something sacramental about rural life."[44] Part of rural life's sacramentality lay in the land itself. The Catholic agrarian worldview taught a rather stringent environmental ethic with transcendent implications. Care for the earth directly reflected one's care for earthly existence; it also influenced care for the soul. "The Worn-out Farm," a poem by J. Gladden Hutton, linked irresponsible farming with spiritual carelessness and national decay.

> Oh, foolish man of high or low estate,
> Through ignorance or lack of vision clear,
> Destroying his most precious heritage,
> Destroying his Hereafter and his Here!
>
> Up, valiant souls who know the race's need,
> Proclaim the truth and faint not while you toil;
> Write plain the words where all who run may read:
> The Nation's life-blood springs from out the soil.[45]

The land possessed salvific qualities for both the natural life ("the Nation's life-blood") and the supernatural. It offered, in a veiled mysterious way, an incarnational relationship with God. "The land," declared John La Farge, S.J., "is the Creator's gift for maintaining the actual existence of the Christian world."[46]

With the acknowledgment that the earth had its own spiritual as well as physical value came the criticisms of one-crop farming. Large-scale farming received unequivocal condemnation, especially with regard to the Dust Bowl and the South's timber and cotton industries. When St. Louis's auxiliary bishop Christian Winkelmann was named bishop of Wichita in 1940, the *Catholic Rural Life Bulletin* commented:

> Anyone conversant with the agricultural tragedy of the last thirty years will realize all too well the tremendous task which will be his. The once rich, fruitful land of Kansas lies near to exhaustion. It has taken a merciless beating. In some places there isn't even a spark of life left. In others, synthetic, inorganic fertilization, get-rich-quick, one-cropping, large-scale, mechanized land-bleeding, not to mention absentee ownership, long ago ridiculed to oblivion any meager attempts to bring about a true ruralism.[47]

"A true ruralism" meant one not invaded by "urban" forms of life, and that included farming methods. The resulting economic and spiritual poverty in rural areas would only resemble further the captivity of the city. "With the general mechanization of life all chance of genuine freedom is suffering," wrote Leo R. Ward, C.S.C., in 1938. "Men lack economic freedom, and in that fix to speak of their being politically free is to use ideal if not ironic words."[48]

The Church, it was believed, played an important role in demanding protection for the environment. Only when that had been secured would people enjoy true freedom, and they would enjoy it "on the land." The precursor to that view, ecological sensitivity, had its roots in a proper religious perspective. Urban Baer, a priest from Wisconsin, insisted that Aquinas had established "the principle that all creatures and consequently all earthly goods, can, of their very nature belong to God alone." Respect of this principle would have prevented the Dust Bowl.

> Considering land as a sacred trust, [the farmer] would not have permitted speculators to make the farmer a chore boy for unhealthy individualism. It must be emphasized and re-emphasized that the very ground the farmer breaks, the very earth he plows, ultimately belongs to God; that the farmer is only the trustee, the guardian thereof, and must one day render an account of his stewardship to the Divine Harvester.[49]

The land also possessed regenerative capabilities that, Catholic agrarians believed, humans had only begun to utilize. Ligutti demanded, "What is the matter with these farmers anyway? Why don't they produce more?" He believed that American agriculture was "able to produce much more food by using its available tillable acreage, labor supply and machinery." Less than a decade after the Dust Bowl stopped swirling, C. E. Wolf claimed that "the very soil is crying out for more human beings—millions of them—to restore its biological balance and preserve its fertility."[50]

Leopold's 1949 *Sand County Almanac* offered a similar, albeit secular, argument: Americans stood to lose more than just topsoil if they continued to farm as they did. The land offered a great deal more, but no one seemed aware of the real wealth beneath their feet. The book described Leopold's experiences escaping from the city to "real life" in rural Wisconsin and his subsequent travels through the Midwest, the Southwest, and the Canadian plains province of Manitoba. Much of the *Almanac* detailed the beautiful and diverse life present in these areas. The descriptions necessarily included criticism of the deleterious effect of agriculture. The residents of these regions rarely seemed concerned about the disaster brewing right in front of them. Riding across Illinois after visiting a state conservation area, Leopold was dismayed by

> the passengers [who] talk and talk and talk. About what? About baseball, taxes, sons-in-law, movies, motors, and funerals, but never about the heaving groundswell of Illinois that washes the windows of the speeding bus. Illinois has no genesis, no history, no shoals or deeps, no tides of life and death. To them Illinois is only the sea on which they sail to ports unknown.

Like the rural reformers, Leopold sensed that part of the problem for the land lay with the people living on it. Still, the land harbored the promise of something better.[51]

Leopold's widely read comments hinted at a basic agreement with the Catholic agrarians' more confessional stance. Immediately after decrying "our Abrahamic concept of land," he wrote: "When we see land as a community to which we belong, we may begin to use it with love and respect. There is no other way for land to survive the impact of mechanized man, nor for us to reap from it the esthetic harvest it is capable, under science, of contributing to culture." Leopold wished to restore, along with the flora and fauna, the natural biotic interrelations disrupted by evolving human agricultural practices. *A Sand County Almanac* concluded with a proposed "land ethic," which "simply enlarges the boundaries of the community to include soils, waters, plants, and animals, or collectively: the land. . . . [This] changes the role of *Homo Sapiens* from conqueror of the land-community to plain member and citizen of it. It implies respect for his fellow-members, and also respect for the community as such." Leopold targeted government that was ineffective and farmers who made self-interested choices as two of the first groups who should implement this new, natural remedy.[52]

What Leopold sought through improved environmental science, the Catholic rural lifers pursued through Christian theology. For their part, the Catholic agrarians had some innovative ideas about the earthly and spiritual manifestations of fertility. An environmental sensibility, if not an explicitly labeled "land ethic," pervaded the Catholic rural life movement. An assumption about American freedom's essentially rural character stood as the basis for the ideas on fertility. Behind that lay a shift in what constituted the "Catholic rural problem." O'Hara's original intent had been to redress lagging awareness of faith among rural Catholics moving cityward. Now "the land" became the focus. Only the land—the stuff on which American rural life was lived—provided a sure foundation for the nation's freedom. A concern with its proper care might not qualify as a prophetic call to contemporary environmentalism, but neither was it an endorsement of current agricultural practices and attitudes.

In this regard the Catholic rural life movement was encouraged by the success of Edward Faulkner's *Plowman's Folly*. Published in 1943, the book became popular in the postwar environmental movement. Faulkner stressed that the use of artificial fertilizers created precisely what it was intended to prevent: a soil base bereft of nutrients. "By imitating nature, man could have enjoyed such benefits as he has never dared hope for; by disregarding the obvious example she set for him, he has courted disaster." The solution hinted at what had created the Dust Bowl: the American farmer's reliance on the moldboard plow. The use of the disk harrow (which did not gouge and overturn the soil) would take advantage of the plant matter on the soil's surface. This would produce a rich, organic, naturally fertilized soil, and "[i]f the men who now are the backbone of commercial agriculture prove to be among the tardy ones to acquire the new information, it will be at their great cost." The *land* in this view, stood as its own entity, free of any need of human adjustment. In fact, Faulkner rejected the notion of human lordship over creation as "the purest propaganda," stating that instead, "plants are the real masters of the earth." Louis Bromfield, with whom Faulkner discussed *Plowman's Folly* before its publication, wrote that Faulkner's ideas "were in one sense revolutionary; in another sense they were as old as time and as old as Nature herself." The Catholic rural life movement agreed. To some extent, it anticipated Faulkner's work when it expanded the "Catholic rural problem" to include reformed views of the land itself.[53]

Freedom's Rural Sanctuary

After 1930 the NCRLC members and other Catholic agrarians realized that they had emerged as the nation's premier church-affiliated agrarian movement. The salvation of rural America had become their responsibility. Therefore, improving Catholic rural life came to mean improving the rural life of other Americans as well.

This agenda harmonized quite well with the growing interest among secular intellectuals in agrarian solutions to the nation's malaise. Characterized by the Twelve Southerners' defiant *I'll Take My Stand*, which upheld the rural and religious traditions of the Old South as paradigmatic, agrarianism enjoyed something of a surge in popularity during the Great Depression. Thomas Hart Benton portrayed in painting what the Catholic agrarians and others were saying: the city's corruption threatened the American way of life. The conformism of the 1920s and the depression of the 1930s served as ample proof of this. Only rural areas refused to buckle under the threat, and even that resistance appeared to be weakening. Neither the Catholic agrarians nor their better-known counterparts in non-Catholic America planned to let that corrosion advance any further. Robert Dorman writes:

> Such was the great peril of life in the modern disenchanted world of the twentieth century—that history would lose its myths, and art its social function, and sociology its ethical thrust, and science its utopian impulse, and the folk their folkness. . . . Willing themselves to be naive, [the regionalists] proposed to reforest, to reenchant the world: to build not merely quaint, impractical, old-fashioned ideological sod houses out in the "wilderness of civilization," but to resettle there, bringing with them a "higher type of civilization"—to build there garden cities.

The paradox of an antimodernist response to modern social dilemmas was precisely what drew together the Catholic rural life movement and secular intellectuals such as Allen Tate and Herbert Agar. Tate's agrarianism, religious yearnings, and acquaintance with Dorothy Day and other Catholic rural lifers led him to convert to Catholicism in 1950.[54]

Many Catholics, including the rural lifers, felt that the Church readily offered the spiritual, social, and intellectual unity desired by so many non-Catholics. Catholic agrarianism received much of its philosophical structure from the Catholic Revival, the revival of Catholicism as an intellectual and cultural force. The codification of neo-Scholasticism as the only system of Catholic thought provided the impetus for this revival. Thomas Aquinas had been officially elevated as the preeminent Catholic thinker by Pope Leo XIII in his 1880 encyclical *Aeterni Patris;* the saint's thirteenth-century integration of philosophy and theology (and that of his commentators), embodied the Christian synthesis of the natural and the supernatural that Catholics hoped to recapture in politics and culture during the late nineteenth and twentieth centuries.[55]

Since Scholasticism included both natural and supernatural knowledge, its adherents envisioned its unitary character as paralleling the similarly univocal position of the papacy as the only religious authority. The one, true Church not only had an infallible leader, it possessed a similarly invincible method of discerning the truths, which that leader would proclaim. In the United States, Jay Dolan has noted, this enthusiasm had a specifically evangelical flavor: "Thomism provided a sense of security in a world of change and furnished the intellectual cement that could bind religion and culture together. The medieval and Thomistic ideal of the unity of religion and life, the natural and divine, became the model for integrating Catholicism and American culture in the twentieth century." A popular book by James J. Walsh, *The Thirteenth, the Greatest of Centuries* (1907), summarized the attitude: reviving what was believed to be the crowning glory of Roman Catholicism—Scholasticism—would bring a similarly glorious moment in America.[56]

The centralization efforts of the Catholic intellectual revival strove to reverse a trend that had continued in European life since the French Revolution: the separation of religion from the public realm. Although such separation was witnessed most dramatically in the waves of anticlericalism that characterized the revolution and many of the political upheavals of 1848, Church authorities believed that the same compartmentalization took place in the workplace and the home. While many papal encyclicals decried the Church's dethronement in political matters, two of them addressed the specific concerns of everyday life. Leo XIII's *Rerum Novarum,* issued in 1891, directed that labor unrest was to be solved by an equitable distribution of property whereby ownership, large or small, might unify opposing elements of society. Celebrating that vision, Pius XI's *Quadragesimo Anno* (Forty Years After), released in 1931, restated the endorsement of independent ownership as a path to a just society. The encyclical also encouraged Catholics to use their integrated vision of faith and life to construct a new Christian order.[57]

Those within the Catholic rural life movement felt their work in American rural life came close to realizing the popes' intentions. Aloysius Muench, who served as bishop of Fargo, North Dakota, believed that the Catholic rural life movement's uniquely Catholic aspects facilitated this success: "The religious principles of Catholic social philosophy keep it on the highway of sound agrarian thought and action. The by-ways of history are strewn with the wreckage of movements because they went astray for a lack of right guiding principles." (Muench may or may not have been directing that remark toward the then-fading ACLA.) Like any other religious tradition, Catholicism offered spiritual guidance. Unlike the others, so the Catholic agrarians thought, the Catholicism of *Quadragesimo Anno* also endowed people with real freedom. This was not just freedom in general; it was freedom *on the land.* Rural America offered the last great chance for private ownership to succeed. Those within the Catholic rural life movement did not overlook the implications this held for their national heritage. In extolling the papal social encyclicals, they had done more than confirm their Catholic integrity; they had also confirmed their agrarian integrity. Others seem to have noticed. The conversion of several prominent American intellectuals, including Tate, obviously added to such confidence.[58]

Pride also came from the knowledge that two Catholics from Europe helped foster much of the American interest, Catholic and otherwise, in agrarianism. Hilaire Belloc, a French Catholic who emigrated to England, had established distributism as an intellectual movement with his 1911 book *The Servile State.* Unswervingly committed to a return of the French *ancien régime,* Belloc praised its small-scale ownership and production under the aegis of a benevolent Christian monarch. He harbored only abhorrence for the modern bureaucratic separation between church and state, as well as that between work and home. This attitude attracted G. K. Chesterton, a journalist of humorous bent who had created his reputation through philosophical arguments with George Bernard Shaw. Chesterton converted to Catholicism largely because of Belloc's Thomistic influence. Together they extolled the medieval Catholic traditions of small-scale farming, property ownership, and industry in which religion penetrated every aspect of life. American decentralist intellectuals, such as Herbert Agar, Ralph Borsodi, and the Vanderbilt Agrarians, followed the "Chesterbelloc" in the condemnation of mass production and intrusive bureaucracies.[59]

During the 1930s the Catholic rural life movement hit its stride, combining these different strands of cultural and religious criticism into an innovative expression of American Catholic intellectual life. Doing so made the Catholic rural lifers appear imminently practical while retaining all of their religious idealism. David Bovée has argued that a crucial shift in the NCRLC's interaction with American culture came in the wake of the Depression. In the early 1930s the conference turned away from its discussion of solving the "Catholic rural problem"—an "irrelevant" and to some extent "nonexistent" problem, according to Bovée—and instead focused on the "hard" questions of rural economic reform. The New Deal, especially its agricultural policies, received much of the attention, as Catholic agrarians were eager to enlist any available help for their programs.[60]

The shift from discussing the "soft" reforms of rural life, such as rural health, community life, and "rural welfare," to the "hard" reforms needed to confront the economic crisis of the Depression was not as large a leap as it might seem. The NCRLC maintained its concern for the "Catholic rural problem" even while it pursued perhaps more immediate projects, such as the establishment of rural credit unions and working with the New Deal's agricultural policies.[61] The NCRLC's solution to the "Catholic rural problem," which included spiritual, social, and economic elements, enabled it to shift emphasis within its overall program without losing its original impetus, as had the Protestant Country Life reformers. Most Catholic agrarians saw the program, and thus rural parishes, as being a unified whole. In an address for the Catholic Hour radio program, Edgar Schmiedeler concluded that

> [f]ew social groups in our present civilization can compare in stability and efficiency with a well-organized rural parish. The latter stands today like a rock of Gibraltar in the midst of the restless and shifting sea of modern life. Its members are drawn together into harmonious unison through a similarity of aspirations and hopes, ideals and ambitions, through sameness of fundamental beliefs in faith and in morals.[62]

Merely by becoming more knowledgeable about their faith, rural Catholics helped themselves and their neighbors. The NCRLC's *Manifesto on Rural Life,* which appeared in 1939, discussed "hard" reforms, such as changing rural taxation laws, along with "soft" ones, such as promoting street-preaching (which would bring in rural converts) and the back-to-the-land movement (which would "plant" Catholics in rural areas).[63]

The farm would provide not only a socially stable environment, but a spiritually safe one as well. Farming combined both physical and mental exertion, eliminating the need for recreation, which satisfied the side of humanity that was neglected with either purely physical or purely mental labor. Besides, farming was, in the words of one commentator, "largely non-competitive." Farmers could all have successful crops without anyone's losing out. "Thus the type of occupation which is characteristic of the land is a type which in every respect fits in with the Catholic conception of the nature and duties of man. And therefore a Catholic can go into this work without stretching his conscience in any way."[64] Milwaukee archbishop Sebastian G. Messmer endorsed a "conservatism that will heed what are not only the teachings of religion and sound philosophy, but also nature's own clear calls and warnings, will easily go hand in hand with a true and beneficent progressiveness, just as nature herself is never revolutionary, yet always progressive and productive." Messmer concluded that "[w]henever country folks have been led into dangerous political experiments, it was done by emissaries of the city."[65]

Consequently, a decade after Catholic Alfred E. Smith's failed presidential campaign, Catholic agrarians still claimed that only rural life assured political freedom. In 1940 Ligutti and John C. Rawe, S.J., published *Rural Roads to Security: America's Third Struggle for Freedom*. The subtitle alluded to the first two struggles—the Revolutionary War (for democracy) and the Civil War (for freedom for all Americans)—in order to situate the third: the struggle against the dehumanizing and environmentally harmful aspects of urban living. A stinging decentralist indictment of modern industrial life, *Rural Roads to Security* offered an accurate expression of the Catholic agrarian theological appreciation of nature. The fertility and stability of "life on the land" stood as the nation's line of defense against the encroachment of a harmful technocratic culture. Achieving the vision of *Rural Roads*, though, required work informed by Catholic agrarian theology, so that the land's fertility and stability, as well as that of believing Christians, might be preserved.[66]

Ligutti, Rawe, and the other leaders of the NCRLC, as well as the Catholic Workers, quoted generously and approvingly from secular decentralist homesteaders such as Ralph Borsodi and Scott Nearing. Both men had exchanged lucrative white-collar city jobs for the hard tasks of subsistence farming, and both had written best-selling books about their experiences.[67] Borsodi's *Flight from the City*, published in 1933, could have lent its title to many a work published by the NCRLC or even *The Catholic Worker*. Borsodi established a "School of Living" in 1934 that instructed willing souls in how—with some help from modern technology—to grow and grind grains for bread, to weave cloth for sewing, and to heat hand-built houses efficiently. When the *Manifesto on Rural Life* called for a "Catholic school of agriculture," Borsodi's institute of subsistence farming and a subtly modernistic "simple life" provided a ready example. An earlier book by Borsodi—*This Ugly Civilization*, published in 1929—had blamed urban pollution and human corruption on the mass production of the factory; in *Flight from the City*, he recommended an escape through "domestic production" on the land.[68] In 1941 the School of Living received praise from both *The Catholic*

Woman's World and the *Catholic Rural Life Bulletin*, which hailed the Borsodi and his wife Myrtle as "the champions of Agrarian-Distributism."[69]

Borsodi and other decentralists, such as Herbert Agar and Allen Tate, kept the virtues of subsistence farming before American readers in the pages of *Free America*, a decentralist publication that enjoyed a decade of circulation before fading in 1947. On their sixty-five-acre farm in Vermont, Scott and Helen Nearing offered a different path "back to the land," one that eschewed every modern convenience Borsodi endorsed as beneficial to homesteading. While Borsodi rejected urban life but not modern convenience, the Nearings dispensed with anything that smacked of modernity, such as electricity and prepackaged goods purchased in stores. This translated into a complete reliance on handcrafted furniture and hand-raised foods; it also made the Nearings' example a difficult one to imitate.[70]

A Catholic agrarian version of the Protestant work ethic had begun to emerge from the rural lifers' myriad efforts. A renewed emphasis on hard work, especially hard *rural* work, would save the nation. However, one place where this work ethic had become conspicuously absent, a matter of concern to many rural leaders, was the education of youth. While agreeing that "Youth" enjoyed "innumerable aids" in the Church and benefited from recent technological and intellectual developments, Joseph Kelly complained that "[w]e are growing up in a seated position, with but one credo on our lips, 'We must be entertained.' We are no longer able to entertain ourselves." The laziness of rural youth now meant a future rural population unwilling and unable to work. "Bad habits, over-indulgence, and constant stepping beyond the rules result in our young-old bodies which cannot stand the strain of a rigorous life." Catholic agrarians had furiously organized numerous attempts to induce rural Catholic youth to remain on the land. These efforts even promoted the very reason that so many were leaving for the cities: that farm life consisted only of hard work. By overlooking the benefits of farm work, rural Catholic young people were avoiding one of their most valuable spiritual inheritances.[71]

The education of young Catholics to appreciate life on the land even extended to marriage preparations. "An essential quality in a future husband is a high respect for womanhood," advised Mildred Daly. However, she counseled that for women, "the ability to adjust to new situations" superseded any other quality. This applied especially to prospective brides, since they would follow their husband's employment.

> Today many young men feel that rural life offers opportunities which they cannot find in industry in the city. Consequently, they take up some type of agricultural work. It is then a necessity for the wife to make an effort to adjust herself to a rural way of living, even though she be an urbanite. Surely most of us agree that the farm is a wholesome and safe place to raise a family.[72]

Of course, family farms needed some economic freedom, too. Although American agriculture had been suffering through a depression for almost ten years before the rest of the nation experienced it in 1929, the NCRLC did not discuss "rural economics" until 1932. This lag may be explained in part by the presidency of W. Howard Bishop from 1928 to 1934. Bishop considered promoting Catholic participation in the idealistic but nonetheless popular back-to-the-land movement as an economic response to the depression. In this he was not alone; a number of Catholic publications, such as *The Catholic Worker, America,* and *Commonweal,* voiced similar opinions. Moreover, he had begun formulating plans to establish a Catholic home missionary society modeled after the Maryknollers (formally named the Catholic Foreign Mission Society) in Asia and Africa. This became the Glenmary Home Missioners.[73]

Bishop's successor as NCRLC president was Joseph Campbell, a priest from Ames, Iowa, the home of Iowa State Agricultural College. Campbell considered rural economics his primary focus, and he expressed a strong interest in creating rural credit unions.

> The credit union is a thrift agency. Through it people can be educated to keep their living cost within their means. . . . In a word, through the credit union parishes and churches can be put in control. Local organization on behalf of social justice is the only way in which social justice can be put in the saddle in the economic order. . . . If people are not willing to pay this price, they are not willing to have social justice.

This solution to rural Catholics' economic woes became the singular focus of the entire conference during Campbell's one-year term. Although the credit union could, in Campbell's eyes, serve as a Catholic basis for improving the entire community, other conference leaders demanded that more attention be paid to other social concerns for the entire rural community, not just Catholics.[74]

Of course, credit unions needed members, and that brought the NCRLC back to the "Catholic rural problem." Catholic agricultural schools, a parallel to state agricultural colleges, would educate rural Catholic youth about the benefits of staying on the land. These proposed schools would have added a rural component to the Catholic educational system, which already stood as an alternative to public schools. As accredited, four-year Catholic colleges, they would have extended beyond Borsodi's School of Living in terms of institutional structure and religious commitment. Many such Catholic schools were discussed, but none was ever fully established. John La Farge, an ardent NCRLC supporter, had founded the Cardinal Gibbons Institute in Ridge, Maryland, to educate African Americans in farming methods. Modeled after George Washington Carver's Tuskegee Institute, La Farge's school opened in 1924, but closed in 1933 because of financial problems. State agricultural colleges directed the rural extension services—one of Edwin O'Hara's favorite suggestions for improving rural life—which had been established earlier by the Country Life Movement. The *Manifesto on Rural Life* endorsed these services as important allies in combating urbanism: "An education in scientific farming and in the arts and crafts will create an interest in rural activities among farm youth that will counteract the lure of the city."[75]

Two problems—location and curriculum—inhibited grand educational plans. Great hopes were pinned on Jesuit institutions for their traditional leadership in Catholic higher education. Jesuit seminarians in West Baden, Indiana, and St. Marys, Kansas, became interested in bio-dynamic farming, but this interest was not replicated at the large undergraduate Jesuit universities, since most of them were located in cities. What precisely would be taught also raised questions. While O'Hara envisioned a curriculum that emphasized agricultural science, other Catholic agrarians, such as Liturgical Movement leader Virgil Michel, O.S.B., argued instead for "the correct rural philosophy." St. Martin's College in Lacey, Washington, offered such a philosophical course in 1946, but lack of interest stifled the original optimism. At least one "rural life school," held in the summer at Oklahoma A & M in Stillwater, attempted a compromise: "soils and soil conservation practices, spiritual and liturgical rural life, and rural education, will share with [the] philosophy of rural life."[76]

Since, according to Chicago's archbishop Samuel Stritch, agriculture was "no mere secular subject," "farming piety" provided the foundation for the reconstruction of the social order that Pius XI called for in *Quadragesimo Anno*. "Christian customs and usages even more emphasize the dignity of farm and farmer. In the farmer's dependence on Almighty God for help and protection he is brought close to God, but Religion inculcates that in a special way the farmer is the cooperator with God in feeding the people." With respect to Pius X's papal motto "to restore all things in Christ," Chicago archbishop Samuel Stritch made the point that farmers stood in a unique position to accomplish such a restoration. By the nature of their vocation, they helped realize Pius's vision. William Gauchat, a Catholic Worker from Cleveland who was involved with the farm communes, agreed: "With prayer, faith, courage, hard work and vision the members of the various Catholic Worker groups are working towards that new Christian society within the shell of the old industrial civilization which has cramped and crippled so many helpless victims."[77]

During the Depression, therefore, the Catholic agrarian worldview held particular veracity, because its call for independent, small-scale farming opposed everything that had created the crisis. Instead of being antimodern or reactionary, Catholic agrarianism's conception of a rural Christian social order appeared to be quite opportune. Wrote C. E. Wolf, "Anyone who has the industry *and the courage to adopt it* as his plan for life will find that it satisfies his fundamental human desires for a livelihood, security, freedom, and happiness. What more has any other occupation to offer?" C. M. O'Brien concluded that "if the Church through the National Catholic Rural Life Conference or other appropriate agencies takes an active part in the settlement and development of the Columbia Basin, she will be but treading in the footsteps of her heroes who have gone before." The Catholic Workers envisioned this rural Catholic self-sufficiency as helping even the most impoverished: Peter Maurin wrote, "With a combination of farming and handcrafts the progress has been phenomenal, and a free and independent and fully human life is within the grasp of these few men who knew only poverty, distress and contempt in the city."[78]

In a true Jeffersonian spirit, Catholic agrarians believed that farming made better people. Since cities had no room for farming, it stood to reason that they could not improve people. The solution lay with the land. If the population shift into the cities could not be stopped, mused Eugene Geissler, this might not be so bad. America "might be sustained, perhaps, far into the future by an influx of young country folk, bringing their truths and traditions with them, into the cities." The farm boy *is something of a philosopher*—a philosopher who has learned a very solid, real and natural philosophy," Geissler commented. "Primarily and paramountly before he discovered anything else on the farm he discovered something great and good behind everything he saw. That was the beginning of his philosophy. Maybe you call it by some other name than he does, or maybe you cannot even see it, but to him it always remains that great and glorious discovery that is God." "Basically," concluded another observer after visiting a particularly successful rural parish in Westphalia, Iowa, "the *unum necessarium* is a vision and a grasp of the good life as God and nature meant it and as the Fathers of America dreamed it for their republic of small land-owners, plus a determination to reduce theory to act."[79] Jefferson's ideal citizen on the land and the one who embodied the social reconstruction desired by the Catholic Church were, in the eyes of Catholic agrarians, the same person.

Salvation through Fertility

When the land received the attention it deserved, and when more citizens appreciated the true freedoms ensuing from life on the land, Americans would, Catholic agrarians believed, recognize the natural physical and spiritual fertility residing there. In an age when more and more homes were receiving electrical service and appliances, the Catholic agrarians seemed to be calling for some forlorn rearguard action against modernity. But by now it is clear that they were not alone in this feeling. Allen Tate had already investigated Southern rural life and Southerners' apparent religious tendencies in his studies of Confederate generals and his well-known modernist poem "Ode to the Confederate Dead." Virgil Michel, the Liturgical Movement leader, also agreed. Michel was a staunch antiurbanite and spoke out against the city's insensitivity whenever possible. His work in liturgical reform, which emphasized regaining a natural or organic sense of Christian worship, could be seen to stem from the same impetus. The Mass, much like the city, had outgrown itself, and now its artificiality threatened the inherent fertility of true Christian worship. All of these perspectives required a certain idealism that such fertility could indeed be recognized in the soul, the farm, and the community. One agrarian critic thought that rural Catholics already possessed this "natural" liturgical sense: "Farm folks are great singers. Why shouldn't they be, with the inspiration of the birds whose companionship they enjoy?"[80]

From this emphasis on life on the land followed another facet of the Catholic agrarian worldview. If cities were sterile and corrupt, rural areas were inherently fertile, physically as well as spiritually. "If it were not for Poseyville, Indiana," remarked one commentator in *St. Isidore's Plow*, "Chicago would disappear. If it were not for Poseyville, Indiana, New York City, New York would disintegrate for lack of leaders." The fertility of the seemingly boundless American farmland reflected the fertility of the American Catholic soul. The city, by comparison, only imperiled life, natural and supernatural, with its industrial pollution and moral corruption. "I exist in the city. I live in the country," Archbishop John Glennon once said. "Sometimes in St. Louis I am not sure I exist, because I can not identify myself on account of the smoke." Of course, part of the motivation behind Catholic agrarianism was that American Catholicism was overwhelmingly urban. Nevertheless, Catholic agrarians condemned the city as a site for any kind of life, religious or otherwise. "I know now," Michel reflected in 1938, the year that he died, "that it is indeed very often a misfortune to be born in a larger city; and subsequent experience and contacts have convinced me that it may become almost an irreparable spiritual calamity to be born in some of our largest metropolitan areas." One pithy phrase captured the sentiment well: "Eden was a farm, Sodom was a city."[81]

Catholic agrarians fashioned a highly stylized rhetoric, but it did not lack practitioners. William Gauchat, the Catholic Worker from Cleveland, wrote, "A farming commune is a farm; it is a community; and it is idealistic." The same might be said of any farm or rural community that adhered to the Catholic agrarian worldview. Therefore, O'Hara concluded, "not only is rural home life most receptive to Catholic principles, but the form of business organization most beneficial to the farmer is essentially a Christian model of industrial organization. The key to successful farm marketing is cooperative organization, and cooperative organization is an expression of Christian principles." Eugene Geissler recalled that the idea for what became the Family Acres community arose from a meeting among graduate students at the University of Notre Dame. Most of them had been students in apologetics (a theological approach that seeks to "defend" Christian beliefs and practices to a wide audience). More than a few of the farm communes associated with *The Catholic Worker* were started by Catholics whose previously closest encounter with rural America had been in school. Geissler remembered the influence of "that big, burly, blue-eyed Italian priest, L. G. Ligutti," as well as reading The *Catholic Rural Life Bulletin* "for the first time and practically going berserk with those wonderful and scrumptious ideas of rural life and community."[82]

Rural life lived properly stood as an independent way of life whose spiritual and physical vitality stabilized an anxious and slipshod modern world. Emerson Hynes, a sociology professor at St. John's College in Minnesota, proclaimed that "farming is first of all a way of life, and only secondarily an

occupation for making an income. Its principal values are of a transcenden-
tal nature. It is not a static, negative system, a mere protest against more
complex ways of living. It is a vital society. It must develop and progress as
well as any other. It is a positive mode of life, with its own end and its own
means for achieving that end." Catholic agrarianism's theological vision of
American rural life certainly possessed an idealistic foundation, but it was
precisely through that idealism that it won many converts.[83]

Consequently, agriculture stood as a unique area in which those interested in Catholic Action could pursue the mobilization of the laity. Farmers
were, of course, laypeople, but the nature of their vocation placed them in
an intimate relationship with the land, which was to rejuvenate both
Church and nation. In describing this relationship, Archbishop Stritch illu-
minated how the Catholic rural life movement's worldview fit into the
broader American Catholic culture. "It is a fact," Stritch claimed, "that in all
countries before the advent of secularism a certain piety attached to farming." Secularism was not merely a word to describe the realm outside the
sphere of religious influence. With it Stritch implied a notion, common in
Catholic circles, that the Protestant Reformation had, in its rejection of
Church authority, torn asunder the innate religiosity in human activity that
that authority had monitored. Hilaire Belloc and Peter Maurin both considered the Reformation an event with terrible consequences.[84]

The Catholic rural life movement did its part to reintegrate human life by
emphasizing a theme long familiar to agrarians: cooperation. In an NCRLC
handbook for Catholic clergy and laity, Thomas Howard wrote that cooperation was "merely the free operation of the Golden Rule in our economy"
and that it gave "sturdy realism to the brotherhood of man and the Father-
hood of God." (Howard was not Catholic, but he was a thirty-second-degree
Mason.)[85] The Redemptorist priest Louis Miller expressed how the neo-
Scholastic Catholic Revival meshed with non-Catholic decentralists:

> Catholics are, of course, concerned primarily—and should be concerned—with
> the religious aspects of the rural problem. But these are so intertwined with the
> cultural and economic problems that we must also devote our attention to
> them. There has been a fine spirit of cooperation among Catholic and non-
> Catholic agrarians in these matters, and it seems to me that spirit should be en-
> couraged by a mutual study of aims and objects.[86]

Cooperation, therefore, characterized how Catholics interacted with others
interested in critiquing modernity and proposing solutions to contemporary
agricultural crises. This interaction also illustrated how the various aspects of
rural life itself were united ("cooperated") around the necessary religious
component.

The NCRLC urged Catholic cooperation in almost every "practical" aspect
of rural life. Its *Manifesto on Rural Life* included sections on "rural health,"
"rural social charity," "farmer cooperatives," "rural credit," and "rural

taxation." Bishop John Peschges of Crookston, Minnesota, himself a farmer's son, described how the *Manifesto*'s suggestions might be realized:

> Burdens must be shared and common problems must be taken up and solved on the basis of the just rights and the proper needs of the individual and of the welfare of the community. No agency is more conductive to this end than the properly organized and managed co-operative. Many co-operatives are such only in name; true cooperatives are both democratic and Christian in spirit.

Peter Maurin made similar claims with respect to the "Green Revolution": "[T]he scholars must become workers so the workers may be scholars." "Co-operation" was how the Catholic agrarians participated in the Catholic pursuit of theological and cultural unity in American life. In doing so, they shared a popular opinion about cooperation and rural life held by agrarian-minded Jews and Protestants.[87]

This pursuit appeared to be on the brink of success in the early 1930s. Agricultural depressions in Canada had been alleviated by Catholics who convinced farmers to abandon economic competition and overproduction in favor of subsistence farming and marketing cooperatives that distributed profits evenly to all. The cooperative work at St. Francis Xavier University in Antigonish, Nova Scotia, received particular attention and praise from American Catholic agrarians. Fishermen in the area had begun to market their catch themselves, while the university trained them in the rudiments of gardening. Raising much of their own food gave the new part-time farmers a previously unknown measure of economic and social autonomy. This made them "able to take advantage of whatever great changes may be forthcoming in the national field for the reconstruction of society."[88] Cooperative experiments in Quebec and Ontario had also proved successful. A priest from Ontario described the efforts for independence in this way: "The object of the community is not to see how much money we can get in from the outside but to see how little we have to send out."[89]

Being inherently fertile, rural life still integrated the physical and spiritual dimensions that both the city and the Protestant Reformation insisted on separating. However, cooperating with that rural fertility held some particularly thorny considerations for rural Catholic women. Catholic agrarians believed that Catholic women, whether they were members of a religious order or not, embodied the fertility of the land. Not only were they physically fertile by producing children, but as mothers they also embodied the family's spiritual fertility. At times the Catholic rural life movement's insistence on this came close to agreeing with one of Friedrich Nietzsche's aphorisms— "Everything about woman is a riddle, and everything about woman has one solution: it is called pregnancy." While Catholic agrarians did not share Nietzsche's misogyny, non-Catholic agrarians such as Ralph Borsodi were not so circumspect. Some secular agrarians were openly misogynistic, as well as racist, viewing rural life as "cures" to both "problems." Catholic agrarians generally avoided such extreme perspectives. Nevertheless, the ways in which they praised what they believed to be the most noble occupation of rural Catholic women imposed some significant constraints on the lives of those women. Religious women did not escape the discussion concerning female fertility and productivity. John T. McNicholas, in reference to establishing rural religious-education programs, commented that the "Sisters will do all the preparatory work and do it only as religious women can do it—with infinite patience . . . with delicacy and tact."[90]

As the soil required particular methods of cultivation, so did parenthood. For many Catholic agrarians, this meant prohibiting artificial birth control. It was, Ligutti and Rawe declared in *Rural Roads to Security,* "the insidious sin. It completes the breakdown of family life. . . . Many young married people feel they are too poor to rear children in the city. They fall into the evil practice of artificial birth prevention." Not surprisingly, hope resided on the land: "On the other hand the small farm demands more helpers; it is the hope of our future generations." Abigail McCarthy reflected (with thirty years of hindsight) that "joyful and unrestrained procreation was basic to the rural life and the family movement." There were many reasons that Edgar Schmiedeler became involved with the Christian Family Movement (CFM); an underlying one was that Catholic agrarianism and the CFM shared a vision of natural fertility that was divinely constructed. Birth control constituted "a serious deviation from an essential and necessary order in creation," according to one Catholic commentator. "In using their reproductive faculties husband and wife supply the human co-principles of life and have the privilege of co-operating with the Creator in the production of new life. This power has been entrusted to them by God; in using it they must respect its sublime character." Just as farming carried specific responsibilities, so did parenting. Raising a family on the land combined these two occupations. In maintaining them, families cooperated with the divine order like no others.[91]

In 1942 a smaller but more direct form of rural Catholic assistance emerged when the Rural Parish Workers of Christ the King began work in Cottleville, Missouri. LaDonna Hermann and Alice Widmer, both alumnae of local Catholic women's colleges, created one of the first "secular institutes" in the United States. Inspired by a speech extolling the archdiocese's rural life program, Hermann and Widmer approached the speaker, Monsignor Leo Steck, about helping the program. Even though neither of them had previously lived in the country, they offered to move to a rural area to assist in the construction of an active rural parish program. Archbishop John Glennon found the two women's project interesting when they asked his permission to pursue it.[92]

A tiny German farming community sixty miles west of St. Louis, Cottleville was not the sort of place that inspired the NCRLC or the ACLA. Farming demanded everyone's attention, leaving little time for "community-building." Hermann and Widmer found the situation as desperate as the NCRLC or the ACLA might have, but the path by which Cottleville would improve differed significantly from the plans of the national organizations.

Instead of prescribing formulaic answers, Hermann and Widmer sought first to discover precisely what the problems were. The utter lack of formal education, especially for young women, caught their attention. A craft class provided an opportunity to teach catechism and reading while also teaching "acceptable" skills such as sewing. Hermann and Widmer's 1929 Model A Ford (nicknamed Isabelle) taxied women to St. Charles for Aid for Dependent Children; it doubled as a mobile library in the summers.[93]

Seven years later, Archbishop Joseph Ritter transferred the Rural Parish Workers to Fertile, located fifty miles due south of Cottleville, and into an 1876 brick house. Now working in an area originally settled by the French in the eighteenth century, Hermann and Widmer discovered a new situation with new problems. In Fertile, the difficulty was not so much recreation as unemployment and a lack of social services. The community was located in what had been a particularly active lead and iron-ore mining area. But with the mines closed, most of the welfare benefits stayed around the county seat of Potosi. The two women realized that this disparity stemmed from ethnic and religious differences. Potosi was largely Anglo-Irish and Protestant, while Fertile and the nearby town of Cadet were French and Catholic. (When Hermann and Widmer arrived in 1949, the local priest still heard the confessions of elderly residents in French.) Widmer's legal training and Hermann's education background helped encourage the area residents to vote and claim their share of the welfare benefits. Under the spiritual direction of a Benedictine abbot familiar with the Liturgical Movement, the Rural Parish Workers had the famed St. Louis liturgist Martin Hellriegel bless their house after its remodeling.[94]

Lay groups such as the Rural Parish Workers assisted with the NCRLC's plans to bolster Catholic rural life because they shared the conference's assumptions about rural life, especially about its fertility. Since the "Catholic rural problem" was a multifaceted one, the response to it likewise needed to be integrated around life on the land. Many Catholic agrarians arrived at this conclusion despite O'Hara's conviction, expressed as early as 1919, that the back-to-the-land movement was "essentially a city movement which seeks to . . . unload on the country groups of individuals who have failed to make a living in the city." For example, neither Hermann nor Widmer had lived in a rural area previously. Yet they moved to Cottleville, firm in their faith that God would provide for them. While the Rural Parish Workers held a perhaps more realistic view than other Catholic agrarians, they all shared the conviction that life on the land would enable Catholics to begin what the modern age seemed to require: a life that integrated religious faith and social concern.[95]

Anchored by the Family Farm

Agriculture was not merely an occupation, but analogous to the soul's relationship with the divine life.[96] Like the Church's seven sacraments, farming conveyed grace in a form unavailable elsewhere. When Catholic agrarians described the fertility of farming and of the land, they recalled earlier traditions of Catholic agriculture, from which it was a short step to endorsing a familiar American icon: the family farm. Not only was it "all-American," it had also, the Catholic agrarians claimed, always enjoyed the Catholic Church's attention. Ignatius Esser, O.S.B., thought that the Benedictine tradition of successful agriculture could be attributed to four factors, but "the biggest secret of all for the success of this agricultural activity lay in the fact that St. Benedict established his community as a *family*." The abbott's patriarchal authority resembled God's love for creation as seen in Christ. Just as the Catholic rural life movement, secular agrarians, and other religious agrarian groups shared the idea that the nation's freedom sprang out of rural America, they also agreed that it grew best out of small-scale, family-owned farms. In the eyes of Catholic agrarians, Thomas Jefferson and Thomas Aquinas spoke with one voice.[97]

The family farm came to be seen as the foundation upon which rural America and the nation would be rebuilt. Alphonse J. Matt predicated the safety of democracy on the family's primacy. The New Deal would succeed, Matt believed, only when "men . . . return to the divinely ordained laws which govern the growth and functioning of the social organism. And the primary cell of that organism is the family, correctly understood not only as the cradle of children but also as the cradle of economy and culture." Out of the concern with families and farming developed a project known as Family Acres. Founded in 1947 by Notre Dame–educated men and their wives, the farming community outside South Bend, Indiana, strove to demonstrate how rural families, living in community, could achieve the integration of life and religion so highly desired by Catholics of the time. Julian Pleasants, one of the Family Acres founders and a biologist employed by the Lobund research laboratory at Notre Dame, concluded that "what the child needs for his spiritual health may very well be what he needs for his physical health."[98]

Family farms not only produced physical sustenance, they provided the surest foundation for inculcating religious beliefs. Another Family Acres resident, Willis Nutting, recalled the modern rural family as a bastion of fertility and stability. "[T]he country offers almost the only opportunity in the modern world for building up a real family life. Elsewhere the home (or rather, the apartment) is scarcely more than a place to sleep. . . . But on the land the family is a real unit geographically, economically, and socially." Being born on the land took on special meaning, since, according to Urban Baer, "Christ Himself wished to emphasize the dignity of the farmer's trust. For He was born, one might say, on the very land itself. . . . Since Christ taught so much of things pertaining to the land how pardonably proud should not the farmer be of his calling and of his trust." Therefore, when Luigi Ligutti quipped (as he often did) "Christ to the Country, the Country to Christ," he spoke more of raising rural America's awareness about a relationship that already existed between the farmer and the land, as well as between Christ and the soul of the rural believer.[99]

Virgil Michel noted a link between family farmers' agricultural methods and their faith. Farming correctly came from holding the correct beliefs—about the land as well as about God. "The evil and unchristian effects of pure commercial farming and of exploitation of the soil, as direct rural counterparts of our citified bourgeois culture, must be convincingly exposed. The family farm must be stressed, and the primacy of subsistence farming." However, Michel pointed out that to live so simply might require technologically advanced assistance. "All the new modern means of self-help, as well as the devices of mutual help among members of the same community, should be studied—rural electrification with all its possibilities, agricultural associations, producer and consumer cooperatives, credit unions, the new agricultural possibilities that we are only beginning to become aware of today."[100]

Spiritual and Physical Remedies from Bio-dynamic Farming

"Bio-dynamic farming" was the primary means by which Catholic agrarians pursued their environmental concern for the social-religious order. Priests John Thomas and James McShane explained: "What do we mean by bio-dynamic farming? The word means methods that conserve the health and fertility of the soil by several means. Among these means are the use of animal and vegetable fertilizer and the avoidance of certain harmful fertilizers." Historian David Bovée has specified what was meant by "fertilizers": manure, legumes, and earthworms. These materials naturally revitalized the land and were, of course, readily at hand. Artificial fertilizers, besides constituting an additional expense farmers could do without, provided merely temporary benefits. When Ligutti advised *Ora et labora,* and use a lot of fertilizer!" he was not simply reinforcing traditional farming practices. He was instead preaching conversion to a different worldview that farmed differently as well. Cognizant of the land's supernatural connection, bio-dynamic farming enhanced its powers of physical regeneration.[101]

"Biodynamic agriculture" (minus the hyphen), though, extended far beyond the confines of Catholic agrarianism. In fact, its origins had at best only a tenuous connection to the Catholic tradition. Rudolf Steiner, founder of the Anthroposophical Society, used the term in 1924 while lecturing to Austrian farmers. Born in 1861 to Austrian Catholic peasants, Steiner became equally interested in science and in romantic mysticism. This led him to become an editor of Goethe's scientific works, and then to join Madame Helena Blavatsky's Theosophical Society. Anthroposophy, which began merely as a fellowship within Theosophy, established its autonomy in 1912. Steiner believed that the material sciences ignored the spiritual reality that physical existence presupposed. A spiritual hierarchy, topped by Christ, animated all physical matter, including humanity. Recognizing this reality enabled one to regain humanity's primordial spiritual awareness, now temporarily lost. Steiner lectured and wrote extensively to advocate his "spiritual-scientific" work that would recognize this unity in life's many pursuits. These included architecture, music and dance, education (the Waldorf schools were founded on Anthroposophy), religion (Steiner's Christian Community resembled the German Evangelical Church, but emphasized the Communion ritual as "the Act of Consecration of Man" and a direct encounter with Christ), and agriculture. Steiner died in 1925, a year after his biodynamic lecture. At least one of his biographers saw Steiner's development of biodynamic farming as the crowning achievement of the work he had begun with Goethe.[102]

Steiner saw biodynamic agriculture as issuing from "the inner, intimate activity which leads directly into the form of the spiritual as this spiritual is present itself on earth." Steiner believed that death, as the counterpart to life, appeared everywhere but was replaced by more life. This rhythm appeared in plants, animals, and even the seasons. Biodynamics employed these rhythms to concentrate and enrich the life forces so that the food produced would likewise enrich the humans who consumed it. Some of the first experiments eradicated chemical pesticides and fertilizers, using instead compost and manure (both being living substances), and paid close attention to seasonal changes to direct planting schedules. (Later biodynamic researchers successfully employed the ancient zodiac signs for their association with the basic elements of earth, air, water, and fire.) Plant life held the key to biodynamic success, for it assisted the farmer in maintaining the soil. In turn, plants, when consumed by different types of animals (cattle, sheep, goats, etc.), returned to the soil as different types of manure to sustain life again.[103]

The biodynamic farm modeled self-sufficiency at every level. "This farm is (or should be) a self-supporting closed organism, in which the different organs such as the fields, the manure, the meadows and the animals all interrelate properly. . . . Foreign elements, such as artificial fertilizers or bought-in feed, which do not belong in this organism, are not constantly introduced on this farm." This natural community with both physical and spiritual levels could serve for more than just food production. The natural rhythms of biodynamics offered a new and therapeutic relationship for those feeling the need to reorient their lives.[104]

This theory coalesced easily with the agrarian and theological traditions prevalent within the Catholic rural life movement. Life produced life, and that was the key for the Catholic agrarians. This notion had deep roots in the history of Christian thought and practice. Christians declared that they received eternal life from their Savior's own life, death, and resurrection. Now the land became a gift to the farmer from God. Bio-dynamic farming replicated that relationship; the farmer produced more life from that which God had already given. The artificial fertilizers of industrialized farming replenished the land only temporarily, and the Dust Bowl was an indication of what the future held if nothing was changed. In 1943, the NCRLC's publication of the time, *Land and Home*, included a piece by Louise Owen that praised earthly bounty and its uses. Entitled "Kill . . . and Cure," the article discussed how rural residents enjoyed a natural abundance unavailable to city dwellers:

> And it is the farmer and his wife who have the upper hand, with the fruits of their orchards, the roots and leaves of their gardens and the edible wild plants of their woods and fields . . . and especially so is the one who has a porker ready to become a part of the larder. For there are more ways to serve up the parts of a pig than any other animal.[105]

Even if one could not farm full-time, subsistence farming could at least supply enough food for a family. Following Steiner (but not mentioning him), the Catholic rural life movement thought that the only "real" food came out of one's own, properly tended ground. *The Catholic Woman's World* noted that "a homesteader believes in the value of live, wholesome foods. Wherever possible, he raises his own, and ignores packaged, devitalized products."[106] *Land and Home* fondly recalled the Pater family, who owned only six acres. Edwin, the patriarch, worked in a nearby factory. "Of the six acres of the Paters' land, they farm only an acre. From this acre they get all the food necessary for their own family."[107]

This success could be replicated anywhere, since both land and human possessed natural capabilities when it came to farming. "Mr. Pater was city-bred and knew nothing of farm life. 'It just seemed to come to him,' says his wife with pride. 'He had never cared for a cow in his life, and yet our cow has never been sick.'"[108] The unreflective productivity of nature, and thus farming, was simply assumed by Catholic agrarians. If one lived correctly on the land, it would provide. "WORK IN THE CITY—LIVE IN THE COUNTRY" blared one NCRLC handout. "Holy Mother Church shows the way to a holier, richer life on the land for farm, small-town, and suburban families through the NCRLC."[109] Often this assumption took on a rather flippant air. "We were just sitting there," Dorothy Day reminisced, "when somebody said, 'let's all go live on a farm.'" Elsewhere, a little reading would suffice. *Commonweal* magazine editor Edward Skillin Jr. wrote in 1942 that "whether your interest in the subject is romantic or you really mean to do something about it, there never was a spring with so many people ready in book form to give advice" on "armchair husbandry."[110]

Unlike the large-scale, one-crop, industrialized farming that had led to the Dust Bowl, "bio-dynamic farming" viewed both crops and livestock as living things requiring respect and attentive care. Utilizing plant and animal fertilizer, concentrating a variety of crops on small acreages, and avoiding mechanized implements, farmers could produce food for the family without doing irreparable damage to the land. Bio-dynamics required hard work, frugality, stability, and religiosity, all of which Catholic agrarians feared were absent in much of American life. Farming according to bio-dynamic methods thus elevated rural Catholics above their urban counterparts as a shining example of American individualism and self-sufficiency. One of Peter Maurin's oft-repeated phrases, "There is no unemployment on the land," might have appeared to be incongruent with the realities of American agriculture. After all, "the children of the Grapes of Wrath" that Ligutti feared might become the nation's future had been displaced from farms, not cities. Nevertheless, Maurin's words aptly reflected the Catholic agrarian opinion that one of farming's benefits was that there was always work. "Honest work is a tradition of the American farmer," Schmiedeler stated. "It is one of the characteristics that give him peculiar worth."[111]

One Catholic agrarian indicated that farm work uniquely augmented Christian faith and practice. "On the land, also, one is very near to our Lord in His earthly life—the toil in the heat of the day, the weariness, the sitting down to rest. Try carrying heavy oak fence posts on your shoulder for an hour, and then see, the next time you say your rosary, how much more the Carrying of the Cross means to you than it ever did before." Such experiences led to a renewed appreciation of the spiritual benefits of simple manual labor. Farming made a person work, and by that work that person would become successful. This explains the Catholic agrarians' praise for the Protestant work ethic (as they interpreted it) wherever it appeared. Leo Ward, C.S.C., observed that "one of the most valuable elements in rural life, an element well ingrained in the normal rural mind, is the conviction that good things cost. Men do not get easy rides on the farm, and they do not look for them."[112]

At the time Ward wrote those words, though, the ride was in fact getting easier on the farm; agriculture had been modernized along with the rest of American life. Catholic agrarians were not united in their views about the technological advances of the day. Some unequivocally opposed them as urbanism run amok. The English priest Vincent McNabb, O.P., whose radical distributism attracted Dorothy Day and many NCRLC leaders, "wore hand-woven clothes, refused to use a typewriter, and traveled nearly everywhere on foot." Technology could resemble industrialization, and thus could be equally condemnable. Of "the advantages and opportunities normally given by life on the soil to man in his elemental quest of fullness of being," Ward listed first "the joy and inner good of working on what, presumably, is one's own, instead of being obliged, as the proletarian is, to work on and with and off what one does not love and could never reasonably be asked to love." The technological industry of the factory lacked the unity between life and work that farming maintained. Ward continued, "[I]t is a good thing to work on the soil. For soil and man are nearly related, and there is something especially normal and healthful and decent about man's working the land."[113]

Other Catholic agrarians, though, allowed farming technology so long as it was used properly. "It has never seemed to me that the machine itself is an evil thing," remarked Skillin. A tractor certainly was more efficient than a horse, although the latter provided natural fertilizer. Purchasing a tractor cooperatively with other neighborhood farmers ensured that it would not be used unnecessarily to the point that the machine separated the farmer from the land being farmed. Ralph Borsodi's School of Living taught self-sufficient living on the land while embracing technology. According to Edward Shapiro, decentralists predicted that electricity "would lead to the dispersal of industry because there was no longer any need for factories to remain concentrated close to sources of coal, and because electricity could easily be adapted to the requirements of small factories and home industries. Electricity also promised to make farm life less onerous and more attractive and, thus, help stem the drift of farmers to the cities." Borsodi demonstrated how a homemade electric loom could weave cloth. Not all Catholic agrarians thought that embracing rural life necessarily entailed rejecting modern comforts; Ligutti's Granger Homesteads featured electric lights and hot water heaters.[114]

Perhaps more important than the physical benefits were the spiritual ones that life on the land bestowed (when it was lived correctly). Living in right relation with the land best prepared one for an equally right relation with God and humanity. In other words, Catholic agrarians used bio-dynamic farming as a tool of cultural criticism as much as for agricultural reform. The Catholic agrarian worldview valued the land, and the created order generally, as a gift from God and believed it should be cared for by the greatest number of people using the correct methods. Walter Lowdermilk, the assistant director of the Soil Conservation Service, declared in an article reprinted in the *Catholic Rural Life Bulletin* that proper use of the soil preceded a just and peaceful social order: "Only by conservation can we be led on to a higher spiritual and physical development which will express itself in stewardship of the earth for the well-being of humanity for all time."[115]

Bio-dynamic farming was at once the foundation and the pinnacle of Catholic agrarianism's antiurban theology. Integrating different crops not only was a wise use of the soil, it brought life out of preexistent natural life, not the artificial existence associated with city living. It required a large number of small, independent farm families who lived off the land they owned. The trend toward large-scale, one-crop farming was especially vilified for its economic and social impact. Thomas and McShane wrote in 1941, "You see that loss of farm families is an economic loss while our birth rate continues to decline. . . . The single-crop planter is a man who does not care for the soil; he is at the other extreme from the man who carefully guards its health." "Animals and crops are living things and they follow laws of nature that we must respect," Rawe argued; "We too are living things—spiritual living things, but rather than adjust ourselves to the laws of life in a material and spiritual being, we have in recent years spent most of our time in an amazingly destructive effort to reduce ourselves to machinery."[116] In agriculture, biodynamic farming crowned the integration of life and religion that other participants in the Catholic Revival sought in literature and other fields. It also revealed the extent to which the American Catholic agrarians had moved beyond the Catholic ghetto and absorbed non-Catholic intellectual and cultural life.

Shortcomings of Catholic Agrarianism

Unfortunately, all the idealism tended to fall flat, far short of the lofty expectations. Few projects of the Catholic rural life movement achieved success. As will be shown in the next chapter, the Catholic Workers' farm communes often created the disasters Catholic agrarians wanted to avoid. The successful attempts, such as the Rural Parish Workers of Christ the King, mixed the Catholic agrarian theology with a good dose of realism. Motor missions, another successful project (to be explored in chapter 4), used the Catholic agrarian worldview as a missionary vision. However, they were far more immersed in rural Protestant culture than some of the Catholic agrarians would have liked. On other fronts, though, the framework of Catholic agrarianism began unraveling.

After Edwin O'Hara became bishop of Great Falls, Montana, in 1930, Kansas native Edgar Schmiedeler replaced him as the Rural Life Bureau director. Theoretically, Schmiedeler became the executive secretary of the NCRLC as well, but there a power struggle awaited him. The power of his position as executive secretary had de facto shifted toward the conference's president, W. Howard Bishop, who was two years into his six-year term. (Schmiedeler's personality apparently did not help; one reporter described him as a "cross between Mussolini and Mr. Milquetoast.")[117] Schmiedeler therefore shifted his focus and applied his bureaucratic acumen to the battle against artificial birth control, and quickly became a leader within the National Catholic Welfare Conference for that apostolate. In 1937 Bishop moved to Cincinnati, where he had an opportunity to establish the Glenmary Home Missioners, a rural religious order the need for which he had argued for years. The increasing specialization of interests within the Protestant Country Life Movement had come to the NCRLC, and with similar effects. As individual NCRLC leaders became attached to particular rural concerns, they pursued their solutions through channels independent of the NCRLC's more general projects.[118]

This left the NCRLC seeking some sort of direction after World War II. Emerging victorious, the United States enjoyed a heady euphoria. The nation stood as a global power, and, at least for many of its religious leaders, this power was not merely military. Led by mainline Protestant denominations, pride in America's preeminence as a global moral power developed quickly. It was shared by American Catholics, whose participation in the war effort attested to their acceptance by other Americans. The postwar years also saw American agriculture become the commercially productive force the National Commission on Country Life had desired forty years previously. There was also an increasing awareness of the international ramifications of American agricultural production. These agricultural developments, as well as the pride in America's moral superiority, received repeated praise from the

NCRLC's longtime executive secretary, Luigi Ligutti, who served in that capacity from 1940 to 1960. Under his leadership, the conference expanded its vision and its programs. By the late 1950s, though, just when the American Catholic Church was enjoying its zenith as a distinct subculture, the NCRLC went the way of its predecessor, the ACLA, dwindling in numbers and relevance. Therefore, while the American Catholic Church relished its recently recognized American character, the ebullience was not shared by the organizations that had earlier insisted on an agrarian basis for that identity.[119]

Ligutti's quasi-monopolistic leadership of the NCRLC resembled that of O'Hara's tenure during the 1920s. In many ways, both of these conference icons call to mind the same images; both have been lionized for their rural pastoral concerns and for their participation in scriptural and liturgical reforms years before the Second Vatican Council mandated them. Both were what a later generation termed workaholics. O'Hara had a sense of down-home wit, but Ligutti raised it to an art form. Much like Peter Maurin's "Easy Essays," "Ligutti-isms" expressed compactly their author's Catholic agrarian outlook. A 1941 audience in Fargo, North Dakota, for example, heard Ligutti's unique rephrasing on a Benedictine motto: *"Ora et labora*—and use a lot of fertilizer!" However, it was Ligutti's persistence in pursuing his expansive goals that led to the conference's membership and financial woes of the late 1950s.[120]

Born in 1895, Ligutti grew up in the Udine region of Italy and emigrated to the United States in 1912. He was ordained at age twenty-two and became the youngest priest in the nation. Ligutti was, as he put it, "interested in the problems of rural life because my people were farmers." His 1926 assignment to Assumption parish in tiny Granger, Iowa, became the springboard for his career in the NCRLC. At first the picture was grim: not only was the parish small, but its members were largely impoverished immigrants working in the bituminous coal mines nearby. The mines operated on a seasonal schedule, leaving the miners without income for months. Taking full advantage of the New Deal's offer of loans through the Subsistence Homestead Division, Ligutti constructed one of the program's most successful agricultural colonies, the Granger Homesteads. This prompted the NCRLC members to elect Ligutti president in 1937, a post he held until 1939; the following year he became executive secretary. In 1949 he was named Vatican observer to the United Nations Food and Agriculture Organization (FAO). In 1960 he became the NCRLC's Director of International Affairs, a position located in Rome. He continued to comment on agricultural and rural life matters until his death in 1983.[121]

The NCRLC underwent a significant change in outlook during Ligutti's tenure as secretary. No longer concerned merely with the "Catholic rural problem" or the economic woes of rural America, the conference came to share the international character of its director. Raymond Miller, a U.S. Department of Agriculture administrator and a longtime friend of Ligutti, wrote:

> First Iowa, then the whole United States, came into the perspective of Monsignor Ligutti. Then apparently Divine Providence cleared the way for a strange

circuit that ended in Rome and led him to follow in St. Paul's footsteps with the whole world becoming the Monsignor's parish . . . and the "county" he served as the Pope's county agent.

Indeed, much like the county agents earlier in the century who sought to improve American agriculture, Ligutti labored tirelessly to involve American farmers in the reconstruction of global agriculture. To this end, he continued the NCRLC's relationship with like-minded agrarian organizations. Besides the ACLA, he brought in the Church of the Brethren's "heifer lift" program, designed to repopulate Europe's decimated cattle herds; this effort aided the NCRLC's organization, CROP (Catholic Rural Overseas Program). He also organized a number of international rural life conferences, the first being convened in Rome in 1951. Father George Hildner, who had moved to a parish in Washington, Missouri, attended—sparking some bewilderment when Ligutti introduced him as "Alfalfa George" to Italian agricultural leaders.[122]

"From the vantage point of his rural community in mid-America, Monsignor Ligutti saw the problems of the world," wrote Miller. Ligutti was able to bring these international concerns to American Catholic farmers because he traveled to these places himself. Not only did he travel extensively, he traveled often. This left the NCRLC headquarters in Des Moines leaderless for much of each year. When Ligutti was in town, the office at 3801 Grand Avenue (the conference's headquarters from 1942 to 1979) became an obligatory stop for visiting Catholic agrarians, much like the Catholic Worker house on Mott Street in New York. More often, though, Ligutti was away. In 1952 and 1954, substitute secretaries were named for the day-to-day operations of the conference while Ligutti traveled.[123]

Ligutti's international visibility made the NCRLC increasingly well known in Catholic circles outside the United States. Ligutti delivered bushels of hybrid wheat to Pius XII in 1950 to demonstrate the possibilities of replicating the Midwest's success in Italy's depleted grain industry. He also expressed some of the most vocal Catholic concern for the large number of war refugees not yet resettled in Europe. And he shared with Edwin O'Hara an interest in improving the quality of rural life in Central and South America. Each visited the areas repeatedly; in 1953 they traveled together to Manizales, Colombia, for the second international conference on rural life. (Aware of Ligutti's efforts, a member of the Presbyterian Board of Foreign Missions congratulated him "on the success of your Rural Life Conference.") Improving the appalling conditions in Latin America, they felt, provided a bulwark against communism.[124]

Stemming communist insurgency preoccupied many Americans during the 1950s. Ligutti's knack for homespun humor served him well in this context. A favorite "Ligutti-ism" ran, "When a farmer and his family own a cow, Communism goes out the back door." Ligutti joyfully provided comic relief to the biting anticommunist frenzy of Wisconsin senator Joseph McCarthy. Behind his flashing smile, though, lay a commitment to fighting communism that was equal to McCarthy's. While the senator detected infiltration, Ligutti, more positively, saw the great productivity of postwar American agriculture as the safeguard against communist promises of a better life. Already in 1945 he asserted that "access to natural resources, created by God for all men to be used for the good of men of every age, color and creed, must be the starting point of a just and durable peace." Much like the Country Life Movement fifty years earlier, which hoped to improve the efficiency of rural America's food production, Ligutti thought the new production would be directed unselfishly toward the goal of feeding the entire planet. In this magnanimous vision, American farmers should use their land more extensively in order to produce even more food for the areas devastated by the recent war. Ligutti also supported "self-help" training in former colonial territories, similar to Dr. Tom Dooley's medical work in Laos, as a step toward independence.[125]

Ligutti's accomplishments placed him and the NCRLC in a very favorable light. One biographer has written that during this time, Ligutti "stood with Fr. John La Farge, S.J., as perhaps the two most vocal spokesmen of the Church's social gospel."[126] However, the internationalization of the NCRLC effectively distanced the conference from its constituency. Anticommunism found sympathetic audiences in rural America before and after the war. But despite these shared feelings, Ligutti and the conference managed to alienate farmers. In 1952 Bishop Edward Daly, O.P., of Des Moines severed the diocese's relationship with the NCRLC over reportedly critical remarks Ligutti had made about the NCWC's endorsement of restrictive immigration. The bishop further charged Ligutti with using NCRLC publications for "propagandizing." Other bishops accused him of pastoral partiality to Italian Americans and, not surprisingly, of being too international and neglecting the concerns of American Catholic farmers.[127] In a decade when the Catholic Church in America began shedding its immigrant identity, Ligutti's apparent ethnic preference for his countrymen recalled an earlier day.[128]

Ligutti left for Rome in 1960, having enlarged the NCRLC's leadership organization. The number of diocesan directors, an office that the conference had encouraged since the 1920s, had grown substantially. When Ligutti departed, many directors operated their own programs somewhat independently.[129] Ligutti's international work had earned the NCRLC the leading role in the Catholic Church's organized efforts to improve global agriculture. Beginning in the late 1940s, there had even been an effort to draft a papal encyclical on rural life. Although that did not happen, John XXIII's *Mater et Magistra* in 1962 more than sufficed for many Catholic agrarians. Nevertheless, David Bovée writes, "even at its most successful, the Conference sensed that it was not very influential among the majority of the nation's 500,000 Catholic farm families."[130]

Likewise, the issue of economic structures always occasioned problems for the NCRLC, for its own finances as well as those of the farmers to whom it sought to minister. O'Hara's one-man Rural Life Bureau ran smoothly, if not extravagantly; but after the NCRLC eclipsed the RLB, the monetary backing of the conference became a perennial topic of concern. The American Board of Catholic Missions began granting five thousand dollars per year in 1930, but that amount shrank as the Depression continued. The publications of the conference—*St. Isidore's Plow, Catholic Rural Life, Landward,* the *Catholic Rural Life Bulletin,* and *Land and Home*—did not produce much income. All had limited subscriptions, since they targeted priests, religious sisters, and educated laypeople. The only attempt to produce a popular farm journal came in 1947 with *The Christian Farmer.* However, the costly format was mismanaged. Although new readership peaked in 1949, by 1951 the *Farmer* ceased publication. The prolonged effect of short funding was revealed in 1957 when the NCRLC became, in Ligutti's words, "virtually bankrupt."[131]

Ligutti's departure in 1960 marked a certain end for the American Catholic rural life movement. While the NCRLC continued to advocate social concerns in rural areas (a conference representative in Washington, D.C., quickly became involved in the farm lobby), the financial and ideological crises of the 1950s had done irreparable damage to the conference's relationship with the rural Catholics whom it was supposed to represent. Ligutti's increasing concern for international agricultural matters enlarged the conference's budget and lent an air of Catholic charity, but it failed to elicit the sustained support from the laity required for such financial endeavors.[132]

The internationalization of the NCRLC followed patterns within earlier agrarian organizations. Had the conference been more aware of the heritage it shared with these organizations, its failure might have been avoided. The ACLA had wilted in the face of farmers' reticence as well. Much like Kenyon Butterfield and the few remaining agrarian optimists, who turned to Europe to forge an international rural life body, Ligutti and the NCRLC insisted on turning American agriculture away from itself at a time when many farmers who survived the Depression faced the likelihood of leaving the farm due to the postwar explosion of agribusiness.[133] (And, like the Country Lifers, Ligutti fretted over the sectarian spirit of many rural Protestant denominations.)[134] What the NCRLC had revived, to recall Walter Ong, was not rural Catholicism in America but a particular cultural and religious interpretation of it.

This similarity between Protestant and Catholic agrarian groups points to an agrarian outlook expansive enough to unify various religious groups that were often in conflict elsewhere. Catholic participation in a vibrant body of American social criticism created a religious worldview of American agriculture unique to the Catholic Church. It characterized the vast majority of American Catholic publications on the "Catholic rural problem," as well as on American agriculture in general, from the 1920s to the 1950s. Tending the soil correctly and praying correctly, both of which the NCRLC taught them, rural Catholics constituted one of the most stable groups in the nation. Ligutti and Rawe's *Rural Roads to Security* served as a fitting *summa* for Catholic agrarians. It described their vision of American rural life and their prescriptive plan for making that prophecy a reality.

Catholic Colonization Projects in Rural America

> Now if God clothe in this manner the grass that is today
> in the field, and tomorrow is cast into the oven; how
> much more you, O ye of little faith?
>
> —Luke 12:28

In rural areas in the United States, Catholic agrarians suggested an alternative Catholic rural life that indigenous rural Catholics either supported and ignored. The Catholic rural life movement's strength in publications, though, created a third party—rural Catholic colonists—who attempted to bridge the distance between the reality facing rural Catholics and the ideal vision offered by the rural life leaders. One NCRLC "Catholic rural life song," entitled "March of Rural Youth," proclaimed:

> We are of that favored band
> Who are living on the land.
> Close to nature's heart we rest,
> Knowing we are truly blest.
> Purple fruit and grain of field
> In a most abundant yield
> Make secure the happy hours
> In this rural life of ours.[1]

Between the lofty ideas and the gritty realities, there were Catholics who attempted to actualize the visions of a new Catholic life "on the land." The colonization movement in the 1930s and 1940s was perhaps the most idealistic attempt to enact Catholic agrarianism's theology of spiritual farming. In 1941 a young Catholic Worker living outside of Cleveland wrote: "And I know with certainty that we with others will be able to prove to others by our way of life that one may attain happiness and a human manner of life here and now. It is no Utopia but reality." With his wife, Dorothy, Bill Gauchat had founded Our Lady of the Wayside farm in an attempt to realize the vision of the "landward movement" that had been discussed for the past ten years.[2]

Catholic agrarianism offered many venues through which Catholicism assumed the cultural forms of rural American life. The most enigmatic were the farm colonies: agriculturally based communities established by those convinced by Catholic agrarianism that "life on the land" possessed virtues unattainable in the city. While other projects brought the Church's sacramental life to rural Americans, the farm colonies, which the Catholic Workers called farm communes, reversed the process, attempting to introduce Catholics to farming. Familiar imagery helped embellish such endeavors; both the medieval village and the early American settlers were recalled as predecessors.

The farm colonies demonstrated the extent to which the Catholic agrarian theology could shape American experience. All the standards of Catholic agrarianism were present, as they were throughout the Catholic rural life movement: an acknowledgment of the spiritual, physical, and economic benefits of rural life coupled with the sobering recognition that Catholics in the United States were overwhelmingly urban. The rural-to-urban population drift was decried as harmful to the nation's health. By gaining what *The Catholic Worker* called a "toehold on the land," Catholic farming communities founded in the twentieth century sought to regain the glory of earlier Catholic settlements. Farming God's creation offered an alternative to modern living in the overcrowded and spiritually bereft city. The colonists' faith in this restorative vision of the land sustained them in the face of the more than occasional difficult moment.

Early Efforts in Catholic Communitarianism

These experiments in creating community established a Catholic presence in an interesting expression of American culture. Communal life runs as a thin but distinctive line through American religious history. "There is," writes kibbutzim historian Iaacov Oved of religious communes, "no equivalent in any of the other countries in the modern world."[3] Perhaps because the principle of life shared in community departs dramatically from the American ideal of individualism, communal living has a certain exotic character that continues to attract new adherents. Regardless of historical period, this impulse toward exoticism has offered Americans innovative lifestyles as alternative expressions of identity. Vegetarianism, regulated sleep patterns and sexual relations, or a restructured pattern of work and recreation, either singly or in some combination, create a privileged and separate sphere of experience. The colonies started by various Catholic rural life aficionados followed this pattern. Those self-styled settlers knew, though, that they were not the first Catholics interested in agricultural communitarianism. While they quickly demonstrated that their efforts were an improvement over the earlier ones, the twentieth-century Catholic agrarians saw themselves as the heirs of that largely neglected historical segment of the American Catholic experience.

Antebellum America witnessed the founding of many religious and utopian communes in the New England and Mid-Atlantic states. Virtually all these communities, such as Oneida, Brook Farm, Fruitlands, and the various Shaker colonies, incorporated agriculture as an essential part of their regulated communal lifestyles. The ability of such colonies to sustain themselves varied greatly, but once the "Great American Desert" was discovered to be fertile, the communitarian phenomenon sprang up in the Great Plains as well. At the turn of the century, homestead communities based explicitly on agriculture returned to popularity. Groups such as the Salvation Army, the Episcopal Church, and the Jewish Agricultural Society extolled Jeffersonian subsistence farming and communal life.[4]

All the while, Catholics had taken up the cause as well. Catholic settlement, though, included more than the complex and diverse patterns of monastic communities transplanting their traditions from Europe. For the laity, immigration was the force behind many of the planned communities throughout the nineteenth and early twentieth centuries. Most of the colonization projects begun before the Great Depression sought to provide certain groups of immigrants with "life on the land" similar to that which they had just left. David Bovée has commented that in "forming communities with utopian purposes, American Catholics were only following a popular American trend in the nineteenth century." It must indeed have been a popular idea, since it seemed as if "almost every bishop in the American hierarchy . . . had a pet colonization scheme."[5]

Both laypeople and clergy organized these projects. James La Ray, a French nobleman, and his son Vincent established eleven Catholic colonies in northern New York between 1800 and 1830. The timber industry augmented farming and drew immigrants from France, Ireland, and Germany. From 1827 to 1836, Boston bishop Joseph Fenwick proclaimed to Irish immigrants that agriculture was the best path to success. A product of rural Catholic Maryland himself, Fenwick purchased land in Maine for an Irish Catholic colony in 1834, calling it Benedicta. Located in the southern tip of Aroostook County, it played an important role in establishing potatoes as northern Maine's cash crop. Escaping urban degeneracy concerned other Catholics as well. In 1842 Catholics from Baltimore and Philadelphia founded the German Catholic Brotherhood to escape the cities' anti-Catholic nativism. Later that year they purchased thirty-five thousand acres in western Pennsylvania to establish a colony. One hundred families soon moved there to hack out of the woods what became St. Marys, Pennsylvania. Further west, Bishop Mathias Loras presented Dubuque, Iowa, as a center for German and Irish Catholic immigrants interested in finding new farmland. North of there, Alexander Faribault, a second-generation fur trader, maintained a French Canadian presence in Rice County, Minnesota, beginning in 1844. Father Ambrose Oschswald founded St. Nazianz, Wisconsin, in 1854.

The community recalled in name and lifestyle fourth-century Cappadocian Father, St. Gregory Nazianzen. Oschswald encouraged all single members of the colony to practice celibacy and view all their possessions as common property. After his death, many St. Nazianz residents joined the Salvatorian order, and a seminary and convent were founded.[6]

Further west, Father Jeremiah Trecy, a priest with a shadowy background but a clear commitment to improving the abysmal conditions of fellow Irish immigrants, founded St. John's City, Nebraska, in 1857. "The only town [in Nebraska] that had been platted for other than commercial purposes," St. John's City nevertheless enjoyed a commercially viable location overlooking the Missouri River twenty miles west of Sioux City, Iowa. Following precedents in eastern states, Trecy envisioned the Nebraska colony as a haven where Irish Catholics might live freely while supporting themselves. Even though most colonists had not farmed in Ireland, the venture captivated their imagination. Leaving Dubuque, Iowa, they decorated their wagons with banners declaring "GOING WHERE NO ONE ELSE LIVES." Upon their arrival, Trecy and the first settlers erected a huge cross on the bluffs for those who followed to see as they came upstream. Trecy traveled widely to recruit more Irish to move to Nebraska. But after the Civil War started, he mysteriously drifted away. Rumored to have served as a chaplain for both the Union and Confederate armies, he never returned to the colony he had established, dying in St. Louis in 1888.[7]

The Civil War played a more direct role in scattering a promising rural Catholic community in southern Missouri. While working missionary territory further north in the state, Father Joseph Hogan realized that many Irish women lived and worked alone in St. Louis while single male Irish immigrants were following the river trade and railroads away from St. Louis. Hogan devised a project for an Irish immigrant farming community as a solution. He acquired some government land between the Current and Eleven Point Rivers near the Arkansas border. While cheaper than farmland further north, it was also remote and heavily forested. Nevertheless, it appeared that the community might prosper religiously and economically. Hogan remembered that

> [t]he little chapel amid the forest trees in the wilderness was well attended. Mass, sermon, catechism, confessions, devotions, went on as in old congregations. The quiet solitariness of the place seemed to inspire devotion. Nowhere could the human soul so profoundly worship as in the depths of that leafy forest, beneath the swaying branches of the lofty oaks and pines, where solitude and the heart of man united in praise and wonder of the Great Creator.

The ferocity of the Civil War in Missouri, though, interfered. Marauding bands of Confederate and Yankee sympathizers repeatedly queried residents about their "loyalties." Such questions were rooted more in attitudes about slavery and states' rights than anti-Catholic nativism, but an incorrect answer might lead to death. Residents eventually scattered, leaving the area with a new name—the "Irish Wilderness."[8]

The desire to preserve ethnic and religious homogeneity contributed to the utopianism of these projects. Planners figured that agriculture would provide the necessary economic glue to hold the community together. Many immigrants had just fled religious and economic upheavals in Europe, and farming supposedly provided the stability they wanted (and, in the minds of the organizers, needed). The early projects anticipated an even grander Catholic colonization scheme. Establishing communities in the 1870s and 1880s, the Irish Catholic Colonization Association (ICCA) inaugurated the most expansive such project of the nineteenth century. Peoria's bishop, John Lancaster Spalding, and St. Paul's bishop, John Ireland, founded the ICCA in 1877 with assistance from Bishop James O'Gorman of Omaha and two wealthy laymen, William Onahan and Dillon O'Brien. Between 1878 and 1883, the ICCA developed settlements across southwestern Minnesota, Arkansas, and Greeley County, Nebraska. A year before the western frontier was declared closed, the Minnesota settlements had already established a Catholic presence vibrant enough to warrant the creation of the diocese of Winona in 1889.[9]

As in many other Catholic colonization efforts, two forms of agrarianism met in the ICCA's plans for immigrant colonization. The association believed—despite the poor showing of Irish agriculture in the first half of the nineteenth century—that those who settled in the rural Irish Catholic communities would be able to recall the agricultural roots of their pious ancestors. The antiurban aspect of Jeffersonian agrarianism also figured importantly for the ICCA. Spalding and Ireland were zealous temperance advocates. Associating Irish alcoholism with urban living, they envisioned the rural communities as opportunities to demonstrate that Irish Catholics, once separated from alcohol, were as capable as any other citizens to contribute productively to American life. Jefferson's claims that the best citizens were those closest to the soil here took on a new meaning: Irish Catholic farmers not only made better Catholics, they also embodied American values better than their urban countrymen.[10]

Despite some opposition from bishops of the eastern states,[11] the ICCA orchestrated a vigorous campaign to arouse interest in moving westward, especially to the favored Minnesota communities. Bishop Ireland first bargained with railroad companies so that the ICCA could be the sole provider of settlers to these communities. The leaders candidly described the rigors awaiting those who chose to move: frigid winters, tornadoes and hailstorms, soil that needed to be "broken" a season before crops could be planted (not having been plowed, the prairie weeds had created a "crust" over the centuries), long intervals between visits by priests, and social isolation. The difficulties necessitated that prospective homesteaders be financially solvent—"men of moderate capital"—before they moved. Ireland and his advisors originally budgeted four hundred dollars for a family of four to get started in the colonies. By 1880, experience had shown that no less than a thousand dollars was needed. Even in 1877, Ireland admitted that "I cannot advise very poor people to come to our colony. Perhaps some day in the near future."[12]

Other ICCA ventures gave similar warnings: without sufficient funding, Catholics were better off staying in the city. Many Irish immigrants lacked the money to transport an entire family to western Minnesota, buy provisions for two years, and acquire the eighty-acre plot designated for each colonist. The settlers also needed housing. Some colonists in Nebraska purchased prefabricated units that could be assembled on-site. An advertisement for these promised that they did "not require a skilled workman to put them together, or take them apart . . . a hurricane can make no impression on them, and, if painted regularly, will last for a century." But dismayed colonists discovered that the flimsy shacks were no match for either winter or summer on the Plains. Lasting less than five years, the portable houses gave way to ones constructed of sod. The material was close at hand, and while sod was neither portable nor attractive, houses made with it provided good shelter.[13]

The housing troubles augured the ICCA's results. Despite the grand plans the communities did not reach the ICCA's utopian goal of creating Irish Catholic regions across rural America—not even with the Minnesota settlements, despite Ireland's seemingly endless optimism. Many of the communities remained small numerically. In terms of religious practice, though, they apparently became quite vibrant. As many other towns on the Plains came to realize, proximity to rail lines provided precarious and fickle support for community life. Many were reduced to ghost towns when the rails were rerouted through another village or the county seat moved elsewhere. Some of the ICCA's communities, and many other Catholic settlements as well, fell victim to these patterns. O'Connor, Nebraska, a project by Bishop O'Gorman, lost a major rail line despite constant pleas to ICCA offices in Chicago. Efforts in Arkansas failed largely because colonists there had to deal directly with the railroad companies, and very few came forth to do so.[14]

Ireland faced his own difficulties. He became particularly alarmed by one group of settlers hailing from Connemara, Ireland. Originally fishing families, they seemed content to serve as day laborers for the other colonists. Even though some of their 160-acre plots had already been plowed, they expressed little interest in developing them. They further offended their neighbors by pestering Ireland for monetary handouts. In contrast, the colonies' German-speaking immigrants were usually success stories. This added to Ireland's frustrations, given his unequaled anti-German sentiments. (As a teetotaler, he particularly despised the importance of beer in German life.) His project to rehabilitate his urban Irish co-religionists had become precisely what he had tried to avoid. Instead of creating a new American identity for Irish Catholic immigrants, to some extent the ICCA

projects drew further attention to the Irish failure in farming while emphasizing the successful tradition of farming by German immigrants.[15]

Improving Rural Catholic Settlement

When the NCRLC first met in 1923, John J. Glennon, St. Louis's reigning archbishop, and his "devotion to the land" repeatedly drew attention
and praise. Glennon was indeed perhaps the most visibly agrarian of all
American bishops. He had been involved in the gritty daily work of agricultural colonization for almost twenty years already when the NCRLC convened. In 1905 Glennon began resettling Belgian immigrants and predominantly German American Catholics from Indiana and Kentucky in
southeast Missouri's Bootheel. Glennonville, the town that emerged, was
lauded as the first step toward recapturing the agricultural traditions
Catholics felt they had lost.[16]

Unfortunately, the location could not have been worse. Glennon purchased more than fourteen thousand acres through an agent, never having
seen the land himself. The agent himself visited the site only infrequently
before he quit, disputing Glennon's refusal to advertise the colonies more
heavily. Built in a swamp along the St. Francis River, the tiny settlement, as
well as the neighboring towns, was a haven for insect-borne disease. Residents of the Bootheel's "instep" were often said to live on "a diet of qui-
nine." Furthermore, the St. Francis flooded backward due to downstream
congestion, and only a small ridge stood between Glennonville and the Mississippi River floodplain. The flood seasons of both rivers ran from February
to May, which meant that water regularly threatened Glennonville. Irregular
levee building exacerbated this problem by further channeling overflow into
the vicinity. Like many nineteenth-century settlers, arrivals to Glennonville
recognized that they now owned land in a less-than-desirable location. In
the words of one settler, "the natives thought the Bishop sent us down here
for penance." Another reflected that "I couldn't say if it were paradise or
purgatory, but I thought it was next door to hell."[17]

Despite the Dantesque circumstances, Glennonville's residents stayed
and, to some extent, succeeded. The first industry—forestry—helped drain
swamps for the production of staves and fence posts. The cleared land could
then be planted with wheat, corn, and cotton, while cattle grazed drier but
still forested areas. After the particularly disastrous flood of 1927 (in which
the Mississippi flooded from St. Louis down through the Atchafalaya River
basin in Louisiana), the Army Corps of Engineers assumed control of the
levee system and maintained it along both rivers. The rich bottomland uncovered by such measures remained relatively protected from flooding until
almost sixty-five years later, in the great flood of 1993.[18]

Glennonville's land reclamation efforts made it unique among Catholic
colonization projects. It also set a certain standard in a category important
for determining the overall success of a colony. St. Theresa's parish, around

which Glennonville was built, was tended for more than fifty years by one priest, Father Frederick J. Peters. The son of Westphalian German immigrants, Peters had attended seminary in Wisconsin with Missouri's conservationist priest, George Hildner. After being ordered by Glennon to build a parish in Glennonville, Peters never left. He stayed through floods, poor farming conditions, and disease epidemics, even after Glennon offered to reward him with a well-to-do parish in the St. Louis suburbs.[19]

Peters quickly gained a reputation among area residents for breaking down long-standing stereotypes of Catholics. Driving over from Malden to say Mass, he gave rides in his horse-drawn buggy to non-Catholics in order to dispel rumors that Catholics had horns. He became a notary public and justice of the peace, and served occasionally as a substitute Latin teacher at the local high school. His success against anti-Catholic bigotry spilled over to his parishioners. One resident who helped ship wood out to market recalled that his boss, Mr. McGilliger, met a woman along the wagon path to Malden.

> She said, "You Catholics ain't got no Bible nohow!" . . . "Well, I think you are mistaken," McGilliger said. "We've got a Bible." The old lady said, "Well, I'd just like to see it." "Well," McGilliger said, "if you would like to see it I'll bring it along tomorrow and let you read it." . . . Well, things went on for about a month. Then one day the old man came out and said, "Here is your Bible, Mr. McGilliger." He said, "The wife said her Bible was so much like that Bible, that she began to think that her Bible was a Catholic Bible, and she threw it in the stove."[20]

Other early arrivals to Glennonville encountered the apparently widespread assumption that all Catholics were Republicans. One settler recounted that, after hearing this so much, one of his father's employees attended a revival to prove otherwise.

> After the preacher got up and went to preaching, and proclaimed that all Catholics were indeed Republicans, a friend of Mr. Angburg [the employee] stood up and declared "Preacher, wait a minute, I've got a Catholic here that will testify that he is a Democrat." He had [Mr. Angburg] stand up, and [Mr. Angburg] said: "Preacher, that [accusation of yours] ain't so." Boy, he said that like to broke up the church meeting.[21]

Peters represented more than a model for ecumenism in small-town Missouri. Residents depicted him as holding the two swords of Glennonville's authority: as the priest, he fully controlled the village's spiritual life, but he also immersed himself in everyday secular concerns. After celebrating Sunday Mass, he was as likely to be found chopping wood, advising farmers about their crops, or tending to victims of the 1928 influenza epidemic (he had attended medical school for two years) as he was reading his breviary. He also assisted the stave factory in its first years of production and maintained a sizable garden in his front yard.[22]

Along with George Hildner almost two hundred miles to the north, Peters earned a reputation as being knowledgeable about many subjects besides religion. Just as Hildner took his prize-winning chickens to the Missouri state fair, Peters advised settlers to avoid farming cotton, unlike the large-scale operations across the ridge. Aware of the soil-depleting qualities of the crop, he reiterated the Catholic agrarian conviction about the superiority of biodynamic farming. He also assisted with obtaining legislation for a levee system along the St. Francis from Lake Wappapello. His connections to Jefferson City resulted in state assistance in building gravel roads from Glennonville to the Dunklin County seat of Malden, as well as to the commercial centers of New Madrid and Poplar Bluff. Area teenagers over sixteen had Peters to thank for a Friday-night dance hall constructed to combat the boredom of living in an isolated community.[23]

Peters, Hildner, Luigi Ligutti, and, as will be seen, Father Arthur Terminiello all demonstrated what Catholics, and not just the agrarian ones, celebrated as the irrepressibly heroic character of the priesthood. Catholics came to believe that a colony's parish needed a strong-willed priest around which the tiny community could unite. Sydney Ahlstrom remarked that instances of American religious communitarianism "were so often but the lengthened shadow of some charismatic leader." Catholic colonization projects certainly fit this category. With the twentieth century and the turn to an explicitly Catholic agrarian perspective, such singular leadership became a de facto requirement. The person best, and perhaps most naturally, suited to assume such leadership was the parish priest.[24]

Strong priestly leadership, in the eyes of many Catholic commentators, prevented in the twentieth century what had happened in the nineteenth: unmonitored settlement. Unless under the watchful, and increasingly agrarian, eye of a priest, Catholic colonists were feared likely to lose their specifically Catholic character and fade indistinguishably into the local religious scene. (This fear was not unfounded, as chapter 3 will show.) Such was the case near Tishomingo, Oklahoma, where in the early 1920s a "Mr. Chapman" started a corporate tenancy settlement. Carved out of Chapman's own thirteen-thousand-acre ranch, the Washita Farm Corporation (so named because of its location along the Washita River) was "plotted into farms consisting of 80 to 100 acres each. On each farm a modern seven-room house, a barn and a garage were erected." A centralized headquarters with farm buildings were constructed as well. Washita's residents shared their crop yields with the corporation. "One-third of the produce would be claimed by the company, while the tenant would be master of the remaining two-thirds." Up to this point, Washita was not a specifically Catholic settlement. In fact, only two families among the forty-eight were Catholic. Chapman apparently was not a good judge of colonist character, and the project suffered accordingly.[25]

After Chapman's death in 1929, though, his successors approached the well-known Extension Society founder and Oklahoma bishop Francis C. Kelley, who promptly dispatched Father Peter Schaefer. Experienced in agricultural projects, Schaefer quickly recruited Catholic families from Oklahoma, Texas, Iowa, and Minnesota to relocate. Most colonists were either former farmers who had moved to cities but lost their jobs, or younger people interested in farming but lacking land. A third group consisted of wheat farmers displaced by the already threatening Dust Bowl. Within two years there were "53 Catholic families, numbering 259 souls, claiming membership in this unique parish. Only a few non-Catholic families remain in the valley."[26]

According to commentators, Washita's improvement came thanks to Schaefer's presence. The coherence of the community depended directly on his efforts. Francis Mellen, a priest who recorded his visit in the *Catholic Charities Review* in 1932, wrote of driving through the Washita River valley "with this zealous and enthusiastic priest": "Now and again men in the fields paused in their toil to wave and call to [Fr. Schaefer] a friendly greeting. As we drove along, pointing to the various homes, he told the histories of the families, referring to mothers, fathers, and children alike, using their given names." Schaefer's clerical enthusiasm created the bond that improved the community. "Almost in exact proportion to the spiritual progress were the results in the rehabilitation of the settlers." Although the community's founder was not able to ensure the farms' financial feasibility, a priest was. With Schaefer the Catholic identity of Washita grew stronger as well. Glennonville, Washita Farms, and other colonies in Minnesota, Montana, North Dakota, and Washington offered proof to many that priestly leadership was necessary for successful rural communities.[27]

The emerging popularity of the agrarian worldview distinguished these attempts to colonize immigrants from those in the previous century. After all, it was Glennon's agrarianism that prompted Edwin O'Hara and Frederick Kenkel to hold holding the NCRLC under his auspices. Significantly, Glennon, while essentially patterning Glennonville after the Minnesota colonies of John Ireland, did not present himself as continuing Ireland's vision, nor did others view Glennon this way. Ireland had sought only middle-class Irish immigrants; Glennon settled whom he could where he could find land. According to one Glennonville resident, it didn't matter who the colonists were or where they were from, "just so long as they were Catholics. That's what he wanted. Didn't want Protestants. He tried to keep them out as much as he could."[28] Glennon's plan was perhaps somewhat more complex. Immigrants were colonized in rural Missouri not because they came from a successful European agricultural tradition, but rather because they might create the idealized rural Catholic life that Catholic agrarians desired but did not perceive in existing farm life.

Glennonville, Tishomingo, and the other colonies represented, for all their failures, a rural Catholic tradition reflecting the specifically Catholic agrarian view that noncolonized rural Catholics lacked. The conflicts over immigrant identity that had bedeviled Ireland were, forty years later, defused by a new desire to create a Catholic rural community with specifically rural characteristics. The push to Americanize immigrants through farming still existed, but now without the specifically anti-German element for which Ireland, Spalding, and others had achieved notoriety. Rural life no longer erased undesirable ethnic elements; it now corrected the "unnatural" state of city living. A priest's leadership was required here as well: "The priest must be the real field man. He must know the principles and he must apply them so as to get results in his own parish."[29] In suggesting this, Catholic agrarian leaders made new, explicit claims about Catholics' becoming exemplary Americans—not because they had been assimilated, but because they "finally" were engaged in the most American of activities—farming.

"Back to the Land!" in the Depression

In 1933 a *Commonweal* contributor reflected that "even though men have chosen temporarily to forsake her, great Mother Earth still waits." In reinvigorating a Catholic back-to-the-land movement, agrarian-minded Catholics hoped she would not need to wait any longer. Catholic agricultural colonization became a serious consideration as the NCRLC and other Catholic agrarians developed their solutions to the Depression-related crises facing rural America. This had not always been the case; Edwin O'Hara had actively opposed colonization as a solution to the "Catholic rural problem." After his interests shifted to the Confraternity of Christian Doctrine, however, the NCRLC doggedly followed a program intent precisely on rural settlement.[30]

Realizing this idealistic "life on the land" took many forms: community services, church programs, and agricultural reforms. At the root of it, though, lay the desire to engage as many Catholics as possible with activities that demanded getting their hands dirty. During the Depression and war years, this conviction centered on "colonizing" rural America. A return to subsistence farming would shore up the dwindling rural Catholic population. An emphasis on cooperation would show both the new arrivals and the inheritors of a century-long Catholic rural presence how to operate their farms more productively. In advocating a return to the land, Catholic agrarians sought to transform American and Catholic rural cultures while preserving the rural Catholic presence that they feared might die off or move away.

Purchasing subsistence "homesteads" came to be discussed by many Catholics. "Rural colonization projects," wrote W. Howard Bishop in 1932, "are not new. America owes its beginnings to such ventures from across the seas." Faced with multitudes of unemployed, Catholic agrarians hoped to turn such projects to a new end, that of economic redistribution. From St. Joseph, Missouri, Albert L. C. France noted the "voluntary communism" employed by the apostles to combat poverty. He then implored, "Why not expand on the plan today by the establishment of voluntary groups of Catholic families on the land, the source of food and fuel, groups picked, organized and directed by capable volunteers, devoted men and women, backed up by authority?" Many noted that the rural-to-urban drift had not subsided. Nevertheless, an editorial in *America* remarked that "while the condition of the farmer today leaves very much to be desired, the plight of the farmer boy who goes to the city is often worse."[31]

A return to farming was seen as one method to relieve widespread unemployment. This return could take many forms. Bishop recommended a "temporary expedient" to urban unemployment and food shortages: "providing garden lots on vacant city land for unemployed men and women to raise vegetables." It would take longer, he thought, to resettle Catholics on the land. Until then, the primarily urban population of the Church could begin the process by growing some of their own food. This "sub-urban" response to the Depression also received attention from Jesuit Daniel Lord's *The Queen's Work*, the publication of the Sodality devotional movement. Fathers Ligutti and Rawe considered garden plots for urbanites as one of the "rural roads to security." The 1949 issue of *The Catholic Worker* that carried Larry Heaney's obituary also held his challenge to readers to "grow your own food." Four years later the paper claimed that Maryfarm near Newburgh, New York, "is fast becoming a 'Garden Enclosed.'" Flower and vegetable gardens surrounded the Worker commune, producing food and decoration for the New York House of Hospitality.[32]

Many came to be convinced, with Peter Maurin, that "the future of the Church is on the land, not in the city; for a child is an asset on the land and a liability in the city." A wholesale return to agriculture became the call of many Catholic agrarians. The benefits of such a transition would be twofold: the unemployment woes would be solved by the variety of labor necessary to operate a farm; and rural religious education, a persistent concern of the NCRLC, would be aided by "seeding" areas near rural parishes with better-trained urban Catholics. Bishop made the back-to-the-land movement the subject of his sixth and final presidential address in 1934. "[I]s there not some way to be found by which these groups of sufferers in the cities and on the farms can work out their salvation together—on the land? We have the strongest reasons for believing that there is." Proclaiming that overproduction of crops, chronic urban unemployment, and farm tenancy might all be solved with such a development, Bishop averred that present farmers need not fear the competition. Since new farms would all be small-scale, subsistence ones, maintained with animal, not mechanized, power, they would be devoted more to garden instead of crop production; their smaller surplus could become part of the commodity market of which all farmers were already a part. Therefore, there would be more buyers and less surplus. "It is time that enlightened farm leaders should see that a wholehearted welcome to the land for distressed families of every type who are willing and able to make good on the land with government help, would be not only a gesture of Christian chivalry but a gesture of business sense as well."[33]

Sending Catholics "back to the land" would help create the rural Catholic community that the NCRLC and others so desperately desired. Fomenting this interest was the knowledge that other religious groups already had carried out such projects successfully. In 1954 John La Farge, S.J., recalled his astonishment "to discover that the Jewish people of the United States had in some ways come closer to a successful answer to the farm problem than had their non-Jewish neighbors." Catholic agrarians had known for ten years of the colonization efforts by American Jews. The Hebrew Emigrant Aid Society had helped build successful agricultural colonies in southern New Jersey from 1881 to 1888. Continuing this tradition, the Jewish Agricultural Society had increased the number of families living on the land from approximately four hundred in 1900 to sixteen thousand by 1930. Other Jewish colonies included the Am Olam in South Dakota and the Sunrise Community, founded by Jewish socialists, in Michigan. Catholic agrarians wanted their co-religionists to develop similar communities.[34]

Before World War II, many Catholic agrarians discussed the back-to-the-land movement primarily as a solution to unemployment. After the war, they envisioned the land as a haven for displaced persons. The Catholic Workers maintained that the land should become a starting point for the creation of a new Catholic culture. "This much is, however, certain," maintained the NCRLC in its 1944 declaration *Rural Life in a Peaceful World:* "civilization will not recover its strength if upon this total war there does not follow a total peace." Catholic agrarianism's insistence on the intrinsically patriotic character of Catholic rural life enabled it to avoid the accusations of disloyalty that had been hurled at Catholics (especially Germans) during World War I. Rural life "naturally" opposed totalitarianism in both politics and agriculture. After all, Thomas Jefferson considered farmers to be the backbone of democracy. Furthermore, the NCRLC declared that rural life held the key to postwar global recovery and security; "[t]he farmer himself can do more than anyone else to bring about this happy condition."[35]

The religious auspices that sparked and directed the landward movement enjoyed an importance equal to that placed on actual farming methods. The necessity of a priest's guiding influence, as in the cases of Glennonville and Tishomingo, was reiterated. La Farge, speaking from his years of experience in southernmost Maryland, wrote:

> But whatever be set on foot in the way of agencies or bureaus, the most essential factor in determining whether good or evil may be expected from the landward movement remains the individual parish priest. An apostolic, rural-minded priest, informed of every phase, spiritual and material, of the rural life problem, will be for his people the compendium of all agencies.[36]

Other Catholic agrarians put scarcely less emphasis on the cleric, connecting his knowledge of Catholic social justice with the technological knowledge of the county farm agent.

The back-to-the-land sentiment of the Catholic rural life movement and other groups provided the ideology necessary for the New Deal's controversial resettlement projects. The Department of the Interior's Subsistence Homestead Division, succeeded by the Resettlement Administration, oversaw an ambitious project to reconstruct American society along rather modernistic lines. M. L. Wilson, the enthusiastic social theorist who led the project, was a disciple of both secular reformist thought and a virulent form of romantic agrarianism. The former assumed it knew better than the masses how to solve their problems, and the latter stood convinced that rural America offered the location on which those solutions would begin. Wilson envisioned a series of federally funded homesteads appearing across the United States, each with affordable, easy-to-build housing and filled with joyous new tenants thrilled to be out of the vicious cycle of work for wages. With small-scale industry nearby and enough land to produce a significant portion of their own food, families would move in a matter of months from tenancy and destitution to ownership and productivity within society. This vision differed little from the earlier projects of secular colonies such as the "Little Landers" of San Ysidro, California, and Catholic projects such as Washita and Glennonville.[37]

In the national debate over the feasibility of the New Deal, the NCRLC stood out among Catholics and non-Catholics as an enthusiastic backer. In its stated support for the New Deal's Agricultural Administration Act, the 1933 NCRLC convention included a resolution declaring that the "back-to-the-land movement deserves our hearty endorsement and encouragement, for we see in it the brightest hope of reestablishing our civilization on a saner, simpler, more wholesome and more enduring basis." Prospective Catholic colonizers were encouraged to avail themselves of any help extended by local, county, state, or federal government, as well as the Church's diocesan rural life bureaus. Other federally funded homestead projects—in Hightstown, New Jersey; Alaska's Matanuska River valley; the "Green" communities outside Cincinnati, Milwaukee, and Washington, D.C.; and some experimental homesteading conducted by the University of Kentucky—drew attention from the Catholic press. In the face of a seemingly endless depression, Catholic agrarians regarded the "landward movement" as the nation's chance to regain its past agrarian glory.[38]

The NCRLC's flagship colony in this process was the homesteads of Granger, Iowa, located just northwest of Des Moines. Granger's economy depended on seasonal work in the local bituminous coal mines. The ebb and flow of money meant squalid living conditions in the surrounding miners' camps. Most unemployed miners and their families lived at or below the poverty level. A 1941 *Commonweal* article reported that one miner spent every winter in the mines; then, "[e]very summer he went on relief. He was never able to make more than five hundred dollars a year and that was spent before it was even made." As pastor of Granger's Assumption parish, Luigi Ligutti saw justification for the anti-industrialism of many agrarians. He also came to understand the criticism of the spiritual and physical squalor some thought was endemic to rural life. The federal homestead grants appeared to be an opportunity to practice much of what the NCRLC had been preaching for the past ten years. The Granger Homesteads became the exemplar, in the words of one NCRLC publication, of "the changing of an industrial and city-minded population into a rural-minded people by pegging Catholic families to the soil." Historian Paul Conkin has noted that the Granger Homesteads thus became the only New Deal homestead project influenced by specifically distributist agrarianism.[39]

Ligutti used the federal funds to establish a predominantly Catholic community of immigrant miners in 1933. Thirty-three of the fifty homesteading families were Catholic; eighteen of these were of Italian origin and twelve were of Croatian origin. After obtaining one of the federal loans, Ligutti purchased 225 acres and divided the land into plots of two to eight acres. Since the coal industry operated seasonally, subsistence farming on these plots would provide food and marketable products whose profits would pay off the federal loans. A diagram in *Rural Roads to Security* showed how Lawrence Oyers divided his three and a half acres: at least 43 rows of corn (sweet and field), one-eighth acre of rye, one-seventh acre of Sudan grass (grown for hay), 1,200 strawberry plants, approximately 1,000 raspberry plants with popcorn planted in between the rows, 18 rows of sweet potatoes, an orchard with 600 tomato plants underneath the trees, at least 30 rows of garden vegetables such as peas, lettuce, spinach, beets, and cauliflower, and a chicken coop.[40]

Granger embodied the assumed superiority of Catholic social teaching, offering an example of almost every Catholic agrarian project. Ligutti received assistance from the extension service of Iowa State Agricultural College in nearby Ames. This helped establish one of the Catholic agricultural schools that O'Hara and the other NCRLC leaders had long desired. Granger's parish school became a field laboratory that taught home economics and scientific farming methods in preparation for life on the land. Following the NCRLC's advice, Ligutti also formed farmer cooperatives. La Farge's description of Granger after his own visit revealed how the homesteads embodied the Catholic agrarian worldview:

> But they can only succeed in buying [houses] in common because they succeed in living in common. And it has taken the leadership of a Catholic priest, the spiritual bond of a Catholic parish, to give each home the *life* that makes this living-in-common possible. It has taken such leadership to overcome the obstacles created by national and racial differences.

Since it was a created community, the Granger Homesteads exemplified the Catholic agrarian insistence on cooperation far more than other cooperative activities made by Catholics elsewhere in the Midwest. Westphalia, Iowa, became the center for the NCRLC's celebration in 1944 of the centenary of the Roachdale cooperatives. In the public expression of what Catholic agrarianism could achieve with cooperatives, though, Granger remained the standard.[41]

Granger's successful cooperative community structure made it a sort of rural Catholic "city upon a hill." Constantly lauded in the Catholic press as an example of Catholic cooperation with the New Deal, the homesteads even received a visit from Eleanor Roosevelt. *Commonweal* editor Edward Skillin Jr. described a visit to Granger as "my pilgrimage." (A few sentences later, however, he complained about the lack of taxicabs at the train stop on the outskirts of Des Moines.) Others came to share this interest. La Farge remarked that Granger "became more or less a rural show-place and a model of what could be done in the way of part-time farming." This success was recognized further in 1941 when Ligutti began his stint as the NCRLC's executive secretary.[42]

A cursory reading of *Rural Roads to Security* and the popular Catholic publications *America* and *Commonweal* might give the impression that Catholic attempts at resettlement consisted solely of the Granger Homesteads. According to Conkin, Granger "was believed by many people to be the nearest thing to Utopia imaginable." Yet even Raymond Witte, C.M., the NCRLC's official historian admitted that "the project was not the work of the Catholic Church, since it was always under the supervision of the Federal government. No attempt was made to make it sectarian but since most of the people in the area were Italian or Croatians, it was natural that two-thirds of the families were Catholic."[43]

Granger's status as an exemplar of the Catholic rural philosophy overshadowed community-creating efforts that were less conscious of who was chosen. Thoroughly Catholic farming towns such as Westphalia, Iowa, and Assumption, Ohio, were lauded as successful cooperative efforts but were not seen as equaling Granger's success. The existence of projects other than the Granger Homesteads bolstered the impression that the Catholic agrarian worldview could accomplish much in the national debate concerning the Depression. As Witte wrote, "[Granger's] success and multiplication is imperative if the Catholic Church is to be successful in establishing herself on the land."[44]

A riskier attempt to create a Catholic community involved Father Arthur Terminiello's St. Teresa's Village near Bolling, Alabama. A Massachusetts native, Terminiello already had participated in the street-preaching apostolate across Alabama. Nationally known anti-Semite Gerald L. K. Smith hailed Terminiello as "the Father Coughlin of the South," complimentarily connecting the two priests' caustic public personalities. Terminello gained his reputation for his defense of the small farming cooperative. St. Teresa's was the only community of its kind in the South. Founded in 1937, the community of former sharecroppers owned 160 acres and leased another 340. A sign at the village's border read, "Founded & Operated on the Principles of Catholic Social Justice." Dorothy Day regarded the young priest as "a man of good will and good spirits, and he needs all the help he can get." Some of St. Teresa's neighbors did not approve, however. One Catholic periodical published a photograph of the village's sign with "KKK" painted across it.[45]

Resembling his neighbors with their Protestant fundamentalism, Terminiello took the universality implied in "catholic" quite literally and, for the location, quite radically. Both of Father Terminiello's Alabama projects—St. Teresa's and the street-preaching services—explicitly sought to include African Americans. However, the farm foreman, Gene Rodgers, was white. Rodgers's family, as well as the other four who began St. Teresa's, were all converts to Catholicism. The new faith appeared even in the community's rather medieval organization of land distribution. Each family tended its own plot while sharing responsibilities for communally held acreage. A better example could scarcely be found of the Catholic agrarian resuscitation of the medieval village centered around the church. Area Catholics joined the villagers for Mass in a circus tent built around the St. Teresa's trailer chapel when it was not in service. Terminiello, like Father Peters in Glennonville, acquired a reputation for teaching by example. In addition to instructing the villagers on the principles of cooperation, he plowed his own land with a team of mules.[46]

The lack of mechanization pointed up an important fact: the residents of St. Teresa's still worked long, hard hours in the southern Alabama sun. The biggest change came in the shift from cotton to tomatoes. Terminiello contracted with a local cannery to process the village's produce. The rest of the land was devoted to bio-dynamic farming, prompting Ligutti and Rawe to proclaim:

> The joy of tilling their own land is now the happy lot of these poor sharecroppers. With almost loving care each man cultivates his tomatoes because they mean food, clothes, shoes, and implements for the village. Before, there was the miserable existence of virtual economic slavery, insufficient food and clothing, profitless cultivation of cotton on exploited land, a shack, and an impossible burden of debt.[47]

The residents of St. Teresa's Village were still sharecroppers (at least until they repaid Mobile's bishop Thomas Toolen for his investment), but Catholic agrarianism had started them on the path out of one of the most intractable problems of the post-Reconstruction South.

Recounting such successes was necessary in light of open opposition to the New Deal, especially Wilson's Homestead projects. Ligutti's glib aphorism—"When a farmer and his family own a cow, Communism goes out the back door"—withered under the opposition that almost every federal homestead project faced. Much like those conspiring to break up the government-camp square dance in Steinbeck's *The Grapes of Wrath,* residents near the homesteads, including Granger, suspected the homesteaders of communist subversion. In fact, Granger came under this particular criticism perhaps more than any other Subsistence Homestead project. Its largely southern and eastern European immigrant flavor spelled trouble to neighboring farmers, many of whom had supported the Ku Klux Klan's "one hundred percent Americanism" only a decade earlier. Making matters worse was that African American families were interspersed with the immigrants and made the greatest leap from mining-camp squalor to homestead success.[48]

Catholic Worker Farm Communes

In most Catholic rural life projects, the clergy managed to maintain a certain degree of control over what was said, sung, and shown within the communities. With the "farm communes" (Peter Maurin's name for them) inspired by *The Catholic Worker,* the story did not unfold quite as neatly. Despite the NCRLC's insistence that "great caution should be observed to avoid indiscriminate herding of families back to the land regardless of their fitness to carry on as farmers," a number of Catholic farm communes sprang up without the suggested authorities. R. Laurence Moore has noted that in America, "if you do not commodify your religion, someone else will do it for you."[49] The Catholic Worker movement founded farms that were not quite the successful commodification that NCRLC leaders might have wanted. Theoretically, the farm communes were identical to the NCRLC's endeavors. Given the Catholic Workers' propensity for being "fools for Christ," the communes founded by them most often became yet another Catholic "sign of contradiction" that Americans both inside and outside the Church struggled to comprehend.

An essential part of Peter Maurin's Green Revolution of "cult, culture, and cultivation," the farming communes offered "a vision of unity for a fragmented world." Maurin's Easy Essays delineated how this might come about. "Bourgeois Colleges," for example, indicated that unemployed college graduates would constitute the advance guard of the revolution. After indoctrination at the Houses of Hospitality with "a very old philosophy, a philosophy so old that it looks like new," they would move onto farm communes:

> On Farming Communes
>   unemployed college students
>   will be taught
>   how to build their houses,
> how to gather their fuel,
> how to raise their food,
>   how to make their furniture;
>   that is to say,
>   how to employ themselves.
> Unemployed college graduates
>   have time
>   on their hands.
> And while time is on the hands
>   of college graduates,
>   their heads don't function
>   as they should function.
> On Farming Communes
>   unemployed college graduates
>   will learn to use
>   both their hands
>   and their heads.[50]

The farm communes constituted the "agronomic universities" that, along with the Houses of Hospitality, would begin the reconstruction of the social order. Maurin's assertion that college graduates, of all people, would learn to employ themselves through agriculture was incongruent with many things, not the least of which were the realities faced by those who tried to live according to Maurin's indoctrinations. The agricultural depression under which the nation had been suffering since the 1920s did not abate until World War II, only adding to the unemployment that agriculture was supposed to remedy. Nevertheless, the farm communes were a substantial part of the Catholic Worker movement both before and after the war.[51]

The Catholic Worker began examining Maurin's idea for farm communes soon after the newspaper began publication in 1933. However, historian Mel Piehl notes, Dorothy Day "had a city girl's doubts about the value of rural life," and Maurin seemed happy with the one-acre vegetable garden that Workers had planted on Staten Island. Maurin's previous attempts to indoctrinate the Workers with the English Dominican Vincent McNabb's decentralist treatise *Nazareth or Social Chaos* did not, as Day recalled, "go over so well, all of us being city people, and Father McNabb advocating a return to the fields." A number of younger Workers soon lost their reserve, however. Larry Heaney, Marty Paul, and Bill Gauchat, from the Milwaukee, Chicago, and Cleveland houses, respectively, and others clamored to try Maurin's Green Revolution on for size. Day admitted the paper should not "write about farming communes unless we had one."[52]

When land near Easton, Pennsylvania, became available three years later, in 1936, Day and others had an opportunity to practice what they had been preaching. Therefore, at much the same time as the "official" Catholic homesteads at Granger were rising above the corn and coal fields of Iowa, a markedly different Catholic agricultural community became reality. Maryfarm, the first Catholic Worker farm commune, was soon joined by Worker farms in Illinois, Michigan, Ohio, and Massachusetts. By 1939 farms also existed in eight other states. After the war, farm communes sprouted in New York and Missouri, while individual families influenced by *The Catholic Worker* worked on the Green Revolution by purchasing their own farms. The Workers' simultaneous rootedness and marginality in the American Catholic subculture was reflected in how the farm communes stood with regard to places such as Granger, Iowa.[53]

James Fisher has written that the Catholic Worker movement was radical only insofar as it was Catholic. The same might be said of the movement's farm communes. Although they exhibited the shortcomings of rural life more than the boosters of Granger would have liked, they were, nevertheless, first and foremost Catholic. The farm communes were perhaps the most avant-garde expression of the Catholic Revival in America. By taking Maurin's Green Revolution in its most literal interpretation, the agrarian-minded Catholic Workers united the Catholic Revival's confidence in self-sustaining Catholic traditions with the American romantic agrarian and naturalist traditions of Thoreau, Whitman, and Jefferson. Unlike the NCRLC, the Workers described their efforts in much the same terminology as did antebellum communitarians such as the Shakers or the residents of Brook Farm.[54]

Since the farm communes were communities united by agricultural work, they exhibited the kind of unity lauded by the Catholic Revival's neo-Scholastic mentors. "Communal life on the land," wrote Milwaukee Catholic Worker Larry Heaney, "is not simply a medieval reality that has ceased to be practical. An organic functional society would have as units self-governing, self-subsistent communities. Healthful intercourse between men is effected by the sharing in common of land, goods and work." In the first year, Mary-farm "sheltered about thirty people at a time—unemployed, invalids, strikers, children,—all races, colors, denominations. There were Gentile and Jew, Catholics, Greek-Catholic, Protestant and atheist, Negro and white."[55] By establishing such communities, the Catholic Workers were creating an example of how the Catholic "Third Front" inspired by the encyclicals of popes Leo XIII and Pius XI might counteract the ills of modern industrialism.

The communes' Catholicity also found expression in their names, much as with ethnic parishes in the city. Throughout the Catholic tradition, a parish's name reflected the community members' respect for the saint whose name they employed. The name also said something about the values the parish expressed to the surrounding world. The Catholic Workers embraced this form of devotional Catholicism far more than did the cleric-led NCRLC. The Benedictine tradition of "ora et labora" (prayer and work), rooted primarily in farming, was honored with farms in Massachusetts and Michigan. The Catholic insistence on Mary's mediation of the Incarnation was recalled in Maryfarm and the Worker farm near Newburgh, New York, that replaced it; Our Lady of the Wayside in tiny Avon, Ohio, outside Cleveland; and Our Lady Star of the Sea Camp, the one-acre vegetable plot on Staten Island. Marian piety had dominated popular Catholic spirituality since the nineteenth century. Like everything else American and Catholic, though, those with agrarian inclinations could claim a little moral high ground. After all, the Nativity took place in a stable. Honoring the Virgin Mother with so many farms, the Catholic Workers perfectly captured the agrarian belief that farming mediated grace, just as Mary herself did. Beyond that, the location names added the requisite rural aspect to the long list of places, such as Fatima and Lourdes, that were especially favored by Mary.

Mary's mediatory role came primarily through her motherhood, and large families were a noticeable feature of all Catholic Worker farm communes. Maurin and the Catholic agrarians, along with the popes and other Catholic intellectuals, had always insisted that the family was the basic societal unit. Since Catholic agrarianism espoused farming as the elementary societal occupation, raising a Catholic family on the land was more important than monetary gain. In the period after Pius XI's *Casti Conubii*, which condemned artificial birth control, the size of commune families often exceeded the farms' resources. Holy Family farm, started by members of the Chicago–Blue Island and Milwaukee Houses of Hospitality, observed this injunction in its name and in reality: two couples produced nine children between them while living in one farmhouse. Marycrest, a postwar effort affiliated with the editors of *Integrity* magazine, became known locally for its herd of dirty children. Mario and Estelle Carota, who established the Agnus Dei farm near Aptos, California, had two daughters and twelve sons by 1958. Dorothy Day's only daughter, Tamar, and Tamar's husband, David Hennessy, began a large family on a West Virginia farm. In a fit of Catholic Revival fervor, St. Joseph's farm at Cape May Courthouse, New Jersey, proposed the "Congregation of the Holy Family," a "Religious Order for married folks living in community."[56]

The farm communes also followed the lead of Catholic agrarian theorists when it came to farming itself. The bio-dynamic farming that Ligutti and Rawe insisted on was familiar to the Catholic Workers; they had practiced forms of it since acquiring Maryfarm in 1936. The integrated use of all available farmland embodied in agriculture what the entire farm-commune experiment sought to demonstrate—that a "community" (in this case, a community of crops, fruit trees, and vegetables) upheld the Christian family far better than the artificiality of city living. *The Catholic Worker* often reserved its last page for articles about the land. Bio-dynamic or organic farming and homesteading received regular attention. The influence of secular agrarians such as Ralph Borsodi, Edward Faulkner, and Scott Nearing was evident. A Catholic Worker in rural Missouri wrote to Ligutti about long-range plans to use the ubiquitous Osage orange (a bushy, thorny regional tree) as a natural alternative to steel-wire fencing. In 1950, sixty-five-year-old Louis McCauley from Washington, Indiana, commented to two Catholic Workers: "But why is a Catholic Worker interested in the laws of plant growth? because a well filled contented body is the greatest place in the world for a holly, [sic] God fearing soul."[57]

Bio-dynamics enabled those who practiced it to live out Maurin's incessant advice to "eat what you raise and raise what you eat." In January 1938 Day wrote that Maryfarm residents were living off the potatoes and carrots raised the previous summer. While two of the three cows were about to calve, thus depriving Maryfarmers of fresh milk (they drank canned instead), they still enjoyed pork sausage, eggs, and the regional delicacy of "scrapple." From the St. Benedict farm in Massachusetts, Arthur Sheehan wrote that "during the first winter, Monsignor Ligutti of the Catholic Rural Life Conference visited us and spent a day with us. He went over the land and estimated that we should be able to support a hundred persons. He advised getting sheep." Later Sheehan wrote to Day that Ligutti "sent us a wheat grinder; we got 25 lbs of grain and we are going to experiment." Another farm resident, Don Palmer (nicknamed "Missouri" after his native state), achieved some notoriety by making four hundred pounds of sauerkraut for the winter rations. Larry Heaney urged all readers of *The Catholic Worker* to "grow your own food," since "[y]ou do not manufacture food then—you grow it or raise it. . . . Somebody must grow your food. You might think about growing your own and even raising some animals. That's a lively thought." Bio-dynamic farming halted the migration (back and forth) between farm and city that Catholic agrarians decried, but its practitioners sometimes found themselves at a bit of a loss. Bill Gauchat diligently studied local edible plant life but found it "hard discouraging work. The simple things that our grandparents knew, are for us hard won discoveries."[58]

If Gauchat's discouragement resulted partly from his own naïveté about agriculture, the other Catholic Workers were no different. They were trying to farm by reading out of a book. Some degree of material, if not spiritual, failure was expected. When the Workers obtained Maryfarm, Day wrote that it overlooked "the cultivated fields of New Jersey."[59] Often such a distant view was as close to successful farming as the Catholic Workers came. The farm communes rarely accomplished the agricultural reclamation projects that their instigators envisioned, despite all the exuberance for bio-dynamic farming.

The farm communes invited failure because too few persons did the needed work. If only one or two families had established the commune, they often buckled under an enormous workload. Larry Heaney, Marty Paul, Bill Gauchat, Carmen Welch, and Arthur Sheehan all wrote to Day of their bewilderment at the variety of tasks simultaneously requiring completion. Welch, a native rural Midwesterner, often included advice for Day concerning the agricultural and societal difficulties at Maryfarm. She reassured Day that "[w]e don't feel that your work with Maryfarm is a failure. Even we who are experienced farmers make mistakes, too—everyone does. You have just made a start there—and what has been done, will just be stepping stones to the future." Marty Paul, a converted Lutheran from Minnesota, offered no such advice, at least to Day. He wanted to learn first, writing Ligutti for information about "European methods of farming." While serving in Europe with the army, he had noticed that "conservation was their life blood, not only of necessity but because of love of the soil and pride in its heritage." Paul admitted that he and Larry Heaney nevertheless "were none too reticent about the opinions we had gleaned from a few books on farming, distributism, and decentralism." On other farms there were plenty of people, but few seemed interested in doing any farm work. Mel Piehl writes that "the farms bred a running controversy over slacking, called in CW terms 'the conflict between workers and scholars.'" In an obituary for a farm-commune casualty, Day referred to John Filliger as "our farmer," implying that he was the only one doing the work. Such, in fact, was the case: Filliger arose at dawn every day and plowed the fields, but little else was accomplished.[60]

If farming per se was not practiced as the vocal farm-commune leaders preached, the raison d'être of the communes emerged elsewhere—namely, the urban Houses of Hospitality. The Workers enlisted both the Communes and the Houses as restorative, not economically successful, ventures. A young man from Fort Wayne, Indiana, queried Gauchat about learning farming particularly from him. In his eyes, Catholic Worker farming was different: "Actually, my impression of your farms is a refuge for those who want a more personalized, thoughtful, and beautiful life, and one more useful to others." The farm communes maintained a policy of unrestricted admission, which flew in the face of the closely regulated homestead projects of Bishop Ireland and, more recently, Monsignor Ligutti. While the open-admission policy caused many communes to gain local disrepute, it created some interesting opportunities for Workers to address the Christian concept of the works of mercy.[61]

Maryfarm set an inauspicious example for the other communes. Although "scholars learning to be workers"—seminarians, city children on vacation, and college students—crowded in during summers, the permanent residents were a motley crew of families, unemployed laborers, and the urban homeless.[62] A more volatile group, unprepared for the problems of communal living and subsistence agriculture, could scarcely be found. Relations were soon strained, at best. One character, a Mr. O'Connell, castigated converts (reportedly bellowing, "ye'd change yer faith for a bowl of soup!") and prevented most repair work by hoarding the tools in his cabin, "where he stood guard over them with a shotgun." In 1942 Eva Gretz wrote to Day that the other residents had taken Day's monetary gift intended for food and spent it instead on liquor. On another occasion at least one visiting priest joined the drinking binge. Local school boards and social services communicated with one of Maryfarm's more skilled managers, Grace Branham, about the farm's shortcomings as an environment for raising children.[63] The addition of family housing to the "lower farm" did not solve matters. (Maryfarm's property extended over a ridge, and buildings stood at both the top and bottom.) Soon residents were sneaking into the "upper farm" during the many Catholic Worker retreats held there to steal food. Day's patience finally reached its limits, and the farm was deeded to the three families of the lower farm in 1946. Another Maryfarm was subsequently established at Newburgh, New York, much closer to the newspaper's headquarters.[64]

Almost all the other farm communes suffered to some extent the same pitfalls as a result of their admissions policy. St. Benedict's in Massachusetts, which served as Ade Bethune's religious-arts studio, also held an unemployed family of four supported partly by the inheritance of the aristocratic Bethune. Nazareth farm in central Illinois became so well known for its reception of derelicts that local Catholics threatened to frame Carmen Welch by disclosing her doubtful Catholic baptism unless she stopped creating such an embarrassment. Day wrote to Dorothy Gauchat of "three mental cases" at the Newburgh Maryfarm in 1948, "recovered all right, but irritating to live with. And yet, I do think they would be just as troublesome in their right minds, if not more so. They are the irritating, critical kind, that needle people and make turmoil. No one else will have them, so there you are." The Gauchats had troubles of their own. In 1940 Bill sent to the other Houses of Hospitality a memo and photo warning of "John McMahon, alias Kane, alias Foster, who disappeared from Blessed Martin House while we were at the Retreat at Easton." McMahon, a fiftyish man with "pleasant and kind manners" to offset his "weakness for the horses," had absconded with more than $250 of the Cleveland house's funds.[65]

Almost any other communal-living efforts would be counted as successful in comparison to these difficult situations, and the tribulations of Maryfarm were compensated for by some earnest attempts to realize simultaneously Maurin's Green Revolution and Day's spirituality focused on Christ's mystical body. The well-known conflict and turmoil at Maryfarm and elsewhere should not obscure the efforts by many communes to use the farms as opportunities for new forms of community. The NCRLC's crown jewel of Granger from the start avoided potentially troublesome elements or those requiring more care, but the Catholic Workers' appropriation of Catholic agrarianism enabled them to invite marginalized people to participate in projects of "Christian social reconstruction."

Widespread unemployment due to the Great Depression provided a millennialist flashpoint for the farm communes. The desire to restore the unemployed and impoverished to a meaningful existence underlay the Catholic Workers' Houses of Hospitality. Communal subsistence farming would sustain these people until they either found work or awoke to the spiritual virtues of farming. As mentioned earlier, Maurin believed that unemployed college graduates would lead the way. Maurin, Day and the others affiliated with *The Catholic Worker,* though, considered any unemployed person a candidate for returning to the land. In 1936 one of Maurin's "Easy Essays" specified the problem as well as its solution "on the land":

> The industrial revolution
> > did not improve things;
> > it made them worse.
> The industrial revolution
> > has given us
> > technological unemployment.
> And the best way
> > to do away
> > with technological unemployment
> > is to place idle hands
> > on idle land.[66]

Heightening the urgency of implementing the Green Revolution was an anxiety straddling the distinction between pre- and postmillennialist tendencies in American Christianity. The return of Americans to the land would not only restore the nation but gradually move it toward the realization of its role in the divine plan of creation. Catholic agrarian theology insisted that subsistence farming in community was a precursor to the heavenly kingdom. A larger number of people participating only brought that next world closer. On the other hand, the sheer number of unemployed Americans now rendered any theoretical discussion outdated. Action was required, and the land appeared, to the Catholic Workers as well as the other agrarians discussed earlier, as the best solution to the nation's problem. At an antebellum revival, accepting one's salvation removed one from the terrors of impending divine judgment.[67] Likewise, it seemed that a quick and sure decision for subsistence farming might avoid the economic and spiritual catastrophe already brewing.

If inviting unemployed individuals while suffering the intolerable ones seems as if it would have been difficult, it often was; and occasionally the unemployed and the misanthropes were the same people. Yet the open-admission policy of the farm communes, despite the conflicts over "slacking," preserved a key tenet of the Catholic Worker radical Gospel. Therefore, the strife-riddled farms contributed as much to the Catholic Worker "downward path to spiritual success" as did the Houses of Hospitality. Committed to an urgently millennialist social vision, the Workers more often than not admitted to their farm communes some of the very people who inhibited the realization of that vision. This policy only reemphasized the "fools for Christ" spirituality popularized by Day and Maurin in the pages of *The Catholic Worker*.

A large number of the marginalized people were people of color. *The Catholic Worker* recognized this with its masthead showing Christ flanked by one black worker and one white one. The farm communes themselves seemed to include more Latino immigrants. Bill Gauchat's Our Lady of the Wayside farm made special efforts to help when Latino immigration swelled after the war. He complained that local doctors, when asked to help, "sounded interested until they heard the name. 'O Mexicans,' and then produced the excuse." Gauchat and St. Benedict's farm in Massachusetts also assisted efforts to relocate Japanese Americans detained during World War II.[68] Efforts with African Americans consisted more of verbal support than invitations to participate. *The Catholic Worker* decried the mass eviction of sharecroppers in the Missouri Bootheel in 1939 and lauded racially integrated cooperative farms there. It also praised the Negro Agricultural School in Camden, Mississippi, Father Terminiello's St. Teresa's Village, and the interracial Koinonia community founded in 1942 near Americus, Georgia. Day visited the last two in her travels across the South.[69]

Redemptive Suffering on Two Farm Communes

Rarely did life flow smoothly on the farm communes. Nevertheless, the fires of agrarian enthusiasm did not die down quickly. Two farms—Our Lady of the Wayside and Holy Family—especially revealed the tension between idealism and reality. Their experiences also gave the armchair farmers who read *The Catholic Worker* a glimpse of what might await them on the land.

In northeastern Ohio, Bill and Dorothy Gauchat took the Catholic Worker concern for the unemployed to an unprecedented level. In the days before state-supported mental health institutions, those not admitted to asylums were condemned to lives of poverty and homelessness. The Gauchats attempted to reverse this fate for many mentally impaired persons by providing housing at Our Lady of the Wayside farm. (The handicapped were not, of course, expected to do any farming.) Bill Gauchat would later remark that this innovative use of the farm commune "fit with our idea of hospitality." It also lent a new flavor to the bio-dynamic subsistence farming they practiced. The Gauchats took in a hydrocephalic baby boy in 1946. Soon they began welcoming unwed teenage mothers, orphan children, and occasionally priests. Dorothy Gauchat explained that after that first child, "we decided that if we were going to take one, we would take one that no one else wanted, a handicapped child. This is how we got into taking care of handicapped children; we took one . . . and people heard about it and we continued taking them in."[70]

The seventy-six-acre Our Lady of the Wayside farm experienced some practical problems and was financially precarious. Bill Gauchat, a native of Windsor, Ontario (also the home of radio priest Charles Coughlin), had spent two years at the Basilian fathers' Assumption College. (The Windsor House of Hospitality bore the name Our Lady of the Wayside as well.) None of this, of course, prepared him for farming, which he started in 1938 after having established the Blessed Martin de Porres House of Hospitality in Cleveland two years earlier. Dorothy Gauchat came from an upper-middle-class Catholic family that promptly disowned her upon her marriage to Bill. Their different social standing mattered little, though, out in the fields where the Gauchats and some residents of Wayside labored.[71]

The Waysiders' lack of farming expertise led to some potentially deadly mistakes. The Cleveland Department of Public Health and Welfare found the farm's well water to be "polluted with intestinal type bacteria," possibly "due to drainage from toilets, barns, chicken runs, pastures or cultivated fertilized land located within the drainage area."[72] A neighbor, moved by an invalid resident's application to link the farm to local electrical service, urged the Cleveland company providing service to "pull a few strings, cut the red tape and get the installment completed this week." The service would benefit many Waysiders: "They provide meals and living quarters for old men whom industry cannot employ and whom it seems no one else is interested in. . . . The farm supplements the home in the city."[73] However, the practice of raising food for consumption at the House of Hospitality in Cleveland won some unsolicited advice from the Lorain County (Ohio) Department of Health: "Farmers who ship their milk to places outside our district are supervised by health authorities in the places using such milk, but we look after what is used here. If you think you want to continue [producing milk,] we shall . . . give you an idea of the requirements." The list included a clean barn with a cement floor, sanitary disposal facilities, a clean water supply, and an annual veterinary examination for the cattle.[74] Even attempts to distribute devotional materials among Catholics were criticized. After asking Gauchat for some sample crucifixes produced by Waysiders, the Liturgical Arts Society secretary Maurice Lavanoux returned them, suggesting that Gauchat "consult someone who has competence as a sculptor and who would give you a few pointers in the design of the corpus as well as the proportions of the cross itself."[75]

These concerns appeared minor to Dorothy Day when she faced the boiling conflicts at Maryfarm. "One of the reasons you don't hear," she wrote Gauchat, "is because your's is one of the places where we are confident everything is going well. . . . Your letters bring us only happiness and inspiration You get along far better than we do in many ways. You are a good manager." Gauchat apparently thought otherwise. In 1953 he reflected that Wayside "was the sorriest CW farm ever conceived. I ought to know—I live here."[76] W. G. felt the farm in Ohio was a failure because it never achieved the (lofty) goals he had set for it.

The unusualness of some farm-commune residents magnified the difference between the communes and their rural neighbors, much as the urban Houses of Hospitality served as a "sign of contradiction" to the Workers' co-religionists. On the farms, however, this separateness came to be elevated to a spiritual level. After all, Our Lady of the Wayside suggested even with its name that grace might be discovered in unexpected areas. Work alone, even if it was farming, could not suffice. Working with marginalized people, as the Gauchats did with the mentally handicapped, pointed toward the spiritual level that all Catholic agrarians treasured. Eva Smith of Maryfarm wrote in 1941 that

> once a year our farm is transformed into a retreat-house, so that we cannot forget the foremost purpose of our work. It is not economic independence, or a more natural life on the land that we are concerned about in the first place, but to love God more perfectly and to find the keys to heaven, that we may pass them on to others.[77]

Smith's candor about Maryfarm's purpose brought into the open the sign of contradiction that threatened all the farm communes. Overemphasis on the spiritual benefits of rural life, perceived as greater than the benefits of farming itself, took Catholic agrarianism down the road to sure failure. Ligutti and the NCRLC insisted that *through* farming, Catholics reaffirmed better than in any other way their relationship with God. The Catholic Workers eschewed rather early the necessity of physical labor in order to focus specifically on the other aspect of Catholic agrarianism: the soul's relationship with God.

Combined with the lack of interest in farming itself, this spiritual self-elevation made for pathetic agricultural returns. Nevertheless, Gauchat, despite his piecemeal farming education, never relented in criticizing the current farming economy and the people who allowed its continuation. Considered a "scholar who became a worker," as opposed to Larry Heaney, "a worker who became a scholar," Gauchat preferred the "spiritual dynamite" of *The Catholic Worker* and bemoaned the postwar drift to suburbia. He blasted modernity for demanding smaller families, while it forced a farmer to sell his last cow to pay his daughter's medical bills. Gauchat then asked mockingly, "Or don't you read GOOD HOUSEKEEPING?"—a jibe at the anesthetized perspective found in the suburbs that were quickly replacing farms in postwar rural America. While admitting that "successful farming takes more special-ized knowledge than any other profession I can think of," Gauchat realized that faith in the virtuosity of farmers did not mean they were all virtuous. "It takes living only a short while in a rural community to become disabused of this fallacy. Horse trading and double-dealing is not only a hobby, but a pas-sion, and highly approved. Those who excel in this rural sport are leaders of the community."[78]

Gauchat's bitterness resulted from the cold realization that rural commu-nities were not inherently Christian, family-oriented, pacifist cells—in other words, Catholic farm communes, opposed to the modern world. Gauchat quoted Samuel Butler's statement in *The Way of All Flesh* that "they would have been equally horrified at hearing the Christian religion doubted, and at seeing it practiced" and then concluded, "it sounded up-to-date to me." In a letter to Day, Gauchat included self-congratulatory descriptions of the Waysiders along with castigation for the lack of charity from himself and oth-ers: "We only want a little store front to house the promise of Christ for the sons and daughters of OUR LADY OF GUADALUPE. And some Holy Name members of Lorain County Catholic Churches to welcome them to hear Mass on Sundays." Gauchat's antitriumphalist superiority did not go unnoticed or unchallenged. Angered over Gauchat's comparison of the troubled farm with Cleveland's Blessed Martin House of Hospitality, "Brother Christopher" asked in 1948, "Did your fingers get caught on one of the Thorns in the Head of the Redeemer whose cross you have been holding so tightly[?]"[79]

Perhaps some of Gauchat's anguished antimodernism stemmed from the indistinct roots of that tradition. Not everybody concerned with preserving subsistence farming was as enraptured with its spiritual dimensions as Gauchat and the Catholic Workers were. Late in life, Scott and Helen Near-ing became something of a tourist attraction for the 1960s counterculture, but the popularity did not sit well with them. Scott emphatically denounced anybody who held a romantic view of subsistence farming, which included most of the young hippies who had come to worship at the Nearings' feet. Much like the anarchist Ed Abbey, whose *Desert Solitaire* describes his sum-mer spent living alone in Utah's Arches National Monument, Scott Nearing lampooned both the modern systems of living against which the couple was revolting and those who would emulate them in that role. If he had had the opportunity to give that same advice twenty years earlier, his antiromantic agrarianism might have benefited some of the farm communes.[80]

The Catholic "culture of suffering," which blossomed between the wars, could scarcely have found a better venue than the farm communes. Even martyrdom was readily available. Holy Family farm, a tragically short-lived colony near Starkenburg, Missouri, revealed the bottomless pit into which any twentieth-century homesteading project could drag its creators. In 1947 Larry Heaney, Marty Paul, and their families moved to 160 acres in central Missouri. Ruth Ann Heaney later recalled that "we decided on Missouri be-cause land was so much cheaper down there, and there were lots of rural

Catholic parishes." A shrine for Our Lady of Sorrows, the oldest Marian shrine west of the Mississippi, and St. Martin's parish were about a quarter-mile walk away.[81]

The Blessed Mother's sorrows would in time come to symbolize the fortunes of the rural living experiment. Heaney wrote to Day that they had some experience with communal farming, but "as farmers we are yet greenhorns and consider ourselves apprentice agrarians." The apprenticeship turned out to be fatal: Heaney died two years later from work-induced pneumonia while living in Nearingesque fashion with both his family and the Pauls' family in an unheated farmhouse lacking both electricity and plumbing. Jack Woltjen later commented about Holy Family farm's troubles: "I don't know of anyone having more of a right to sing [a] song [of woe], for Marty, like Job, had the book thrown at him."[82]

Before then, though, "our little experiment in saving a shell-shocked social order," as Paul described Holy Family farm, demonstrated how even "fools for Christ" could participate in the Catholic agrarian appreciation of rural America. Heaney wrote in *The Catholic Worker:*

> We are not here merely to farm. We are living and working on this farm in order to build a community—a community about a church. It is a new society we desire, based on Holy Mass and personal sacrifice for the common good. . . . Our pioneering is unique. . . . Those Nineteenth Century pioneers came west to conquer a wilderness—to harness the natural forces of God's creation. We Twentieth Century pioneers are out to conquer ourselves—to harness all our natural powers and have them supernaturalized by God and His Church.

Heaney and Paul might have been better off had their pioneering been less unique. The sheer amount of farm work that they insisted on doing by hand threatened to bury them. Their lack of agricultural experience magnified this problem and made them contradict even the guidelines set forth in *Commonweal,* by no means an authority on the subject. Wrote Paul, "Our limited knowledge and even more limited funds didn't make it feasible for us to buy livestock, so for several months we farmed without horses or livestock of any kind." Their assumption that life on the land would, by some supernatural means inherent to living in a rural location, sustain them through difficulties shattered against successive waves of failure.[83]

Improper and untidy conditions completely wiped out the first flock of chickens. Heaney and Paul put up hay by hand in a time when most of their neighbors were purchasing their first tractor-drawn balers. The garden, which produced most of the food, took up so much time that "we were learning gardening instead of the rudiments of farming, which we set out to do," wrote Paul. In the spirit of Edward Faulkner's *Plowman's Folly,* they decided to disk, not plow, the few acres they devoted to crops, and almost killed their two-horse team in doing so. Logs were sawed by hand into boards to build additional housing for all the children. Ruth Ann Heaney, herself a native of rural Nebraska, later remarked that "I knew more how to run the farm when we went down there than anybody, just because I knew something about the seasons and what kind of crops."[84]

The antimachine farming practices (inspired by Vincent McNabb's writings) fit wonderfully the Catholic agrarian work ethic as well as the "culture of suffering" in which the Holy Family farmers had been formed before coming to Missouri. The hard work sacramentally conferred grace, much like the daily Mass for which they walked a quarter mile each day. Toil also confirmed the rectitude of the farm, which they themselves felt but which the neighbors doubted. However, in 1949 providence became difficult to discern even for the farmers. After a train ride back from St. Louis, Heaney arrived at nearby Hermann with a February blizzard coming down. A ride could not be found, and since Holy Family farm lacked a telephone, he walked the ten miles back wearing only street clothes.[85]

Pleurisy developed into lobar pneumonia. Heaney was in St. Mary's Hospital in St. Louis for about three months. In a *Commonweal* article, Marty Paul finished the story: "After many X-rays it was decided that he had a lung abscess and needed surgery. Larry didn't survive the operation and died in the hospital in St. Louis. He was thirty-seven. His wife, Ruth Ann, had just borne her sixth baby." Dorothy Day attended the funeral in Rhineland and wrote Heaney's obituary for *The Catholic Worker*. (It shared the front page with two other obituaries, one of which was Peter Maurin's.)[86]

Day's eulogy for Heaney became an opportunity to create the hagiography that the Catholic Workers needed. If Maurin was the mind behind the Catholic Workers, Heaney had become his most ardent disciple. (Ruth Ann Heaney, Marty Paul, and the Gauchats would all later agree with Day's description of Larry as a Catholic Worker "saint.") At Maryfarm, newlyweds Larry and Ruth Ann made themselves a reputation for integrating their Catholic faith, their love for each other, and communal life on the land. "I remember how shocked everyone was when they saw Larry and his wife living up to the ideas Peter Maurin was always talking about in connection with farming communes," Day wrote.[87]

Although Day had excoriated some Maryfarm residents for "the peculiar heresy of the family,"—the tendency to be concerned not for other family members and thus not first for the wider community—she recommended the Heaneys' life of voluntary (and involuntary, she reminded readers) poverty as a more wholesome family life. With no outside luxuries, their family members' love for one another stood as an example for all, much as with the early Christians. The Heaney children created their own imaginative play worlds (once asking Day herself to play Herod for a Nativity reenactment) and ended each evening in the living room—heated by a wood stove—praying together "for all children . . . who were orphans, and who were hungry and cold." Such scenes contradicted outsiders who might have dismissed Heaney's death as an avoidable, unnecessary sacrifice. "No, we do not believe that Larry died of hardships and overwork," Day wrote, "but because he had reached that stage of perfection pleasing to God, as his pastor said at his funeral Mass and so he took him. And we rejoice in the suffering and know it to be the gentle rain to water the crop. He is with God."[88]

Heaney's death embodied the air of martyrdom enveloping the early days of *The Catholic Worker*. After all, Heaney had died establishing a farming community, like the nineteenth-century pioneers he extolled in the pages of the newspaper. Ruth Ann took a farmer's comment at the funeral that Heaney "*would* have made a good farmer" as support not only for a grieving family, but also for the agrarian ideal that he had died trying to realize. The 1953 *Commonweal* article in which Marty Paul recounted Holy Family farm's tenure seemed to mock Heaney under the well-meaning subtitle "From Chicago to a Farm in Missouri: Two Families' Trials, Tribulations and Promise for the Future"; Holy Family farm, like Catholic agrarianism itself, seemed to have very little promise in the mid-1950s as the detriments of rural living came to be the only news from the farm. In 1940 John Magee had written Dorothy Day that "anyone who takes responsibility in this work gets it in the neck." The Heaneys and Pauls discovered paradigmatically the painful limits of what such responsibility might entail.[89]

Farm Communes and Catholic Culture

Certain forms of Catholic spirituality infused the NCRLC, the Granger Homesteads, and, as will be shown in chapter 4, the motor missions. Similarly, a distinct Catholic Worker spirituality surrounded the farms and the urban Houses of Hospitality. Peter Maurin's spiritual preference was to be a "fool for Christ." Imitating Christ's passion, the road to Christian success was paved with contradiction and suffering. When followed in rural communes, however, this path led to lousy farming. James Fisher writes that the "farm communes simply became rural houses of hospitality: flophouses in the country." Although they shared the Catholic tradition of communal living, the Catholic Worker farms certainly were not the Granger Homesteads.[90]

A case may be made that the tinge of rural decadence was actually what Day and other urban-oriented Catholic agrarians desired. This pertains especially to the spirituality surrounding both the newspaper and its farm communes. A seam in *The Catholic Worker* garment that caused a fair amount of consternation was the participation of many, including Day herself, in the retreat movement. Retreats focused on cultivating a deeper sense of personal piety and community with like-minded others through long periods of silent prayer over the course of a week or five days. Critics labeled the practice "Jansenistic" for the almost exclusive insistence on salvation through personal faith. Although the retreats strengthened the bridge between the paths of Day's personal spiritual journey and the institutions of the Catholic Church, not all Catholic Workers participated. Much like the military conscription debate, which began to erupt at the same time, the Catholic

Worker participation in the retreat movement created a de facto segregation between the spiritual haves and have-nots.

Increasingly after 1940, Day and others immersed themselves in retreat practices: longer periods of prayer, an even more ascetic lifestyle in the Houses of Hospitality (where life was already lived on the edge of physical and monetary peril), and, most importantly for this study, increasing amounts of time on retreat at Maryfarm. The land in Easton quickly became the center for these retreats, bringing a seemingly unending stream of visitors. Some of these were quite notable: Paul Hanly Furfey and Virgil Michel, O.S.B., two leading clerical intellectuals who unreservedly endorsed the Catholic Worker personalism; the famous convert couple Jacques and Raisa Maritain; and many others. Many retreatants were Easton-area Catholics or other residents of Pennsylvania, New York, or New Jersey. Infrequently, a Midwestern or Southern visitor participated.[91]

The priests who led the retreats were often quite colorful personalities. For example, Father John Hugo, a popular spiritual author and director, came to have an iron grip on Day's spiritual development. Extolling an uncompromising vision of Christian faith, Hugo had gained a reputation as a clerical thorn in the side of postwar religious complacency. Ruth Ann Heaney would later remark that "Father Hugo messed up Dorothy's liturgical sense, probably." His insistence that all work be done to the glory of God revealed how conflicted the retreats were themselves. While he stalked Maryfarmers demanding "Stop smoking, for the love of God!" two Irish priests followed him with cigarettes, snickering "Have a cigarette, for the love of God!" Occasionally the chancery office in Philadelphia withheld permission to conduct a retreat, an injunction that the priests, Day, and the rest would promptly disregard.[92]

Maryfarm, unlike the other farm communes, came to be the untamed spiritual resource to which Day and others repeatedly turned for succor. Conveniently located near New York, the rough-hewn character of rural life and its corresponding "natural" spirituality were never far away when needed. In this sense, Maryfarm ceased to be an "agronomic university," or anything corresponding to an agricultural economy. It more resembled a recreational resort for the spiritually gifted, much like President Roosevelt's retreats or vacation areas for the privileged few. Day wrote much of *On Pilgrimage*, a 1948 book about her spiritual retreat experiences, while at Maryfarm, and the retreats came to hold a central place in her spiritual outlook for the rest of her life.[93]

Being a convert, Day was already somewhat separated from the Catholic mainstream. By plunging headlong into the deep spiritual traditions of Catholicism, she separated herself even further from the culture most American Catholics knew. Certainly the Masses that concluded each retreat departed notably from the usual whispered Latin. Most of them were dialogue Masses in the Maryfarm barn, often accompanied by the sounds of belled cattle and sheep munching on hay in the stalls below. That retreat participants perceived this as a spiritual virtue, one that recognized the crucial link between liturgy and life on the land as described by the Liturgical Movement, suggested how distant Maryfarm and the Catholic Workers had grown from the culture of many American Catholics.[94]

David Bovée writes that "with the resumption of the farm-to-city trend of the population in the late 1930s, any real hope among Catholic agrarians for a large-scale back-to-the-land movement just about died out." For a short time, though, farm colonies realized the NCRLC's vision of rural America; they demonstrated that the Church could save rural America on the Church's own terms. The farm colonies were the rural life movement's most idealistic (not to mention brave) contribution to the vibrancy of the Depression-era American Catholic Church. Again, Granger provided the example for the Catholic Church across the nation. Looking to the past, Frederick Kenkel commented in 1936 that "there is no reason for believing that the Government should not be able to accomplish in an Iowa community of today what benevolent autocrats of the Enlightenment, such as Frederick the Great of Prussia, acting on theories supplied by Mercantilism, succeeded in doing frequently in the 18th century." An enthusiastic Edward Skillin thought Granger "looks like the chief element in a long-range solution of the scourge of the last ten years."[95]

The pedestal on which Catholic agrarian leaders placed the farm colonies and communes had much to do with this optimism. Despite the fact that one in five Catholics already lived on the land, the NCRLC and prominent Catholic publications such as *America* and *Commonweal* elevated the idiosyncratic colonies in all their perfectionist glory as the standard that *all* Catholics should follow. Skillin advised that "Catholics who see the Church wasting away in our American cities should be particularly interested, but every socially minded American should take the challenge of [Granger's] achievement to heart." A 1948 article in *The Catholic Worker* thanked God "for Maryfarm, where people can come and be silent at least for a while, where people can meditate and be rejuvenated for the struggle of life in the city."[96]

This separation of the colonies from the surrounding rural Catholic population, which occasionally was sizable, did much to reinforce the colonists' perception of themselves as exemplary. *Integrity* magazine devoted an entire 1953 issue to rural life; in an article entitled "Adjusting to Life in the Country," Harry and Kate Donaghy wrote: "Some country Catholics are downright resentful if you outline the ideas of the rural apostolate to them. As one honest parishioner told us years afterwards, she felt insulted that someone from New York should presume to show her how to be a Catholic."[97]

The condescension extended to all rural Americans as well. The Catholic colonist in the rural apostolate, the thinking went, lived in the upright sort of way that rural life naturally sustained.

> You are now in the limelight, a new member of a village body with definite responsibilities to the Mystical Body, among these to remember your divine sonship and to behave as royal children of God the Father. In the rural areas where

there are very few Catholics this is of supreme importance. Pray, and be sure you are up to this challenge, and up to long separations from friends and families. And even to the loss of unimportant things like the convenience and excitement of the corner delicatessen and Macy's and the foreign movies.[98]

The Donaghys subtly and crucially linked "divine sonship" with the cultural benefits of city life that Catholics increasingly enjoyed after World War II. The "incarnational," that which demonstrated "divine sonship" on earth, ultimately remained urban life. By temporarily forgoing such graces, the Catholic rural apostolate cemented its self-perception as prophet to a rural America seeking to find a path in postwar life different from that of the tainted city.

Some of this condescension worked itself out in the establishment of the communities. Glennonville and Washita Farms in Tishomingo, of course, were created with people invited to settle in a certain location. The 1933 NCRLC convention resolved that

> great caution should be observed to avoid indiscriminate herding of families back to the land regardless of their fitness to carry on as farmers. We also recommend that prospective settlers be protected from falling into the hands of unscrupulous or well intentioned but incompetent promoters and saved from the calamity of settling on poor, unproductive land or from pursuing farm methods that are sure to end in failure.[99]

Granger and the other Depression-era communities, therefore, subjected all applicants to a screening process. Queried about their ethnic background and possible criminal record, as well as undergoing an assessment interview by Ligutti and other Homestead officials, those wishing to go "back to the land" found that the road leading there had checkpoints.

Such winnowing perhaps dimmed the glowing rhetoric that described Granger and its implications for American Catholicism. However, such a process might have helped the Catholic Worker farm communes to rise above being seen simply as "flophouses in the country." Whether in Illinois, Ohio, Massachusetts, Missouri, or New York, neighbors of the communes, Catholic or not, saw less "Christ" and more "fools" than felt comfortable. When commune residents reversed this judgment to argue that precisely such disorder and lax farming practices constituted a "new order," they only exacerbated what was already a tenuous relationship. From California, a Catholic Worker wrote that "the world is in a terrible way and there will be the abomination of desolation—but there will also be the elect." Ruth Ann Heaney recalled that farmers in the parish referred to Holy Family farm as slightly strange, while from her perspective there "was no one to share . . . to talk ideas with" in the neighborhood. Even Father Minwegen, the priest who regularly held dialogue Masses at St. Martin's parish near Holy Family farm, often dismissed the Catholic Worker notion of charitable work, saying "let someone else take care of these people."[100] Three hundred years after the Puritans declared Boston to be a "city upon a hill," that same sense of election surfaced in the followers of Catholic agrarianism.

Despite Heaney's death, going back to the land was still encouraged. The NCRLC continued to press such projects, especially for remaining European refugees. The efforts of Dr. Paul Sacco in the diocese of Dubuque, Iowa, were viewed in the early 1950s as yet another sign of the imminent return to subsistence farming by many Americans. *The Catholic Worker* received letters from many readers, Catholic and non-Catholic alike, asking for opportunities to farm or offering land on which to do so. A young French Canadian woman wrote in 1953 that she discovered "the profound beauty of our exquisite country 'The United States'" while visiting the new Maryfarm in Newburgh, New York.[101]

The communal component that Catholic agrarianism continually extolled as being necessary, however, had faded. All the Catholic Worker communes either shrank or ceased operation altogether in the late 1950s. The new enthusiasts of the 1950s insisted that "you can't read your way to the farm," but that was precisely what most of them did. Farming communes had become nothing more than a personal model for holy living, not an imperative for all Americans. The New Deal communities, including Granger, had lost most of their cooperative identity by the time historian Paul Conkin wrote his still worthy study of them in 1959. Maryfarm retained a large vegetable garden but little else. In the decade when all but a handful of American farmers obtained the electrical service and mechanization needed to convert farming into agribusiness, the difference between them and the colonization efforts of Catholic agrarians could scarcely have been more evident. That some of these modern farmers were themselves Catholic only emphasized this distance.[102]

Writing about the "communitarian impulse" in American religious history, Sydney Ahlstrom remarked that "most of the new communities, of course, remained simply the ideas of 'reading men,' yet six score of them were actually founded, a few dozen of them became celebrated though transient successes, and . . . became a major American cultural force." The Catholic farm colonies of the early and mid-twentieth century were not what Ahlstrom had in mind (he was writing of the Mormons), but they might have qualified as "celebrated though transient successes." They certainly offered examples of how Catholics could participate in a truly "American" form of religious practice while maintaining, often stridently so, a Catholic identity.[103]

The communes incorporated all the hallmarks of American communitarianism: perfectionism, millennialism, concern for sexual practice, charismatic leadership, and even one of the most Protestant features, the priesthood of all believers. Yet they did so within the context of the Catholic Church, which at times was solidifying its "otherness," and in locations that greatly abetted this sense of separateness. *The Catholic Worker* at its roots was a separatist Catholic publication, and the farm communes, from Easton to West Nyack to Rhineland, followed this pattern. Ligutti's Granger Homesteads, which offered the righteous "success" that the Catholic Workers could not hope to duplicate, was the only federal homestead community founded by a religious organization. Jews, Protestants of all sorts, and those more secular, when looking for an example of how a religious body could interact successfully with the federal government, looked first to the plots outside Granger, Iowa. Other communities such as Westphalia, Iowa, and Assumption, Ohio, proved to many Catholics that "twenty-five years of crusading" by the NCRLC had had concrete results, and that more would be forthcoming. The Green Revolution, in all its millennial fervor, seemed imminent, and the Catholic Church appeared to be poised to show the nation the way.[104]

Yet for all that, in the words of Marty Paul, "[h]ow close we come to the spiritual ideal we started off with depends much on how well and how wisely we treat the natural elements we work with."[105] Generally speaking, the natural elements could have been used more wisely. The farm communes were peopled with those lacking a rudimentary knowledge of agricultural skills. Even Granger's settlers were familiar only with outdated farming methods, warranting the establishment of what were essentially technical schools to teach "better" methods.

This lack of skill at farming underlined the essentially intellectual structure and popularity of the Catholic rural life movement. The colonies, communes, and homesteads, which were touted as the high tide of Catholic agrarianism, revealed at the same time the inherent shortcoming of that outlook: in trying to move more Catholics back to the land, the Catholic agrarian perspective overlooked the fact that the rural Catholics sympathetic to such a pattern did not need to move anywhere, since they already lived in rural areas. Urban Catholics captivated by life on the land soon awoke to the realities of that life, physically and spiritually. Most discovered what their neighbors who never left the city streets knew all along: city life looked better and better. Not only was rural life filled with tedious labor punctuated by periods of dire want and financial concern, it was also peopled with characters who could be ignored in an urban context. The benefits of rural living could often be achieved in the suburbs, where undesirable people were kept at bay and private gardens might be tended. Like most other entries in the arcane history of American communalism, the Catholic farm colonies faded as the outside world, which had once been renounced so vigorously, persisted in its seductive whispers. Except for the most dedicated among them, the colonists surrendered to that call.

In a way, then, Heaney's death in 1949 signaled the twilight of American Catholic agrarianism. Scarcely forty-five years earlier, Catholics had begun settling in southeastern Missouri. The development of a specifically Catholic rural life began soon afterward. In the middle of the same state, the Holy Family farm failed, largely because the exhausting labor that Glennonville's residents did out of necessity the Heaneys and Pauls did out of spiritual desire. The difference was that such works of supererogation had become not so much reality as a narrative for forming an American identity. What was significant was that Heaney, a third-generation Irish American from the streets of Milwaukee, became as enraptured with that narrative as any other American. What was tragic was how short its life, and Heaney's life, was. After Heaney succumbed, Father Peters lived another seven years in the Bootheel's slowly drying swamps. Despite the different outcomes, Heaney's words echoed the sentiments surrounding the New Deal's Granger Homesteads. In contrast to the "siege mentality" prevalent in urban areas, the Catholic farming colonies were opportunities to encounter overlooked expressions of American culture while simultaneously "supernaturalizing" them. With the colonies, the Church was finally "rooted" in America.

Nevertheless, the Catholic agrarianism that spurred the homesteaders to go back to the land faded quickly once they arrived. Other Catholics were experiencing similar reversals. Allen Tate, a consistent supporter of agrarianism from his days at Vanderbilt up through his conversion to Catholicism in 1950, found in neo-Thomism the religious and philosophical structure for which his cultural criticism had been searching. Unfortunately for Tate, the very intellectual trends that had drawn him into the Church were not to enjoy many more days there. The Second Vatican Council and its particular impact in America put an end to many of the aspects of Catholicism that Tate had favored. Agrarianism, a style of thinking that enjoyed a much broader audience than neo-Thomism, and the projects of communal living it inspired were similarly fated. In 1953 Father H. A. Reinhold, a German emigré priest conducting an apostolate in the Seattle shipyards, concluded glumly, but not without some relief, that "there is no longer room, where I live, for sustenance and richly diversified farming, except someone decided to be a martyr of his conviction or has so much capital that he can afford time and labor to make his farm into something like an educational institution."[106]

Tate and other converts of the time entered the Church only to stumble upon a vast reorganization. So, too, Catholics intoxicated with the spiritual virtues of farming rushed back to the land to find that often such virtues came only with the exorbitant price of hard labor and deprivation, and that the very people living closest to those spiritual virtues seemed unaware of their sacred surroundings.

CHAPTER THREE

Part of the Scenery

Catholic Experiences in Rural America

> And I will plant them upon their own land: and I will no
> more pluck them out of their land which I have given
> them, saith the Lord thy God.
>
> —Amos 9:14

While the Catholic agrarian vanguard colonized rural America, the National Catholic Rural Life Conference took steps to spread the good word among Catholics already there. In October 1947, the inaugural issue of *The Christian Farmer* appeared with its headline proudly touting "Christian Farmer News Letter—Precursor to Christian Farm Monthly." A left-hand column entitled "The Monsignor Says" featured Luigi Ligutti's picture. The column opened: "It's about time! We have over 500,000 Catholic families living on the land in the United States, but no Catholic magazine or paper is written for them. This is a start, and believe you me, we'll have a real good one some of these days." Simplicity in vocabulary and style dictated the new format. "We'll write it so the ordinary farmer won't need a dictionary to look up every other word. . . . Above all, we want to hear from you. It's going to be your paper."[1]

Plans for *The Christian Farmer* were, to say the least, grandiose. Previous NCRLC publications had been directed toward priests, members of religious orders, and educated laypeople. While these publications included some of the clearest statements of Catholic agrarianism, they also had notably low subscription numbers. *The Christian Farmer,* according to one of its planners, intended "to do for the readers practically what *Land and Home* [the NCRLC's previous publication] does for them theoretically, to be concretely what *Land and Home* is abstractly." Ligutti estimated that national circulation might reach one hundred thousand. With advertising projected to fill half the magazine, one planner suggested "copying the format of the popular secular magazines or the more popular Catholic magazines," adding that *Better Homes and Gardens,* also based in Des Moines, might be a good place to start. The first issue of *The Christian Farmer* featured photographs, a farm women's page, and devotional petitions. But the magazine never fulfilled the hopes of Ligutti and the NCRLC leadership. In October 1948, its circulation rose to fifteen thousand, but two years later paid subscriptions accounted for less than half its printing of ninety-six hundred copies. By February 1951, *The Christian Farmer* ceased publication due to lack of interest and unpaid production costs. Despite its best efforts to reach America's rural Catholic population, it suffered the same fate as previous NCRLC publications.[2]

The failure to maintain a popular outlet for Catholic agrarianism illustrates its adherents' ambiguous relationship with the rural Catholics they intended to help. At certain points, such as the early 1930s, the Catholic agrarian message reached a sympathetic and needful audience. Yet after World War II this enthusiasm could not be recaptured. The NCRLC's membership fluctuated dramatically before and after the war.[3] Groups such as the Central Verein and the Catholic Workers likewise could not sustain the same level of membership or interest, despite constant calls to embellish American Catholicism with Catholic agrarian principles. The frustration Catholic colonizers experienced came in part from the frequent reluctance of rural Catholics to trade their existing lives for the purportedly improved one offered by Catholic agrarians. The transformations within American rural life and the means by which rural Catholics created their own identities established a certain insular mind-set that Catholic agrarians only infrequently affected. Examining the origins of the Catholic presence in rural America reveals the depth of rural Catholics' independence, as well as the reasons for their readiness, frightening to many Catholic leaders, to simply blend into their surroundings instead of maintaining their faith as a distinct one.

Catholic Settlement Revisited

Before the Catholic rural life movement and its colonial legions arrived, rural America possessed its own Catholic flavor. In some ways the roots of Catholic rural America closely followed the specifically planned settlements discussed in the previous chapter. Still, Catholic settlement in rural America consisted of far more than what the planners had in mind. Clergy and missionary aid societies worked together to found ethnic communities. These, though, rarely exhibited a utopian or idealistic character. They served more as a solution to the problem of Catholics moving about independently—another source of Catholic settlement. Occasionally this rural Catholic population could be gathered into a specific community, but just as often not.[4] Either way, Catholic settlement by accretion sparked more than a few worries back East. Congregationalist Lyman Beecher despised the "uneducated" revivals sweeping the hinterlands, just as much as he feared the alarming rate of Catholic growth out there. An 1834 lecture series in Boston was published the following year as "A Plea for the West." Catholic rural settlements, Beecher claimed, possessed sinister roots and conspiratorial intentions:

American travelers at Rome and Vienna, assure us, that in the upper circles the enterprise of reducing our western states to spiritual subserviency to the see of Rome is a subject of avowed expectation, and high hope, and sanguine confidence . . . the correspondence of Catholic bishops and priests in this country . . . are full of the same predictions and high hopes.

Beecher's lectures have become better known for the inspired crowd that burned the Ursuline Convent in Charlestown, Massachusetts.[5] Meanwhile, the Catholic hierarchy fretted instead about a possible loss of faith caused by all the freewheeling Catholic settlement. Conspiracy or apostasy fears aside, Catholic rural America had already in the nineteenth century come to be seen as a place full of peril and ignorance. This prepared the ground for the Country Life Movement and for the Catholic rural lifers following in its footsteps.

For some of the freelance Catholic rural settlers, ethnicity remained a primary concern. Often they concentrated themselves in particular states (e.g., west-central Nebraska, Michigan's Upper Peninsula, northern Wisconsin, central Minnesota). Immigrant aid societies, an important source of direction and assistance, proliferated in the nineteenth century. While many served primarily as benevolent organizations, some directed funding toward the specific purpose of rural immigrant colonization in America. In 1822 French Catholics established the Society for the Propagation of the Faith at the prompting of Bishop William DuBourg of St. Louis and New Orleans. Propaganda Fide became widely known as a source of missionary personnel and funding among American Catholics. The Irish benefited primarily from the Irish Catholic Colonization Association and Thomas D'Arcy McGhee's Irish Immigrant Aid Society, founded in 1856 in Buffalo, New York. In 1848, Dutch Catholics began emigrating to northeastern Wisconsin under the direction of Father Theodore Van den Broek. The priest had seen the territory previously as a missionary to the Menominee Indians. Upon their removal by the federal government, he began canvassing both the Netherlands and eastern American cities for Dutch Catholics interested in farming. Green Bay and the surrounding Fox River valley became the most popular destination. The Polish Roman Catholic Union emerged in 1873 and included rural colonization with its insurance and philanthropic concerns.[6]

No group, though, settled a particular region as heavily as German Catholics did the Midwest. The American interior offered land enough for them to build communities centered around agricultural vocation, ethnic identity, and religious practice. Teutopolis, Illinois, a pan-Germanic community established in 1839, offered Catholic immigrants to Cincinnati an opportunity to escape from the city. Oldenburg, Ferdinand, Fulda, and Jasper all grew as German Catholic colonies across southern Indiana. Father Joseph Kundek, who organized Ferdinand, grasped how rural America ensured religious freedom. "Many a German Catholic is agreeably surprised to find he can travel four, five, or even ten miles in a wooded region settled by

Catholic families and discuss matters pertaining to religion without fear and without contradiction. Here a German is really independent and respected."[7]

The communities arose with the assistance of German immigrant aid associations, such as the Leopoldine Missionary Society (Leopoldinen-Stiftung), founded in Vienna in 1829. Originally the society sought the conversion of the Ojibwa Indians living around the upper Great Lakes. Soon it began assisting Slovenian and German Catholics to settle in the same areas. Father Francis Pierz did the most to create such ethnic enclaves. One such area, Stearns County in Minnesota, has been described as "probably the most rural Catholic county in the United States."[8] In 1857 the Swiss Colonization Society of Cincinnati purchased land in Indiana for a colony named Tell City (after the Swiss hero William Tell).[9] In 1835 the German Catholic Colonization Association of Philadelphia established the town of Hermann along the southern bluffs of the Missouri River west of St. Louis. Frustrated by the same anti-Catholic nativism that later sparked the settlement of St. Marys, Pennsylvania, colonizers defiantly made Hermann's main street ten feet wider than Philadelphia's. The town became so successful in preserving German cultural practices that enclaves of German Lutherans and Reformed immigrants began to establish themselves in the town as well. In the area that became known as the "Missouri Rhineland," Hermann stood as the capital.

More than a hundred years later, of course, the Heaneys and Pauls moved to the area to "start" a rural Catholic community. Before that, Hermann realized what one observer called the New Germania by reproducing in an antebellum Missouri town the religious diversity of the homeland.[10] Just to the west, a purely Catholic village named Westphalia was settled in 1835 as well. Jette Bruns, who at age twenty-three moved to Westphalia in 1836, wrote home in 1839: "Westphalia is coming up in the world, it is a town. Now all who live here seem to get ahead." By 1848 Jette and the rest of the town could worship in the new stone building of St. Joseph's parish. (Catholics from Westphalia in Germany seemed particularly fond of naming their colonies after their former home; a Westphalia arose in south-central Michigan in 1836 and another one appeared in Iowa.) The pattern of German community-building in the Midwest continued into the 1880s, when German-speaking immigrants from Russia moved into McIntosh County, North Dakota, and Hays County, Kansas.[11]

While priests were often the most successful recruiters for immigrant resettlement, their presence in the communities themselves was far from guaranteed. While Oldenburg in southeastern Indiana did not enjoy a resident priest, Ferdinand, further west, did. Father Kundek served as the town's priest, community planner, exemplary farmer, and best recruiter among German Catholics living in eastern states or abroad. Other locations were not so blessed. Only a few miles away in Jasper, a German Catholic community began building a chapel while waiting for a German-speaking priest to serve them. Catholics in New Vienna, Iowa, waited for three years after completing their building before a priest arrived in 1851. Belgian priest Ferdinand

Helias, S.J., served as Westphalia, Missouri's first resident pastor, but only after a period of traveling between it and a host of similar parishes in central
Missouri. Like the Methodist circuit riders, whose popularity was just beginning to wane, Helias rode from town to town, administering the sacraments
as he went. In between visits, Westphalian Catholics gathered to socialize
and recite the Mass prayers. Father Edward Jacker traveled among the mining towns of Michigan's Upper Peninsula until a permanent parish could be
obtained in Calumet.[12]

Customarily, the colonization projects of St. Paul's bishop John Ireland
are seen as the high tide of rural Catholic success in the nineteenth century,
despite his eventual disillusionment with them. This focus obscures the
rural Catholic communities that developed independently of such organized colonization projects. David Bovée has written that the "record of
Catholic colonization in the nineteenth century shows some successes, but
mostly failures—especially in the most grandiose projects." Success came
elsewhere, but not in the form that Bishop Ireland or even the immigrant
aid societies envisioned or desired. Perhaps the most truly successful rural
Catholic settlement occurred when Catholics simply moved west on their
own. After all, one of the first rural Catholic colonies was "founded" in
1799 when Father Demetrius Gallitzin petitioned Bishop John Carroll to become the pastor for a group of Catholics already living near what was later
named Loretto, Pennsylvania.[13]

The family of NCRLC founder Edwin O'Hara provides a good example of
this sort of settlement by accretion. Both of his parents left Ireland in the
1840s. Before Edwin's birth in 1881, they and their older children had
moved west, first from Indiana (where Edwin's mother was trained as a cate-
chist by Holy Cross Father Edward Sorin) and then Iowa. They headed toward Minnesota after hearing of even better settlement opportunities there,
landing near Lanesboro in 1870. The American wheat market had drifted
west as well, from New York's Genesee Valley in the eighteenth century to
southeastern Minnesota at the same time the O'Haras arrived. Other
Catholic settlers in Minnesota had also apparently migrated to wherever the
wheat grew best. Apart from any clerical direction, a rural Catholic population accumulated. In 1878 when Bishop Ireland opened up the colonies, the
unregulated migration of Catholic farmers from southeastern Minnesota to
the richer soil of the western part of the state increased rapidly. Ireland finally had to state explicitly that the colonies existed only for recent immigrants and colonists from eastern cities:

> I have been informed that in several districts of Minnesota, Catholic farmers are
> preparing to sell their lands with the intention of moving to Swift County [in
> west central Minnesota]. I beg leave to say . . . that no Minnesota farmer will
> from this date be admitted into the Swift County Colony. I have organized this
> colony for the benefit of men without homes, more especially for Eastern peo-
> ple, and I will rigidly adhere to my first plan.[14]

Southern Minnesota, with its largely autonomous Catholic settlements along the Mississippi River and Bishop Ireland's colonies in the west, therefore held both patterns of the growing rural Catholic presence in the nineteenth century.[15]

It was this elusive, free-settling Catholic presence in rural America that created so much consternation about the loss of faith outside the city. Priests serving Catholic colonies, while doing mission work in the surrounding area, would discover Catholic enclaves previously unknown to them. Philip Vogt, a Benedictine in southeastern Nebraska, encountered a whole array of Catholics:

> From Nebraska City I have gone into the interior of the region as far as Turkey Creek six miles or more away. Eight Catholic families there who speak German. A little more than a mile away is another creek, Yankee Creek where there are six English speaking Catholic families. . . . Then on to Rulo where in the vicinity live many Catholics, English, French, and German speaking.

On their way to St. John's City, Nebraska, Father Jeremiah Trecy's settlers met a group of French Canadians living outside Sioux City, Iowa. Trecy later discovered a Catholic community living around South Dakota's Fort Randall. Roger Finke and Rodney Stark have argued that Trecy's experience was not uncommon; as American settlers moved westward, they met the Catholic presence that had preceded them.[16]

In the case of colonies, the priest led the people into the wilderness, but more often the wilderness lured the people first. Upon gathering together, they petitioned for a priest. Within forty miles of the German immigrants at Hermann, Missouri, Catholics settled in piecemeal fashion. A village named Armagh began with those

> who slowly but surely made fields of the forests, and who laid the foundation of civilization and prosperity in the foothills of the Ozarks. . . . Many of these early settlers were Catholics, some of whom had come hither from Ireland, others from New Orleans, and from the Eastern states. That the spiritual welfare of these isolated children of the Roman Catholic Church might be provided for, the first missions in these parts were established.[17]

St. Joseph's parish in Edina, Missouri, appeared in this spontaneous fashion, although here parishioners at least enjoyed local non-Catholic support. Area Protestants contributed to the parish building fund, and the "church-raising" in 1844 was attended by residents of three counties. Dubuque, Kansas, like its namesake in Iowa, became a center for rural Catholic settlement. Polish and German-Russian immigrants from Minnesota, Wisconsin, and Iowa arrived first. Daniel Fitzgerald's list of "original surnames" in Dubuque includes "Woydziak, Redelzkes, Polzin, Murray, Driscoll, Schauff, Harrington, Neys, Kehough, Huberty, Scharpf, and Weber. Dubuque was always a community of

mixed nationalities." In Arkansas, the single-nationality towns of St. Benedict's and Warren (Swiss German and Polish, respectively) were two of the
communities that convinced the ICCA that the state might also support Irish
Catholic colonization.[18] In the 1870s Platte County, Nebraska, first settled by
German Catholics, began receiving more and more Polish Catholics. So many
from Galicia arrived that in 1890 one town changed its name from Burrows
to Tarnov, the provincial homeland's principal city. In 1895 Franciscans who
had originally settled in Clontarf, Minnesota, petitioned to leave: "The Brothers think that Nebraska, owing to its natural advantages over this place, will
prove more encouraging to persons coming to join them from other states."[19]

Serving these communities with the Church's sacraments proved to be a
difficult task. A recurring narrative from rural priests was having to race long
distances on horseback to someone's deathbed in order to administer extreme unction. One notable instance occurred in 1877 when Father John
Daxacher rode from St. Helena, Nebraska, to Deadwood City, South Dakota,
for the hanging of Jack McCall, the convicted murderer of Wild Bill Hickok.
Daxacher arrived in time to accompany McCall to the gallows. Confirma-
tions, weddings, and baptisms were often scheduled for when the priest visited. One particular baptism in 1879 in Fremont, Nebraska, included the entire Borglum family. Their son Gutzon, the future carver of Georgia's Stone
Mountain and South Dakota's Mount Rushmore, was nine.[20]

On the other hand, some Catholic communities refused a priest's services
unless he spoke their language. Slovenian Catholics in central Nebraska were
particularly firm in their stance against the German-speaking priests sent by
Omaha bishop James O'Gorman. "Volga-Germans" in Victoria, Kansas,
clashed with other German Catholics in the area over which German dialect
was to be used in prayers. Such incidents resembled the controversy among
the Church hierarchy over how quickly immigrants should assimilate into
American life. In rural areas, there were similar battles concerning assimilation within ethnic Protestant churches, too. This allowed Catholics to blend
into the religious landscape more easily than in the city. It was quite possible
for a rural Catholic parish to be at odds with its bishop but at peace with its
Protestant neighbors, whether ethnic or old-stock American.[21]

The "persistence of ethnicity," as Rob Kroes calls it, was found in ethnic
Protestant denominations such as the Lutheran Church—Missouri Synod and
the Christian Reformed Church. Much like ethnic Catholic parishes, these
churches believed that language did save the faith, and rural settlement in
turn helped preserve that language. Accordingly, a variety of ethnic Protestant
churches settled rural areas. Sometimes this occurred after Catholic settlers
had already arrived. Twenty years after Catholicism established itself in northeastern Iowa, the area became predominantly Swedish Lutheran. Finnish immigrants found northern Wisconsin suitable for the preservation of their
Lutheran faith and ethnic identity; those who worked in the area's copper
mines labored alongside Czech and Slovakian Catholics. Christian Reformed
Dutch immigrants in Wisconsin were three times as likely to settle in rural

areas as Dutch Catholics. These differences in confession and ethnicity resided within a rural matrix where one group could be more "American" in one situation and less in another. German Lutherans in Kansas and Missouri were more "American" by virtue of being Protestant, but as a church they were far more concerned with preserving the German characteristics of their faith than were German Catholics.[22] In 1957 James Shannon, writing about Catholic rural settlements, claimed that "as parochial centers . . . their numbers and success have measured up to the most sanguine predictions of their founder. In each of these settlements a common religion is still the principle of social cohesion." The same could be said for ethnic Protestants. Religious preservation through rural settlement was far from a specifically Catholic concern.[23]

Rural Catholics also shared experiences with another seemingly unlikely group: old-stock Americans. Many of the unregulated Catholic settlers, like the more numerous Protestants, obtained their land through squatters' rights. This loose pattern of settlement accounted for many of the Catholic groups "discovered" by the traveling priests who arrived later. Rural Americans, especially those from the "frontier" Baptist and Methodist churches, have most often been cast as the intractable opponents of anything "Romish." However, there were some similar experiences as the areas these groups settled created new regional identities.[24]

In the antebellum period, many Americans—recent immigrants as well as old stock—had headed westward across the Appalachians and beyond. The fears of many nativists that with the new immigrants lawlessness would reign in the cities paralleled similar fears in the Midwest concerning the many poor Southern white settlers (already bearing the nickname "rednecks") who were moving northward. Those who held such fears stigmatized both "new" groups as violent threats to a stable society. Rural settlements emerged just as many cities gained large Irish neighborhoods. St. Louis, for example, had the "Kerry Patch" on its near north side, and central Missouri became known as "Little Dixie" for its settlement by migrants from Kentucky, Tennessee, and Virginia. The "good folks" in Missouri started to feel surrounded.[25]

The popularity of Jesse James justified, to some extent, the fear of the "pukes" (another derogatory term for the Southern settlers). His earliest training came as a Confederate guerrilla in northwestern Missouri and eastern Kansas. After the war, Jesse, his brother Frank, and the Younger boys graduated to armed robbery. While the urban elites wondered whether the law even existed anymore in Missouri, James received popular absolution from area residents, who considered him their defender against wealthy corporations and landowners. The son of a staunchly Landmark Baptist mother, James shared some connections with Missouri's Catholics. Geographically, Little Dixie's borders overlapped with the western edge of New Germania. Little Dixie also earned its name from the fact that its counties had the largest slave populations in the state. Slave ownership signaled that one stood above the socioeconomic level of the pukes, and Catholics as well as Protestants possessed the means to do so.[26]

Another example from postwar Missouri demonstrated the cultural assimilation of rural Catholics. Near the end of the Civil War, Missouri's legislature enacted the Test Oath, a law by which all ministers were required to register with the state before performing any religious duties. This infuriated all sorts of Christians, Catholic as well as Protestant. Father Joseph Hogan declared in his travels across northern Missouri:

> To the Catholics of Brookfield and Linn County belong the honor and high distinction of being the first, and so far as I know the only people in the State of Missouri, to call a public meeting, to denounce, oppose and resist, the infamous, anti-Christian measures of the State of Missouri. . . . And if there be any who doubt that those who first unfurled the flag of religious liberty in America, do not mean to keep that flag with its proud folds fluttering defiantly in the breeze, let them read what the people of that Faith have put on record at Brookfield.

Hogan had supported the North in the war, but the Test Oath was another matter. Methodist circuit riders across the state, whose constituencies were often pro-Southern, spoke of the "martyrs" who opposed the Test Oath on the grounds of "Christian freedom."[27]

Through this ad hoc migration, Catholics established significant rural communities, though less numerous than those of their Protestant counterparts. Baptists, Campbellites, and Methodists are usually considered more "frontier" denominations than Catholics. In some states, Roman Catholics were not only the "frontier" denomination, they were the only organized church in the county. Even where they were not, such as in Little Dixie, there were often unifying cultural factors that overrode confessional differences. David Bovée has calculated that by 1900, the Catholic population in some regions was in fact predominantly rural. One such region was the Upper Midwest—Iowa, Wisconsin, Minnesota, North Dakota, and South Dakota—while another was the Southwest—Arizona, New Mexico, and Texas. Louisiana, another part of the South, contained perhaps the largest rural Catholic population in the country. Nationally, there certainly was a rural Catholic minority.[28] In some locations, though, a rural Catholic majority might be said to have existed. The varieties of Catholic settlement throughout the nineteenth century created such complexities. Catholics held some degree of strength in rural America despite eruptions of nativism. Rural Catholics were certainly no less Catholic than their urban counterparts in terms of religious observance. From the perspective of Jeffersonian agrarianism, they could have been perceived as more "American," because they engaged in what the nation's forefathers had seen as the national occupation: farming. In terms of divisive matters such as preserving doctrinal purity or ecclesiastical unity through a foreign language, ethnic Catholics were no different from—and were sometimes more assimilated than—recently arrived ethnic Protestants. The farming life cycle formed a common core that Catholics shared with their neighbors.[29]

This rural Catholic presence, to some degree independent from the institutional Church, is important to remember, because the first sixty years of the twentieth century were filled with attempts by the Church to reorganize and strengthen a Catholic rural life that Church leaders felt was left fallow. In reality, rural Catholics had succeeded in creating an expression of American Catholicism already very similar to other patterns of American life. It had succeeded as well in surviving blizzards, prairie fires, and the arduous labor involved with establishing farms and communities. The twentieth-century Catholic rural life movement began from the premise that the rural Catholic Church was weak. That obliviousness to an existing vibrant rural Catholic presence revealed the extent of the Church's participation in the nation's increasingly urban outlook.

Transformations in American Rural Life

The Catholic agrarians had hoped to reform American agriculture according to their theological image of farming. Apart from this or any other intellectual debate concerning it, agriculture itself underwent dizzying changes during the first half of the twentieth century. Catholics who farmed and those who lived in areas dependent upon agriculture were affected by these transformations as much as any other group. In some regions (e.g., Louisiana, central and northern Minnesota, southern Indiana, and along the Missouri River in Missouri, Kansas, and Nebraska), they had maintained their strong communities since settling there in the previous century. Agriculture and its varying fortunes served as a unifying experience, as did technological advances and the national image of rural life itself. With the exception of religious affiliation, therefore, rural Catholics shared a great deal of their lives with their non-Catholic neighbors.

The Midwest—the region with the most rural Catholics—serves as a good example. Variations in agricultural success were due to the disparate fortunes of the region's farmers. The areas furthest north received one climatic blow after another. The Dakotas and western Minnesota began the 1920s with a severe drought and plummeting postwar prices. The 1930s brought little relief. Crops withered in triple-digit heat, and the resulting lack of animal feed struck down many herds not felled by the frigid Dakota winters. (In 1936 Steele, North Dakota, experienced a summertime high of 120 degrees and a January low of sixty below zero.) Farmers abandoned their holdings, and small-town merchants, dependent upon farms' buying power, closed as well.[30]

The weather that tortured agriculture in one region could benefit farmers elsewhere. The area that in the 1930s would become the Dust Bowl—southwestern Kansas, eastern Colorado, and the panhandles of Oklahoma and Texas—enjoyed a mini-renaissance during the 1920s. This region's nightmares of the 1890s had been erased by the once-again burgeoning wheat crop—this time augmented with increasing mechanization—and the advent of exploratory oil drilling. The disastrous conditions in the Dakotas seemed far away. By the time farmers realized that less and less rain had fallen, it was too late. Soon the midday sunlight in towns such as Liberal, Kansas, was completely blocked out by boiling dust storms. The NCRLC presaged a better day after Christian Winkelmann became Wichita's (and thus Liberal's) bishop. His earlier success with the St. Louis archdiocesan rural life program gained him a measure of respect from Catholic agrarians as a cleric capable of handling such rural problems. Winkelmann was not the only person moving to Kansas against a torrent of those leaving. The popular images of Dust Bowl migration have merged with Steinbeck's *Grapes of Wrath:* herds of dilapidated pickup trucks filled with dirty children and lean, flinty-faced parents. However, Pamela Riney-Kehrberg has shown that during the Dust Bowl, most residents remained in Kansas and did the best they could.[31]

Of course, Steinbeck's celebrated novel focused on the cotton sharecroppers of eastern Oklahoma, not the dust-choked wheat farmers further west.[32] Tenant farming persisted across the nation until World War II. In the Deep South, it survived until the 1950s.[33] Midwestern tenant farmers were not nearly as numerous or poor as their Southern counterparts, but they certainly existed. Concentrated most heavily in the Great Lakes states of Illinois, Indiana, Michigan, and Ohio, farm tenancy had been a constant factor in Midwestern rural life.[34] Ideally, it was believed to be fine preparation for actual farm ownership; hard work and frugal living honed farming skills and saved money. But regardless of region, tenant farmers shared similar experiences: as they sank into destitution, they devoted more and more of their rented land to producing cash crops and less to their own subsistence needs. Caught in the tightening vise of needing to buy more products but receiving dwindling profits, many tenants drifted into cities.[35] This cityward trend, which threatened to turn into a torrent, was what had frightened O'Hara, Ligutti, and other Catholic clergy about the "Catholic rural problem." Although their caustic antiurbanism forecast a dire end for cities, Catholic agrarians felt that the "children of the grapes of wrath" were offered a bleak future as well.

The experiences of rural Midwestern Catholics, therefore, depended upon their location and what they farmed (if they farmed at all), among other factors. Rural Protestants, African and Mexican Americans, and the very few rural Jews faced the same problems. Catholics in Wisconsin shared more with Lutherans there, such as fluctuating dairy prices, than with Catholics in Louisiana or at the edge of the Dust Bowl in central Kansas. Rooted in the previous century's settlement patterns, this subtle rural heterogeneity made for a variety of "rural Catholics." The Catholic rural life movement did not encounter a monolithic rural Catholic population, even though its plans were geared toward one.[36]

One assertion that may be made about rural America, Catholic and non-Catholic alike, concerns what David Danbom calls "the universality of hard work." Life on the land was based on long hours of manual labor, and it included every member of the family over the age of five or six. If this labor pool failed to produce a subsistence income, family members resorted to working for other local farmers. Carmen Welch explained this in *The Catholic Worker* for those considering taking up farming:

> The usual pay check that you have been used to having every week or every two weeks won't be there. But perhaps you can figure out other means to make extra money. . . . Here, a man gets from seventy-five cents to one dollar and fifty cents per day now and you are asked to bring your dinner. Hired girls from one to two dollars per week and you are expected to do and know everything from milking the cows to chopping wood and running the house, cooking three meals a day, the laundry and caring for the children too.

Such jobs could be picked up in addition to work on one's own farm, although Welch's work with her rural House of Hospitality in Ramsey, Illinois obviously monopolized her time. Many commented on the bleak future that a life of such work held. James Agee's popular *Let Us Now Praise Famous Men* described the lives of three Alabama sharecropping families, the Gudgers, the Ricketts, and the Woods. What he wrote about them could easily have been extended to all rural Americans: "The family exists to work . . . and children come into this world chiefly that they may help with this work."[37]

Hard manual labor, of course, was not unique to rural America. Nor was the ambivalence with which rural Americans viewed the New Deal from the beginning. Catholics were at first quite enthusiastic, but they became disenchanted with the New Deal's bureaucracies and lack of attention to poverty issues. To rural Americans, receiving WPA (Works Progress Administration) benefits seemed particularly odious, since it indicated that people were no longer the independent, hard-working citizens they thought themselves to be. Carmen Welch wrote, "[D]uring the days of the early depression, nearly every bank failed, farmers, once well-to-do could no longer crest the wave, and today, they are either gone, no body knows where, some took suicide as the way and others, swallowing their pride for the sake of the 'woman and kids' asked for relief. There are no charities here, despite the many churches that call themselves such."[38]

As discussed earlier, Catholic agrarians seemed aware of the rural obsession with work, as well as the lack of rural charity. While the Catholic rural life movement sought to fill that gap with practical planning, romantic visions of what constituted rural work remained. C. E. Wolf, one who "left college to become a farmer," suggested that "a young man should *not* start out farming on rented land." Instead, land should be purchased first and then gradually improved with buildings. Wolf realized this might take two or three years. During that period, the farmer should plant according to bio-dynamic methods; a "garden, orchard, vineyard, [and] berry patch" were all to be started.

> The first improvement should be a well, after that should be the barn, then the other outbuildings and finally the house. Financially speaking, this sounds like

a big order. You must remember, however, that the buildings on a forty or fifty acres farm will be much smaller than those on a quarter or half section of land. Much of the building material can be second handed. Old buildings can be bought and wrecked and the lumber used again.

Bio-dynamic farming thus applied to a farm's construction, not just care for crops and livestock. With recycling of building materials, immediate costs remained low and the natural world was not further damaged. Keeping to a tight budget was essential, since such a farm was not intended to be commercially productive. It went without saying that all this would be achieved with manual labor. However, it had already been noted that buildings constructed this way actually raised farm costs, especially for small-scale farmers. Bio-dynamic farming seemed to require significant starting costs. Constant repairs and small amounts of land nullified any savings that Wolf's advice might have brought.[39]

Meanwhile, agriculture was becoming an industry like any other. This meant that economic survival depended in part on maintaining farm buildings and equipment. Facilitating this transition were innovations such as John and Mack Rust's mechanical cotton picker; an International Harvester model advertised that it accomplished the work of fifty field hands. The technological and economic changes that accompanied the New Deal and the years following World War II were of such magnitude that it is no exaggeration to discuss the period in terms of a paradigm shift for all rural Americans, including Catholics. Better machinery usually meant better returns (if the weather allowed). But it also added to unemployment, as sharecroppers and small-scale farmers became extraneous or uncompetitive.[40]

The most influential change in rural America was also the most deceptively simple: electricity. Electric service revolutionized both farm and home life. Barns shone at night. Electric motors powered fans and milk coolers. Although many of the new household appliances (toasters, mixers, sewing and washing machines) cost far more than any farm or working-class family could afford, they appeared constantly in popular magazines such as *Good Housekeeping*. Many rural areas did not receive full electrical service until after 1945, but the New Deal's Rural Electric Administration did alleviate this situation somewhat. Once installed, electric service became a matter of pride, even for Catholic clergy. In 1940 George Hildner wrote of his Missouri parish that "new and complete installation of equipment for all buildings and the flood-lighting of the grounds was effected by inducing the Union Electric Company of MO. to extend their service to the church and entire community."[41]

The ease of work with electricity and better machinery in turn transformed agriculture itself. The global food shortages following World War II gave American agriculture the opportunity to show its productive might. The distinguishing characteristic of agribusiness—massive production of food—came as the result of the modernization of rural America. This new ethic of efficiency vilified anything that entailed *too much* work. As both house and farm became increasingly efficient, a sort of inversion occurred. Those farmers who remained on the land could look disdainfully on the immediate nonindustrial past. "We used to eat inside and shit outside. Now we eat outside and shit inside!" one southern Illinois woman commented. After homesteaders moved into the Granger properties that Ligutti directed, Edward Skillin noted that neighborhood boys had taken to tipping over the abandoned outhouses, even under the threat of gunfire. The triumph of modernization was all but complete.[42]

Yet as rural America modernized itself, cultural critics emerged to indict its intransigence and lack of refinement. Sinclair Lewis's popular *Main Street,* published in 1920, upbraided the Midwest's pettiness and isolationism. Across the region, boosters leaped to defend the "real" Midwest. The uproar grew particularly strong in Stearns County, Minnesota, the center of rural Catholic settlement less than one hundred years before. Inside its boundaries lay Sauk Centre, Lewis's childhood home and the basis for his novel's fictitious Gopher Prairie, as well as St. John's archabbey of the Benedictines. It seems that Lewis not only was aware of the abbey, but incorporated it in the novel's criticism. When the protagonist, Carol Kennicott, questions the town's complacency, she receives the following reply:

> Anyway, Gopher Prairie isn't particularly bad. It's like all villages in all countries. Most places that have lost the smell of earth but not yet acquired the smell of patchouli—or of factory smoke—are just as suspicious and righteous. I wonder if the small town isn't, with some lovely exceptions, a social appendix? Some day these dull market-towns may be as obsolete as monasteries.

The reality of Gopher Prairie belied the myth of rural vitality and moral purity. Unconnected to either land or factory, the small town, like the monastery, was a bygone image best relegated to the past.[43]

Main Street's widespread success announced Lewis as a novelist worthy of notice. It also codified an undercurrent of sentiment among American intellectuals that rural America was a backwater deserving only derision and rejection. Three years later, Robert and Helen Lynd's *Middletown* appeared and only reinforced the conclusion that Midwestern wholesomeness and religiosity were more myth than reality: "It appears that there is a strong disposition to identify the church with religion and church-going with being religious." Middletown was as unobservant in religion as anywhere else, and the facade only exacerbated the hypocrisy of small-town religiosity. The Lynds made such claims after concentrated sociological research in the small Midwestern city of Muncie, Indiana. Rural reformers such as the Catholic agrarians sought to improve rural America in order to ensure its production of food, or children, or both. *Main Street* and *Middletown,* on the other hand, lent credence to those who believed that rural America should simply be abandoned and forgotten.[44]

Understandably, a siege mentality quickly established itself among Midwesterners, much as it had among Southerners smarting from their Civil

War losses. (Disparaging all things Southern, of course, continued apace. At roughly the same time, H. L. Mencken labeled the region the "Sahara of the Bozart.") Because *Main Street* took place in a small town, national discussions of the Midwest focused almost exclusively on its rural aspect, despite the presence of urban production centers such as Chicago, Detroit, and St. Louis. Ten years later, when the Depression caused widespread unemployment, the nation's conception of rural America reappeared as a healing vision. David Danbom explains this transition in national perception:

> People beset by depression needed someone white with whom they could iden-
> tify and who was worse off than they were, someone they could feel sorry for
> and who could make them count their blessings, and the Okies filled the bill.
> For the first time in the history of the country, a substantial body of rural Amer-
> icans were the subject of urban pity. It was an important milestone on the road
> rural America was traveling from majority to marginality.[45]

Catholics traveled that road alongside their rural neighbors. Unlike their urban co-religionists, who built monumental parish churches and surrounded
them with schools and convents as cultural barriers, rural Catholics, perhaps
particularly so in the Midwest where many of them lived, were grouped together with other rural Americans as part of the backwater that lacked cultural and intellectual vigor.

The Blending In of Rural Catholics

The Catholic agrarians' antiurbanism committed them to restoring the vision of rural America that Lewis, the Lynds, and H. L. Mencken incessantly
lampooned. However, Thomas Carey's sermon before the 1925 NCRLC convention in St. Paul, Minnesota, suggested the ambivalence with which many
rural reformers viewed their subjects. "It is time for [the Church] to venture
forth, as the Church of ancient times, to evangelize the countryside. Even in
this twentieth century she will find there pagans and heathen without number, who seem to think that man lives by bread alone." In that last sentence,
Carey might have been referring to Catholics as well as Protestants. In ways
other than agriculture, Catholics had their own rural lives that they constructed without recourse to Catholic agrarianism. There was, therefore, another sort of "Catholic rural life": rural Catholics became quite similar to, even
occasionally indistinguishable from, their non-Catholic neighbors. A grave-
stone epitaph for one citizen in Edgar Lee Masters's Spoon River claimed that
when all of the town's church bells rang, he "could no longer distinguish . . .
any one from the others." Likewise, rural Catholics could at times become just
another religious group competing in the rural American religious market.[46]

Cultural historian Warren Susman has observed that the "communications
revolution," made possible by technological developments such as the radio
and telephone, created a number of contradictory impulses in American

intellectual and cultural life. The 1920s, for instance, developed as "the great age of the community study" (such as that by the Lynds), but the decade also saw an increase in expressions of self-identity. "Life by association" character- ized much of American culture as people expressed their individual identities by joining a variety of social, political, and religious communities (and thus confirming the criticisms of Lewis and Mencken). No other group, though, combined the emphasis on community and self-awareness with the identity of small towns as thoroughly as did the Ku Klux Klan.[47]

The early 1920s saw the high-water mark of Klan membership. Committed to a social-reform program they touted as "100 percent Americanism," Klan members vigorously sought to "protect" the white Anglo-Saxon Protestant (WASP) population. The organization was "vehemently and violently anti- union, anti-Semitic, anti-Catholic, anti-prostitution, anti-smoking, anti- dancing, anti-'petting,' and anti-liquor." While certainly racist, the Klan of the 1920s spent more time pursuing its agenda for social reform and legislation. Its motto, *non silba, sed anthar* (not for self but for others), came from the twelfth chapter of Paul's letter to the Romans. (Ironically, the same passage alluded to the "Mystical Body of Christ" doctrine so treasured by Dorothy Day.) In the 1920s, the motto emphasized the self-sacrifice that Klan members thought nec- essary to combat what they believed to be "infiltration" by "non-Americans" and to restore the threatened sense of WASP community and identity. Catholi- cism was seen as one of the most serious threats to this identity.[48]

The Klan's message found a sympathetic audience. Approximately five million men paid their ten-dollar registration fee and donned the white hood, and women joined similar organizations. Ruth Ann Heaney remem- bered her childhood in rural Nebraska as being marked by Klan marches. She observed, as did others, that the hooded order was not as anonymous as it wished; children often could identify members by their shoes. At the height of its popularity, the Klan appeared to be a primarily rural phenomenon, or at least filled with rural Protestants who had recently immigrated to the city. For example, Perth Amboy, New Jersey, and Chicago each saw a spate of Klan-related violence; and the Indianapolis city government, with the excep- tion of the mayor, was filled with Klan members.[49]

Klan vigilante violence possesses legendary status in American life. Leonard Moore, however, has challenged the conclusion that "the very dy- namics of Klan organization dictated violence," emphasizing instead the Klan's ordinariness. For example, Indiana, the state where it captured the most political power, witnessed very little Klan-related violence. The Klan appealed to a wide spectrum of people who desired greater "law and order" in their communities, not just to the white underclass. Its "Americanism" seemed to support precisely such goals. Scandals involving embezzlement and sexual depravity by state Klan leaders, especially Grand Dragon David C. Stephenson of Indiana, destroyed this appeal. By the mid-1920s the state of Indiana, in which almost 40 percent of the male population had once been Klansmen, held only a few thousand.[50]

Kansas City's Archbishop Edwin O'Hara blesses parishioners at the dedication of St. Su-
sanne's Church in Mt. Vernon, Missouri, 17 July 1945. The church had been built with
Extension Society funds. (Courtesy Loyola University, Chicago Catholic Church Extension Society Papers, photograph collection)

Peter Maurin (second from left), Father Pacifique Roy (fourth from left), and retreat participants stand in front of Maryfarm's barn, Easton, Pennsylvania, 6 May 1945. (Courtesy Marquette University Archives)

Monsignor Luigi Ligutti (second from left), Ralph Borsodi (third from left), and home-steaders near Borsodi's School for Living, Suffern, New York. (Courtesy Marquette University Archives)

LaDonna Hermann (center) teaching sewing, Cottleville, Missouri. (Courtesy Rural Parish Workers of Christ the King)

Cover for National Catholic Rural Life Conference homesteading pamphlet. (Courtesy Marquette University Archives)

Vincentian motor mission advertisement. (Courtesy DeAndreis-Rosati Memorial Archives)

SAINT·ISIDORE·PLOWING·WITH·ANGELS DOES·THE·WORK·OF·THREE·FARMERS

St. Isidore

St. Isidore prayer card. (Courtesy Marquette University Archives)

Mass at a Vincentian motor mission along
the Eleven Point River, Riverton, Missouri,
1943. (Courtesy DeAndreis-Rosati Memorial
Archives)

(left) Parishioners attending consecration of St. Suzanne's parish, Mt. Vernon, Missouri, July 1945. (Courtesy Loyola University of Chicago Archives)

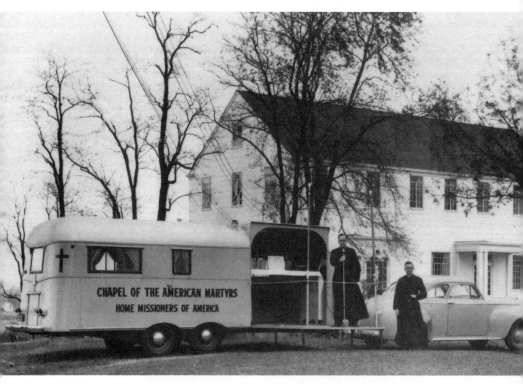

W. Howard Bishop and Raphael Sourd with the Chapel of the North American Martyrs, Glendale, Ohio, 1941. (Courtesy Glenmary Home Missioners of America Archives)

National Catholic Rural Life Conference emblem. Shaped like a Communion host, the emblem symbolizes the simplicity and fertility of rural life repeatedly praised by the Conference. (Courtesy Marquette University Archives)

W. Howard Bishop, founder of the Glenmary Home Missioners
of America and president of the National Catholic Rural Life
Conference, 1928–1934. (Courtesy Glenmary Home Missioners
of America Archives)

Vincentian street-preaching service held in front of a country general store. (Courtesy DeAndreis-Rosati Memorial Archives)

Catholic motor mission held on the steps of the Russell County courthouse, Seale, Alabama. Courthouses were often the setting for the services. (Courtesy DeAndreis-Rosati Memorial Archives)

Eleanor Roosevelt (with broad-brimmed, flowered hat) visits the Granger Homesteads near Des Moines, Iowa, 8 July 1936. To her right stands Monsignor Luigii Ligutti, who received national acclaim for his management of the federal funded homestead project. (Courtesy Marquette University Archives)

Across the nation, the Klan suffered the same fate. Only the 1928 presidential campaign of New York Catholic (and anti-Prohibitionist) Al Smith could spark a small Klan revival. Two incidents, also from Indiana, indicated why the Klan's supposedly ironclad rural roots could be quite tenuous. In 1923 a rumor spread that the Pope had arrived in Chicago and subsequently boarded a train to North Manchester to begin his conspiracy to overthrow America. The Klansmen in that small Indiana town dutifully suited up and met at the train station to greet the pontiff. When the Pope failed to disembark, the bewildered yet relieved Klansmen dispersed, stopping only to harass an unfamiliar salesman. (Apparently they were worried that the Pope might be disguised.) The anti-Klan newspapers in the state and the nation gleefully derided the Klan as small-town buffoons. Just to the north that same year, Knute Rockne embellished the reputation of the "Fighting Irish" when he ordered the Notre Dame football team to dispatch a Klan march in South Bend.[51]

However, the Ku Klux Klan did not hold a monopoly on fraternal organizations in rural America. The Klan's anti-Catholicism, combined with the nation's antirural sentiment, prompted rural Catholics to muster their own organizations with their own identities. Besides the Notre Dame student body, some of the Klan's most vigorous opposition came from Catholic fraternal societies, such as the German Catholic Central Verein and the Knights of Columbus. Both sought widespread social reform, as did the Klan, but for these groups such reform included eradicating anti-Catholic bigotry. This agenda won them praise from the first NCRLC convention in 1923.

David Chalmers has suggested that "America has long been a nation of joiners, of men bound together for companionship and community purposes. American fraternalism has often been a path to assimilation and Americanization of a heterogeneous society, but as often as not, the concept of fraternity has often stood for exclusion." Fraternal organizations were one element of rural culture that revealed how closely Catholics—in contrast to other religious groups—resembled their neighbors, despite some conflicts. Missouri Synod Lutherans, who were as concerned with maintaining their ethnic and religious heritage as were Catholics, expressly forbade membership in secret organizations. The Indiana district of the Church of the Nazarene forbade Klan membership on similar grounds. The Ku Klux Klan and the Knights of Columbus often denounced each other as a threat to American identity and national security. Still, the presence of such conflicts in small Midwestern towns reflected how rural Catholics were involved in the everyday life of rural America in ways that some other religious groups were not.[52]

If the Ku Klux Klan arose from the historical exigencies of the post–Civil War South, the Knights of Columbus traced its roots to the religious and cultural environment of immigrant enclaves in urban New England. Although two more bitter rivals could scarcely be found, they shared similar concerns of uniting men in a group sworn to protect certain cultural and religious values. The Knights of Columbus provided a specifically Catholic fraternal alternative to the Ku Klux Klan and other groups such as the Masons, the International Order of Odd Fellows, and the Shriners' Temple. A young priest, twenty-nine-year-old Michael McGivney, founded the Knights of Columbus in New Haven, Connecticut, in 1881. It followed a number of fraternal and social organizations that promoted insurance benefits for members' families in the event of death. Such insurance societies were common among the working class, especially when they—and not the insurance companies—survived an economic depression in the early 1870s. Groups such as the Ancient Order of Hibernians, the Catholic Knights of America, the Western Catholic Union, the Massachusetts Catholic Order of Foresters, and the Catholic Benevolent Legion of Brooklyn all shared goals of mutual support between members and some form of secretive ritual.[53]

McGivney incorporated existing total-abstinence societies that had taken root among Catholic immigrants and a number of Catholic militia groups left over from the Civil War to establish a society directed by and for laymen. The name they chose reveals how Catholic immigrants and their children brokered their position in American culture. "Knights of Columbus" reclaimed the Catholic share in Christopher Columbus—the heritage of all "Americans"—and wedded that to the growing popularity of ritualistic secret societies intent on preserving some sort of group identity. Within twenty-five years, the Knights had established councils in every state and most Canadian provinces and were preparing to do so in Cuba and the Philippines. In Kansas, the Knights had been present in the state's oldest parish, St. Joseph's in Flush, since 1904. At the other end of the state, the German-Russian immigrants around Victoria established a council in 1912. (Another cause for pride in that area came the same year when William Jennings Bryan called their St. Catherine's parish church "the Cathedral of the Plains.")[54]

The Knights recalled their militia roots as they attacked signs of anti-Catholicism in American culture. Indications of their success came from their opponents as much as from other Catholics. *The Menace,* a furiously anti-Catholic newspaper published in Aurora, Missouri, presaged the Klan's conspiracy theories, boasting in 1917, "For five years *The Menace* has waged a war versus political Romanism, declaring that 'the Roman Catholic political machine is the deadliest enemy to free institutions and liberty.'" The Knights and other Catholic groups, it was said, sought to promote "the interests of the Roman Catholic hierarchy and the papal system of government through legislative channels." (In 1920 *The New Menace* surfaced in nearby Branson, making similar claims.) Opponents of Catholicism also circulated a false but notorious "Loyalty Oath," in which Knights supposedly swore to subsume American government to the Pope and kill non-Catholic babies. During the height of Klan power, Edwin O'Hara and the Knights combined their efforts to fight Klan-sponsored legislation requiring all Oregon children to attend public schools. They launched a pro-Catholic advertising campaign in the state's newspapers as well. When O'Hara organized the 1923 St. Louis meeting of the NCRLC, he asked the Knights to send a representative; part of the proceedings included a discussion of the Knights' other rural activities.[55]

The origin of the Knights of Columbus as a temperance society had its equivalent in the twentieth century. Catholics contributed significantly to the temperance cause up through Prohibition. Jay Dolan has observed that "temperance was to late-nineteenth century Catholicism what birth control was to mid-twentieth century Catholicism: the *cause célèbre* of moral reform." The NCRLC from its inception condemned the influence of alcohol in rural communities. On the parish level, Catholic agrarians wished that the example of St. Hubert's clubhouse in Westphalia, Iowa, might be followed elsewhere:

> Most rural pastors today sooner or later face the problem of taverns and their effect on neutralizing the work. . . . No young man in Westphalia need travel to another town seeking the sort of recreation that taverns and pool-rooms provide: no pagan tavern could survive in Westphalia today. . . . Yet there is none of the oppressive air of a self-righteous "temperance bar" about St. Hubert's: the regulations are kept, as it were, automatically because they are the natural expression of the kind of social life the people of Westphalia appreciate and want.

Catholic agrarian temperance advocates, like most Catholic "drys," differed from Protestant reformers in their reliance on community self-regulation, not legislation. Either way, nothing seemed to work. In November 1926, *Catholic Rural Life* included a quotation from the Anderson, Indiana, *Herald*: "It's hard to believe in a corn surplus, when you hear a wet telling how many stills are operating."[56]

The Knights of Columbus had begun as a benevolent society among Irish Catholic immigrants, but it quickly moved beyond ethnic boundaries. Even within ethnic boundaries rural Catholic organizations created their own American Catholic identities. Camaraderie mattered as much as, if not more than, moral reform. In discussing "Bohemian Catholic rural activities," Father V. F. Mikolasek endorsed the "gradual Americanization through social clubs for youth in literary and dramatic societies." He also listed five "enemies of the spiritual life": anti-Catholics, apostates, "Americanization by force," indifferent societies, and an insufficient number of Bohemian-speaking priests. Writing in the midst of the Klan's anti-immigrant fervor, Mikolasek considered the second and third enemies the worst; these worked together to draw Bohemian Catholics away from the Church. The Klan and like-minded people, he thought, usually had the opposite effect: their hatred actually strengthened Bohemian ethnic and religious identity. The Central Bureau of the Central Verein, which controlled the German equivalents to the Irish benevolent societies, also directed the rural life projects of the state vereins. The Minnesota chapter of the Central Verein (which supplied the NCRLC with Joseph Matt, one of its prominent lay members) conducted its own "practical farmers conferences." Held at St. John's abbey in Collegeville, the conferences were one of the few attempts to procure actual Catholic farmers for the NCRLC's programs. The Missouri Catholic Union of America, under the direction of the Central Bureau, managed a lecture series for 140 rural parishes.[57]

Thus, a network—sometimes strong, sometimes weak—addressed rural Catholic issues before the Catholic rural life movement emerged to unite things. While profiting from NCRLC programs, the same network remained after Catholic agrarianism faded. In 1954 the Knights' combination of Catholic identity, American fraternalism, and social awareness remained undiminished in Flush, Kansas. J. E. Biehler wrote, "In keeping with this splendid spirit of the past, the Knights of the present continue to manifest the same spirit of cooperation and aggressiveness. Their enthusiasm and good will are not limited to the four walls of the council chamber; they extend to every project that is for the good of the parish and the community." Catherine Albanese has argued that "whatever their ascribed religious identity, Americans were professing religions that bore the signs of contact with those who were other and different. American religions were *changed* religions, and they were *new* religions, even if they evoked the stuff of tradition and the trappings of former cultures and times." Rural Catholic fraternal organizations, whether they squared off against the Ku Klux Klan, preserved ethnic identity, or both, placed their members in new relationships through cultural and religious forms familiar to their non-Catholic rural neighbors.[58]

Familiarity characterized the ways in which rural Catholics interacted with their neighbors, even in matters of religion. In *Middletown* the Lynds noted that "preoccupation with the daily necessities together with the pressure for civic solidarity, tends soon to dull such occasional acute doctrinal self-consciousness."[59] Even as the Catholic agrarians strove to solve the Catholic rural problem, their desire for cooperation helped ensure familiarity among rural residents.

The Knights and other fraternal groups operated on a parish system, and that meshed nicely with the Catholic agrarian emphasis on strong rural parishes as centers of rural reform. Beyond the fraternal groups, rural Catholic parishes, as much as the rural Protestant churches on which the American Country Life Association focused, could serve as sites where a rural community could be built. For example, George Hildner's contacts with the University of Missouri School of Agriculture won his tiny parish both local and national attention.

> Helpful has been the good fortune of having the Soil Conservation Demonstration Area here established and the church farm designated as a demonstration unit. This unique distinction has signalized St. John's church farm, it being the only church demonstration farm in this entire part of the United States. The demonstration area in its work throughout the community has directly benefited every farm of this district, has helped change the farming methods and practices, stimulated milk production as a new means of livelihood in the community, and promoted wild life management.

Farmers interested in developing new techniques of soil conservation therefore visited St. John's parish, but not for any explicitly religious function.
The parish doubled as well as a union hall for a local of the Sanitary Milk
Producers.[60] A 1943 article by James T. Meehan, S.J., describing a "Catholic
Oberlin" likewise illustrated how Catholics could become rural community
leaders. St. Patrick's parish outside of Stevens Point, Wisconsin, with the
help of its Protestant neighbors, raised the entire church building in order
to construct a community center in the basement. "Early 1938 saw the
opening of Saint Patrick's Community (not parish) Hall, free to any meeting of general benefit to the district or parish. Now began a new era of
community life." The Catholic parish had become "catholic" as well—that
is, all-inclusive. "The people have put themselves into the hall they built.
They are proud of it. They are proud of their Catholic faith. Protestants
think kindly of Catholic neighbors and all help one another in time of
need. Prejudices have been destroyed, and a fine community spirit is making steady growth."[61]

Such church-centered, interdenominational activity was not limited to
Catholic parishes. The Catholic women's club of St. Martin's parish in Caldwell, Kansas, met one November day in the basement of the Christian
Church (Disciples of Christ) for a turkey dinner.[62] This interaction illustrated
the rural cooperation that took place on an ad hoc basis before the ACLA or
the Catholic agrarians began espousing it. For the residents of Caldwell, having to deal with the Dust Bowl at their doorstep further ensured community
interaction in this town located just across the state line from Oklahoma.
The Depression created an opportunity to institutionalize such spontaneous
rural cooperation, as the NCRLC did in Westphalia, Iowa. "The American
farmer is normally the most rugged of individualists and is not to be shaken
out of that attitude by talk, but Father Duren seized the right moment to begin talking economic cooperation, when adverse conditions made his people
ready to think of some new way out."[63] By 1948 the NCRLC's historian
counted Westphalia as one of the conference's "victories" in its "crusade" for
rural life, "one of the best rural communities in the United States."[64] The
tiny village of 150 had incorporated "cooperation" at almost every level of
community life, "the result of a happy combination of drouth [sic], depression, and the wisdom of Father Duren."[65]

The Catholic rural life movement knew that rural issues encompassed
more than men and farming. "The problem of the hour is the problem of
the land," proclaimed Dominican priest Vincent McNabb, "and the problem
of the land is the problem of the woman."[66] The solution to these problems,
though, often departed significantly from the ideal family farms envisioned
by Catholic agrarians. Work done by women in farm communities constituted another avenue by which rural Catholic familiarity was maintained.
The Catholic agrarian worldview placed special emphasis on the spiritual
and physical fertility of women, but rural Catholic women shared other bur-
dens with their non-Catholic neighbors. Hard work, again, provided the

link. Expected to manage the household and raise children, they also worked regularly alongside their husbands on the farm itself.

Catholic agrarians nevertheless seemed more interested in stressing the woman's role in the productive rural home. The Catholic establishment in general agreed; Catholic publications on marriage and family life reasserted the view that women worked at home, not outside of it. One of Edgar Schmiedeler's books on the subject decried the "heartless homes" where women worked (and played) elsewhere. Catholic agrarian publications readily followed suit, since their other pages already advocated rural fertility and productivity in other forms. Susan Frawley Eisele's column for rural women in *The Christian Farmer*, entitled "My Fair Lady," began: "Welcome to the home page of THE CHRISTIAN FARMER! We farm women are to have for our very own use and enjoyment, this section of the paper, where we are going to gather once a month and talk about the things closest to our hearts." After this came suggestions to make round pot holders instead of square ones, as well as applesauce cake "with plenty of raisins and nuts" instead of fruitcake for the upcoming Christmas season.[67]

"Real" work for women, according to Catholic agrarians, apparently had more to do with food preparation than production. The Catholic agrarian worldview considered the natural world to be already productive in some ways. In June 1944 *Land and Home*, quoting the *Science News Letter*, reminded readers, especially women, that picking "the wild greens that grow along roadsides and even, sometimes, on the front lawn" was a convenient way to avoid wasting ration points. Besides dandelions and watercress, "housewives may be able to serve, as a change from spinach and lettuce, stinging nettle, marsh marigold, dock, milkweed, chicory, wild onion, lamb's quarter, summer mustard, pokeweed, sorrel and purslane or parsley." If the Catholic agrarians prescribed bio-dynamic farming for farming men, for rural Catholic women making use of God's good bounty seemed to be in order.[68]

Louise Owen's 1943 "Kill . . . and Cure" article, which focused on the multiple uses of pork, made a similar point: much could be accomplished with little. Owen included four recipes for cures and brines, one for sausage, and one for headcheese. "Certainly the porker is a valuable and versatile addition to our table, and what a pleasure, satisfaction and economy comes from dishing up our own hams, sausages and bacon!" However, Owen's remarks clearly assumed that her readers were beginners: "If you want to make head cheese—and you should—it is necessary to keep the pig's head separate from the rest of the sausage meat and scraps."[69]

Some of Owen's readers might have already known this, as did many rural Catholics who did not subscribe to *The Christian Farmer*. Carmen Welch mentioned in passing, "No one here rarely butchers a beef yet we have often wondered why. We think the chief reason is they are not so experienced in killing and cutting up a calf, as they are with a pig—that is about the first thing farm boys and girls learn about, where there are many hogs, how to butcher them, render the lard, make the sausage, the heads' cheese, liver wurst, mincemeat and all the rest of it." On the other hand, Owen prefaced her recipes for brines and headcheese with the remark that "anyone who is not inclined to do the actual killing himself can probably find an obliging farmer or butcher" to do it.[70]

In other words, rural Catholics already knew many of the paths by which rural neighborhoods and communities were maintained before Catholic agrarians began to recommend them. Everyday rural life allowed for such interaction between Catholics and non-Catholics, and occasionally necessitated it. Even seemingly significant differences in religious practice could be acknowledged without the bigotry that others assumed rural life bred. Advertisers in a Kansas parish's jubilee history included a grocer who boasted "Fresh Fish for Fast Days," and another advertisement sent "Best Wishes to Our Catholic Friends." Patrick McGosgrove, a mail carrier in Edina, Missouri, for fifty years, suited himself and his horses up in green for his last St. Patrick's Day in 1921. That McGosgrove, who "had lost none of his Irish emotionality during the many years he had lived in America," could stand equally as a community figure and as a Catholic parishioner reflected this often overlooked familiarity in rural experience.[71]

Recreation provided another example. It was one aspect of rural life in which Catholic agrarians experienced more success connecting with rural Catholics. The ACLA linked recreational activities to retaining the youth population of rural areas, and the Catholic agrarians followed suit. Since the parish served as the foundation for Catholics, any such activities were opportunities for the Catholic community to present itself to others. Occasionally, "rural dramatics" or a "rural orchestra" was discussed as a means of combating rural boredom, thought to be a chief reason that young people migrated to the city. The Rural Parish Workers of Christ the King eventually created a complete educational agenda in Cottleville and Fertile, Missouri. Often, two programs overlapped. In the early days at Cottleville, LaDonna Hermann included religious instruction with sewing lessons for local girls.

Sports were also quite effective, particularly baseball. The sport's major professional teams were, of course, located in cities, but its setting recalled the nation's rural, agrarian heritage. Played on a large, open, green field suggestive of rural areas, baseball rewarded individual work as well as team effort. This resembled the cooperation between farmers and their communities that was so much desired by the Catholic agrarians and other rural reformers. Baseball's unyielding refusal to expand represented what was characterized as the stubbornness and unchanging nature of rural America. Like that place, baseball also offered an avenue of assimilation for ethnic Americans. Players such as Joe DiMaggio, Josh Greenburg, and Jackie Robinson demonstrated that Catholics, Jews, and African Americans could "make it" in America like anyone else.[72]

Across rural America, Catholic players illustrated the same point. In 1936 St. Mary's parish in Westphalia, Michigan, included a baseball-team photograph in a booklet celebrating the town's centennial; other pictures showed a brass band and the church building. In Westphalia, Iowa, a crowning achievement of the town's cooperative structure was its baseball field. "The baseball field is more directly the product of cooperative enterprise in that its construction, from leveling the ground and felling the timber to driving the last nail in the bleachers, was done by the people themselves." Such facilities were intended for one gender only, of course; Catholics in New Cleveland, Ohio established a boys' baseball team and a "canning club" for young girls.[73]

Father Ligutti recognized the assimilative power of this and other sports. At his first rural parish in Magnolia, Iowa, recreation during summer catechism classes included "baseball, tree climbing, boxing." While Ligutti separated the students by sex for their classes, apparently they participated in the same recreational activities. The Knights of Columbus council in Flush, Kansas, boasted of having "sponsored a baseball team for over forty years and a basketball team for the past ten years." St. Joseph's parish in Edina, Missouri, featured a communitywide Labor Day picnic with boxing matches and a contest in which entrants tried to whistle while eating as many soda crackers as they could. Such activities were avenues through which rural Catholics interacted, or competed, with non-Catholic Americans. A 1925 article in *Catholic Rural Life* remarked: "The boys and girls (big and small) think that New Cleveland is the best place on God's earth and very few leave it to go to the city. Our amusements are base ball, horse shoe pitching, picnics, and parties, dramatic plays, yes—and even social dances." While Catholic agrarians approved of such activities for their value in keeping youth on the farms, rural Catholics themselves used them in order to construct their own communities.[74]

The technology that came with the agricultural revolution provided another way for rural Catholics to foster familiarity with their non-Catholic neighbors. If wired for electrical service, the rural household possessing a radio encountered a whole new world as entertainment, news, and politics poured in. The Grand Ole Opry, for instance, became a Southern and then a national weekend institution; its product—country and western music—expressed a very accessible form of agrarianism. The NCRLC sponsored radio programs in the cities that hosted its annual convention. Carmen Welch wrote to Dorothy Day about hearing the radio broadcast of Pope Pius XII saying Mass.[75]

Father Charles Coughlin, of course, serves as the best example of Catholic participation in religious broadcasting. The popularity of the "radio priest" preceded that of more genial evangelists such as Fulton Sheen and Billy Graham. Taking a page from *Quadragesimo Anno,* Coughlin called for independent property ownership, small-scale production, and traditional morality. He established the National Union for Social Justice (NUSJ) at his Shrine of the Little Flower outside Detroit. Because Coughlin broadcast from Detroit and because his bombastic attacks often included paeans to Irish Catholic nationalism, he has been viewed primarily as an urban Catholic version of the Great Commoner, William Jennings Bryan; neither was thought to have said much of originality or substance. Coughlin, though, explicitly included agrarian interests in his radio addresses. At the height of his powers, he allied himself with the National Farmers' Union (NFU), which shared his growing dislike for Roosevelt's New Deal. Officials within the NFU introduced Coughlin to William Lemke, a North Dakota Catholic who was sympathetic to farm interests and whom Coughlin later chose as the candidate of the Union Party (which was affiliated with Coughlin's NUSJ) in the 1936 presidential election.[76]

The NCRLC's broadcasts also contributed to creating a link between Catholicism and agriculture.[77] A year after Lemke's overwhelming defeat, Ligutti broadcast a series of addresses over WHO in Des Moines. The series, about rural life and the NCRLC, was quite a success. A closing suggestion to write Ligutti for transcripts brought in dozens of requests. A man from Des Moines remarked that he heard one address while at a barber shop. "You know what kind of entertainment the barbershops prefer, something light and snappy, at least not Beethoven or dissertations on economics. However, when your talk came on . . . everyone stopped talking and listened to the whole speech." A woman from Iowa Falls wrote that Ligutti's talks "certainly refer to the most perfect type of existence for the human race; and since the most perfect, the one where (all other things being equal) we can come the nearest to enjoying that, 'Peace which the *world* cannot give.'" Across the Missouri state line, a vocational-agriculture instructor commented that "there is a great need to interest youth in the advantages of farm life. It doesn't appeal to many in its present condition." A bank cashier from southern Minnesota echoed that concern.[78]

Ligutti's less caustic broadcasts characterized rural Catholicism's identification with shared rural values. "Motor missions," the Catholic street-preaching services (covered in the following chapter), used the radio occasionally as well. Priests in the Concordia, Kansas, diocese operated the "Catholic Hour" radio program. Only the Paulists, who were founded to convert Americans, used the radio waves with any breadth. Edgar Schmiedeler reported that in 1940 the group in Winchester, Tennessee, began a program that "goes out over the powerful station, WSM, an NBC outlet in Nashville. It is directed to the country people and follows immediately the National Farm and Home Hour." The same station broadcast the Grand Ole Opry every Friday and Saturday night. (This happened before the Opry moved to the now famous Ryman Auditorium, which was quickly labeled "the Mother Church of Country Music.") Just as Catholic as Father Coughlin, and certainly less shrill, few associations between religion and rural life could have been stronger than these radio broadcasts.[79]

Catholic Agrarianism and Rural Catholics

The popularity of Coughlin's and Ligutti's radio broadcasts illustrates the complex relationships among rural Catholics, their non-Catholic neighbors, the pervasive new technological developments of the time, and the proponents of Catholic agrarianism. When Catholic agrarians were successful in getting their suggestions accepted, they gave rural Catholics an increased awareness of themselves as a particular religious group. When unsuccessful, the Catholic agrarians appeared rather unrelated to and unconcerned about the group they claimed to support.

More than in any other way, Catholic agrarians aided rural Catholics by creating an increased sense of identity. To do so, they built upon existing parish-level organizations such as the Knights of Columbus and the Central Verein. Priests who became public figures, such as Coughlin, Hildner, Ligutti, and O'Hara, augmented this heightened self-awareness of rural Catholics, though they did not create it. Even here the priests used cultural media already familiar to rural Catholics. Hildner's agricultural knowledge cast him in much the same light as a county extension agent teaching new farming techniques. A radio station could broadcast a discourse on Catholic doctrine one night and air the Carter family bluegrass band the next. Baseball games pitting parish teams against local teams came to resemble the major-league games heard on the radio. Contests with local teams recalled federal government programs intended to make rural life more appealing; while competitive, the games fostered community awareness and togetherness. In some places, this enhanced identity included the impression that Catholics belonged to one of the few churches willing to address the needs of rural Americans. Carmen Welch wrote to Dorothy Day and Ade Bethune that it was "8 miles to the nearest Catholic church and there are 3 Protestant sects here, but few members. Only those who consider themselves the 'aristocrats' can afford to belong to them—and those families, like my own, who have been found to ask for relief, aren't welcome or either they intimate you don't need to come again."[80]

Problems arose not over a Catholic presence itself, but whether certain expressions of it seemed conventional by rural standards. Welch, for all her work with Nazareth House, did not have good relations with the Catholics of Ramsey, Illinois, and the surrounding area. She had been raised Catholic, but her six children had not yet been baptized. Her husband, Jesse, was not Catholic and did not care to be. Consequently, Nazareth House's status as a Catholic institution sparked something of a controversy in the small Illinois town. Besides receiving threatening mail (one letter apparently read, "All WPA people should be taken somewhere and shot"), the Welches were rumored to be defrauding the public through pleas for charitable donations in *The Catholic Worker.* Day even received a letter from an Illinois state postal inspector asking her to "please advise your attitude in the matter and whether or not your office sanctions the operation and appeals through your paper from institutions operating under the guise of Catholicism."[81]

More positively, Catholic agrarians created devotions specifically for rural Catholics, based on devotions available to all Catholics. The "Little Flower," St. Thérèse of Lisieux, became quite popular before her 1931 canonization.

Catholic agrarians rarely missed an opportunity to emphasize the floral saint's symbolic union of natural life and supernatural piety. W. Howard Bishop's first rural life organization bore the name, as did Coughlin's suburban Detroit shrine. *The Catholic Worker* repeatedly published Ade Bethune's woodcut prints of biblical images; "The Sower" and "Christ the Tree of Life" were visual counterparts to Maurin's Green Revolution. The Liturgical Movement also created specifically rural images for all American Catholics. The natural simplicity of rural life embodied the purity that liturgical reformers sought. Shorn of all human accouterments, not cluttered and crowded like a city, the new Mass would offer a purified spiritual experience, just as rural life offered an authentically "natural" one.

Ligutti's dislike for prayerbooks that were "too urban" led him to create a more suitable version. Published in 1956 and edited by Alban Dachauer, S.J., *The Rural Life Prayerbook* contained translated sections of the Mass, prayers, and blessings. The character of these items reflected how Catholic agrarianism had combined traditional Catholic devotional prayers with specifically rural ones. "A Prayer for the Wood-Lot" appeared in between "A Prayer to Simon of Cyrene" and "To My Friend Jesus." There were blessings for candles on the feast of St. Blaise, diseased animals, bees, and tractors, as well as a "reserved" blessing to "ward off destructive insects and other small animals"— for which, Dachauer noted, the priest must receive his Ordinary's approval.[82]

One particular devotion stood above all others in its embodiment of Catholic agrarianism and its popularity among rural Catholic laypeople: St. Isidore the Farmer. Isidore was a devout peasant and dutiful husband whose faith had been rewarded when, after he was rebuked by his overseer, two angels helped him plow the fields. The patron saint of Madrid, he was canonized the same day as Francis Xavier, Teresa of Avila, and Philip Neri. Despite the obvious suitability, the NCRLC did not start encouraging Isidore's devotion until Virgil Michel and the Liturgical Movement became involved. A petitionary prayer was written and widely circulated:

> O God, who didst teach Adam the simple art of tilling the soil, and who through Jesus Christ, the true vine, didst reveal Thyself the husbandman of our souls, deign we pray through the merits of St. Isidore, to instill into our hearts a horror of sin and a love of prayer, so that working the soil in the sweat of our brow, we may, with Christ our Lord, enjoy eternal happiness in heaven.

Pius XII named St. Isidore the NCRLC's patron saint in 1948. The following year, the NCRLC began conducting pilgrimages to Isidore's shrine in Madrid. The national shrine was located within the NCRLC headquarters in Des Moines.[83]

With this devotion, Catholic agrarians made their clearest mark on the postwar devotional high tide. (The NCRLC also actively promoted Marian piety through Our Lady of the Fields, but this did not draw the same level of devotional attention.) The St. Isidore devotion became one of the conference's biggest successes as the laity joined the Company of St. Isidore. "An outdoor shrine" to the saint, one conference advertisement stated, "is a sign of God." *The Christian Farmer* included petitionary prayers and notes of gratitude to Isidore. Some of the "suggested family practices" for the Company of St. Isidore included "[d]aily recitation of the prayers of St. Isidore, the Christian Farmer, the Rosary, and the Rural Family Prayer." Devotees were encouraged to consecrate their homes to the Sacred Heart. Urban Catholics from Chicago and Brooklyn as well as rural ones became enraptured with the devotion. In 1956 one hundred thousand people participated in the St. Isidore novena. Two years later, over ten thousand had become conference members.[84]

However, 1958 turned out to be the high-water mark of the conference's presence among rural American Catholics. The latter, David Bovée writes, "seemed mainly attracted by the Conference's spiritual program, not its rather self-sacrificing economic message. Thus, when the Church entered the era of Vatican II, with its emphasis on modernization and social justice, not old-fashioned devotions, NCRLC membership declined rapidly." Laypeople had not constituted a large part of the conference's membership. Yet once rural Catholics began to join the NCRLC and the Company of St. Isidore, the Church turned its attention away from the very niche created for rural laypeople by the conference that claimed to minister to their needs. Ironically, this transformation was due in part to the heirs of the Liturgical Movement, which had originally organized the devotion. Just when the NCRLC recorded its largest membership, the conference's internal conflicts over finances and Ligutti's leadership prevented any further action. The recent gains were therefore lost as quickly as they had been made. James Hudnut-Beumler has remarked that "while Vatican II made eating meat on Friday permissible for Roman Catholics it did not necessarily make them feel good about it." Something similar might be said about the piety replaced by the Second Vatican Council. Devotional life was certainly reformed, but, at least in the case of the NCRLC, the difference between the intended effects and the actual fallout was greater than expected.[85]

The spiritual separation between the NCRLC and rural Catholics that occurred in the late 1950s masked rural Catholic liturgical traditions that had preceded, and then coexisted with, devotion to St. Isidore. As with much else in Catholic rural life, these public devotions often served a unifying purpose for the entire community as they celebrated a specifically Catholic religious identity. In the small Missouri town of Edina, "[t]he happiest event of the spring of 1939 was the crowning of the May Queen." With one young woman chosen as queen and another as her crown bearer, "Father Mullins gave the ceremony for a large audience of Catholics and non-Catholics. It was the kind of affair that Edinans loved and the crowd looked forward in anticipation of a new annual event." The Ku Klux Klan had employed a formidable array of outdoor pageantry in its marches and cross-burnings. Outdoor Catholic processions, Marian or Corpus Christi, or the Rogation Days celebrations established parish boundaries with a similar liturgical flourish. The crucial difference lay in the Klan's exclusionary vision; its ceremonies proclaimed clearly who did not belong. Catholic processions instead offered an inclusive experience. The boundaries could be crossed through conversion or, more frequently, by instances of rural neighborliness. By establishing themselves with such rituals, rural Catholics helped strengthen their own community.[86] It was not surprising that Protestants attended a St. Isidore outdoor devotion in Kingsville, Ohio, in 1953. Among the "ten little churches" in southwest Missouri that Edwin O'Hara consecrated with great ceremony, two stood in towns neighboring Aurora, former home of *The Menace*.[87]

The rupture between the NCRLC and the rural Catholic laity over St. Isidore reflected greater distances between the realities of American Catholic rural life and the images after which Catholic agrarians wished the laity would pattern their lives. Unaware, perhaps, of the ACLA's intellectual origins, the Catholic agrarians replicated its mistake of distancing itself from the farmers who supposedly needed its help. The neo-Thomistic structure of the Catholic agrarian worldview meant that its adherents separated themselves from the rural Catholic laity on more than just a spiritual level. When the worldview failed, it did so completely. No longer connected with Catholic farmers politically, regionally, or spiritually, Catholic agrarians found themselves with a message but no audience.

Sometimes the rhetoric stood diametrically opposed to rural Catholic experience. Disgruntled with the undifferentiated nature of farm work, John McNamara wrote, "We all insist that whenever possible the place for the mother is in the home, operating the household and attending to the spiritual education of her offspring." Farming had spiritual benefits, but motherhood did as well. McNamara desired a division of labor that respected this outlook. Such a view of rural Catholic life, with clearly defined gender roles, hoped to deny the ambivalent reality. The August 1926 issue of *Catholic Rural Life* announced an essay contest as a means to include more laypeople in the discussion of Catholic agrarianism. Asked to consider rural life "not merely from an economic standpoint, but also from the social, cultural, and religious side," adult essayists were to respond to "Do you wish your boy to be a farmer?" while those aged fifteen to twenty were asked to respond for themselves. The winning essays, which were published in the November and December issues, illustrated the ambivalent relationship between Catholic agrarians and rural Catholics. Clarence Umschied of St. George, Kansas, and Lawrence Greiner of Panama, Iowa, received first and second place for their reasons why they wanted to become farmers. The parents' winning essays were both written by women: Mrs. Samuel B. Hill of Walnut, Kansas, and Mrs. Joseph Iffrig of Vinita, Oklahoma. Since for Catholic agrarians farming was a spiritual activity, McNamara might have approved. However, Hill's and Iffrig's responses also indicated that women were as involved with farming as were men, and fairly conversant with it as well. Like many other Catholic agrarian attempts to improve rural life, the essay contests showed that rural

Catholics could manage their own religious and cultural identities differently, even using the Catholic agrarian channels to do so.[88]

That independence could be found elsewhere in rural Catholic life. McNamara complained: "What chance has the priest to gather children for instruction and devotions when he must contend with a litany of extra-curricular activities of the school and elsewhere? They make quite a long litany: band practice, Boy Scout meeting, Girl Scout meeting, basketball practice, games, practice for plays, plays, shows, dances, parties, sales, practice for this and practice for that until the thing becomes nauseating."[89] The very structures that Catholic agrarians strove so diligently to implement in rural parishes became the expressions of rural Catholic life that parishioners found interesting, not the "correct philosophy of rural life" that Catholic agrarians hoped they might accept.

On the other hand, farmers hesitated to change farming methods. Catholic agrarians recognized this reluctance but dismissed it as stubbornness to be overcome.

> The intelligent, industrious farmer knows the value of all these bio-dynamic methods from experience. Thousands of other farmers "had to be shown." . . . The plan was put through by means of inexorable firmness. The objection of the farmers "I'll try that next year" was met with the insistent "No, do it this year." The farmers acceded and found their cash income going up almost immediately.

Country Lifers had previously attempted to change farming methods, and the process that they helped start—the industrialization of agriculture—had become the Catholic agrarians' most formidable enemy. Faced with planting for the financial future or planting on the basis of theological principle, most Catholic farmers did the former and went to Mass as usual. Their spiritual relationship with the land and the Church expressed itself in a way different from that prescribed by Catholic agrarianism.[90]

Ligutti's increasingly international agrarian vision for American Catholic rural life, filled with admirable references to social justice and Christian charity, ran aground on the developments within American agriculture itself. During one of his trips to Europe, Ligutti saw a barefoot man carrying a handicapped child and commented: "Most people don't want too much—some work, a little bread, a prayer and a smile. Why should not society arrange to satisfy such humble requests?" The "culture of abundance" in America, though, dictated that rural Catholics would want more. Participating wholeheartedly in what became the nation's largest agriculture boom, Catholic farmers and their co-religionists in small towns disregarded the self-denial of their clergy's agrarianism out of financial necessity and a wish to recognize fully their long-standing place in rural American culture.[91]

In 1925 one Catholic agrarian described a visit to a local psychiatric ward and then commented:

> I have been thinking . . . that about three-fourths of the small towns of America
> have one thing in common with the asylum folks—they can't get together.
> They cannot organize for the public good. They break up into little antagonistic
> social, business and even religious factions and neutralize each other's efforts.

In the 1940s things seemed not to have changed much. An NCRLC booklet
on homesteading directed: "Do not hesitate to become acquainted with your
new rural neighbors. They are one of the finest assets of rural living. Rural-
ists are not isolationists."[92] The exasperation of rural reformers often approx-
imated that of the social and literary critics who lampooned rural life for its
cultural stagnation. The lack of visible change came to be blamed on the
rural residents themselves. Further care for them needed to take into account
their apparent handicaps, since in the minds of many Catholic agrarians,
most rural Catholics neither wanted to reform nor took advantage of all that
had been offered them.

In Rome to assume his position as the NCRLC's director of international
affairs in 1960, Ligutti reflected, "Last year I was so concerned with Des
Moines—now forget it!"[93] Although criticism of clerical distance from the
laity erupted after the Second Vatican Council, this distance had already
doomed the most concerted efforts to organize rural Catholics as other
groups had been organized within the Church. Before 1960, rural American
Catholics had communicated their discontent with the discrepancy between
rhetoric and reality by refusing to join or support the organization that
Church leaders had constructed for their benefit.

When the Company of St. Isidore failed to retain its members, the
Catholic agrarian worldview lost the constituency it was supposed to have
encouraged. This occurred as American agriculture completed its metamor-
phosis into agribusiness. One NCRLC administrator wrote to another in
1953, "Personally I think the rural cause would be in a better way if we could
have 'shot' or deported a few labor czars ten years ago."[94] Agriculture had become just another business, despite the efforts of the Catholic agrarians.
Now, when "abundance" could accurately describe American agriculture, the
specifically Catholic endorsement of such a goal deteriorated.

During the 1925 Scopes "monkey trial," H. L. Mencken had noticed the
striking and enraptured worship practiced by rural Protestants in the hills beyond Dayton, Tennessee. He later recognized that everyone knew these
groups existed but avoided acknowledging their presence.[95] The same could
not have been said of rural American Catholics; many knew of them, and
spoke often and vociferously in their defense. But in doing so, the proponents of Catholic agrarianism constructed their own version of rural Catholic
identity, one that was removed from the diverse experiences of rural
Catholics. Meanwhile, a Chicago priest with a budding sociology career came
to one of what would be many shocking conclusions about the American

Catholic laity: "In the externals of life there is little to distinguish the Catholic suburbanite from his Protestant neighbor."[96] At one level, Catholic agrarianism's loss of appeal occurred because the same conclusion had already been true of rural Catholics for most of the twentieth century.

Despite its misperceptions, Catholic agrarianism harbored an irrepressible sense of innovation. This engendered a pastoral pursuit that best exhibited the adaptability of Catholicism to rural America. This was Catholic street-preaching, what the Catholic press often labeled "motor missions." Unlike the colonization efforts, the motor missions revealed the degree to which Catholic agrarianism could interpret American culture accurately. The success of this alternative rested in part with the ability to attract the rural Catholic laity, which demonstrated every day its unique blend of independence and communal neighborliness.

CHAPTER FOUR

Muddy Roads and Rolling Stones

Catholic Motor Missions

> And other sheep I have, that are not of this fold: them also
> I must bring, and they shall hear my voice, and there shall
> be one fold and one shepherd.
>
> —John 10:16

In Flannery O'Connor's novel *Wise Blood*, Hazel Motes announces a new denomination—the Church of Christ without Christ—from the bumper of a battered Ford. "I'm member and preacher to that church where the blind don't see and the lame don't walk and what's dead stays that way." When his audience, unconvinced, decides to move on, Motes explodes: "Listen, you people I'm going to take the truth with me wherever I go. . . . I'm going to preach it to whoever'll listen at whatever place." Other Christian ministers take a dim view of Motes and his new endeavor. After meeting Hazel only briefly, Asa Hawks, another itinerant preacher in town, mutters: "Goddam Jesus-hog."[1]

Wise Blood appeared in 1952. In the decade or so before that, Catholics had pursued very similar evangelization projects in O'Connor's home state of Georgia and twenty-seven other states. Since their message was Catholicism and not some ecclesiastical idiosyncrasy, they did in fact preach Christ. They hoped that many rural Americans, heretofore "blind" to Catholic Christianity, would now see. Just like Motes, the Catholics involved in this missionary project were willing to preach Catholic truth wherever people were willing to listen. Rural America seemed to be just such a place. "The countryside of the United States," wrote Edgar Schmiedeler, O.S.B., in 1938, "offers one of the most inviting missionary fields in the world to-day. There are in these rural parts vast numbers of sheep that are outside the Fold."[2] Although most observers would have been averse to using Asa Hawks's profanity, many judged these Catholic missionary efforts with much the same disdain.

Souls outside the Church always ignited pastoral worries, but now the Church had acquired a new method for retrieving them: motor missions.

These were five or six evenings' worth of informative talks and hymns that proclaimed the truths of Roman Catholicism on the streets of small towns. Laypeople as well as clergy participated, but only the latter employed the "trailer chapel" (or "motor chapel"): a trailer outfitted with a sound system, a generator, living quarters for two priests, and a fully functional altar. A Paulist priest called his outfit a "rectory on wheels,"[3] and many motor missioners described their worship services as "revivals." While that form of Christian worship had long been associated with rougher edges of American life, a rural Catholic revival seemed almost inconceivable to many Americans, Catholic or not.

Used only in rural areas, the Catholic trailer chapel became a fixture across the United States during the interwar period and the decade after World War II. The Catholic agrarian worldview valued rural life for its spiritual and physical benefits: it produced more and better Catholics. Many hoped the Catholic rural life movement would also produce new ones. If the "seeds" were "properly sown," rural America would produce a missionary harvest unequaled in the Church's history. The motor missions and trailer chapels served as the plow, breaking the new ground to be cultivated later. Edward Stephens, a priest from Richmond, Virginia, explained the new pastoral approach:

> The automobile has hastened food supplies, medical aid and the morning papers to those who, by choice or compulsion, live in the isolated rural sections of the country. The same motor now becomes the efficient means of bringing the Gospel of Christ, His sacrifice and His sacraments to the same people in the rural districts. The Church, in employing the motor chapel, simply displays her age old adaptability to conditions without sacrificing either doctrine, discipline or dignity.

"Selling God" through the necessary, and often ingenious, use of culture has characterized American religion since the beginning of the nineteenth century. Combining timeless truth and the latest generator-powered technology, the trailer chapels united the evangelical revival with the Catholic "parish factory" of the nation's largest cities. The transformations of twentieth-century American rural life were both the impetus for and the ultimate demise of this quintessentially American expression of Catholicism.[4]

The Origins and Development of Catholic Motor Missions

To some extent, Catholic motor missions already existed. The Catholic Church Extension Society, whose work in rural America preceded the National Catholic Rural Life Conference, had employed "chapel cars" (pulled by train) and motor chapels as early as 1907. Using eighty-four-foot Pullman cars (bearing the names St. Anthony and St. Peter) outfitted with an altar, a confessional, and seating for seventy-five, Extension conducted missions throughout the Great Plains and western states where no parish buildings existed or where Catholics lived without sacraments. The chapel car itself was an idea borrowed from Protestants. Francis C. Kelley had drawn up plans for the Catholic trailer chapel after seeing a Baptist one displayed at the 1904 World's Fair in St. Louis. The attendant, much to Kelley's surprise and delight, credited Pope Pius IX with owning the first version. "The immediate purpose of the Chapel Cars," an Extension pamphlet read, "is to bring the consolations of their religion to Catholic people scattered in small numbers in little railroad towns where no church as yet exists." Since Extension sought to establish Catholic parishes in rural areas, the mobile chapels helped elicit interest and funding. A 1910 report from Brogan, Oregon, concluded: "Here too a Church is needed and all independent of creed have expressed willingness to assist in the erection." Baptists and Episcopalians also used chapel cars in their own pursuit of denominational expansion.[5]

The emergence of the Catholic agrarian worldview articulated the difference between Extension's efforts (which continued throughout the twentieth century) and those of the Catholic rural life movement. Writing in the *Homiletic and Pastoral Review,* Conleth Overman, C.P., categorized the difference: the street-preaching movement was "(1) entirely clerical, (2) specifically rural, and (3) envisaged by the priest street-preachers as a pastoral function." Non-Catholics had been included in the social and agricultural reforms of Catholic agrarians, but in the motor missions the reformers gave non-Catholics their undivided attention. However, the NCRLC had relegated street-preaching and other such activities to the diocesan directors. With the exception of an occasional conference or "street preachers' institute," the motor missions lacked a permanent and recognizable national organization.[6]

They did not, though, lack charismatic clerical leaders. Oklahoma native Stephen Leven became the first of many priests motivated to preach Catholicism to other rural Americans. While completing his doctoral studies at Louvain, Belgium, Leven had worked with the London-based Catholic Evidence Guild. Having provided priestly supervision and theological training for the lay organization, Leven realized that the method might be effective against anti-Catholic bigotry in America as well. After he returned in 1928 to his hometown of Tonkawa, he began driving one day a week to neighboring towns to deliver informational lectures on Catholicism. Although not the worst area, Oklahoma had seen spates of Ku Klux Klan violence earlier that decade. Leven's solitary missions in a thicket of Klan strength showed that other Americans could match the hooded order even on its own ground.[7]

Further proof came in the development of Leven's methods across the United States throughout the 1930s. Members of the Congregation of Mary (also known as the Vincentians) working out of Perryville, Missouri, began a series of missions across the southern half of that state in 1935. The Vincentians then began similar work across the Midwest, reaching as far west as Denver. At the same time, diocesan priests conducted motor missions in Nebraska, Kansas, Illinois, and Virginia. By the early 1940s, annual reports by

Schmiedeler on the motor missions were appearing in the pages of *Homiletic and Pastoral Review*, a journal designed to help Catholic priests hone their preaching skills. In 1940 Schmiedeler trumpeted that "the motor mission in rural parts is to-day an established institution. Scarcely five years of age, it shows a lusty growth and gives every impression that it is here to stay."[8]

The nomenclature quickly became interchangeable; street-preaching, motor missions, and trailer chapels all referred to the same phenomenon. Nevertheless, some distinctions remained. "Street-preaching" described something like Hazel Motes's ministry: a layperson or priest speaking from a car or a truck bed. "Trailer chapels" brought the Church's full sacramental ministry to the weeklong services. In addition to rural white Americans, the motor missions included work among African, Mexican, and Native Americans, across seventeen states and eighteen dioceses. A 1943 article by Schmiedeler listed motor missions in thirteen states, despite wartime rationing. The number might have been larger, but, as Schmiedeler noted, "there was no motor mission work in the Diocese of Springfield in Illinois during the summer of 1942, the equipment so efficiently used in former summers by Msgr. David L. Scully and his co-workers having been loaned to the Diocese of Natchez for 1942." War rationing did have its effects, but the apostolate recovered a little in the late 1940s. By the mid-1950s, though, attendance had dropped noticeably. The Vincentians had ceased street-preaching across southern Missouri by 1965.[9]

Leven regarded parish street-preaching as one of the cheapest paths priests could take to reach the non-Catholics of their parishes. A fine example was just to the north in Caldwell, Kansas, where Thomas Green of St. Martin's Church took to the streets for four straight summers, 1935 through 1938.[10] Father Arthur Terminiello, the founder of St. Theresa's Village, joined a motor mission band of diocesan priests in central Alabama. Edward Stephens, formerly a lawyer in Connecticut, organized and led the "Diocesan Missionary Fathers" around Richmond, Virginia.[11] Depending on the area, seminarians also attended. The motor missions became a required activity in the Vincentian novitiate in Perryville, Missouri, as well as for the subdeacons from the Kenrick Seminary in St. Louis. The missions were praised as an excellent opportunity for the future priests to hone their preaching skills and stoke their evangelical zeal into a blaze. A number of religious orders joined the Vincentians in the street-preaching apostolate. Two became noticeably widespread. The Paulists, founded in the nineteenth century by the convert priest Isaac Hecker for the conversion of America, operated first from Winchester, Tennessee, where they had tended a parish since 1900. They later expanded to Utah, the Texas panhandle, and coastal South Carolina. The Glenmary fathers and brothers gained notice for their work in southern Ohio, southwestern Virginia, and Kentucky. W. Howard Bishop sent Glenmary novices to train with Leven, the Paulists, and the Vincentians.[12] Benedictines, Capuchin Franciscans, Jesuits, Oblates of Mary Immaculate, and Passionists also participated.[13]

Laypeople participated as well, but obviously they were limited to public speaking. Only priests managed the trailer chapels' sacramental functions. The Catholic Evidence Guild (which operated in England and the United States) and David Goldstein's Catholic Truth Guild (which later became the Catholic Campaigners for Christ) limited their endeavors to the cities. In the late 1940s, some female college students from Illinois did make repeated trips to rural North Carolina and Oklahoma. Another role for laywomen recalled the more clearly defined gender roles common to the Catholic agrarian world-view. Dr. Bessie League, a faculty member of Texas Tech University, received praise in one of Schmiedeler's articles for keeping the Paulists who were operating out of Amarillo supplied with "clean altar linens and other necessities." Hugo Hahn, a Redemptorist priest working out of Newton Center, North Carolina, likewise remarked that by week's end the local women usually saved the priests from their own cooking on the trailer chapel's tiny stove.[14]

Regardless of who spoke, the Catholic motor missions created a unique religious and cultural exchange in rural America. Since most of the agents in the Catholic motor missions were celibate priests with years of theological training and were likely to be infatuated with Catholic agrarianism, it may appear that they were somewhat removed from the rural population to whom they preached. However, the small-town setting blurred the lines between a priest and the laity. Much like farming, priestly involvement in rural missions brought the pastor closer to nature and thus, in an incarnational turn, closer to God. Just as the NCRLC insisted that "there is something sacramental about rural life," the priest involved in motor missions engaged in "spiritual farming."[15] Francis Wuest, a Glenmary novice who later served a mission church in Norton, Virginia, relied on the familiar pastoral scenes in Scripture.

> The fields have been planted by the Master Missionary. They were cultivated by the Apostles. Down through the centuries the priests of that Apostolic Church have reaped a rich harvest. But the fields are still ripe for the harvest. Many barns are still empty. How is that harvest to be reaped? How are those barns to be filled?[16]

The answer, of course, was by Wuest himself and priests like him who spent their summers in the trailer chapels.

The Motor Missions' Holy Simplicity

More than anything else, simplicity governed the motor missions. Ralph Egan, a priest from Rulo, Nebraska, boiled them down to "music, an apologetic discourse and questions." Each night usually began with twenty minutes to an hour of often blaring music to attract a crowd. A Glenmary novice with Father Leven categorized the choices: "a) Band Marches, Fast and Stirring; b) Slower, quieter—Foster's folksongs; c) Protestant hymns." "The Bells of St. Mary" announced the beginning of the Vincentians' missions. The

Paulists began their Tennessee motor missions with five to seven minutes of "comedy" music, or with songs such as "Great Speckled Bird," "Old Rugged Cross," and "I'm S-A-V-E-D."[17]

Despite Father Egan's description, motor missioners usually delivered two or three talks. Although the order and duration varied with each mission, usually one priest gave a ten- to fifteen-minute presentation and then a second priest followed with a twenty- to thirty-minute lecture. After that came approximately fifteen minutes of answers to the question-box entries. Training manuals, private correspondence, and published accounts all stressed that in the week's very first talk, the priests would thank all for attending and especially the civil authorities for granting permission for the event. Lecture topics usually fell into one of three groups: biblical characters or saints' lives, Catholic practices and doctrines, and general Christian themes. For example, on Monday evenings the Paulists spoke of Abraham as one who prayed to know the truth and then did so. Following this was a longer "sermon" on "salvation," stressing one's obligation to seek the true religion. Father Leven, who always began "with a forceful sign of the Cross" and a prayer to the Holy Spirit, used the shorter talk to cover "any of the lighter doctrines of the Church" and the "main" speech to develop "a major point of doctrine." The Vincentians used four series of talks, each of which progressed from humanity's relationship to God onward through redemption and finished with the roles of Mary and the Church highlighted in salvation. The Lord's Prayer and a hymn closed each evening's mission. Afterward the missioners invited the audience to inspect the trailer chapel, ask more questions, and possibly request information about the Vincentians' well-publicized correspondence course on the Catholic faith.[18]

The attempt to establish a link with the non-Catholic audience could make or break the week's efforts. Besides employing attention-drawing spectacles, the missioners appealed to their listeners' native theological sensibilities. Normally, the King James Version (KJV) of the Bible served as the translation of choice. This indicated many things: a basic willingness to embrace Protestantism's biblicism as well as a certain bravado for using a non-Catholic translation precisely to explain and defend Catholic doctrine. This use of the Bible took different forms. The Paulists used the sixth chapter of John's Gospel to explain Catholic doctrines of the Eucharist. The Redemptorists operating in North Carolina took a different tack, reading for ten minutes from the Douay version and then lecturing for an hour on Catholic doctrine using the KJV.[19]

The emphasis on Scripture came from the motor missioners' English predecessors. Catholic Evidence Guild founder Frank Sheed wrote, "A Catholic apologist who is not soaked in the Gospels is an anomaly in himself, and in his work doomed to aridity." This attitude moved easily across the boundary between lay Guild member and motor priest. Henry Lexau observed that the theological method for priests training for street-preaching in southwest Missouri consisted of the following: "You're in town to discuss the Catholic religion, not any other. Speak simply. *Infallibility, Incarnation, sanctifying grace* are words in a foreign language to most Protestants. Quote Scripture. Quote Scripture. Quote Scripture." After one particular mission in Richville, a woman remarked that she "never heard so much Scripture preached in all my life." In Missouri's southeastern Bootheel, an African American pastor similarly praised the Vincentians' scriptural approach. The reliance on biblical texts developed less as an attempt to devalue the basis of Protestantism than as a demonstration of how Catholic doctrine shared common ground with, and even superseded (or preceded, depending on the lecture), the various forms of Protestantism.[20]

Using the KJV Bible also kept the motor missioners focused on their pursuit of homiletic simplicity. The street-preaching manual compiled by the Denver-based Vincentians addressed the matter this way: "The subjects which ought to be presented to a street crowd are the basic truths of natural and revealed religion. They can all be summed up under the general heading—GOD AND MAN." The manual's authors emphasize that the vocabulary used should be "the simplest possible, such as is suited to the age level of the twelve year old child. Long and involved sentences should be assiduously avoided. The street-preacher should regard his audience as religiously or theologically illiterate—and undoubtedly a large portion will be so." The "Specimen Street Lecture" hinted at how these directions might take shape.

> [God] settles forever for us the question of religion. For only God has the right to say how we are to worship Him. No one else has the right to set up a church, for the Church is simply God's way of safeguarding the religion and the teaching He originally gave to mankind. The question of the true Church is settled once for all.[21]

This sermon adhered doggedly to the quest for simplicity while making a nonbelligerent case for the primacy of the Roman church. The insistence on homiletic simplicity resonated with a similar insistence throughout Catholic agrarianism on the inherent simplicity and superiority of rural life. With the motor missions, the need for simplicity arose as well from the desire to communicate Catholic truth as clearly and enticingly as possible.

Other motor mission veterans reiterated the points of simplicity and nonconfrontation. In doing so, they demonstrated how engrossed in rural America Catholicism could become, even without mentioning Catholic agrarianism explicitly. Father Leven, who worked with both the Evidence Guilds and the various motor mission groups, debunked the apparently common assumption "that to preach out of doors to an audience of non-Catholics one must be a combination of St. John Chrysostom and the *Summa Theologica*," because "experience has shown that most of the questions asked at the outdoor meetings can be answered by one having a grade school knowledge of Catholicism. . . . The burden of all preaching must be 'Jesus Christ and Him Crucified.'" Proclaiming this triumphantly, though, was categorically prohibited: "The audience must never be considered as opponents of the Church. One should not aim primarily at answering charges against the Church nor even at proving Catholic claims." A Paulist revealed that members of his order "emphasize what the Catholic Church *has* rather than what other churches lack. And so we set forth in a simple way some doctrine which is so coördinated with the moral theme as to be almost unconsciously assimilated by those who listen."[22]

The ways in which the motor missioners discussed their vocation rarely rose to the level of intellectual creativity. Instead, their remarks constituted a conversation among working pastors and, infrequently, some particularly articulate laypeople. Instead of discussing speculative theology, they focused on the ways in which they delivered that message to new groups of Americans. In this way, the motor missioners became merchants of a particular religious "good" with a keen sense for advertising. Often missions would be held every night, except for Sunday so as not to conflict with other services. Each stop—preceded by a week of handbill advertising—followed roughly the same schedule: on Monday, after checking first with the authorities, the two or three priests staffing the mission trailer would park it in the best location they could find in town. A question box with a sign inviting inquiries was set up, usually some distance away from the mission site to ensure privacy. Electricity for the microphones and loudspeakers was obtained by asking a nearby household or business for use of an outlet, or later by using a portable generator. The Vincentians' street-preaching manual mentioned a further possibility: "In case there is no connection at hand, the Public Service Company is, as far as our experience goes, glad to send a man to install a connection with the proper voltage."[23]

Leven stressed that "the first human step in convert-making is to establish contact with non-Catholics in a way which will make it possible to give them Catholic instruction." This was the justification for the sound system. The Denver Vincentians claimed that "with a good loud-speaking set the speakers have been heard as far away as ten blocks, and thus, many are brought within his audience besides those who are visibly present before him. People sitting on their lawns, clerks in stores, the sick in their beds, within a radius of from eight to ten blocks, can and do hear the message."[24]

The trailer chapel itself emerged in 1937 with the Paulist fathers in Tennessee. Soon the other groups procured them as well. Motor missioners took pride in the impression their wheels made. The appearance alone of the trailer chapel did much to prepare the crowd for instruction, as Leven wished. After one sojourn across south central Missouri, Orville North, C.M., reflected: "Interesting sight—three Vincentians clad in black coats, collars and straw hats, pulling into a little country town called Myrtle in a huge White Trailer with the words 'CATHOLIC CHURCH' written on the side." Another Vincentian, Patrick O'Brien, remarked that a "Chapel Car was a grand advertisement. When we roll into town, heads nearly turn right off shoulders. The whole thing ablaze with light and tootling away on the Marine

Hymn is something to see and hear." Since its design did put the Church on wheels, the trailer chapel could now bring the entirety of the Church's sacramental life to isolated Catholics. Outside the supposedly Catholic-controlled industrial cities, the sight of priests driving a shiny metal trailer was enough to draw the curious as well.[25]

Like the Extension missions decades earlier, the motor missions sought to discover and retrieve "lost" Catholics. If Catholics were found in the town, the trailer's function as chapel became all the more important. Baptisms and marriage solemnizations were commonly needed in areas that had not been visited by a priest in perhaps more than a year. Saying Mass itself, or assisting through prayer, often took on an entirely new significance in a motor mission. Richard Ginder, who accompanied a chapel trailer in rural Washington, noted that many people knelt in the grass of an open field to receive Communion. However, "in some places, the people had been away from Mass so long that they forgot the simple stand-sit-kneel routine." The Vincentians operating the St. Anthony trailer chapel in Missouri said Mass at the trailer at least once in the course of a week's mission. Apparently this benefited Catholic and non-Catholic alike:

> [The priest] celebrates Mass in the open . . . while one of the assistants reads everything in English over the loud-speaker, step by step with the celebrant and server, so that anybody who comes near can understand every single word. The missionaries' diaries report that this "feature" is especially appreciated and commented on frequently. (Supposing the same thing were done five or six times a year in all our churches, what a difference it would make in both Catholics' and non-Catholics' appreciation of the Mass!).

Even when Mass was not celebrated, the altar and vestments still attracted attention in one of the motor missioners' most popular demonstrations: while one priest vested himself at the altar, another stood at the podium and explained every action and item.[26]

The trailer's technological attractions had additional benefits. Those who could not attend a motor mission were often able to hear it because of the powerful sound systems used. Father Francis Broome, C.S.P., remarked that the Paulists' St. Lucy Trailer Chapel (one of three or four trailers that also featured a movie projector and screen) had "been heard at a distance of three miles, and questions have been sent in by people who were listening to the service at a distance of over a mile." The deafening sound occasionally helped the priests handle unexpected difficulties. Enveloped by a thick fog descending from the Rocky Mountains, a Vincentian mission in Victor, Colorado, succeeded only because the loudspeakers reached those sitting on their porches. Walter Burke, writing of his "rectory on wheels," noted that the "powerful public address system carried well on the night air, indeed so well that it dominated the whole town. It was a rare front porch that did not have more than one set of ears cocked to hear every word of Catholic truth that punctuated the quiet summer evenings." Hecklers and other troublemakers could simply be drowned out. After residents in one northern Texas town attempted to strong-arm the Paulists into turning the volume down, Burke triumphantly wrote: "On the last night during the talk on 'Why I Am A Catholic' we turned up the volume dial to its highest notch and shook the trees on the nearby hills with the reasons why the Catholic Church was the true church."[27]

This confidence, equally technological and theological, provided some motivation on occasions when the equipment was not working. The motor mission service included the possibility of speaking without amplification in such cases. Father Terminiello served as his own repairman for car and trailer. Having been denied access to electrical outlets by the two homeowners in an Alabama village who had service, Terminiello reportedly said, "We'll preach without their lights." The story continued: "And he did so. With a strong voice and a good supply of flashlight batteries." Broome, on the road up to thirty-seven weeks out of the year, commented that "only rain can stop the trailer service, and even when it rains we sometimes carry on in a schoolhouse or tobacco barn." As Stephens suggested, the trailer chapels allowed the Church to adapt to new situations without diluting its message of salvation.[28]

Showings of filmstrips or movies, though rare in many rural areas, offered explanations of the sacraments or the Church's apostolic roots. The free shows were not merely for catechetical purposes; they often became the motor missions' biggest attraction. Those shown most often were *King of Kings*, *The Ten Commandments*, and *The Life of Christ*. Since all three were silent films, the priests usually played "reverential" background music and provided explanatory comments with each scene. Such commentary was found to be an effective pedagogical tool. Broome remarked that "it would be impossible to find a more impressive way of setting forth our belief in the Real Presence . . . than by giving that explanation as the scene of the Last Supper is portrayed on screen." A Paulist working in North Carolina reported that "we just explain what Christ meant when he said 'This is My Body' and 'My Blood, shed for you and many unto the remission of sins.' And when Peter is singled out in the last reel to 'feed My sheep,' it is simply a question of filling in the blanks to point out that here Christ is making the first Pope."[29]

Many accounts in both clerical and lay publications insisted that "in evaluating results, numbers mean something but not very much."[30] This certainly applied to the number of converts: most missions yielded only one or two a year, and many none at all. The buoyant vagueness of the written accounts also downplayed the array of difficulties that could be encountered with every night's proceedings. Mechanical problems, troublesome audiences, and the weather affected the motor missioners' success.

Heckling was the most common annoyance. Usually this involved only an occasional shout from the far reaches of the audience. In Missouri, some hecklers repeatedly drove their cars by the motor mission site in an attempt to drown out the Vincentians with engine noise. In Virginia, a priest had the free literature he was distributing thrown back in his face. Obscene questions could appear in the question box. A recurring query that the Vincentians faced throughout southern Missouri was whether the Catholic priest, not the groom, was expected to spend the first night with the bride. Others questioned what were perceived to be lax Catholic attitudes toward alcohol, dancing, and gambling. (One brave soul even asked if two boys could fall in love with each other.) Less confrontational queries wondered why priests wore their collars backward, whether nuns shaved their heads, and whether dating between Catholics and Protestants was permissible. In Tennessee, the Paulists were asked what appeared to be a legitimate question: what were their views on tobacco usage? It was a trick, Father James Cunningham realized, for "when I reached for the cover of the motion picture machine, I found it covered with tobacco juice. A farmer in the crowd had used it for a target all evening, and was a good shot."[31]

The reliance on Scripture did not preclude opposition from local religious leaders. In Utah, Mormon frostiness received constant mention by the Paulists operating the St. Paul the Apostle trailer chapel. In Sylva, North Carolina, the women from Rosary College encountered a Holiness preacher "who threatened to 'come loaded for geese and ducks' because we needed our 'feathers plucked.'" In the diocese of Crookston, Minnesota, the priests learned that local Lutheran ministers often prohibited their congregations from attending the motor missions, while they themselves did attend. Other encounters with Protestants were opportunities to rejoice. A priest in Arizona exuberantly wrote Father Schmiedeler: "On the way here . . . we passed a Protestant trailer rolling in the opposite direction. Evidently the religious trailer idea is growing in favor. We thank God and our friends that we have the privilege of being in the vanguard of this movement."[32]

Although always downplayed when mentioned, violence occasionally did occur. The Glenmary fathers seemed to be particular targets. Raphael Sourd, the first priest to join Howard Bishop in Glenmary, was on the receiving end of a brick thrown in Sunfish, Kentucky. Known for his sense of humor, Sourd wrote Bishop that "the blood of the first martyr in the conquest of rural America has been shed." Elsewhere, a young man fired a shotgun at Sourd after suspecting the priest of trying to convert his father. In a later visit to the same area, Sourd and the newly ordained Francis Massarella found they were rumored to be spies for "stealing blueprints and taking pictures." Actually, they were looking for land on which to build a small mission church. Residents around Lubbock, Texas, feared that the Paulists' St. Rita trailer chapel might house Nazi spies plotting to poison the water supply. Near Dayton, Tennessee, the Paulists' St. Lucy trailer chapel was "bombed" by a drunken youth throwing stones. Father Terminiello's "Catholic revival" in Mount Moriah, Alabama, weathered "two cyclones, continual rain and much opposition among the natives who at one time came up to burn the tent."[33]

These incidents, however, were relatively isolated. Local police often voluntarily watched over the missions to ensure they were not interrupted. In Advance, Missouri, a Vincentian priest who asked the sheriff about his holstered pistol heard in response: "If you knew some of these people from the sticks, like I do, you'd know that anything may happen." When the Paulists applied for permission to use the school grounds at Marble Plains, Tennessee, a town official remarked, "Several complaints have come in from the Methodists nearby asking me to refuse you permission. If you want to use the school, however, go right ahead. You Catholic people pay taxes same as the Protestants. I've never heard of any harm coming from your trailer work." When the civil authority was not present, the audience often regulated itself. For instance, the crowd at Dayton doubled after the "bombing," and insisted on making reparations. Afterward, those attending repeatedly asked the priests to return, assuring them of future good hospitality. Leven, Schmiedeler, and other motor mission popularizers stressed again and again that "heckling in the Midwest is unknown," and that more often than not the crowd, finding itself sympathetic to the priests, handled its own unruly elements.[34]

Occasionally the motor missioners' enthusiastic use of their equipment impaired their own proceedings. In Lynchburg, Virginia, Father Stephens realized that the trailer chapel exerted quite a pull on his car's engine. Traffic following "Our Lady of the Highways" up the hill quickly snarled. Stephens remarked that it was "an embarrassing incident and caused us some delay, but it was a fine advertisement for us. It was the first time that the Catholic Church completely halted traffic on Ninth Street." Sometimes they found that the sound system was too effective. In Colorado, the police were sent to "inform the speakers that their public address system was so loud that it interfered with people listening to their radios seven or eight blocks away."[35]

Catholic Ambivalence concerning the Motor Missions

The motor missions in rural America followed a basic tenet of the Catholic Church's evangelization strategy: if non-Catholics lived there, then the Church must preach there, too. "If the great masses of outsiders cannot be intrigued into the Church to hear her Gospel there, it is obvious then that the only way in which to reach them is to carry the evangel to them in the market place and the highways, and wherever they congregate under the canopy of the sky." By 1927, the Catholic Evidence Guild and David Goldstein's Catholic Campaigners for Christ had been doing just that for as many as ten years. A year before Al Smith lost the presidential election, largely because of his faith, Goldstein claimed that "it was safe to say that the average American is interested in what Catholic laymen have to say of the faith that is in them."[36]

Still, for most Catholics, the image of any Catholic haranguing a street-corner crowd bordered on outlandishness.[37] Marian Rauth asked readers of *The Catholic World*, "What would you do if, walking down Main Street in a small North Carolina town one afternoon, you saw three girls standing on the back platform of a station wagon, and heard them singing 'You Are My Sunshine'? Would you pass by. . . . Or would you stop and listen?"[38] That priests participated in, and usually led, these events only exacerbated the matter. A 1942 article in *The Sign* began:

> Suppose you were driving through these United States and, arriving at twilight in some very small town, you saw a crowd gathered in front of the general store listening attentively to a Catholic priest. Wouldn't you be surprised? You might expect to find the barker for a traveling circus, or a medicine man selling Pink Pills for Pale People, but not a Catholic priest, Roman collar and all, on a platform out in the open street, talking through a microphone to a crowd of American farmers and businessmen about the Marks of the Church.

Along with trailers made into "churches on wheels," it was a picture that most American Catholics could barely begin to comprehend; for them, "Catholic street preaching" was an oxymoron. The article in *The Sign* continued: "For, if you are a conventional Easterner like myself, you have a vague notion that street preaching by priests must be dangerous and inadvisable, or at least out of date."[39]

Apparently other Catholics thought the same. Accounts of the motor missions, whether authored by priest or layperson, usually dedicated some space to deflecting such concerns. The dignity of the priest involved received the most attention. Father Stephens of Virginia acknowledged the argument of some that "in employing such a mode of preaching, we become as politicians and medicine men." Not surprisingly, he did not put much stock in such a complaint:

> The dignity of a priest has greatest value when he employs that dignity of priesthood for the good of souls and the advancement of Christ's kingdom on earth. . . . If politicians and medicine men have employed the pulpit of the highway to sell their commodities, does that make it wrong for a priest to do so? His is a Divine commodity. Should he be more vain and less zealous?[40]

Experience on the mission circuit proved that dignity also belonged to the motor mission services themselves. The trailer chapel competed with Protestant revivals for the ears and souls of small-town residents, but that did not mean they resembled "the Billy Sunday shouting service." The Vincentians' motor mission manual argued that skeptics instead would find the motor mission's audience

> eagerly drinking in the words of sound doctrine that flow in a gentle, refined and convincing manner from the lips of an intelligent young priest equally refined and convincing, whose neat appearance befits the dignity of his calling and whose presence suggests that of a professional man, a leader, a gentleman, and excludes anything redolent of hellfire and brimstone methods, of revival-tent shindigs, anything that would detract from the dignity of one called to Holy Orders.

Finally, motor mission defenders suggested, questioning the dignity of Catholic street preachers in effect prejudged the crowd as well. A writer for *The Sign* hoped to change such attitudes, pointing out that "a crowd in the street is a vest-pocket edition of America, lovable as Mr. Chips, affable as your Congressman, human as the Bumsteads. . . . These outdoor meetings are genuinely American. . . . [T]hey've a flavor and a warmth that is New Englandish and breeds cordiality."[41]

In the same decade that included Charles Coughlin's diatribes and the Catholic Workers' gentle anarchism, the motor missions carved out a space where the Church and American culture could interact without the extremes of either bombast (in Coughlin's case) or pacifist anarchism (in Dorothy Day's case). The trailer chapels had their own prominent figures and wealthy laypeople likely to make charitable donations. These, just as much as the chapel names or the defense of the missions' dignity, placed the motor missions in the midst of the burgeoning world of American Catholicism in the 1930s.

Those defending the aplomb and popularity of the motor mission could scarcely have chosen a better exemplar than Monsignor Fulton Sheen. Immersed in a popular radio and publishing apostolate and on his way to a television career, Sheen was associated with motor mission work in various ways. He donated, delivered, and blessed the second trailer chapel (named St. Bridget) to the diocese of Mobile. His popularity as a nonthreatening but effective Catholic speaker could be seen in Henry Lexau's description of Father Robert Ready, a Benedictine street preacher in southern Missouri: "From the way his friends had talked, I had expected a giant edition of Fulton Sheen and a megaphone voice that would carry for miles. Instead, Father Ready turned out to be short, shy, very quiet." The Vincentians used Sheen's approach in writing their own lectures. In southern Nebraska, copies of Sheen's prayerbook were available for those who were interested.[42]

The positive qualities that Sheen's association reflected on the motor missions dimmed somewhat in the late 1940s when Arthur Terminiello, Alabama's well-known motor mission priest, was indicted for an inflammatory speech he made in Chicago. Assailing both Jews and Eleanor Roosevelt, Terminiello's words sparked a minor riot among those protesting the event's main speaker, noted antisemite Gerald L. K. Smith. Nicknamed "the Father Coughlin of the South" by Smith, Terminiello successfully appealed his conviction to the Supreme Court. A minor legal furor surfaced in the pages of *America* and *Commonweal*, two publications sympathetic to the motor missions but not to any right "to be unruly," in the words of one editor for *America*.[43] Although injurious to clerical dignity, the scandal apparently did not harm the image of those involved in the motor missions. Wealthy laypeople who had underwritten the first trailer chapels continued to contribute money to those involved, and the accounts of Terminiello's conviction did not mention his motor mission work.[44]

Like their Protestant counterparts, Catholic clergymen sought to cultivate a persuasive missionary image, and their motor missions certainly helped with that. They marketed a new Catholic identity among a largely non-Catholic rural America. From his office at the National Catholic Welfare Conference, where he directed the Rural Life Bureau and authored motor mission articles, Schmiedeler wrote that "*the* prime objective of Rural Catholic Action is the promotion of the farmer's religious life." Since the priest took care of the Catholic farmer, it followed, according to Catholic agrarians, that the priest would at least introduce the neighbors to the Church as well. The NCRLC's 1941 convention in Jefferson City, Missouri, included an entire session on Catholic street-preaching. Across the street from the Missouri state capitol, four priests—including the Vincentians' motor missions director Joseph Lilly, C.M., and Thomas Green, one of the first motor missioners in the Wichita diocese—familiarized convention participants with the techniques and styles of their apostolate. Schmiedeler's first article for *Homiletic and Pastoral Review* intertwined the trailer chapel and Catholic agrarianism: "The time is ripe for action. And the harvest promises to be exceedingly great." Although no NCRLC leader attracted as much attention as Sheen, the conference's presence lent the motor missions some of the dignity that critics felt was lacking. This helped the motor missions preserve Schmiedeler's optimism and agrarian vision, while defusing their potentially controversial position within the Church.[45]

Harvesting the Success of Motor Mission Efforts

Seasoned motor missioners continually mentioned the intrinsically long-range character of the work. Amid all the stories stood the desire to see some returns, but that often went unfulfilled. Most motor missioners would have agreed with the conclusion of Paulist priest Richard Walsh: "Fortunately, in the work of saving souls, you can't pay off on statistics." Since the missions took place where few or no Catholics lived, it would take time for concrete results to emerge. Speaking before an assembly of the Confraternity of Christian Doctrine, Father Broome illustrated the situation he faced in Tennessee:

> People often think that the Catholic Church does not want to receive members, just because we do not have "altar calls" for membership or a "mourner's bench" on which those new members are to sit. Many of our hearers want to become Catholic after hearing our services for one or two evenings. That may be flattering, but we know that those same eager ones became Baptists two months ago at a revival. They will probably become Campbellites a month from now when that group holds a "protracted meeting." Indeed, we hear men bragging of the number of times they have "got religion." When we explain that such is not the way of becoming a Catholic, they feel that something is wrong.

Experiences such as these could be pointed to as successes in the more moderate goal of diminishing anti-Catholic bigotry. Making converts would take more time, requiring perseverance in the face of such confusion.[46]

Despite repeated assurances that the motor missions were working even though there were no wholesale conversions, a near obsession with numbers permeated the written accounts. In 1938 Vincentian father Daniel Kane conducted motor missions in six towns throughout the diocese of Lincoln; the average attendance each week was "between 8,000 and 9,000; and 1,880 pieces of literature was distributed." Upon returning to St. Mary of the Barrens in Perryville, Missouri, the Vincentians filled out reports for each town visited; grades were given ("fair," "good," or "excellent"), and all questions asked by attendees were recorded verbatim. Success was also measured by the return of "fallen-away" Catholics. Seventy-three-year-old Bud Kennedy had been baptized in 1874 by Southern "Lost Cause" poet-priest Abram Ryan but made his first confession and Communion at the Paulists' St. Lucy trailer chapel in 1938. Kennedy's return inspired hope, but the experiences of Richard Ginder and others in Washington state may have been more common. Ginder fretted over how many "fallen-aways" had done so out of their own laziness, not the absence of the Mass.[47]

If the tangible success of the motor missions was questionable, they exhibited considerable ingenuity in presenting Catholic sacramental life to the nation's rural populace. Although the United States lost its status as Catholic missionary territory in 1908, traveling mission priests remained a fixture throughout the first half of the twentieth century. With the trailer chapels, the priests were still traveling, but in a fashion that attracted and held the attention of non-Catholics while supplying the sacraments to Catholics isolated from normal parish life. During the same period, Catholic agrarians began pursuing their desire to improve all of American rural life. The trailer chapel's growing ubiquity in America represented one more step in the Church's eschatological hope of truly being present in all places and all times. A trailer chapel's entry into a new town marked a new public presence of the Church that many rural and small-town Catholics had not experienced. Not everyone agreed with the method chosen to accomplish this. Motor missions encountered a great deal of opposition within the Church. Despite the reservations, though, the trailer chapels occasionally resembled the critics' urban Church more than they did the rural one they were supposedly strengthening.

Catholic street-preachers united the two through language that recalled the Mystical Body of Christ theology used by Dorothy Day and the Catholic agrarians. Evidence Guild leader John McAniff encouraged fervor and enthusiasm, for street-preachers "must be able to see in every stupid question a human soul groping in the dark for truth . . . in every angry denial, a human soul shrinking for the Sacrifice of the Cross . . . and in every listener, the image and likeness of God." Reflecting on his training with the Vincentians, Glenmary novice Francis Massarella wrote that

> as a result of these wonderful experiences I am convinced that it is my vocation to be amongst these simple loving souls. They are so responsive, and so appre-

ciative for everything that you try to do for them. I think I have benefited immensely by these experiences. I have had clear contacts with souls and have
come to know their problems better. This work has created in me a real sympa-
thy for souls and a desire to be with them all the time.

Massarella's words recalled the pastoral tone that frequently characterized
discussions of the motor missions. Despite the crowd's occasional hostility or
indifference, they were the ones with whose care the motor mission priests
had been charged. Truth Guild member Paul Dearing wrote that "for many
such souls, Catholic street preachers, lay and clerical, have served as an effective instrument of Divine Grace." Father Burke claimed that "the natural
virtue of these country people is good ground for the seed of faith to grow, if
it be God's will that it take root." Christ's mystical body became more and
more visible as the trailer chapels turned the "naturally Christian aspira-
tions," as Father Broome put it, of rural Americans toward Catholicism.[48]

Not only did motor mission theology spring from a mission that was mobile, it also encompassed a public different from that of the urban Church. In
rural Washington state, said Ginder, "the Mass and divine grace work won-
ders. And, psychologically, the colorful vestments and ceremonies—the rever-
ence of the staff—renew the train of fading associations." The motor missioners appeared among marginalized people as well as isolated Catholics. A
brochure for the Vincentians proclaimed boldly: "He said: 'OTHER SHEEP have
I who are not of this fold, THEM ALSO MUST I BRING.'" In a letter to W.
Howard Bishop, Father Donald Barry, C.S.P., wrote: "I am convinced that
among the so-called white trash who are lower socially than the tenant farmers and sharecroppers is to be found the hope of Catholicism in the South. . . .
Social activities are the doctrines that the poor understand." Barry's conviction also alludes to the reason for such flurried motor mission work among
African, Mexican, and Native Americans. The conversion of these groups
would proceed more smoothly by this method, and once accomplished
would provide the basis for converting the rest of the nation.[49]

If theological inclusiveness took the trailer chapels to the edges of
Catholic culture, their names rooted the enterprise solidly within that culture. As with the parish, the name chosen for the trailer chapel emphasized
certain aspects of the Catholic faith. Father Terminiello's St. Theresa trailer
bore the name of one of the patron saints of Catholic missions. The pioneering Vincentians used the St. Anthony trailer chapel, named after one of the
first anchorite monks. The Glenmarians' Chapel of the North American Martyrs, named after their patron saints, recalled the Jesuit missionaries' willingness to introduce Catholicism to hostile areas. The Redemptorists in North
Carolina named theirs Our Lady of Perpetual Help, after a devotion associated with their order. The Paulists' first two trailer chapels, St. Lucy and St.
Rita, recalled early female martyrs. Lucy also stood for Lucia, the young Por-
tuguese girl who received the vision of the Blessed Mother at Fatima in 1917,
which itself was becoming a popular devotion. Other examples of Marian

piety were Father Stephens's St. Mary of the Highways, Father Joseph Cassidy's Queen of the Apostles in Georgia, and Holy Family, one of two Dominican auto chapels in South Carolina.[50]

Since the 1960s, the public character of American Catholicism has shifted from largely privatized devotions to involvement with social-justice movements including all sorts of Americans. Ann Taves has argued that, surrounded by a Protestant culture steeped in mistrust of all things "Catholic," the most distinctive forms of nineteenth-century Catholic piety were turned inward as matters of personal, not public, faith.[51] The motor missions of the 1930s and 1940s, however, took devotional confidence to a new level. Not only was the Catholic faith openly preached, it was carried to the doorstep of rural America, the very area that epitomized anti-Catholic sentiment. Nowhere was this bravery more pronounced than in the trailer chapels, bearing the signs of Catholic devotional piety and draped with an American flag.

What was perhaps most significant about the trailer-chapel names was what was excluded. No trailer was named Immaculate Conception, even though the devotion had been popular among American Catholics for almost one hundred years. The omission was significant; Catholics had long regarded Mary's meek purity as a contradictory sign of the Church's triumph in the world. In the minds of many laypeople and clergy, Catholic street-preaching and motor missions degraded the Church unnecessarily. The opposition centered on the propriety of a priest's acting "like a Catholic Salvation Army," in the words of Catholic convert and street preacher David Goldstein. In their own defense, the street preachers appealed to the Catholic version of the spirit of the times; motor missions and trailer chapels seemed to be what the moment required. They sought to make converts, thus involving them in a widely discussed topic among American Catholics before Vatican II. In fact, the motor missioners confirmed what many Catholic Revival devotees already sensed: America was no longer a firmly Protestant country; there seemed to be a lack of any religious influence at all. Many intellectuals had read their way into the faith, but what about everybody else? The neo-Scholastic succor of Catholicism had to be delivered to the people, since they did not seem disposed to go find it. In *The White Harvest*, a collection of essays on convert-making, Father John O'Brien wrote that the "restrained conservative methods sufficient for the Ages of Faith must be supplemented by vigorous, aggressive, radical measures to halt the onward sweep of irreligion like a great avalanche across the countryside of America." Much like the rest of the Catholic rural life movement, the motor missioners ventured beyond the confines of the Catholic ghetto to realize that their opponents apparently had conceded the field.[52]

Broadened Horizons for American Catholics

The high tide of motor mission activity represented on a smaller scale the optimism with which the entire American Catholic Church approached its surroundings. A significant instance of the unity that Catholics valued so highly came in the judicious efforts to include minority groups. Attention paid to African, Mexican, and Native Americans within the Church had previously consisted of little more than underfunded churches and schools, brought to the minds of most urban Catholics only in occasional pleas for donations. In displaying its "age-old adaptability to conditions without sacrificing either dignity, doctrine, or discipline," as Father Edward Stephens described earlier the Church mounted what might be called an evangelical outreach through the motor missions to these marginalized groups. Not only were they souls to bring inside the fold, they also expressed the incipient unity that many Catholic leaders wished rank-and-file Catholics would recognize in their own lives.[53]

Although fewer African Americans than Latino and Native Americans were baptized Catholics, motor missions focused most heavily on converting African Americans. Schmiedeler mentioned Terminiello's work in the Mobile diocese in articles covering 1938 and 1939. However, he failed to mention that since 1937 Terminiello had conducted motor missions specifically for African Americans, almost none of whom were Catholic. For the 1940 article in *Homiletic and Pastoral Review*, Schmiedeler recorded the efforts of Joseph Cassidy and the Queen of the Apostles trailer chapel in rural Georgia. Hopes were especially high in Lakeland, where Cassidy drew an average of four hundred attendees each evening. The follow-up catechism class was so popular that it began to meet five nights a week, and Cassidy was hoping that a church might be built soon. Only after these remarks did Schmiedeler acknowledge that "the group under discussion here is colored."[54]

Schmiedeler's word choice indicates that discussions of minority inclusion in the motor missions often carried paternalistic undertones. W. Howard Bishop's biographer draws attention to Bishop's "gradualist" attitude toward overcoming the bitterness of Southern racism. The African American cleaning woman at his first parish in rural Maryland was required to sit in the balcony during Mass. Bishop likewise turned away a young black man interested in Glenmary and the priesthood because Glenmary missionaries were to proceed with circumspection, not direct action, so as not to offend any observers. The Catholic Conference of the South often devoted an entire panel discussion to "the rural Negro." In one session, Terminiello commented that he and the other Alabama mission priests "let them say 'Amen' while we preach." A 1939 Paulist motor mission in Tullahoma, Tennessee, apparently brought out most of the black community, prompting this account:

> On several occasions . . . the five hundred and more colored folk who sang with our records, said "Amen!" during the sermon, and wept and protestated their love for Our Saivour [sic] as the "King of Kings" was shown upon the screen. It was unusual for us to look out from the footlights on the trailer and see the moon shining down in all its glory on a sea of black faces—with ivory teeth and sparkling white eyes making a severe and noteworthy contrast.[55]

The motor missions nevertheless represented one of the few attempts by Catholics to invite African Americans into the Church. Unlike efforts in cities, which depended mainly on the decision of interested blacks to present themselves to the Church, the motor missions brought the Church to them. With another nod to "age-old adaptability," the motor missions exhibited a remarkable fluidity with the cultural forms surrounding the Catholic message. Though Terminiello's words certainly reflect a degree of paternalism, they also reveal a savvy missionary sense: "We have also found that it adds to the interest of the meeting—especially among the colored—if we allow them to sing some of their own hymns such as, 'Give Me the Old Time Religion.' This hymn, for example, can well be used to illustrate the Apostolicity of the Catholic Church."[56] The inclusion of different hymnody was simply an extension of Catholic street preachers' use of the King James Version Bible to demonstrate principles of Catholic doctrine. Just like their Bible, an audience's hymnody could be employed to support Catholic truth.

Experiences such as these prompted, perhaps unintentionally, the reconsideration of racial segregation. Although the motor missions enjoyed their heyday before the civil rights movement, accounts of missions held in black communities expressed a certain surprise at how readily the established forms of racism could be transformed into a unifying religious experience. A Vincentian concluded that the proceedings in Caruthersville, Missouri, had been quite successful:

> The people quoted texts right along with us, punctuated the citation of texts with "That's right" and affirmed the correctness of our citation when we would lean out of the pulpit and ask whether they didn't think that was right. . . . The Street Preachers could not help, on leaving, wishing that they could spend a full week among these neglected people . . . people who wondered themselves why they were being neglected.

Some of that neglect was Catholic self-projection resulting from more than two hundred years of anti-Catholic bigotry in America. But if the black audiences reminded Catholics of indignities once suffered, Native Americans stood as one of the "triumphs" of Catholic participation in the building of the nation. The motor missions of the 1930s and 1940s also offered American Catholics an opportunity to return to the adventurous times of the earliest missionary activities on the continent. In 1938 Oblate Father Vincent Arbiter began using the trailer chapel at the Fort Apache reservation in Arizona. By 1940 Schmiedeler could report that four other trailer chapels were being used in Washington state, as well as elsewhere in both Arizona and New Mexico.[57]

Like the accounts of missions to rural blacks, those concerning Native Americans reverted to stereotype in describing their subject audience. Usually this meant emphasizing how the Indians were always "wandering," "roaming," or otherwise temporarily located. The trailer chapel was depicted as a surefire method of keeping the Church's sacraments nearby. Father Cyril

Feisst, operating a unit out of Twisp, Washington, wrote that the trailer chapel "has been a great help to me in getting my Indians to go to the Sacraments. It gave me an opportunity to camp at the people's homes." His success prompted him to plan for a permanent church at Monse; Schmiedeler's article a year later, in 1941, indicated that the structure had been built. The "frontier" imagery, which so often characterized other endeavors to recall Catholic participation in the nation's settlement, returned in the accounts of the motor mission efforts among Native Americans. As one hundred years earlier, Catholics enjoying a more developed parish life could read of constantly mobile missionaries bringing the Church to the Indians, culminating in the completion of a permanent church. Having a church of their own signaled that Native Americans were on their way to "Americanization," like immigrants from Ireland, Italy, Germany, and elsewhere a generation or two earlier.[58]

If African Americans represented surprising new missionary fields and the Native Americans traditional ones, both served by the trailer chapels, Mexican Americans were perhaps the neglected missiological stepchildren. The Mexican Catholic Church underwent periods of violent persecution by an anticlerical revolutionary government earlier in the century. The consequent migration northward was met largely with indifference on the part of American Catholic leaders, the efforts of Father Kelley's Catholic Church Extension Society notwithstanding. There may have been ethnic prejudice at work. Apart from efforts to establish a Mexican seminary in exile, the unique expressions of Latino Catholicism, especially those connected with Native American peoples living in isolated areas, received little attention from the Euro-American hierarchy. Schmiedeler listed only the efforts of a Father Urbanowski and his trailer chapel named Espiritu Sanctu working with the Mexican population surrounding Houston, Texas. Schmiedeler measured Urbanowski's success, which repeated the formula of Father Feisst with the Native Americans, by the first stirrings of ethnic parish life beginning with a small church near Bryan. The only other activity involving trailers with Mexican Americans took place in Texas as well. Like the Paulists with their St. Rita trailer chapel, the Missionary Catechists operated out of Amarillo and used a "house trailer" in their catechism lessons for migrant farm workers. Apparently this trailer served only to house the Catechists and was not used in celebrating Mass. Finally, the motor mission could assimilate as well as instruct. Albert Haverkamp, George Spiegelhalter, and Matthew Hall, all priests at St. Benedict's Church in Atchison, Kansas, started an apostolate in the northeastern corner of the state in 1936. Schmiedeler wrote that in 1940 Bishop Paul Schulte of Leavenworth asked that communities of Mexican immigrants be included "in the belief that they would thus become more quickly Americanized." Elsewhere in the state, that process had already begun. In 1951, St. Patrick's parish in Chanute celebrated its fiftieth anniversary with a parish history that included pages written in Spanish and dedicated to Our Lady of Guadalupe.[59]

It only made sense that the motor missioners would include descriptions of the religious sensibilities of their audiences. The most recurrent one was "pagan." In a 1939 article on the motor missions, Schmiedeler reported that "the people with whom they come into contact . . . are non-Catholic rather than Protestant." The inaugural issue of *The Challenge*, published by the Glenmary Home Missioners, prominently included a map of counties in the United States; those without a resident priest were shaded and ominously named "NO PRIEST LAND." This graphic depiction of lack of priestly ministry (in approximately one-third of the nation's three thousand counties, located overwhelmingly in the Southeast) was intended to shock complacent urban Catholics into realizing that, though their name was legion in the cities, the countryside lay fallow. The duty to change this placed Catholic readers in a state of existential angst. The tide could be turned and rural America made Catholic—or another influence could sway the nation's rural denizens toward another faith, and the long-feared anti-Catholicism would erupt again in rural areas.[60]

To describe non-Catholics as "Protestant" no longer sufficed, since, in the minds of most trailer-chapel priests, their listeners had lost the vestiges of even that form of Christian faith. Yet rural Americans were not the anti-Catholic hatemongers ready, as many urban Catholics still feared, to accept the old stories of conspiracy and abduction told by Maria Monk in the nineteenth century. Instead, rural non-Catholic Americans appeared to be in a state of spiritual limbo where all religious beliefs were regarded as equal. In other words, they were "pagan"—not really anything. From Texas, Father Walter Burke, C.S.P., wrote:

> [J]udging from their own statements, the substitute [to Roman Catholicism] they propose seems nothing more than a syncretism of other religions and a hodgepodge of Kantianism, psychology, and modern "science." At the heart of it is a new form of emotionalism with a superficial facade formed by a rich embroidery of Scripture.

Of course, Burke revealed more about his own attitudes toward non-Catholics than about their actual beliefs, but he was not alone in his assessment. Frederick Coupal, C.M., one of the first motor missioners in Missouri, traveled north in the summer of 1940 to the diocese of Marquette, Michigan. His only description of the "religious influences" in Menominee mentioned the "usual heresies with Lutherans predominating." A month later, in Marquette itself, he encountered only "usual heretical sects." Commenting on "the humble hill-hemmed folk" of Kentucky, Raphael Sourd wrote that "meaningless jargon and foolish sensuous tantrums overworked the imaginations of these simple folk. Strange how human nature deprived of the full light of the Gospel can be imposed upon."[61]

The apparent uniform blandness of rural Protestantism merely further convinced the motor mission priests that success lay ahead. The only obstacles were the vast amount of territory to be covered and the relatively small number of trailer chapels. Schmiedeler's readers became very familiar with "parishes" that included towns more than a hundred miles apart. A Paulist writing from Clemson, South Carolina, took the hyperbole even further: The diocese of Charleston, he reported, had "fewer Catholics proportionately than the State of Mongolia in China, generally accepted to be almost an entirely pagan territory." The implication that South Carolina was more "pagan" than a foreign country was, of course, unsettling. Despite the fragility of that situation, the motor missions and trailer chapels offered hope that the state and others like it might soon be brought back into the Catholic fold.[62]

The motor missioners' belief in the impending success of their work emerged in comparisons with foreign missions. At the 1937 NCRLC convention in Richmond, Virginia, W. Howard Bishop could not have stated this fervor more clearly:

> Why this discrimination against our non-Catholic fellow-countrymen when we are so eager to win non-Catholic foreigners? If the Chinese and Africans are worth converting to the Church, why not the American mountaineers, farmers and farm tenants, colored and white? . . . Let us get busy on an offensive program, taking the "fallen aways" along with the "never-weres" and working indiscriminately for both.

Bishop's militancy was unmistakable; it showed in the very language describing his work. When the Glenmarians received their trailer chapel in 1941, Bishop labeled it "our latest acquisition in Motorized Missionary Artillery." Burke spoke of "invading" small towns in the Texas hill country. The trailer chapel was the key weapon in this "invasion," since it was already a familiar part of American life. The extension of this form of militancy abroad was evident when Schmiedeler reported in 1941 that a completely outfitted trailer chapel had been shipped to the Conventual Franciscan missions in China.[63]

Motor Mission Catholicism as American Religion

Introducing her study of nineteenth-century American Catholic devotion to Our Lady of Lourdes, Colleen McDannell writes that those "who are caught up in the holy rarely notice the institutional and cultural structures that construct, define, and even distribute the sacred."[64] McDannell's remark may be extended to the motor missions and their audiences. While the trailer chapels redefined the public character of the Catholic Church and consequently endured internal criticisms, they engaged American culture in new ways. The distribution of "the holy"—in this case, the sacraments and doctrines of Catholicism—carried out through the use of cultural and technological forms that American Catholics had previously overlooked as tools of evangelization. Where and how the motor mission priests employed these tools resembled in many ways their use by the "usual heretical sects" and the cultural patterns of American religion.

Catholic opposition to the motor missions stemmed from the desire to maintain distance between the priesthood and the scatological ramblings of evangelical Protestantism. This latter resided in the very locations to which the motor missions brought the Church. One of Schmiedeler's articles included a list of stops that sounded something like an underworld journey:

> Little towns are rapidly coming to the fore to-day in the work of the Church in the United States. They are helping to make church history. One hears their names over and over again. Among them are the following: Alto (Tennessee), Bolling (Alabama), Cape Girardeau (Missouri), Caldwell (Kansas), Greenfield (Indiana), Monse (Washington), Powhatan (Virginia), Tonkawa (Oklahoma), Valdosta (Georgia), Vernal (Utah). Still others could easily be added to the list. The number is rapidly increasing.

Catholics, of course, lived in every state of the nation when Schmiedeler wrote this in 1940. But areas such as these were the supposed harbors of the Church's enemies, particularly the Ku Klux Klan. Rural America, despite its proximity, was often as foreign as another continent for many Catholics. "It didn't take us long to find out," wrote Paulist priest Richard Walsh, "that St. Paul's technique would work in South Carolina as it worked in Asia Minor. The best way to get into their minds was through their hearts."[65]

The transformation of the perception of rural America from small-town idyll to indolent backwater was complete by the time the St. Lucy trailer chapel rolled out of Alto, Tennessee. If the intellectual disillusionment of the 1920s offered Catholics anything, it was the reassurance that the urban addresses that most of them held were preferable to what lay beyond the city limits. The confidence fostered by the Catholic Revival was based largely on the culture of urban Catholicism and its large parishes and usually easily recognized urban presence. The motor missions instead preferred the small town, the farmer's barn, and the dirt road—scenes that many Americans, Catholic or not, had come to consider backward at best.

To counter this impression, motor mission priests resorted to descriptions of their actual rural experiences, as they had in answering the criticisms concerning the Church's dignity. They argued that the positive stereotypes, not the negative ones, were the accurate assessments of rural America. In Utah, a Paulist vacation school had attracted a large non-Catholic audience, including "two great-grandsons of Brigham Young, who ninety-three years ago founded Mormonism." Southern hospitality meant "more than eating fried chicken on the veranda of a plantation. It does mean making folks feel at home," wrote Walsh. Still, "a New York accent is no asset in the southern mountains where the memory of Sherman's march to the sea is dying very slowly—but after you show them that you are interested, the Southerners respond warmly."[66]

With memories of burning crosses and Klan marches still fresh, even in the northern urban streets of Newark and Perth Amboy, successful motor missions in southern states seemed especially spectacular. Cassidy's Queen of the Apostles based itself in Georgia, the same state the Ku Klux Klan once called home. In fact, the Klan's Imperial Palace was purchased in 1936 by Cassidy's superior, Bishop Gerald O'Hara, as the rectory for Atlanta's new Christ the King Cathedral. Although Terminiello received the most press, he was but one of many priests running missions in Alabama. Apart from Arkansas and Florida, trailer chapels covered some part of every state in the old Confederacy. They did encounter some cultural difficulties—but not the sort most Catholics expected. Father John Renehan, C.S.S.R., wrote that offering open-air Mass in North Carolina was often hard because "it is almost impossible to start services before 9 P.M. The rural people work till the sun goes down, then have supper, and come out to the service." The real "difficulty is that people in the rural South just don't know the Church as she really is," wrote Father Robert Ready, O.S.B., of Mountain Grove, Missouri. Besides street-preaching, Ready planned to counter such ignorance by joining the town's Chamber of Commerce.[67]

The concern that motor missioners showed for the communities they visited took them a long way toward reaching the hearts of non-Catholic rural Americans. Throughout the South, Walsh found "that it is just as important to be sympathetic to the people in the afternoon as to give a good talk at night." This meant mixing with the farmers and merchants in the area. Walsh wrote that he and his Paulist brethren

> would stop a cotton farmer while he was plowing and listen to him talk about the boll weevil. His eyes would light up as he took us through his watermelon patch, and then he would point out the harm done by the last frost to his peach trees. We would let him talk and ask interested questions. And as we took leave of him to stop on the next farm for a glass of well water, he would assure us that he would not only come to our "trailer meeting" but would bring his brother too.

The trailer chapel's mobility facilitated interaction between the motor mission priests and their audiences. When Catholicism came to a small town, the message needed to be delivered in a fashion that suited the setting. Father Broome remarked that "[w]e have preached to them while attired in hunting boots and leather jackets, when it was so cold that we marveled that anyone would stand outside and listen to us."[68]

"Man's ingenuity, however many times it may have served Mammon," wrote Eoin McKiernan in *The Catholic World*, "has frequently given striking, if not bizarre, service to God." This certainly applied to the trailer chapels. Meeting local farmers meant more than simply demonstrating neighborly concern or trying to drum up attendance for that night's services. Part of the motor missioners' success lay in their resemblance to the ubiquitous county farm agent who attempted to "extend" information from the state agricultural college to the farmers. Most farmers, though, doggedly clung to what agents referred to as "antiquated" methods. This "stubbornness" did not prevent large crowds from gathering at demonstrations of new techniques for hog butchering, field tilling, or fruit canning. Many just watched for entertainment. County extension agents had become a fixture in farm culture a decade before the Catholic motor mission "invasion," and they had helped build the foundation for the surprisingly positive reception of the motor missions. Glenmarian John Marquardt's account of a Kentucky sorghum stir-off indicated how this might have happened: "I reckon that those citizens of the hills found out that day that a city feller can talk to a critter and 'git him a movin'" mighty nigh as well as a country feller." Both the agent and the priest demonstrated new techniques, whether of plowing or praying, and both came from outside the immediate area. Part of the trailer's attraction was its novelty; people would attend a service just to figure out how an altar, sound system, movie projector, water tank, stove, and two priests could fit into it. An extension agent with a new tractor and plow would receive much the same reception; both would be thanked, but not completely accepted. Father Broome's audience had probably gathered previously in similar settings for an introduction to purportedly better methods of harvesting tobacco or preserving topsoil.[69]

The motor mission enjoyed perhaps a better reception than the extension agent, who was widely regarded as the best source of *mis*information. After all, Walsh and the other Paulists merely listened to the farmers of the South Carolina piedmont; they did not suggest that the frost damage could have been avoided with better planning. The lack of expressed condescension (though it surfaced elsewhere, such as in the published accounts) made the difference. The priests tried to appear as much like the farmers as they could. Father Broome wrote that "our first job when we stop is take off our collars. . . . If we spoke to a more critical group, I'm afraid we would be known as the priests with dirty hands, because nobody has yet discovered a lubricant for our trailer pitch that will wash off with cold water."[70]

The motor missions, a novelty among American Catholics, attracted non-Catholics for the same reason: a trailer chapel simply had not been seen before. While the Extension Society had operated chapel cars and trailer chapels for thirty years before the Paulists commissioned the St. Lucy, only the 1930s and 1940s witnessed their nationwide use combined with a Catholic agrarian perspective. Improved roads, although many were still dirt, facilitated this expansion. So, too, did the increasing availability of automobiles. Participation in building the American love affair with cars is certainly not something readily associated with the Catholic Church, but a case could be made that the motor missions did contribute to it. More importantly, the trailer chapels were one instance in which the American Catholic Church achieved a surprisingly high degree of assimilation to rural America without diminishing its own identity. They introduced Roman Catholicism to rural America in all its forms—doctrinal, liturgical, and devotional. To do so required a certain material aspect and the entrepreneurial skills to market the religion. The motor missions possessed both in abundance. They were superseded only when the technological and cultural mores of America changed in the postwar years.[71]

Those recognizing the material significance of the trailer chapel included some who would have been least likely to use it. In the midst of the modernist movement in architecture, the trailer chapels drew attention from primarily urban-dwelling, aesthetically sophisticated Catholics. *Liturgical Arts*, a journal featuring some of the most innovative work in creating worship space, featured the first two trailer chapels (the Paulists' St. Lucy, operated in Tennessee, and St. Mary of the Highways, operated in Virginia by Father Stephens) next to other architectural innovations of liturgical space, such as the Chapel at Rosary College in Illinois and modernist-influenced church structures in Germany. More significantly, it added another voice to the debate over motor mission dignity. Adherents of the Liturgical Movement could affirm the trailer chapel's centeredness on the Eucharist, not "distracting" devotions. The altars in both trailers could swivel to face either into the trailer or out toward the attending crowd. Mass "facing the people" thus became a rural phenomenon two decades before it officially debuted in the parishes. The support by the Liturgical Movement cast the trailer chapels with the Catholic avant-garde in a debate over Catholic aesthetics. The Liturgical Movement's affiliation with Catholic agrarianism could not have appeared more clearly. The rhetoric and artwork alone endorsed the "natural" worship of God's Son where He was born (a rural area). In practice, this emphasis on rurality emerged in the Company of St. Isidore, the Rogation Days processions, Martin Hellriegel's blessing of the Rural Parish Workers in Fertile, Missouri, and the renegade services in Maryfarm's barn. The trailer chapels removed any remaining reservations about the Church's adaptability and sophistication, demonstrating publicly how American, how modern, and how mobile it could become while remaining both "natural" and traditionally Catholic.[72]

Along with those concessions to modern American life came the movies, perhaps the Church's biggest adaptation of all. The motor missions used only silent ones, especially the three mentioned above directed by Cecil B. DeMille. *The Ten Commandments*, Schmiedeler reported in 1939, "has been made available on 16mm film through the kindness of Mr. DeMille, who requested the motion picture company to put this film at the disposal of the missionaries." According to the motor missioners, the movies' effectiveness rested on their novelty. Apparently, many a small town was first introduced to motion pictures by the motor missions. The priests held their audiences' attention much as the county extension agents did: by appealing to their curiosity. Determining whether the crowd's receptivity was due more to the speeches or to the movies that followed was difficult. At least one priest sensed that it might be the latter, but he worried little, since the result was the same.

One of the lasting joys that fills the heart of the trailer missionary is to move through the crowd in the dark as they watch Christ being scourged and

crucified—and hear the quiet weeping of these simple souls. They are more affected by the scenes of Calvary and Gethsemani than by any sermon.

The Vincentians often encountered some of their strongest opposition not
from competing evangelists, but from special features at a local theater. In
one town the missionaries arranged to use the theater themselves, in order
to prevent such competition. The informational speeches were given outside, followed by the film inside. The project failed miserably; instead of the
fifty to one hundred people who usually attended outside, only ten stayed
long enough to move inside for the movie.[73]

The decline of the trailer chapel lay in the transformations of American
rural life, not those of the Catholic Church during the 1960s. After acknowledging its importance, the NCRLC's national conventions left most of the
work to the diocesan directors. Even among its advocates, motor mission
work often failed to sustain itself for long after the war. The Glenmarians,
who were the last to acquire a trailer chapel, were the first to abandon it in
1946. Bishop had never considered street-preaching to be his order's vocation. He focused instead on the greater mission to convert rural America.
When the Chapel of the North American Martyrs appeared to have outlived
its usefulness, something better replaced it. "Christ Week" became Glenmary's primary evangelization method—a week's worth of hymns and
preaching in the best tent-revival tradition. The advertisements for it proclaimed, "All *real* Americans love to hear about Jesus!" Apart from that, the
technology that made the motor missions so attractive to rural Americans
soon produced newer, more seductive attractions that rendered the trailer
chapels obsolete. As in American rural life generally, it was the most mun-
dane innovation that posed the biggest threat: electricity. Most importantly,
this meant that rural and small-town Americans could now have air condi-
tioning. In the mid-1950s, motor missioners in the St. Louis archdiocese began reporting low attendance due to people staying inside where it was
cooler. Another culprit was, of course, television. While twenty years earlier
radio broadcasts could be woven into a night's services, apparently no
speaker could compete with televised Cardinals baseball games.[74]

The mixture of confidence and confusion surrounding the motor missions
raised questions about their Catholicity—that is, their religious identity—as
well as their "catholicity," or inclusiveness. Whether urban or rural, the
Catholic Church in the United States concerned itself with both of these issues. But unlike urban American Catholicism, which pursued each issue sep-
arately, the Catholic agrarian agenda envisioned the two as being intertwined around the unifying concept of a spiritually and physically rewarding
rural life. While this vision took many forms, the motor missions made particularly fine examples. From their devotional names to the orthodoxy of
their preaching, the motor missions sought to deliver undiluted Catholicism

to their rural Protestant (or, in the missioners' eyes, almost pagan) audiences. Yet at the same time the motor missions exuded an inclusiveness unmatched in the cities. There, non-Catholic America was mostly held at arm's length. The motor missioners, though, practically embraced American culture even as they offered a religious message that they believed transcended that very culture. Hazel Motes remarks that "no one with a good car needs to be justified." Brian Abel Ragen has claimed that Motes appropriately enough preaches from a car hood, since doing so denies the continuity of Catholic churches demonstrated by their names and the past glories those names evoke. However, in the motor mission services, good cars dispensed justification. They managed to imitate Motes's preaching style while maintaining the very theological continuity he denied.[75]

Although they lasted only thirty-five years and found success for perhaps only ten of those, the Catholic motor missions constituted an important landmark in the history of American Catholicism. Failure simply seemed impossible to those engaged in the work:

> Here, then, is a great adventure as we go off the main road in search of the other sheep. Here is a real drama, a vital contest with eternal souls as the prize of victory. And our weapons are prayer and grace and goodwill. And also gaily colored pamphlets and Mickey Mouse cartoons and the Hollywood epic of the life of Christ. Throw in sympathy and understanding of the problems of the cotton-pickers and make all these converge in a 22-foot box with four wheels that is equipped with up-to-the-minute loudspeakers and projectors—and there you have the trailer mission. If anything comes to be the 1945 version of a mission of the Apostle of the Gentiles, this is it.

In its forays into rural America—either "NO PRIEST LAND" or simply a town without a Catholic parish—the American Catholic Church employed a wealth of modern technological tools such as cars, loudspeaker systems, record players, and movies in an attempt to present the Catholic faith where it had not yet been seen and heard. Like the circus and the county farm agent, the Catholic motor missions and street revivals were a spectacle that broke up the monotony of small-town life. Father Hugo Hahn's summary of the Redemptorists' work in North Carolina applied to all the motor missions: "First, we must convince people that the Catholic Church is really a work of God and not some sinister thing out of hell. If the trailer chapel can create interest and a benevolent attitude about the Catholic Church, our work has been done." Motor missions painted a different picture of what it meant to be Catholic in America before the seismic restructuring of Vatican II. In the midst of charges that Catholicism was an alien and un-American faith, the motor missions brought Catholicism literally to the doorsteps of rural America, or at least within earshot.[76]

The Wheat and Chaff
of Catholic Agrarianism

Behold this child is . . . a sign which shall be contradicted

. . . that, out of many hearts, thoughts may be revealed.

—Luke 2:34–35

By the end of the 1940s, the integration of agriculture and religion sought by Catholic agrarians had started to unravel. The motor missions struggled to regain their prewar audiences. The National Catholic Rural
Life Conference watched successive publications suffer from lack of interest,
despite their attempts to market Catholic agrarianism to the farmers. Some
newcomers tried their hand at farming but likewise found the path increasingly difficult. While starting a farm in Pennsylvania, James Kenny also
taught English at the Jesuits' newly established LeMoyne College in Syracuse,
New York. With no small amount of disgust, he wrote to *The Catholic Worker*:

> Frankly I am tempted to become a little skeptical of the human material that
> goes into the making of a Commune. Of the persons of your acquaintance, who
> talk of Communes, how many are eager to bend over a hoe in the hot sun,
> while sweat streams into your eyes, or sneeze in the stifling air of a hay-loft in
> haying time, or do without gas, electricity, and running water (we do not have
> any of those three "services" here), or carry wood for the stove, or pull weeds,
> or any other of the real work connected with farming?

Fewer Catholic agrarians were willing to confront the realities of the images
that their religious view of agriculture inspired. Some discovered this the
hard way. Ruth Ann Heaney recalled that "we were left with the problems of
how to interpret or to apply Peter [Maurin]'s ideas in this situation. It was up
to us to work it out."[1]

This comment recapitulated the rural life that the Heaneys and the Pauls,
isolated geographically from their confreres in the cities and separated spiritually from their neighbors in the Missouri countryside, had—along with many
other American Catholics—tried to improve. They faced an unbridgeable gap

between the lofty descriptions of rural life and the hard reality down on the farm. Like many rural Americans, they did the best they could. In doing so, they succeeded (as Larry Heaney's well-attended funeral showed) in creating the community that so many agrarians desired but could not sustain.

By that time, though, the agrarian impulse in American Catholicism was swiftly becoming nothing more than an idea held only by the most dedicated. By 1951 *The Christian Farmer* had ceased publication. By the mid-1950s, all of Granger's cooperative ventures, save the credit union, had ended as well. It was the decade when rural America completed its electrification, thus depriving the motor missions of their audiences. By the late 1950s, only the devotional Company of St. Isidore remained to promote the Catholic agrarian worldview, and its days were numbered.[2]

Robert Dorman labels the immediate postwar years the "Pickett's Charge" of the Regionalist movement among American intellectuals and artists. Catholic agrarianism made up one of the proud units in this final, grand, headlong but ultimately doomed assault against modernity. The history of British and American intellectuals converting to Roman Catholicism is, according to Patrick Allitt, "a monumentous [sic] and protracted failure." The Catholic rural life movement's antimodern agrarians certainly experienced defeat, but perhaps not so grandly as Allitt's subjects (among whom were a few agrarians). The Catholic agrarians returned only in remnants from their crusade. How those remnants have developed since then indicates a certain bio-dynamic action itself: they keep fostering new growth.[3]

Maryfarm provided an interesting setting in which to realize the symbolic relationship between the liturgical life of the Church and "life on the land." Although few other Catholic parishes would celebrate Mass in a converted barn with the animals downstairs munching on hay, the dialogue Mass said in the local vernacular quickly became normative after the Second Vatican Council. The innovation surrounding the trailer chapels also characterized American Catholic life soon after the Council. The difference was that what the motor missioners had done to inculturate Catholicism to rural America—using English translations of the Mass, performed "facing the people" and accompanied by popular, folksy songs—was now understood to be what Catholic liturgical life should be in the modernistic 1960s. Some critics have charged that the apparent tastelessness of the situation at Maryfarm, and perhaps also in the motor missions, may have carried over as well. With liturgical innovation, they argued, came blatant disregard for tradition, transcendent spirituality, and anything resembling ecclesiastical dignity.[4]

Similarly, the simplicity of rural life that William Gauchat, the Heaneys and Pauls, Frederick Kenkel, and Luigi Ligutti all extolled in the 1930s and 1940s returned full force in the 1960s. The Camphill movement, based first in eastern New York and then Pennsylvania, promoted the heritage of Rudolf Steiner's "biodynamic agriculture." "The Farm," established in 1969 near Summertown, Tennessee, by Stephen Gaskin and 250 followers, replicated the Catholic farm colonies' countercultural critique of American acquisitiveness. Apparently, though, Farm residents were not dissuaded from marketing organically grown vegetables. The Farm's success, therefore, resembled that of Granger, while its rhetorical spirit apparently shared more with the Catholic Workers. Certainly the ecological concerns of the Farm and other groups resembled, despite some clear distinctions in theological preference, the earlier claims by Catholics about the sacramentality of life lived intimately with nature. Catholic attempts at land colonization failed, but in this they took their place alongside other American communitarians. What survived the colonies' convolutions did so more in the wider patterns of American culture. These affinities, however unintentional, might have been the colonies' greatest legacy.[5]

Environmentalism, another less specifically Catholic remnant, wove concern for the earth with experimental forms of spirituality and lifestyles. It offered Farm-like communal experience to those not inclined to give up their individuality for life in south-central Tennessee. Writings from Kentucky farmer Wendell Berry, Passionist priest Thomas Berry, and others provided renewed inspiration. Bill Devall and George Session wrote that "Deep Ecology" advocated "biocentric equality," wherein "all things in the biosphere have an equal right to live and blossom and to reach their own individual forms of unfolding and self-realization within the larger Self-realization." This led to the recognition "that we, as humans, and as communities of humans, have vital needs which go beyond such basics as food, water, and shelter to include love, play, creative expression, intimate relationships with a particular landscape (or Nature taken in its entirety) as well as intimate relationships with other humans, and the vital need for spiritual growth." Devall and Sessions have contrasted the dominant worldview, which endorses "dominance over Nature," with deep ecology's insistence on "harmony with Nature," "biospecies equality," and the acknowledgment that "earth 'supplies' [are] limited." This viewpoint could be pursued to surprising, even threatening, extremes. Earth First! has engaged in "monkey-wrenching": tree-spiking, "decommissioning" of bulldozers, and other acts of "ecotage" designed to thwart any environmentally harmful project, be it housing construction or tree-harvesting. Such activities demonstrate how far the perception of the spiritual benefits of nature apart from human usage could be taken. Many in the Earth First! movement, Martha Lee has noted, view monkey-wrenching as a religious, even sacramental, activity. Participating in ecotage manifested outwardly one's inner spiritual growth.[6]

This "earth first" spirituality made a significant point: most of the world's major religious traditions did not provide much help for the earth. Rupert Sheldrake indicates that even praiseworthy acts were usually merely symbolic: "The pope's honoring of the earth as mother is expressed through his custom of kissing the ground as soon as he alights from planes. It seems a shame that this is usually tarmac." Buddhism, especially in its expressions among Euro-American converts, offered an exception. Gary Snyder's "Smokey the Bear Sutra"—with its refrain "DROWN THEIR BUTTS CRUSH THEIR BUTTS"—demonstrated that a religious concern for the environment need not lack humor or commitment. "Now those who recite this Sutra and then try to put it in practice . . . Will save the planet Earth from total oil slick . . . Will enter the age of harmony of humans and nature . . . AND IN THE END WILL WIN HIGHEST PERFECT ENLIGHTENMENT."[7]

The "right attitude" and "right occupation" of the Buddha's Eightfold Path lurk behind Snyder's creative blend of ecological activism and American popular culture. Along with them stands the notion that defending the earth delivers its own salvation. The "religion of nature" has always existed in American religious history. The emergence of environmentalism enabled this subculture to develop fully into its own tradition. Roger Gottlieb describes deep ecology as "a passionate, spiritually oriented, mystical communion with the earth and its many beings, a recognition of kinship with those beings that requires no more philosophical justification than does the connection we feel with our parents, pets, or lovers. As such, deep ecology is a spiritual philosophy; and the deepest experiences that animate its adherents are profoundly mystical." Like any other tradition, deep ecology uses this fundamental religious experience to prompt its followers to action. "You are more than your profession and race and religion and even gender. In your cells and sinews and even your atoms there is a tie to all this [nature] which surrounds you. Open yourself up to this source of grace and peace and love. More important, open yourself up to the love you feel for it." Just as the Christian tradition insists that "faith without works is dead," Gottlieb indicates that following deep ecology necessarily includes acting upon one's experience of nature.[8]

Chastened, Christian theologians joined the endeavor, noting the Christian tradition's "ambiguous promise" for ecology. The tradition contains more than excuses for the domination and exploitation of nature for human ends. Paul Santmire has noted that other voices celebrate the natural world. This ecological motif creates a mutual network among God, humanity, and nature. It departs significantly from more familiar theological models, in which humanity seeks God above and beyond nature. Santmire describes the resulting vision "of an enormous diversity of living forms and material shapes charged with wonder and awe." This "metaphor of fecundity" could be traced in Scripture (such as the Psalms) and the Christian tradition (the Puritans' vision of America as a New Eden). In Santmire's and other accounts, St. Francis of Assisi stands out as a laudable example of one Christian who embraced and appreciated nature instead of following the custom of exploitation. The path, though, need not always lead to the antiestablishment friar. Within the Christian tradition, animals also deliver this alternative ecological message.[9]

Catholics writing on environmental issues strove to avoid anything androcentric—perspectives that valued the environment primarily in terms of its benefits to humans. Erstwhile Dominican Matthew Fox discussed "creation spirituality," and Rosemary Radford Ruether described an "ecofeminist theology of earth healing." Both attempted to rejuvenate interest in how supernatural benefits could be derived through an appreciation of natural phenomena. Fox even dated the divine "original blessing" at almost twenty billion years before "original sin." Later he produced a book of "conversations" with Aquinas on the matter. Catholic or otherwise, Christian theology began sharing some of deep ecology's sensibilities. After writing about the "greening of science and God," Rupert Sheldrake concluded: "As soon as we allow ourselves to think of the world as alive, we recognize that a part of us knew this all along." Before all this, though, came the Catholic agrarian emphasis on bio-dynamic farming as both a spiritual and physical activity. The soul's fertility reflected that of nature. Increasing demands for environmental protection echoed what Catholic agrarians had often voiced forty years before: that humanity existed along with other life forms on more than a physical level. If Catholic agrarians spoke of how that relationship could improve humanity's relationship with God, the various voices of current environmentalism decried the betrayal of that trust.[10]

These similarities—admittedly distant, but nonetheless present—could extend even further. In 1978 Mary Daly's *Gyn/Ecology* offered a radical feminist "metaethics." An exclusive community of women-identified women, according to Daly, could re-envision how they interacted with global life. Liberating women from patriarchy's "necrophilia" necessarily entailed freeing the rest of "global life" and vice versa. With reference to Rachel Carson's *Silent Spring*, Daly wrote: "I am affirming that those women who have the courage to break the silence within our Selves are finding/creating/spiraling a new Spring. This Spring within and among us makes be-ing possible, and makes the process of integrity possible." To parallel the ancient fertility goddess's Triple Spiral as "maiden, mother, and crone," Daly encouraged her sister journeyers to "spin, spark, and spook." Taken together, these ventures empower women to move beyond mere equality to the rebirth and celebration of the "gynergy" repressed for so long. Daly's radicalism (literally, in this case, since both she and Peter Maurin stressed the word's original meaning of "returning to the roots") paralleled that of Earth First! Daly later wrote that "*Gyn/Ecology* can be Seen/Heard as a Thunderbolt of Rage that I hurled into the world against the patriarchs who have never ceased to massacre women and our Sister the Earth." Her celebration of "biophiliac gynergy" also bore a slight thematic resemblance to the Catholic agrarians' adulation of female (physical and spiritual) fertility. Clearly, the ends to which they pursued this shared insight could not have been more different. Daly sparked a reawakening to women's self-awareness and social awareness, while the Catholic agrarians hoped that women would literally deliver the future agrarian economy. Both, though, sensed some connection between this issue and the land. The rupture between American Catholicism and anything rural might be what makes such similarities between Catholic agrarianism and socially and religiously progressive endeavors appear so outlandish. Writings motivated by ecologically sensitive principles, the endorsement of small, self-sufficient communities, the celebration of earthly fertility and motherhood (at the cosmic and/or personal levels), organic farming, and the pursuit of "pure" and healthy lifestyles have been seen by a wider readership than one might assume.[11]

On the other hand, another set of comparisons seems quite "natural." The sudden and complex transformation of American Catholicism following

Vatican II is a large and oft-told story. At the time, rejecting the immediate past—which of course included Catholic agrarianism—seemed more than merely preferable; some indicated that it was the only real choice available. The preconciliar prominence enjoyed by Catholic intellectuals such as Hilaire Belloc, G. K. Chesterton, and Jacques Maritain not only dwindled; current fashion dictated outright rejection of them. The intellectual giants of the past now seemed only to provide fodder for sarcasm or derision. In the new situation, the satirical and insightful agrarian Chesterton resurfaced as the obese and flatulent buffoon Ignatius P. Reilly in John Kennedy Toole's uproarious *A Confederacy of Dunces*. Martin Cruz Smith's *Gorky Park*, a murder mystery featuring the weary and cynical Russian detective Arkady Renko, contained a passing insult of the Catholic Workers: in a crowded Moscow bar, Renko hears from a hard-boiled New York cop about "the limp-wrist Catholic Marxist movement, with all their cute magazine names like *Work, Worship, Thought*—as if any of them worked harder than lifting a sherry glass or passing a fart—or sniveling-after-Jesus names like *Orate Fratres* or *The Gregorian Review*." Even the farm communes are included: "Of course, we had our own retreat—Joe Hill House, Maryfarm—deep intellectual conversations around the fireplace. . . . Oh we were weekend monks. Did the Gloria with tom-toms, stained glass, gilded ikons." The Catholic rural life movement—indeed, the whole Catholic Revival—seemed to be a minor, utopian, but still rather pathetic story in American life that was better left in the past.[12]

Nothing, though, sounded the alarm to abandon ship as loudly as Paul VI's *Humanae Vitae*. Appearing in 1968, the encyclical reasserted the Church's prohibition of artificial birth control and the subsequent endorsement of natural family planning. Marriage, far from being merely the product of evolution, came as a gift from God. Those supernatural origins, though, included natural guidelines whose observance the Church reiterated. Pope Paul wrote that "to experience the gift of married love while respecting the laws of conception is to acknowledge that one is not the master of the sources of life but rather the minister of the design established by the Creator." Paul had wanted to make a definitive statement on the Church's teaching. Instead, the pope's words, Mary Jo Weaver writes, "stimulated the largest and most serious movement of public dissent from Catholic teaching in the modern period." The popular fallout naturally prompted a conservative counteroffensive. Discussions of what constituted "natural" family life sprang readily out of the rhetoric provided by Catholic agrarianism. Human life should be given every opportunity to produce; this fertility reflected what the Creator had given every other living thing. By then, though, the subset of American Catholic intellectual and cultural life providing some of the most original views on fecundity and God's plans for nature had receded far from the now consciously urban-focused Catholic majority.[13]

Something similar occurred in the Catholic heartland. During the heyday of Catholic agrarianism, the Midwest had served as a breeding ground for expansive and risky Catholic thought and liturgical innovation, but it was now viewed as a backwater (as it had been for decades by non-Catholic intellectuals). The Society of St. Pius X, a schismatic traditionalist Catholic movement led by French archbishop Marcel Lefebvre (1905–1991), refused to recognize Vatican II's liberal developments. The resistance centered on the Latin Mass, which Society members regarded as permanent and irrevocable. While the Society established parishes nationally, it located its headquarters in Kansas City, Missouri, and its college just to the west in St. Marys, Kansas. Other conservative Catholic communities established themselves in similar settings across rural America. Saving the Catholic tradition from its appalling modern developments seemed to require withdrawing to the hills.[14]

Similar shoots growing out of the Catholic agrarian compost were the racist and antisemitic Christian Identity movement and the "constitutional fundamentalist" Posse Comitatus, a group that recognized the county sheriff as the highest legal official. Rulo, Nebraska, a home to nineteenth-century Catholic settlement and twentieth-century motor missions, witnessed a standoff in 1985 between the local Posse community and law enforcement concerning a custody battle over Catholic children from Kansas. Gerald L. K. Smith, Father Terminiello's advocate and speaking partner, avidly endorsed Christian Identity after World War II. So did Bob Mathews, who founded The Order (also known as the Bruders Schweigen, "the silent brotherhood"), a right-wing militia responsible for armored-car robberies and the 1984 murder of Denver radio personality Alan Berg. Taking "land spirituality" in another direction, Mathews hoped eventually to establish an all-white territory in the Pacific Northwest, the "natural" home of the race. (Other Christian Identity members had similar plans.) Before being killed in a standoff with federal authorities, he signed his last letter "As always, for blood, soil, honor, for faith and for race." The "soil" here served to anchor Mathews's hope for a certain and (in his mind) peaceful future. The Catholic agrarians had harbored hopes for the land, too, but obviously not along the lines of Mathews's racist ideology. Still, both began (and ended) with the land. Here the similarities with Catholic agrarianism leaned right, instead of left toward deep ecology and radical feminism. The association of rural America with things backward or outdated handily obscured an earlier day when the Catholic rural life movement contained both "liberal" and "reactionary" (by today's standards) elements.[15]

Meanwhile, Catholics had gradually embraced the urban areas where most of them had lived for so long. At one level, this had been occurring for quite some time. James Farrell's Studs Lonigan trilogy celebrated the gritty realities of Irish Catholic life in Chicago, while the festival surrounding Our Lady of Mount Carmel in Italian Harlem provided evidence of the clear vitality of "street Catholicism." Only later did this shift come at the academic level. In 1962 Robert Cross's article "The Changing Image of the City among American Catholics" appeared in *Catholic Historical Review*. The article demonstrated how painfully antiquated the antiurban vision of Catholic agrarianism seemed in the age of the "managerial priest." Cross specifically named Schmiedeler, Kelley, and O'Hara as some of those Catholics who led the Church "in the 1920's [to] adjudge the urban impact primarily as it compared with a romanticized rural impact." Every aspect of the Catholic agrarian worldview went under the blade of Cross's historical assessment in light of "wiser answers about the urban impact": the insistence on urban sterility and decay, rural fertility, and the inherent religious superiority of rural inhabitants.[16]

Cross noted, however, that with the emergence of improved sociological research, the city in the late 1950s and early 1960s appeared in a far more positive light. "Several studies have shown that among city dwellers there is a higher level of religious observance with higher amounts of education." "Trying to secure decent physical and moral conditions for their flocks," Catholic agrarians "scanted the task (incumbent on all who live in a heterogeneous city) of developing procedures for working equally with non-Catholic groups." Since urban sociology had removed the Catholic agrarian wool away from their eyes, Catholics stood to take their rightful place in shaping the nation's urban areas. "Now that urban Catholicism is part of the Establishment, a more active, confident role would seem plausible . . . Catholic churchmen have a special incentive to abandon a defensive tradition toward the urban impact on religious life." Three years later Harvey Cox's *The Secular City* appeared, extolling urban anonymity and mobility as signs of new freedoms and possibilities for religious development. Catholic agrarianism had run its course.[17]

Back on the farm, Catholic agrarianism and rural Catholicism continued to enjoy strange friendships, such as that with country music. Salvific messages have taken many forms in rural America, but few matched country music's popularity. The nostalgia and condescension that characterized Catholic agrarians appear as well in what one critic has called "the camouflage music by which a historically mobile nation continues to grieve the losses of departures."[18] What has been lampooned as "redneck music" veils an acute existential conflict. Yearnings for something better than one's present lot battle with the intense anguish over willfully separating oneself from that "down-home" community. This tension between the horizon of opportunity (the city) and home (often a farm or small town) replicates the dialectic of American individualism. The drive for individual freedom rends the communal fabric that formed the person experiencing that very impulse.

Country music enjoyed its first success in the rural South as an expression of popular religious and cultural values. It achieved national status without, for the most part, losing its roots as "working people's music." Within country music reside those mutually exclusive values just discussed: respectability and freedom from social conformity, the "home" and the "road," salvation and damnation. Hank Williams Sr. perhaps best personified these conflicts, in his private life as well as in his songs titled "Honky Tonkin'" and "I Saw the Light." The pattern had emerged even earlier, in the tragically short life of railroad worker and country singer Jimmie Rodgers. Born in Meridian, Mississippi, Rodgers pioneered some of the characteristics of the genre during the 1930s: the high-pitched nasal yodel, the images of transitoriness in one's emotional and spiritual life, and the inclusion of working-class experiences. Even Rodgers's death from tuberculosis, which he fought valiantly while making his last record, embodied one of country music's clearest antitriumphal messages: through death, one is able to transcend obstacles (whether personal, occupational, or spiritual) insurmountable in one's earthly existence. Little more than a decade later, Larry Heaney provided the Catholic Worker version of the same story.[19]

While country's uniquely American blend of music, culture, and region was developing, the motor missions crisscrossed the same region with a slightly different message but carrying many of the same themes. As with much in the motor missions' relationship to rural America, few things seemed further apart than Roman Catholicism and country's emerging religious sensibilities. The religiosity of country was (and still is) individualistic Protestant Christianity, which emphasizes personal experience and scriptural imagery. Beyond that, little seems similar between the motor missioners' sermons on marriage, the audience's questions on interreligious dating, and the occasionally blatant sexual appeal of male country stars such as Hank Williams Sr., whose personal magnetism and stage performances had female listeners swooning years before Elvis Presley or the Beatles. Still, the Paulist fathers in Tennessee used radio shows to spread their message when not traveling with the St. Lucy trailer chapel. As noted earlier, WSM, the station that carried these shows, was the same one that later began broadcasting the Grand Ole Opry on Saturday nights. This two-hour show was the primary venue for the nation's country musicians and, apparently, for Catholicism too. After the motor missions faded, rural Catholics still had the music. A late-1960s continuum might be imagined to stretch from the anti–Vietnam War protests of the Berrigan brothers to Merle Haggard's "Okie from Muskogee"; each end of the span captured some element of the rural Catholic experience.[20]

Strands of religious (or romantic) agrarianism survived elsewhere, but often shorn of the specifically Catholic content that was so important between the wars. Only a woman's gold cross earrings distinguish the one Catholic character in Carolyn Chute's *Letourneau's Used Auto Parts*. That book and Chute's other novels, particularly her popular *The Beans of Egypt, Maine,* describe the gradual encroachment of modern, anonymous, corporate America into a tiny rural New England community. As more and more Boston professionals purchase bankrupt farms, the lights of their newly constructed houses fill the previously starlit Maine nights with an artificial and unearthly glow. Conversely, the native Mainers, regardless of profession or education, inevitably end up residing in Lucien Letourneau's "Miracle City," an unzoned jungle of mobile homes and shacks lacking electricity and plumbing. Displaced from their old world and not welcome in the new, the residents of Egypt, Maine, resort to a variety of cruelties and relationships in their pursuit of a surrogate relationship with the land. Ana Castillo's characters in *So Far from God* experience a similar situation in New Mexico. Sofie, the mother of four girls and the long-suffering wife of a compulsive gambler, struggles to maintain her household, the family butcher shop, a barn full of animals, and the garden. Since the Church rarely intrudes or comforts, Sofie finds refuge, as do all her *comadres,* in popular Catholic spirituality and the folk medicinal remedies of the local healing woman Doña Felicia. Her daughters are not so lucky. Divorced from their ancestral ties to the New Mexico countryside, they find work elsewhere, and the results never provide the same level of support and permanence. For Sofie's daughter Esperanza, leaving the land ultimately leads to her death. The other three daughters stay in the area but end up dying anyway.[21]

Conscientious attempts to recapture the preconciliar Catholic agrarian unified vision rarely rise to the same level of literary skill. Some contemporary Catholic fiction still readily endorses the Catholic agrarian image of women as physically fertile and spiritually virtuous, and thus a bulwark against the insidious poisons of modern life. Christy Cousino observes that only explicitly Catholic literature still confidently links land and faith. "Feminine fertility, especially in the agricultural utopia serves as a sign of closeness to nature and as foil to the mechanization of urban life." Cousino notes that, despite some popularity among reviewers on the Internet, this reconstruction never overcomes its noticeable artificiality. Castillo's fleeting reference to St. Isidore seems quite natural in comparison: "He was the patron saint of farmers, and to not revere him could bring a farmer the worst punishment of all: bad neighbors. A farmer could survive droughts and bad crops, but not an ill-willed neighbor."[22]

Instead of spinning nostalgic or saccharine tales ending with (notably productive) familial bliss, Chute and Castillo begrudgingly acknowledge the suburbs' metastasis into hitherto untouched rural areas. Not only is the appreciation of rural America fading, rural America itself is shrinking as the new enemy—the franchised banality of the suburbs—inches further and further over the farmland. Catholic agrarianism had once embraced the possibility that most Catholics, while they could not "escape" the city, might be able to garden bio-dynamically in their suburban enclaves. Today, though, the Catholic community of Genesis Farm in western New Jersey, for example, stands as an isolated bastion of ecologically sensitive agriculture and spirituality surrounded by rapidly expanding New York suburbs. Instead of supporting the postwar Catholic flight from the city, Genesis Farm uses the earlier, apocalyptic voice of Catholic agrarianism to emphasize bio-dynamic farming and ecofeminist spirituality. Contemporary Catholic environmentalists, no longer "agrarians," and their counterparts demand repentance instead of redemption. When so much of American life seems so comfortable, solace may only be found, Belden Lane has suggested, in "fierce landscapes." Lane has in mind those few remaining places untouched by human design. Genesis Farm and other environmental groups seek to reclaim a similar ferocity in lifestyle and agriculture.[23]

Nevertheless, the land still maintains a certain evocative hold on the American imagination. One of William Least Heat Moon's characters in *Blue Highways* sagely advised that "[l]iving in rural America without land is to be without strength. . . . To an American, land is solidity, goodness, and hope. American history is about land." A recent sociological survey indicated that while fewer Americans farm, a sizable majority retain similar beliefs about living on the land. Neither Chute nor Heat Moon is Catholic, but Bruce Springsteen, the Catholic balladeer from New Jersey, used the name of what some have called the quintessential Midwestern state—Nebraska—as the title for a sparse album of brooding songs. Song characters are trapped in a spiritual and social landscape that is alternately as bleak or as hopeful as the Great Plains are thought to be.[24]

Attempts to minister to those living on the land or close to it still continue as well. Despite the transformations of the 1960s, the NCRLC has never ceased its advocacy for family farmers. Catholic Workers still draw inspiration from Peter Maurin's Green Revolution. The NCRLC once claimed that the real American Catholics lived in rural America. Now it has been suggested that the surviving small towns in the United States that have created their own local theologies exemplify a "Christian base community" better than the Latin American villages that inspired the term. Nevertheless, even a compliment such as that bears some resemblance to the ACLA's and NCRLC's colonial attempts to teach rural Americans how they could better themselves. Local rural American theology now "comes from the people," and admitting that one anoints sick farm animals no longer seems odd or quaint. Rural America, though, refuses to surrender itself so easily. Some still decline to join the rush for efficiency, development, and improvement, even when those pursuits are now led by their neighbors. Jim Goad's *Redneck Manifesto* concludes with a satirical prophecy: "The trash is only starting to strike back. The fog lifts. The sun burns through the clouds. The necks slowly sizzle to red."[25]

The land still retains both sides of the romantic image—Edenic utopia and howling wilderness—that Americans have, since the time of the Puritans, projected onto rural America. Before the seismic shifts of the 1960s, many Catholic agrarians not only agreed with this image, they attempted to ensure the realization of its positive aspects for future generations. Anthony DeCurtis commented in 1991 that the new decade seemed "characterized by an eager sense of penitence driven by a secret fear that it really may be too late to turn things around. Suddenly, after a ten-year rape of the earth, everyone is an environmentalist." Peter Berger once wrote that "[i]n a world full of Nazis one can be forgiven for being a Barthian." It seems that a parallel to Berger's comment might apply to the material studied here. Leaders of the Catholic rural life movement may not have enjoyed the success they sought, but their crusade did possess a rare integrity. David Danbom has claimed that while "romantic agrarianism" seems forever to be losing a battle with "rational agrarianism" over how best to understand American agriculture, the former nevertheless helps Americans understand how such matters are approached. For roughly thirty-five years, rural Catholics made some of the keenest observations concerning romantic agrarianism and thus contributed to the dynamism and richness of American Catholicism. Often their rural idealism appeared doomed in the face of the modern world. However, like the Redeemer born in a barn, their concerns eventually rose with renewed life.[26]

Notes

Introduction: Catholic Rural Life?

1. All Bible passages in this book come from the Douay-Rheims English Bible (New York: P. J. Kenedy & Sons, 1914).

2. Douglas Slawson, "Thirty Years of Street Preaching: Vincentian Motor Missions, 1934–1965," *Church History* 62 (1993): 69; Edgar Schmiedeler, O.S.B., "Motor Missions," *Homiletic and Pastoral Review* 38 (1938): 582–83; "Tour in Diocese Is under Direction of Father Ralph Egan," Photocopy of newspaper clipping, Diocesan Archives of Lincoln, Nebraska.

3. Walter Ong, S.J., *Frontiers of American Catholicism: Essays on Ideology and Culture* (New York: Macmillan, 1957), 8.

4. Peter A. Huff, *Allen Tate and the Catholic Revival: Trace of the Fugitive Gods* (New York: Paulist Press, 1996), 24.

5. Ibid., 64–70.

6. George J. Hildner, *One Hundred Years for God and Country: St. John's, the Church and the Community, 1839–1940* (Washington, Mo.: Washington Missourian, 1940), 125.

7. Philip Gleason, *Keeping the Faith: American Catholicism Past and Present* (Notre Dame, Ind.: University of Notre Dame Press, 1987), 140. Cf. Arnold Sparr, *To Promote, Defend, and Redeem: The Catholic Literary Revival and the Cultural Transformation of American Catholicism, 1920–1960* (New York: Greenwood, 1990).

8. Three of the many wonderful studies of urban Catholicism are Robert A. Orsi, *The Madonna of 115th Street: Faith and Community in Italian Harlem, 1880–1950* (New Haven, Conn.: Yale University Press, 1985); Paula M. Kane, *Separatism and Subculture: Boston Catholicism, 1900–1920* (Chapel Hill: University of North Carolina Press, 1995); and John T. McGreevy, *Parish Boundaries: The Catholic Encounter with Race* (Chicago: University of Chicago Press, 1997).

9. Gleason, *Keeping the Faith*, 213–15; Leslie Woodcock Tentler, "On the Margins: The State of American Catholic History," *American Quarterly* 45 (March 1993): 115–16.

10. Similar claims concerning assimilation into the American mainstream have been made about other Catholics during the twentieth century. See James Terence Fisher, *The Catholic Counterculture in America, 1933–1962* (Chapel Hill: University of North Carolina Press, 1989), 250; and Kane, *Separatism and Subculture*, 319–24. Robert P. Swierenga notes that mistaken assumptions about rural life have also characterized the field of rural history; see "Theoretical Perspectives on the New Rural History: From Environmentalism to Modernization," *Agricultural History* 56 (1982): 497–99. On the Catholic Church in Latin America, see Penny Lernoux, *Cry of the People: The Struggle*

for Human Rights in Latin America—The Catholic Church in Conflict with U.S. Policy, rev. ed. (New York: Penguin Books, 1991).

11. See Leslie Woodcock Tentler, "'A Model Rural Parish': Priests and People in the Michigan 'Thumb,' 1923–1928," *Catholic Historical Review* 78 (1992): 413;

12. James Davidson, *Courtesans and Fishcakes: The Consuming Passions of Classical Athens* (New York: St. Martin's Press, 1998), xxvi.

13. See William C. Placher, *Unapologetic Theology: A Christian Voice in a Pluralistic Conversation* (Louisville, Ky.: Westminster/John Knox, 1989), 19, 105–18, 168.

14. Thomas Jefferson, "Notes on the State of Virginia"; Jefferson to James Madison, 20 December 1787; Jefferson to Jean Baptiste Say, 1 February 1804, all in Thomas Jefferson, *Writings* (New York: Library of America, 1984), 301, 918, 1144; Jim Goad, *The Redneck Manifesto: How Hillbillies, Hicks, and White Trash Became America's Scapegoats* (New York: Simon & Schuster, Touchstone, 1997), 23. On the portrayal of rural America in popular culture, see J. W. Williamson, *Hillbillyland: What the Movies Did to the Mountains and What the Mountains Did to the Movies* (Chapel Hill: University of North Carolina Press, 1995).

15. José Lutzenberger and Melissa Halloway, "The Absurdity of Modern Agriculture: From Chemical Fertilizers and Agropoisons to Biotechnology," in *The Meat Business: Devouring a Hungry Planet,* ed. Geoff Tansey and Joyce D'Silva (New York: St. Martin's, 1999), 6 (quotation); Kevin Flynn and Gary Gerhardt, *The Silent Brotherhood: The Chilling Inside Story of America's Violent Anti-government Militia Movement* (New York: Signet, Penguin, 1995), 22; Edward W. Said, *Orientalism* (New York: Vintage, 1979) 3, 5–7, 11–15, 24–28; Williamson, *Hillbillyland,* 20.

16. Michel Foucault, *The Archeology of Knowledge,* trans. A. M. Sheridan Smith (New York: Pantheon, 1972), 17.

Chapter 1: Fertile Land and Fertile Souls

1. Edwin V. O'Hara, *The Church and the Country Community* (New York: Macmillan, 1927), 24. See R. Laurence Moore, *Religious Outsiders and the Making of Americans* (New York: Oxford University Press, 1986), 35–71, for a discussion of Catholic "strength" and "weakness" in American life.

2. Roger Joseph Scheckel, "The Origins of the National Catholic Rural Life Conference: A Historical and Theological Analysis" (M.A. thesis, Catholic University of America, 1984), 31, 49–50.

3. David S. Bovée, "The Church and the Land: The National Catholic Rural Life Conference and American Society, 1923–1985" (Ph.D. diss., University of Chicago, 1986), 119–21.

4. David Danbom, *The Resisted Revolution: Urban America and the Industrialization of Agriculture, 1900–1930* (Ames: Iowa State University Press, 1979), 23–50; Merwin Swanson, "The 'Country Life Movement' and the American Churches," *Church History* 45 (1977): 358–73; Swanson, "The American Country Life Movement, 1900–1940" (Ph.D. diss., University of Minnesota, 1972), 189–90.

5. Swanson, "The 'Country Life Movement' and the American Churches," 360; Danbom, *The Resisted Revolution,* 51–74; Deborah Fink, *Agrarian Women: Wives and Mothers in Rural Nebraska, 1880–1940* (Chapel Hill: University of North Carolina Press, 1992), 25–29, 159.

6. James H. Madison, "Reformers and the Rural Church, 1900–1950," *Journal of American History* 81 (1987): 649–50, 656; Roger Finke and Rodney Stark, *The Churching of America, 1776–1990: Winners and Losers in Our Religious Economy* (New Brunswick, N.J.: Rutgers University Press, 1992), 207, 208–9; Bradley J. Longfield, *The Presbyterian*

Controversy: Fundamentalists, Modernists, and Moderates (New York: Oxford University Press, 1994), 54–76, especially 54 and 58–64.

7. Danbom, *The Resisted Revolution,* 47, 49.

8. Ibid., 88–89. T. J. Jackson Lears, in *No Place of Grace: Antimodernism and the Transformation of American Culture, 1889–1920* (New York: Pantheon, 1981), 107–17, discusses the "worship of force" in the 1890s and the attempts to use it in various projects of social control (often racist in orientation).

9. Finke and Stark, *The Churching of America,* 207, 212–16; Swanson, "The American Country Life Movement," 351, 371.

10. Edwin O'Hara, quoted in Raymond Witte, "The Rural Problem in Its Bearing on Catholic Education," quoted in Raymond Witte, S.M., *Twenty-five Years of Crusading: A History of the National Catholic Rural Life Conference* (Des Moines: NCRLC, 1948), 54.

11. Bovée, "The Church and the Land," 83–103, 105; Timothy M. Dolan, *Some Seed Fell on Good Ground: The Life of Edwin V. O'Hara* (Washington, D.C.: Catholic University of America Press, 1992), 64–65, 81–84, 85.

12. Edwin V. O'Hara to J. P. Howard, printed in *St. Isidore's Plow* 1 (October 1922): 1; Bernard M. Baruch, "Solution to Rural Credits," *St. Isidore's Plow* 1 (March 1923): 1; Carl Phillips, "Catechism Summer Schools," *St. Isidore's Plow* 1 (May 1923): 2. Cf. William Monahan, "Farm Demonstration as a Method of Extension Teaching," *St. Isidore's Plow* 1 (January 1923): 1.

13. James O'Toole, *Militant and Triumphant: William Henry Cardinal O'Connell and the Catholic Church in Boston, 1859–1944* (Notre Dame, Ind.: University of Notre Dame Press, 1992), 132, 134, 199–200; Witte, *Twenty-five Years of Crusading,* 62, 63; Bovée, "The Church and the Land," 118, 126–28; "Two Rural Life Conferences," *St. Isidore's Plow* 2 (October 1923): 2; Edwin V. O'Hara, "The Clergy and Rural Life," *St. Isidore's Plow* 2 (October 1923): 3; O'Hara, "The Church and Rural Life," *St. Isidore's Plow* 1 (October 1922): 1.

14. Swanson, "The American Country Life Movement," 252–56, 273–76; Witte, *Twenty-five Years of Crusading,* 61 n. 8.

15. Swanson, "The American Country Life Movement," 372–73. A notable Protestant voice of ecumenism within the ACLA was Arthur Holt, a Congregationalist pastor and ethics professor at Chicago's Christian Theological Seminary. Holt published numerous articles in *The Christian Century.* See Jacob H. Dorn, "The Rural Ideal and Agrarian Realities: Arthur E. Holt and the Vision of a Decentralized America in the Interwar Years," *Church History* 52 (1983): 53–55.

16. "Missionary Work in Rural Parishes," *Catholic Rural Life* 3 (May 1925): 5.

17. Francis Clement Kelley, *The Story of Extension* (Chicago: Extension Press, 1922), 5, 9, 18–49; James P. Gaffey, *Francis Clement Kelley and the American Catholic Dream* (Bensenville, Ill.: Heritage Foundation, 1980), 1:75, 77, 79–80.

18. Kelley, *The Story of Extension,* 117, 143; Gaffey, *Francis Clement Kelley,* 1:83–97. The Lapeer parish church was finally completed in 1901. When Kelley transferred to the Chicago archdiocese in 1906 to direct the Extension Society, a debt of seventy-three hundred dollars remained.

19. Kelley, *The Story of Extension,* 113–14. Pius X lifted the missionary status of the United States in the papal document *Sapienti Consilio.* Historian James Hitchcock writes that many of the twentieth-century Catholic intellectuals were in fact converts, and "the remarkable fact is that the distinguished converts . . . were attracted to the Church, not in spite of the condemnation [by Pius X], but almost, in some cases, because of it." Hitchcock, "Postmortem on a Rebirth: The Catholic Intellectual Renaissance," *American Scholar* 49 (spring 1980): 212.

20. Kelley, quoted in Witte, *Twenty-five Years of Crusading*, 67; Bovée, "The Church and the Land," 128–30. The correspondence between O'Hara and the Extension Society concerning the churches in southwestern Missouri is in the Loyola University of Chicago Archives, Catholic Church Extension Society collection, series D/D3D, box 1, folder 1-3, 1-5. See also Timothy Dolan, *Some Seed Fell on Good Ground*, 220–22. Leslie Woodcock Tentler covers Carey's success in Lapeer in "'A Model Rural Parish,'" passim.

21. Witte, *Twenty-five Years of Crusading*, 71.

22. Christopher J. Kauffman, *Mission to Rural America: The Story of William Howard Bishop, Founder of Glenmary* (New York: Paulist Press, 1991), 38–39, 67–68; Victor Day, "The Correspondence Course in Christian Doctrine," *St. Isidore's Plow* 2 (January 1924): 2.

23. Philip Gleason, *The Conservative Reformers: German-American Catholics and the Social Order* (Notre Dame, Ind.: University of Notre Dame Press, 1968), 140, 223.

24. Witte, *Twenty-five Years of Crusading*, 62, 78–79; Matthew Hoehn, O.S.B., *Catholic Authors: Contemporary Biographical Sketches, 1930–1947* (Newark, N.J.: St. Mary's Abbey, 1948), 674–75. Cf. Edgar Schmiedeler's *A Better Rural Life* (New York: Wagner, 1938). On the Matt family publishing tradition and *Der Wanderer*, see Michael W. Cuneo, *The Smoke of Satan: Conservative and Traditionalist Dissent in Contemporary American Catholicism* (New York: Oxford University Press, 1997), 49–58.

25. Patrick Allitt, *Catholic Converts: British and American Intellectuals Turn to Rome* (Ithaca, N.Y.: Cornell University Press, 1997), 152; Fisher, *Catholic Counterculture*, 25–43.

26. "N.Y. Milk Strikers Ask for Greater Share of Profits," *The Catholic Worker* 1 (September 1933): 1, 4; Mel Piehl, *Breaking Bread: The Catholic Worker and the Origin of Catholic Radicalism in America* (Philadelphia: Temple University Press, 1982), 57–143. See also Peter Maurin, *The Green Revolution: Essays on Catholic Radicalism, 1949* (Chicago: Francis of Assisi House, 1976); Anthony Novitsky, "The Ideological Development of Peter Maurin's Green Revolution" (Ph.D. diss., State University of New York at Buffalo, 1977).

27. Alden Brown, *The Grail Movement and American Catholicism, 1940–1975* (Notre Dame, Ind.: University of Notre Dame Press, 1989); Fisher, *Catholic Counterculture*, 94–95. Dennis Michael Robb, "Specialized Catholic Action in the United States, 1936–1949: Ideology, Leadership, and Organization" (Ph.D. diss., University of Minnesota, 1973); Grailville staff, *Restore the Sunday: The Christian Concept of the Sunday and Practical Suggestions for the Sanctification of the Sunday in Lay Life* (Loveland, Ohio: Grailville, 1949); Craig R. Prentiss, "Taming Leviathan: The American Catholic Church and Economics, 1940–1960" (Ph.D. diss., University of Chicago, 1997), 141–58. The Grail had attempted to inaugurate its programs in Chicago before moving to Loveland.

28. The map appears in *Land and Home* 9 (June 1946): 31. An insert on page 5 of *Catholic Rural Life* 3 (November 1925) ranks the states according to number of subscriptions to the publication. It listed in descending order Iowa ("with four hundred names"), Michigan, Missouri, Illinois, Minnesota, "and thirty-five states, Canada, and South America." On NCRLC attendance, see Bovée, "The Church and the Land," 271, 323.

29. Edwin O'Hara, quoted in Raymond Witte, "The Rural Problem," quoted in Witte, *Twenty-five Years of Crusading*, 49. Witte (pp. 3–9) has numerous charts depicting the low birthrates of heavily Catholic states, such as Massachusetts and Rhode Island, compared to the higher rates of "weak" Catholic states, such as North and South Carolina. He includes, but does not comment on, the high birthrates of "strong" Catholic states with large rural Catholic populations, such as Wisconsin and Louisiana.

30. Rudolf B. Schuler, "Cooperation in the St. Louis Archdiocese," *Catholic Rural Life Bulletin* 4 (August 1941): 70. Apparently Schuler was referring to support much like that offered for "pagan babies." *Rural Parish Workers of Christ the King Newsletter* 1

(November 1946). Cf. John La Farge, S.J., "Catholic Agrarians Swing into Action," *America* 56 (14 November 1936): 129–30; and La Farge, "Unity of Mankind through Creation and Redemption, Basis of Interracial Justice," *The Queen's Work*, December 1934, 1, 7, 10.

31. Christian H. Winkelmann, "The City Church Helps the Country Church," in *Rural Catholic Action: Diocesan Director's Series* (Washington, D.C.: National Catholic Welfare Conference Rural Life Bureau, 1936), 53–56.

32. O'Hara, "The Clergy and Rural Life"; Thomas Carey, "Presidential Address," *Catholic Rural Life* 3 (November 1925): 3.

33. Luigi Ligutti, "Cities Kill," *Commonweal* 32 (2 August 1940): 301.

34. W. Howard Bishop, "Presidential Address," in National Catholic Rural Life Conference, *Proceedings of the Eleventh Annual Convention, 1933* (Washington, D.C.: National Catholic Welfare Conference, Rural Life Bureau, n.d.), 13.

35. Charles Morrow Wilson, "American Peasants," *Commonweal* 20 (8 December 1933): 147.

36. Willis D. Nutting, "The Catholic College and the Land," *Catholic Rural Life Bulletin* 1 (November 1938): 22.

37. David Shi, *The Simple Life: Plain Living and High Thinking in American Culture* (New York: Oxford University Press, 1985), 215–23; Warren I. Susman, *Culture as History: The Transformation of American Society in the Twentieth Century* (New York: Pantheon, 1984), xxv; Witte, *Twenty-five Years of Crusading*, 129. Fisher, *Catholic Counterculture*, 106, describes a similar outlook among the editors of *Integrity* magazine.

38. Nutting, "The Catholic College and the Land," 22–23; Joe Fratelli to John and Sally, n.d., Marquette University Archives (MUA), Milwaukee, Wisconsin, Dorothy Day–Catholic Worker movement collection (DD-CW), W-4.2, box 1; Eva Smith, "Vision on the Farm," *Commonweal* 34 (27 June 1941): 228.

39. Ignatius Esser, O.S.B., "Significant Chapters in Benedictine History," *Catholic Rural Life Bulletin* 1 (November 1938): 21.

40. Timothy Dolan, *Some Seed Fell on Good Ground*, 154–55; Steven Avella, "Sanctity in the Era of Catholic Action: The Case of Pius X," *U.S. Catholic Historian* 15 (1997): 58, 68–74.

41. Paul H. Hallett, "Giuseppe Sarto's Boyhood," *Land and Home* 7 (1944): 50; Steven Avella, "Sanctity in the Era of Catholic Action: The Case of Pius X," *U.S. Catholic Historian* 15 (1997): 58, 68–74.

42. John La Farge, S.J., "Agriculture and Vocation," *Christian Rural Fellowship Bulletin* 34 (September 1938): 5. Cf. William Kerrigan, "The Trappists and the Prairie," *Land and Home* 7 (September 1944): 64–65. Pius's rural origins have been stressed by Protestant church historians as well: "[O]f humble origin . . . Pius X was a faithful parish priest whose parish had become worldwide." Williston Walker et al., *A History of the Christian Church*, 4th ed. (New York: Charles Scribner's Sons, 1985), 673.

43. Aldo Leopold, *A Sand County Almanac* (London: Oxford University Press, 1949), viii; Robert L. Dorman, *The Revolt of the Provinces: The Regionalist Movement in America, 1920–1945* (Chapel Hill: University of North Carolina Press, 1993), 315–17, 319.

44. Wehrle quoted in Dolan, *Some Seed Fell on Good Ground*, 58.

45. J. Gladden Hutton, "The Worn-out Farm," *Catholic Rural Life Bulletin* 2 (August 1939): 2.

46. John La Farge, S.J., "The Land: The Hope of the Future," in National Catholic Rural Life Conference, *Proceedings of the Eleventh Convention*, 71.

47. "Notes and Comments: Bishop Winkelmann," *Catholic Rural Life Bulletin* 3 (February 1940): 15.

48. Leo R. Ward, C.S.C., "The Land and Human Values," *Catholic Rural Life Bulletin* 1 (August 1938): 3.

49. Urban Baer, *Farmers of Tomorrow* (Sparta, Wis.: Monroe Publishing Company, 1939), 37–38.

50. Luigi M. Ligutti, "What's Wrong with Farmers?" *America* 69 (24 April 1943): 66; C. E. Wolf, "I Left College to Become a Farmer," *Catholic Rural Life Bulletin* 4 (February 1941): 1.

51. Leopold, *A Sand County Almanac*, 119.

52. Ibid., viii, 204.

53. Edward H. Faulkner, *Plowman's Folly* (Norman: University of Oklahoma Press, 1943; reprint, Covelo, Calif.: Island Press, 1987), 100, 128, 35, 36; Louis Bromfield, *Pleasant Valley* (New York: Harper & Brothers Publishers, 1945), 165.

54. Mary L. Schneider, "Visions of Land and Farmer: American Civil Religion and the National Catholic Rural Life Conference," in *An American Church: Essays on the Americanization of the Catholic Church*, ed. David J. Alvarez (Moraga, Calif.: St. Mary's College of California, 1979), 106; Huff, *Allen Tate and the Catholic Revival*, 50–71; Dorman, *The Revolt of the Provinces*, 29–53, 105–42.

55. Huff, *Allen Tate and the Catholic Revival*, 11–12; Gerald McCool, S.J., *Nineteenth-Century Scholasticism: The Quest for a Unitary Method*, rev. ed. (New York: Fordham University Press, 1989), 1, 14–15, 135–44, 226–40.

56. Jay P. Dolan, *The American Catholic Experience: A History from Colonial Times to the Present*, rev. ed. (Notre Dame, Ind.: University of Notre Dame Press, 1992), 352; Hitchcock, "Postmortem on a Rebirth," 217–19; James J. Walsh, *The Thirteenth, the Greatest of Centuries* (New York: Catholic Summer School Press, 1907); William M. Halsey, *The Survival of American Innocence: American Catholicism in an Era of Disillusionment, 1920–1940* (Notre Dame, Ind.: University of Notre Dame Press, 1980).

57. Michael J. Schuck, *That They Be One: The Social Teaching of the Papal Encyclicals, 1740–1989* (Washington, D.C.: Georgetown University Press, 1991), 42–93. Claiming that the Catholic rural life movement stood as one of the best examples of the Catholic "organic unity" sought before Vatican II, Craig Prentiss points to the Catholic agrarians' constant referrals to *Rerum Novarum* and *Quadragesimo Anno*. Prentiss, "Taming Leviathan," 81, 95–98.

58. Aloysius J. Muench, "Religion and Agrarianism," *Catholic Mind* 38 (8 November 1940): 438; Luigi M. Ligutti, "The Popes and Agriculture: A Brief Survey of Papal Documents Relating to the Soil and the Principles of Rural Life," *Commonweal* 31 (1 March 1940): 397–99; "Notes and Comments: The Popes and Agriculture," *Catholic Rural Life Bulletin* 4 (May 1941): 44; "Notes and Comments: The Papacy Forever!" *Catholic Rural Life Bulletin* 2 (May 1939): 14.

59. Jay P. Corrin, *G. K. Chesterton and Hilaire Belloc: The Battle against Modernity* (Athens: Ohio University Press, 1981), 1–28; Huff, *Allen Tate and the Catholic Revival*, 13–14; Prentiss, "Taming Leviathan," 82–87; Allitt, *Catholic Converts*, 163–65, 172–77, 181–83.

60. Bovée, "The Church and the Land," 198–200. Witte, *Twenty-five Years of Crusading*, 89, made the same point: the devastation of the Depression provided the conference with an unprecedented opportunity. See also Edward S. Shapiro, "The Catholic Rural Life Movement and the New Deal Farm Program," *American Benedictine Review* 28 (1977): 307–32; and Shapiro, "Catholic Agrarian Thought and the New Deal," *Catholic Historical Review* 65 (1979): 583–99. Cf. Fisher, *Catholic Counterculture*, 73–76. Catholic agrarians later grew disenchanted with the New Deal—as did other Catholics such as Dorothy Day and the radio priest Charles Coughlin—over its em-

brace of government bureacracy and its neglect of the poor. On the opposition to the New Deal prompted by Coughlin, see chapter 3.

61. Shapiro, "Catholic Agrarian Thought and the New Deal"; Shapiro, "The Catholic Rural Life Movement and the New Deal Farm Program," 318–23; National Catholic Rural Life Conference, Edgar Schmiedeler, O.S.B., "Beyond the NRA," *Commonweal* 19 (22 September 1933): 485–87;

62. Edgar Schmiedeler, O.S.B., *Rural Catholic Action* (Huntington, Ind.: National Council of Catholic Men; Our Sunday Visitor, 1932), 19;

63. *Manifesto on Rural Life* (Milwaukee, Wis.: Bruce, 1939), 13–17, 63–70, 132. On the NCRLC's sustained discussion of farm prices along Catholic agrarian lines, see Prentiss, "Taming Leviathan," 111–14.

64. Nutting, "The Catholic College and the Land," 3.

65. S[ebastian] G. Messmer, "Some Moral Aspects of Country Life," *St. Isidore's Plow* 1 (March 1923): 2.

66. Luigi Ligutti and John C. Rawe, S.J., *Rural Roads to Security: America's Third Struggle for Freedom* (Milwaukee, Wis.: Bruce, 1940). Peter McDonough includes many of the points made here in an explication of the expression in *Rural Roads to Security* of the Jesuits' search for a new social order in midcentury American life. McDonough, *Men Astutely Trained: A History of the Jesuits in the American Century* (New York: Free Press, 1992), 89–95.

67. Shi, *The Simple Life*, 228–30, 241–45. Edward Skillin Jr. noted in a visit to the School of Living that "the majority of [the students were] Quakers or Catholics." Skillin, "Homework that Pays," *Commonweal* 34 (5 September 1941): 465.

68. William H. Issel, "Ralph Borsodi and the Agrarian Response to Modern America," *Agricultural History* 41 (April 1967): 157–59. Ralph Borsodi, *Flight from the City* (New York: Harper and brothers, 1933); *This Ugly Civilization* (New York: Simon, 1929).

69. Mildred Jensen, "Back to the Land," *The Catholic Woman's World* 3 (January 1941): 43, 48–49; "Notes and Comments: Mr. and Mrs. R. B.," *Catholic Rural Life Bulletin* 4 (May 1941): 45.

70. Huff, *Allen Tate and the Catholic Revival*, 69. Agar's and Borsodi's books received favorable reviews in prominent Catholic publications such as *America, Commonweal,* and *The Catholic Worker.* The first three appendixes of Ligutti and Rawe's *Rural Roads to Security* (pp. 313–31) dealt with Borsodi and the School of Living. All were reprints from previous publications or pamphlets produced by the School of Living. On the Nearings, see Shi, *The Simple Life*, 255–56, 230; and Rebecca Kneale Gould, "Getting (Not Too) Close to Nature: Modern Homesteading as Lived Religion in America," in *Lived Religion in America: Toward a History of Practice,* ed. David D. Hall, 217–42 (Princeton, N.J.: Princeton University Press, 1997).

71. Joseph Kelly, "What Does Youth Want?" *Catholic Rural Life Bulletin* 4 (February 1941): 12.

72. Mildred Daly, "Youth Seeks Quality in Choosing Spouse," *Catholic Rural Life Bulletin* 4 (February 1941): 13.

73. Bovée, "The Church and the Land," 211; Kauffman, *Mission to Rural America,* 87–88, 111–14; John C. Rawe, S.J., "Homesteading Solves the Problem of Farm Decline," *America* 60 (3 December 1938): 200–201; Wilson, "American Peasants," 147–49. The column "Farming Commune," usually authored by Eva Smith, appeared often in *The Catholic Worker* after 1936.

74. J[oseph] M. Campbell, "Credit Unions," in National Catholic Rural Life Conference, *Proceedings of the Eleventh Annual Convention,* 28; Bovée, "The Church and the Land," 296–98.

75. Cyprian Davis, O.S.B., *The History of Black Catholics in the United States* (New York: Crossroad, 1990), 226–27; "Negro Agricultural School," *The Catholic Worker* 15 (September 1948): 1, 4; Bovée, "The Church and the Land," 99; McGreevy, *Parish Boundaries,* 39, 45; National Catholic Rural Life Conference, *Manifesto on Rural Life,* 21.

76. Gilbert J. Garraghan, *The Jesuits of the Middle United States* (New York: America Press, 1938), 3:448–50; McDonough, *Men Astutely Trained,* 75; Huff, *Allen Tate and the Catholic Revival,* 60; "News from the Field," *Jesuit Educational Quarterly* 2 (March 1940): 207; "News from the Field," *Jesuit Educational Quarterly* 3 (June 1940): 52–53; Virgil Michel, O.S.B., "Christian Education for Rural Living," *Catholic Rural Life Bulletin* 1 (August 1938): 19; "The Rural Pastor's Page: Priests and Seminarians," *Land and Home* 7 (June 1944): 46. "Agricultural College" folder, MUA, NCRLC, series 1/1, box 1; See also Pope Pius XII, "Address to the International Catholic Congress on Rural Problems, July 2, 1951," reprinted as "Problems of Rural Life," *The Catholic Mind* 49 (October 1951): 708–11.

77. Archbishop [Samuel] Stritch, "A Christian Day: A Sermon Preached at the Opening Mass of the 20th Annual Convention of the NCRLC, October 4, 1942, Peoria, Illinois" (Des Moines: NCRLC, n.d.), MUA, series 8/1, box 4, folder 21, pp. 10–11; William Gauchat, "Cult, Culture, and Cultivation," *Catholic Rural Life Bulletin* 4 (August 1941): 66.

78. Wolf, "I Left College to Become a Farmer," 4 (emphasis in the original); C. M. O'Brien, "Economic and Sociological Aspects of the Columbia Basin Project," *Catholic Rural Life Bulletin* 2 (November 1939): 29; Peter Maurin, "Idle Hands and Idle Lands," *The Catholic Worker* 3 (February 1936): 1; See also Gauchat, "Cult, Culture, and Cultivation," 66.

79. Eugene S. Geissler, "Shaw, Chesterton, and the Country Boy," *Catholic Rural Life Bulletin* 3 (November 1940): 24, 25 (emphasis in the original); Donald Hayne, "Westphalia: Pattern and Promise," *Catholic Rural Life Bulletin* 2 (August 1939): 28.

80. Huff, *Allen Tate and the Catholic Revival,* 34–56; Paul B. Marx, O.S.B., *Virgil Michel and the Liturgical Movement* (Collegeville, Minn.: St. John's Abbey–Liturgical Press, 1957), 255; "Notes and Comments: Songs and Singing," *Catholic Rural Life Bulletin* 2 (May 1939): 15.

81. Ralph Parlette, "The Cities Do Not Make Their Own Steam," *Catholic Rural Life* 3 (November 1925): 6; Archbishop John Glennon, quoted in *St. Isidore's Plow* 2 (December 1923): 2; Virgil Michel, O.S.B., "City or Farm?" *Orate Fratres* 12 (1938): 367. "Eden was a farm" appears on a flyer, circa 1930, from the University of Georgia School of Agriculture, possession of author.

82. Gauchat, "Cult, Culture, and Cultivation," 64; Edwin O'Hara, "The Clergy and Rural Life," 3; Eugene S. Geissler, "Family Acres," part 1, *New Heaven/New Earth,* 1984, 7. See also Julian Pleasants, "Apologetics and Catholic Action," *The Notre Dame Scholastic,* 1940, 8.

83. Emerson Hynes, "Consider the Person," *Catholic Rural Life Bulletin* 1 (May 1939): 7.

84. Stritch, "A Christian Day," 5; Corrin, *G. K. Chesterton and Hilaire Belloc,* 93; Novitsky, "The Ideological Development of Peter Maurin's Green Revolution," 85.

85. Thomas E. Howard, *Agricultural Handbook for Rural Pastors and Laymen: Religious, Economic, Social, and Cultural Implications of Rural Life* (Paterson, N.J.: St. Anthony's Guild, 1946), 31. Raymond W. Miller describes Howard's Protestant and Masonic heritage (as well as his own) and its interaction with Ligutti in *Monsignor Ligutti: The Pope's County Agent* (Washington, D.C.: University Press of America, 1981), 20–22.

86. L[ouis] G. Miller, C.Ss.R, "Some Agrarian Beginnings," *Catholic Rural Life Bulletin* 3 (November 1940): 23.

87. National Catholic Rural Life Conference, *Manifesto on Rural Life,* 43–51, 60–62, 66–70; John Peschges, quoted in Catholic Cooperative Committee, *Catholic Churchmen and Cooperatives* (Huntington, Ind.: Our Sunday Visitor, 1944), 15; Maurin, *The Green Revolution,* 27; Samson Liph, "Jewish Farm Settlement," *Land and Home* 7 (September 1944): 64; Gabriel Davidson, *Our Jewish Farmers and the Story of the Jewish Agricultural Society* (New York: L. B. Fischer, 1943), 122; Mark A. Dawber, *Rebuilding Rural America* (New York: Friendship Press, 1937), 48–72. Dawber, who held a chair in rural ministry at Boston University's School of Theology from 1919 to 1925, included in his book supplements on rural ministry from the Northern Baptist Convention's Board of Education.

88. M. M. Coady, "Cooperation in Nova Scotia," in National Catholic Rural Life Conference, *Proceedings of the Twelfth Convention, 1934* (Washington, D.C.: National Catholic Welfare Conference, Rural Life Bureau, n.d.), 175. See also Coady, *Masters of Their Own Destiny: The Story of the Antigonish Movement of Adult Education through Economic Cooperation* (New York: Harper, 1939).

89. Francis J. McGoey, "The Canadian Landward Movement," in *Rural Catholic Action,* Diocesan Director's Series No. 1 (Washington, D.C.: National Catholic Welfare Conference, Rural Life Bureau, 1936), 37. On Quebec, see "Superior School of Agriculture, Ste. Anne-de-la-Pocatière, Quebec," *Commonweal* 30 (15 September 1939): 484; and C. E. Couture, "Colonization in Quebec," *Land and Home* 9 (June 1946): 48–49. See also Gregory Baum, *Catholics and Canadian Socialism: Political Thought in the Thirties and Forties* (New York: Paulist Press, 1980), ch. 7, passim; and William Westfall, "Voices from the Attic: The Canadian Border and the Writing of American Religious History," in *Retelling U.S. Religious History,* ed. Thomas A. Tweed (Berkeley: University of California Press, 1996), 194–95.

90. Friedrich Nietzsche, *Thus Spoke Zarathustra,* trans. R. J. Hollingdale (New York: Penguin Books, 1969), 91; John T. McNicholas, "Experiments in Solving Rural Catholic Problems," *St. Isidore's Plow* 2 (January 1924): 4. The view of women as mothers, spiritually or physically, was not restricted to rural areas; see Orsi, *The Madonna of 115th Street,* 129–49, for an urban Catholic perspective. Cf. Prentiss, "Taming Leviathan," 147–54.

91. Ligutti and Rawe, *Rural Roads to Security,* 64; Abigail Q. McCarthy, *Private Faces, Public Places* (Garden City, N.Y.: Doubleday, 1972), 81. Cf. Bovée, "The Church and the Land," 373. John L. Thomas, S.J., *The Catholic Viewpoint on Marriage and the Family* (New York: Hanover House, 1958), 116. In the 1960s, when the "population myth" became a powerful argument for artificial birth control, the NCRLC debunked this 'Myth' largely on the grounds that the planet could hold still more people.

92. Alice Widmer and LaDonna Hermann, *Bits of History* (n.p., 1992).

93. *Rural Parish Workers of Christ the King Newsletter* 2 (November 1947); 1 (November 1946); LaDonna Hermann, *Memories of "Isabelle": A 1929 Model A Ford Who Loved Life* (privately published, 1991).

94. "A Year with the Rural Parish Workers," *Review for Religious* 12 (September 1953): 242–48; Natalie Villmer, *History of the Old Mines Area, Washington County, Missouri* (Old Mines, Mo.: Old Mines Area Historical Society, 1973), 9; *Rural Parish Workers of Christ the King Newsletter* 6 (1951).

95. O'Hara, quoted in Witte, *Twenty-five Years of Crusading,* 48; Widmer and Hermann, *Bits of History.*

96. On the use of analogy in theology, see David Tracy, *The Analogical Imagination: Christian Theology and the Culture of Pluralism* (New York: Crossroad, 1981), 404–38.

97. Esser, "Significant Chapters in Benedictine History," 21. Cf. Rembert Sorg, O.S.B., *Towards a Benedictine Theology of Manual Labor* (Lisle, Ill.: Benedictine Orient,

1951), especially 95–123. On Jefferson and Aquinas, see Paul Conkin, *Tomorrow a New World: The New Deal Community Program* (Ithaca, N.Y.: Cornell University Press for the American Historical Association, 1959), 24.

98. Alphonse J. Matt, "The Family and Social Security," *Catholic Rural Life Bulletin* 2 (May 1939): 8; Julian Pleasants, quoted in Donald Thorman, "Experiment in Christian Living," *Voice of St. Jude,* November 1960, 20; Pleasants, letter to the author, 25 January 1998.

99. Nutting, "The Catholic College and the Land," 2; Baer, *Farmers of Tomorrow,* 39.

100. Michel, "Christian Education for Rural Living," 20.

101. John Thomas and James McShane, "Farmers Must Reform Methods of Farming," *Catholic Rural Life Bulletin* 4 (November 1941): 101; Bovée, "The Church and the Land," 259. Cf. John C. Rawe, S.J., "Biological Technology on the Land," *Catholic Rural Life Bulletin* 2 (August 1939): 1–3, 20–22; Rawe, "What, Where, and Why of Bio-Dynamics," *Land and Home* 6 (September 1943): 67–68.

102. Guenther Wachsmuth, *The Life and Work of Rudolf Steiner from the Turn of the Century to His Death,* 2d ed., trans. Olin D. Wannamaker and Reginald E. Raab (Blauvelt, N.Y.: Garber Communications, 1955), 8–19, 70–71, 158–59, 547; Robert S. Ellwood and Harry B. Partin, *Religious and Spiritual Groups in Modern America,* 2d ed. (Englewood Cliffs, N.J.: Prentice Hall, 1988), 87–89; Willy Schilthuis, *Biodynamic Agriculture,* trans. Tony Langham and Plim Peters (Hudson, N.Y.: Anthroposophic Press, 1994), 39–41.

103. Wachsmuth, *The Life and Work of Rudolf Steiner,* 418–22, 468–70, 548; Schilthuis, *Biodynamic Agriculture,* 24–34.

104. Schilthuis, *Biodynamic Agriculture,* 32, 79–83, 88–89.

105. Louise Owen, "Kill . . . and Cure," *Land and Home* 6 (June 1943): 52.

106. Jensen, "Back to the Land," 48.

107. "Cracked Corn: Part-Time Farming Works," *Land and Home* 8 (March 1945): 20.

108. Ibid., 20.

109. MUA, NCRLC, series 7/1, box 13. The same image and phrase of "Work in the City, Live in the country" served as the front cover for Reverend Patrick Quinlan's *Standing on Both Feet: The Rural Homestead, a Necessity for an Era of Reconstruction* (Des Moines: National Catholic Rural Life Conference, n.d.), copy in MUA, NCRLC, series 5/1, box 8.

110. *The Long Loneliness: The Autobiography of Dorothy Day,* rev. ed. (New York: Harper & Row, 1981), 285; Edward Skillin Jr., "Armchair Husbandry," *Commonweal* 35 (27 March 1942): 554.

111. Edgar Schmiedeler, O.S.B., "Why Rural Life?" in National Catholic Rural Life Conference, *Proceedings of the Eleventh Annual Convention,* 7.

112. Nutting, "The Catholic College and the Land," 3; Ward, "The Land and Human Values," 4.

113. Corrin, *G. K. Chesterton and Hilaire Belloc,* 98; Ward, "The Land and Human Values," 2, 3.

114. Edward Skillin Jr., "Granger Homesteads," *Commonweal* 32 (24 May 1940): 94; Edward S. Shapiro, "Decentralist Intellectuals and the New Deal," *Journal of American History* 58 (March 1972): 941; Issel, "Ralph Borsodi," 164–65.

115. Walter C. Lowdermilk, "'Lebensraum'—Agrarianism vs. War," *Catholic Rural Life Bulletin* 3 (November 1940): 21.

116. Thomas and McShane, "Farmers Must Reform Methods of Farming," 102; John C. Rawe, S.J., "The Home on the Land," *The Catholic Rural Life Bulletin* 2 (February 1939): 25.

117. "Leaders Meet at Kansas Monastery," *Landward* 5 (Spring 1937): 11.

118. Bovée, "The Church and the Land," 288–95. See also Jeffrey M. Burns, *American Catholics and the Family Crisis, 1930–1962: The Ideological and Organizational Response* (New York: Garland Press, 1988).

119. James Hudnut-Beumler, *Looking for God in the Suburbs: The Religion of the American Dream and Its Critics, 1945–1965* (New Brunswick, N.J.: Rutgers University Press, 1994), 18–21; Patrick W. Carey, *The Roman Catholics*, Denominations in America, no. 6 (Westport, Conn.: Greenwood Press, 1993), 90–91, 94; James Hennesey, S.J., *American Catholics: A History of the Roman Catholic Community in the United States* (New York: Oxford University Press, 1981), 280.

120. Timothy Dolan, *Some Seed Fell on Good Ground*, 104; Vincent A. Yzermans, *The People I Love: A Biography of Luigi G. Ligutti* (Collegeville, Minn.: Liturgical Press, 1976), 20, 58. "Ora et labora" (prayer and work) is a motto used by religious orders (particularly Benedictine ones) to reflect the interrelationship of the spiritual and the physical realms. Paul Marx, *Virgil Michel and the Liturgical Movement*, 173 n. 76, quotes a 1930 letter from O'Hara to Michel concerning the Liturgical Movement in O'Hara's class on "parish sociology." Bovée, "The Church and the Land," 328, connects the NCRLC's interest in the Liturgical Movement with Vatican II's new liturgical sensibilities.

121. Yzermans, *The People I Love*, 4–10, 22, 33–39, 51, 84; Witte, *Twenty-five Years of Crusading*, 116. Ligutti died on 28 December 1983 in Rome; he was buried in Granger, Iowa. "'Apostle of Rural Life' Dies at 88," *National Catholic Reporter* 20 (13 January 1984): 25.

122. Miller, *Monsignor Ligutti*, 39, 79–82, 99–106; Witte, *Twenty-five Years of Crusading*, 128–29; Yzermans, *The People I Love*, 108–10. An example of CROP's organization in Illinois is described in Susannah Crowe to Rev. H. J. Miller, 11 September 1948; and Leo Kroll to Luigi Ligutti, 14 September 1948, both in MUA, Luigi G. Ligutti collection (LGL), box D-1. Ligutti organized six international conferences on rural life: Rome (1951 and 1962), Manizales, Colombia (1953), Panama City (1954), Santiago (1957), and Caracas (1961).

123. Miller, *Monsignor Ligutti*, 201; Bovée, "The Church and the Land," 304–6, 309.

124. Miller, *Monsignor Ligutti*, 95–98; Yzermans, *The People I Love*, 102, 158–60; Timothy Dolan, *Some Seed Fell on Good Ground*, 206–16; W. Stanley Rycroft to Ligutti, 7 February 1953, MUA, LGL, box D-1. Ligutti was apparently aware that the Central Intelligence Agency funded agrarian-reform conferences in Central America. Lernoux, *Cry of the People*, 291–93.

125. Luigi Ligutti, "The Pope of Peace," *Catholic Rural Life* 7 (October 1958): 14; Ligutti, "No Room for Others," *Land and Home* 8 (June 1945): 23; Bovée, "The Church and the Land," 379. On Dooley, see James T. Fisher, *Dr. America: The Lives of Thomas A. Dooley, 1927–1961* (Amherst: University of Massachusetts Press, 1997). In a 1954 issue of *St. Isidore's Plow* (which reappeared after the demise of *The Christian Farmer*), Ligutti praised the 1939 victory parade by Franco's forces in the Spanish Civil War, concluding that "the Spanish nation, which seems rather small to Americans, is the only nation which has defeated the armed forces of communism, and driven them back." Original in MUA, NCRLC, series 6, box 1.

126. Yzermans, *The People I Love*, 161.

127. Yzermans, *The People I Love*, 80–81, 139–44, describes these aspects of Ligutti's troubles. Ligutti also maintained relations with the Scalabrini Fathers, a religious order concerned with care for Italian immigrants. Italian American concerns figured prominently, along with plans for the upcoming NCRLC convention, in a letter from Ligutti to Monsignor E. E. Swanstrom, 8 August 1951, MUA, LGL, box C-2.

128. On the decline of European ethnic identity in America during the 1950s, see Gleason, *Keeping the Faith,* 35–81.

129. An example of what the NCLRC considered a successful diocesan rural life program appears in Rudolf B. Schuler's "The St. Louis Archdiocesan Program," *Rural Catholic Action: Diocesan Director's Series* (Washington, D.C.: National Catholic Welfare Conference Rural Life Bureau, 1936), 5–12. Bovée, "The Church and the Land," 318, 320–21.

130. Yzermans, *The People I Love,* 269–70.

131. Bovée, "The Church and the Land," 276–77, 313–15, 401. During the mid-1930s, Bishop and Schmiedeler refused to petition NCRLC members for direct funds; Bishop paid for the production of *Landward* out of his own expense allowance. Kauffman, *Mission to Rural America,* 86–87.

132. National Catholic Rural Life Conference, *1957: Serving Rural America 35 Years, National Catholic Rural Life Conference* (Des Moines: NCRLC, 1957); Jay Dolan, *The American Catholic Experience,* 417.

133. Swanson, "The American Country Life Movement," 212, 371.

134. Ligutti wrote in 1950, "It is to be regretted, however, that a very cheapening appeal is being made by some Protestants. . . . The real leaders in the Protestant rural life field are not of this mind, and are doing a splendid piece of work for the good of rural people in the U.S. We need dynamic leadership and not mutual mistrust and recriminations. That holds good for Catholics as well as Protestants." Ligutti, memo, 6 January 1950, attached to letter of Ligutti to Dr. Harry Richardson, 5 January 1950, copy in Catholic Central Union of America archives (CCUA), Catholic publications files.

Chapter 2: Catholic Colonization Projects in Rural America

1. National Catholic Rural Life Conference, *Catholic Rural Life Songs* (Des Moines: NCRLC, n.d.), 13–14.

2. William J. Gauchat to Carlos, 5 September 1941, MUA, DD-CW, W-46, box 1.

3. Yaacov Oved, *Two Hundred Years of American Communes* (New Brunswick, N.J.: Transaction Books, 1987), 3.

4. Daniel J. Boorstin, *The Americans: The National Experience* (New York: Vintage Books, Random House, 1967), 230; Daniel Fitzgerald, *Ghost Towns of Kansas: A Traveler's Guide* (Lawrence: University Press of Kansas, 1988), 130–33; Violet Goering and Orlando J. Goering, "Jewish Farmers in South Dakota—the Am Olam," *South Dakota History* 12 (1982): 232–33, 246–47; Conkin, *Tomorrow a New World,* 11, 18–20; David Danbom, *Born in the Country: A History of Rural America* (Baltimore: Johns Hopkins University Press, 1995), 189; Shi, *The Simple Life,* 154–74. The communitarian regulation of diet, reproduction, and ritual practices is described in Laurence Veysey, *The Communal Experience: Anarchist and Mystical Counter-Cultures in America* (New York: Harper & Row, 1973), 18–73.

5. Lawrence J. McCrank, "Religious Orders and Monastic Communalism in America," in *America's Communal Utopias,* ed. Donald E. Pitzer, 204–52 (Chapel Hill: University of North Carolina Press, 1997); Bovée, "The Church and the Land," 13, 9.

6. Mary Gilbert Kelly, O.P., *Catholic Immigrant Colonization Projects in the United States, 1815–1860,* United States Catholic Historical Society Monograph Series, no. 17 (New York: United States Catholic Historical Society, 1939), 19–26, 37–47, 120–22; Hennesey, *American Catholics,* 128–29; Edward McCarron, "A Brave New World: The Irish Agrarian Colony of Benedicta, Maine in the 1830s and 1840s," *Records of the American Catholic Historical Society of Philadelphia* 105 (1994): 1–15. Both Kelly and McCarron noted that at least three German families were listed as part of the original

Benedicta settlement. Fenwick planned to establish a seminary and college near the farms, much like Mount Saint Mary's in Emmitsburg, Maryland. However, in 1843 he obtained land instead near Worcester, Massachusetts. The College of the Holy Cross, staffed by Maryland Jesuits, began that same year. On Oschswald and St. Nazianz, see Mary Kelly, *Catholic Immigrant Colonization Projects,* 190–91: the residents of St. Nazianz "claimed they were suffering from annoying restrictions imposed by Protestant authorities, but they really wished to establish in the United States a free Catholic community in accordance with their own ideas."

7. Henry W. Casper, S.J., *The Church on the Northern Plains,* vol. 1 of *The History of the Catholic Church in Nebraska* (Milwaukee, Wis.: Bruce, 1960), 72, 75, 79, 86–97.

8. John J. Hogan, *On the Mission in Missouri, 1857–1868* (1892; Glorieta, N.M.: Rio Grande Press, 1976), 37–39, 60–63. Another example of how Civil War issues divided communities appears in Fitzgerald, *Ghost Towns of Kansas,* 77–86; Fitzgerald describes Big Springs, a free-state town, and Lecompton, a pro-slavery one. The two towns were in the same corner of Franklin County.

9. James P. Shannon, *Catholic Colonization on the Western Frontier* (New Haven, Conn.: Yale University Press, 1957); Sister Mary Evangela Henthorne, B.V.M., *The Irish Catholic Colonization Association of the United States* (Champaign, Ill.: Twin City, 1932); William I. Crozier, *Gathering a People: A History of the Diocese of Winona* (Winona, Minn.: Diocese of Winona, 1989), 87. The ICCA settlements included, in Minnesota, Graceville, Sweetman, Ghent, Minneota, Avoca, Adrian, DeGraff, and Clontarf; in Nebraska's Greeley County, Greeley Center, O'Connor, Spalding, and Scioto. No sizable communities were raised in Arkansas despite apparently good soil and low prices. Henry W. Casper, S.J., mentions that many Midwestern clergy opposed the ICCA. Casper, *Catholic Chapters in Nebraska Immigration, 1870–1900,* vol. 3 of *The History of the Catholic Church in Nebraska* (Milwaukee, Wis.: Bruce, 1966), 46–47. Crozier, *Gathering a People,* 41–42, notes that southwestern Minnesota had been cleared of Native Americans after a Sioux uprising in 1862 was brutally suppressed.

10. Shannon, *Catholic Colonization on the Western Frontier,* 51–52.

11. Archbishop John Hughes of New York had united many of his brother bishops to oppose Catholic frontier settlement by heightening fears that Catholics lost the faith soon after they passed the city limits. In 1857 Hughes used this concern to heckle Father Trecy's presentation on St. John's City before a colonization convention at Buffalo, New York. Mary Kelly, *Catholic Immigrant Colonization Projects,* 251–53. Finke and Stark, in *The Churching of America,* 110–15, 141, argue that Hughes's opposition was rooted in the mistaken assumption that "millions" of Catholics had fallen away from the faith. His calculations for this conclusion rested on faulty numbers from many observers, all of whom greatly overestimated the size of the Catholic population.

12. Ibid., 107.

13. Ibid.; Henthorne, *Irish Catholic Colonization Association,* 148.

14. Shannon, *Catholic Colonization on the Western Frontier,* 52, 57, 66; Casper, *Catholic Chapters in Nebraska Immigration,* 63–85; Henthorne, *Irish Catholic Colonization Association,* 121, 128–29. Big Springs, Kansas, suffered the same fate as O'Connor, Nebraska, when the railroad shifted its lines in 1869. Fitzgerald, *Ghost Towns of Kansas,* 86.

15. Crozier, *Gathering a People,* 96–101, discusses Ireland's anti-German sentiments when the diocese of Winona and archdiocese of St. Paul were established. Russell Gerlach, *Immigrants in the Ozarks: A Study in Ethnic Geography* (Columbia: University of Missouri Press, 1975), 107, describes a similar situation of German immigrant success (although these were Lutheran Germans) among the old-stock, English-speaking farmers of Lawrence County, Missouri.

16. Donald F. Molitor, "The History of Glennonville and Adjacent Catholic Colonization Ventures in Southeastern Missouri: A Study in Changing Rural-Urban Patterns, 1905–1947" (M.A. thesis, Saint Louis University, 1967), 31–33 (copy in Saint Louis University Archives).

17. Ibid., 54–55, 61, 64–68, 69–80, 120–22, 146–51, 263 (Molitor interview with George Fortman, 8 March 1966), 369 (interview with Ben Siebert, 8 March 1966).

18. Ibid., 98, 100–103, 154–56, 198–200.

19. Ibid., 137–46, 192–98, 221–22, 253 (interview with George Hildner, 3 March 1966).

20. Ibid., p. 263 (interview with Fortman).

21. Ibid., 175–90, 263 (interview with Fortman, 8 March 1966), 341–42 (interview with John Peters, 9 March 1966).

22. Ibid., 175–90, 291–92, 293–94, 301 (interview with Mary Kettman, 1 July 1966), 308, 319–22, 369–70 (interview with Mena Siebert, 8 March 1966), 390 (interview with Joseph Stenger, 9 March 1966).

23. Ibid., 231–36, 253 (interview with Hildner), 266–68 (interview with Fortman), 295, 301–2 (interview with Kettman), 330–34 (interview with J. Peters).

24. Sydney Ahlstrom, *A Religious History of the American People* (New Haven, Conn.: Yale University Press, 1972), 491. Molitor quotes a newspaper as remarking, "Father Peters is Glennonville, and to a very large extent Glennonville is Father Peters." Molitor, "The History of Glennonville," 225.

25. Francis Mellen, "A Farm Colonization Experiment," *Catholic Charities Review* 16 (1932): 288; Bovée, "The Church and the Land," 242.

26. Mellen, "A Farm Colonization Experiment," 288.

27. Ibid.; Bovée, "The Church and the Land," 242; John La Farge, S.J., "What May We Expect of the Landward Movement?" *Catholic Action* 14 (September 1932): 11.

28. Molitor, "The History of Glennonville," 276 (interview with Fortman).

29. Archdiocesan Archives of St. Louis, Donald F. Molitor papers, ch. 5 file: NCRLC publication.

30. Wilson, "American Peasants," 147; Bovée, "The Church and the Land," 240; Conkin, *Tomorrow a New World,* 36–37; Robert D. Cross, "The Changing Image of the City among American Catholics," *Catholic Historical Review* 48 (1962): 40; National Catholic Rural Life Conference, *Proceedings of the Eleventh Annual Convention,* 14, 47–50, 68–70, 84–85. Cf. W. Klinkhammer, "Opportunities for Catholic Farmers in the Red River Valley," MUA, NCRLC, series 8/1, 1934 convention folder.

31. W. Howard Bishop, "A Step toward Rural Colonization," *Catholic Action* 14 (September 1932): 19; Albert L. C. France, "Economics and Authority," *Commonweal* 14 (14 October 1931): 581; "The Drift from the Farm," *America* 45 (19 September 1931): 558.

32. Bishop, "A Step toward Rural Colonization"; Ligutti and Rawe, *Rural Roads to Security,* 158–62; Larry Heaney, "Grow Your Own Food," *The Catholic Worker* 16 (June 1949): 4; Dorothy McMahon, "Maryfarm," *The Catholic Worker* 19 (May 1953): 2. *The Queen's Work* featured a "rural project" once a year throughout the 1930s and 1940s. Cf. McDonough, *Men Astutely Trained,* 85–89.

33. Peter Maurin, "Outdoor Universities," in *The Green Revolution,* 129; W. Howard Bishop, presidential address, delivered before the twelfth annual convention of the NCRLC, St. Paul, Minn., 6 November 1934, MUA, NCRLC, series 8/1, 1934 convention folder, 6, 8–9.

34. John La Farge, S.J., *The Manner Is Ordinary* (New York: Harcourt, 1954), 237; Conkin, *Tomorrow a New World,* 256–61; Davidson, *Our Jewish Farmers;* Ellen Eisenberg, *Jewish Agricultural Colonies in New Jersey, 1882–1920* (Syracuse, N.Y.: Syracuse

University Press, 1995); Pearl W. Bartelt, "American Jewish Agricultural Colonies," in Pitzer, *America's Communal Utopias*, 352–74. Cf. Oved, *Two Hundred Years of American Communes*, 316–31.

35. National Catholic Rural Life Conference, *Rural Life in a Peaceful World*, statement of principles and methods adopted at the Wartime Meeting of the NCRLC executive committee and advisory board (Des Moines: NCRLC, 1944), 1, 9.

36. La Farge, "What May We Expect of the Landward Movement?" 12.

37. Conkin, *Tomorrow a New World*, passim; Judith K. Fabry, "The Surplus Farm Population: Agricultural Policy-Makers and the Program for Older Rural Youth, 1935–1940," *Journal of the West* 31 (October 1992): 27–28; Harry McDean, "Western Thought in Planning Rural America: The Subsistence Homesteads Program, 1933–1935," *Journal of the West* 31 (October 1992): 15–21.

38. Resolution V.1, National Catholic Rural Life Conference, *Proceedings of the Eleventh Annual Convention*, 84; "Back to the Country," *America* 48 (12 November 1932): 127; "Back to the Farm," *America* 47 (23 July 1932): 368; "Ed. S.J." [Frederick P. Kenkel], "Granger Subsistence Homesteads," *Central-Blatt and Social Justice* 29 (January 1936): 305–6; Lawrence Lucey, "A Cooperative Town: Resettlement Administration at Hightstown, New Jersey," *Commonweal* 25 (18 December 1936): 210–12; Henry W. Clark, "Resettlement on the Last Frontier," *Commonweal* 28 (1 July 1938): 266–68; Walter J. Marx, "The Matanuska Colony," *Commonweal* 46 (23 May 1947): 139–41; Edward Skillin Jr., "Decentralization and the Land," *Commonweal* 31 (19 May 1939): 88–89; Skillin, "Coop's End in Hightstown," *Commonweal* 32 (3 May 1940): 31.

39. C. Edward Wolf, "Granger's Fifth Birthday," *Commonweal* 34 (24 January 1941): 348–49; NCRLC publication, MUA; Conkin, *Tomorrow a New World*, 294.

40. Ligutti and Rawe, *Rural Roads to Security*, 335.

41. Bovée, "The Church and the Land," 240, 243; John La Farge, S.J., "Granger Prospers on an Iowa Prairie," *America* 68 (31 October 1942): 97. Bovée remarks that by the mid-1950s, only the credit union remained of Granger's extensive cooperative system. For essays read at the Westphalia celebration, see Catholic Cooperative Committee, *Catholic Churchmen and Cooperatives*.

42. Conkin, *Tomorrow a New World*, 302; Bovée, "The Church and the Land," 244; Skillin, "Granger Homesteads," 95; La Farge, *The Manner Is Ordinary*, 233.

43. Conkin, *Tomorrow a New World*, 303; Witte, *Twenty-five Years of Crusading*, 192, 194.

44. Witte, *Twenty-five Years of Crusading*, 215–18. Witte describes Queen's Acres (outside of Cincinnati, Ohio), Assumption, Ohio, and Westphalia, Iowa after other "victories" such as Granger, the Glenmary Home Missioners, and Father Ray Marchino's Rural Uplifters of Evansville, Indiana.

45. Ligutti and Rawe, *Rural Roads to Security*, 331; Leo Ribuffo, *The Old Christian Right: The Protestant Far Right from the Great Depression to the Cold War* (Philadelphia: Temple University Press, 1983), 181; Dorothy Day, "Priest Starts Farm Co-op," *The Catholic Worker* 5 (January 1938): 7; "St. Theresa's Village Is Run on Principles of Democracy," *Action: A Catholic Pictorial News Monthly* 1 (June 1938): 6–10 (this issue includes the photograph of the sign for St. Theresa's Village).

46. Ligutti and Rawe, *Rural Roads to Security*, 331; *Father Terminiello's 25th Anniversary*, 9, Archdiocesan Archives of Mobile, Alabama. Even though agricultural technology was sweeping through the South, mules remained a fixture for many farmers. A 1930s flyer from the University of Georgia's School of Agriculture announced a lecture by a Mississippi farmer who after a disastrous flood began using tractors instead of his twenty mules (flyer in possession of the author).

47. Ligutti and Rawe, *Rural Roads to Security,* 331–32.

48. Ligutti, "The Pope of Peace," 14; John Steinbeck, *The Grapes of Wrath* (New York: Viking, 1939), 402–72; La Farge, "Granger Prospers on an Iowa Prairie," 97. Danbom, *Born in the Country,* 219, notes about the federal homestead projects add that "all too often, the answer was to provide marginal farmers with new farms that were only slightly less marginal."

49. Resolution V.1, National Catholic Rural Life Conference, *Proceedings of the Eleventh Annual Convention,* 84; R. Laurence Moore, *Selling God: American Religion in the Marketplace of Culture* (New York: Oxford University Press, 1994), 10–11.

50. Maurin, *The Green Revolution,* 93–94.

51. Fisher, *Catholic Counterculture,* 42.

52. Piehl, *Breaking Bread,* 128–29; Day, *The Long Loneliness,* 183, 185. Day remarked that her daughter Tamar, when asked her opinion of *The Catholic Worker,* "wrinkled up her nose and said she liked the farming-commune idea, but that there was too much talk about all the rest." Day, *Loaves and Fishes* (New York: Harper, 1963), 42–43.

53. Piehl, *Breaking Bread,* 128–29, 132. The July 1939 issue of *The Catholic Worker* lists Houses of Hospitality, "Catholic Worker Cells," and "CW Farms"; in addition to Our Lady of the Wayside in Ohio, St. Benedict's in Massachusetts, Nazareth in Illinois, and Maryfarm in Pennsylvania, farms are listed for Michigan, Missouri, Arkansas, Minnesota, Vermont, California, New Jersey, and Louisiana. The Zarrellas, one of many couples at Maryfarm, later "retired" to Alice Zarrella's hometown of Tell City, Indiana, where they pursued much the same agenda. Joseph and Alice Zarrella, interview with William Miller, 10 July 1967, MUA, DD-CW, W-4, box 1. In the 1950s Dorothy Day and the *Catholic Worker* editors received a stream of mail from individuals who had purchased farms with much the same intentions as the first farm communes twenty years earlier, but it was not until the 1960s that agrarian communitarianism saw a revival of its popularity. MUA, DD-CW, W-4, box 1.

54. Fisher, *Catholic Counterculture,* 71.

55. Larry Heaney, "Work on the Land," *The Catholic Worker* 8 (September 1941): 8; Dorothy Day, "Idea for a Farm Commune," *The Catholic Worker* 5 (January 1938): 8.

56. See Novitsky, "The Ideological Development of Peter Maurin's Green Revolution"; Day, *The Long Loneliness,* 179, 234, 239; Schuck, *That They Be One,* 79, 91; Proposal for "Congregation of the Holy Family," MUA, DD-CW, W-4, box 3; Fisher, *Catholic Counterculture,* 101–30, especially 123–25; Mario Carota to Dorothy Day, various letters, MUA, DD-CW, W-4, box 1; Estelle and Mario Carota, *We Shall Raise Our Voice Again: The Conflict between Doctrine and Canon Law* (Santa Cruz, Calif.: Christian Economic Networks, n.d.).

57. Marty Paul to Luigi Ligutti, 21 September 1947, MUA, LGL, box D-1; Louis McCauley to Bill [Gauchat] and Marty Paul, 7 May 1950, MUA, DD-CW, W-46, box 1.

58. Day, *The Long Loneliness,* 176; Day, "Idea for a Farm Commune," 8; Arthur Sheehan, "A History of St. Benedict's," MUA, DD-CW, W-4, box 2; Sheehan to Dorothy Day, 7 April 1939, MUA, DD-CW, W-4, box 2; Heaney, "Grow Your Own Food," 4; William J. Gauchat to Leo Branick, 11 February 1942, MUA, DD-CW, W-46, box 1.

59. Day, *The Long Loneliness,* 197.

60. Carmen Welch to Dorothy Day, undated, MUA, DD-CW, W-4, box 1; Marty Paul to Luigi Ligutti, 21 September 1947, MUA, LGL, box D-1; Marty Paul, "Diary of a Romantic Agrarian," *Commonweal* 57 (2 January 1953): 328; Piehl, *Breaking Bread,* 130; Dorothy Day, "Death of an Apostle," *The Catholic Worker* 16 (June 1949): 1, 6.

61. Ray Knight to William Gauchat, 26 December 1945, MUA, DD-CW, W-46, box 1; Fisher, *Catholic Counterculture,* 43.

62. Day wrote that when commune members were working side by side, "no one knows which are the unemployed workers and which the student or scholar." Day, "Idea for a Farm Commune," 8, Piehl, *Breaking Bread*, 130.

63. Day, *Loaves and Fishes*, 55; Eva Gretz to Dorothy Day, 16 March 1942, MUA, DD-CW, W-4.2, box 1; Rev. Joseph Wood to Dorothy Day, 4 August 1940, MUA, DD-CW, W-4.2, box 1; Grace Branham to Easton school board, 10 September 1941, MUA, DD-CW, W-4.2, box 1.

64. "Although they [the Catholic Workers] admitted that this failure showed there was a 'contradiction' between 'the two ideas of performing the works of mercy at a personal sacrifice and saving to provide for one's own,' the Workers felt that there was more 'glory' in 'suffering for a cause' than in making a living as farmers." Piehl, *Breaking Bread*, 131.

65. Dorothy Day to Dorothy Gauchat, 28 October 1948, MUA, DD-CW, W-46, box 2; Bill Gauchat to Directors, Catholic Worker Houses of Hospitality, 16 September 1940, MUA, DD-CW, W-46, box 1.

66. Maurin, "Idle Hands and Idle Lands," 1.

67. Catherine Albanese, *America: Religions and Religion*, 3d ed. (Berkeley, Calif.: Wadsworth, 1999), 424–27.

68. William Gauchat, "Our Lady of the Wayside Farm," *The Catholic Worker* 16 (June 1949): 5; on Catholic Worker assistance with Japanese American relocation, see Ralph M. Galt to William Gauchat, 8 December 1942, MUA, DD-CW, W-46, box 1. Other Catholic agrarians feared antiimmigrant sentiments. Ligutti's talks on WHO radio prompted one listener to ask: "Could you tell me where or how I could get some Jap help or would Mexican help be better? I have heard the Japs are fine help." A. J. Corrigan to Ligutti, 8 December 1937, MUA, LGL, box C-1.

69. Day, "Priest Starts Farm Co-op," 1, 7; Lee Carter, "Sharecroppers Homeless; Seek Free Land," *The Catholic Worker* 6 (March 1939): 1, 2; "Missouri Cooperative," *The Catholic Worker* 10 (March 1943): 8; "The Negro," *The Catholic Worker* 15 (September 1948): 1, 4; MUA, DD-CW, W-6.1, box 1, Koinonia Farm file. John Egerton, *Speak Now against the Day: The Generation before the Civil Rights Movement in the South* (Chapel Hill: University of North Carolina Press, 1994), 127, notes that Koinonia lay near the peanut farm of future president Jimmy Carter. On Clarence Jordan and the other Koinonia founders, see David Stricklin, *A Genealogy of Dissent: The Culture of Progressive Protest in Southern Baptist Life, 1920–1995* (Lexington: University Press of Kentucky, 1998).

70. Piehl, *Breaking Bread*, 130; William and Dorothy Gauchat, interview with William Miller, 1967, Avon, Ohio, pp. 16, 18, MUA, DD-CW, W-9, box 1. Day, *The Long Loneliness*, 232–33, describes the Gauchats' entire apostolate stemming from Our Lady of the Wayside farm.

71. "Catholic Worker Cells," *The Catholic Worker* 6 (September 1938): 7; William and Dorothy Gauchat, interview with William Miller, 1967, pp. 1, 12.

72. W. H. Hay, Chief of Laboratories, Division of Health, to William Gauchat, 11 July 1940, MUA, DD-CW, W-46, box 1.

73. L. M. Greany to E. G. Crawford, 27 July 1942, MUA, DD-CW, W-46, box 1. Greany wrote that the applicant, twenty-year-old Betty Clendenning, was "an invalid for life, being able only to move two fingers on each hand and her head slightly, lives on a specially constructed bed from which she never leaves."

74. F. W. Vincent, Acting Health Commissioner, to William Gauchat, 31 August 1945, MUA, DD-CW, W-46, box 1.

75. Maurice Lavanoux to William Gauchat, 16 March and 30 March 1942, MUA, DD-CW, W-46, box 1. See also Eugene McCarraher, "American Gothic: Sacramental

Radicalism and the Neo-Medievalist Cultural Gospel, 1928–1948," *Records of the American Catholic Historical Society of Philadelphia* 106 (spring/summer 1995): 7–8.

76. Dorothy Day to Bill Gauchat, 13 July [1940], MUA, DD-CW, W-46, box 2; William Gauchat, "Reflections on the Green Revolution," *The Catholic Worker* 20 (May 1953): 5.

77. Eva Smith, "Farming Commune," *The Catholic Worker* 8 (September 1941): 8.

78. Ruth Ann Heaney, interview with Rosalie Troester, 14 July 1989, MUA, DD-CW, W-9, box 4, p. 33; Gauchat, "Reflections on the Green Revolution," 5.

79. Gauchat to C. L. Devilbiss, 21 September 1951, MUA, DD-CW, W-46, box 1; Gauchat, "Reflections on the Green Revolution," 5; Gauchat to Day, "Feast of Our King" [October] 1950, MUA, DD-CW, W-46, box 2; Brother Christopher to Gauchat, [c. May 1948], MUA, DD-CW, W-46, box 1.

80. See Shi, *The Simple Life;* Edward Abbey, *Desert Solitaire: A Season in the Wilderness* (1973; rev. ed., New York: Bantam Books, 1990); Gould, "Getting (Not Too) Close to Nature."

81. Ruth Ann Heaney, interview with Troester, 20. The shrine at Rhineland, Missouri, is mentioned in Dolan, *The American Catholic Experience,* 234–35, as a devotional site for Kansas and Missouri Catholics.

82. Larry Heaney, "Toehold on the Land," *The Catholic Worker* 14 (June 1947): 3; Jack Woltjen to *The Catholic Worker,* 1955, MUA, DD-CW, W-6.1, box 1. Twelve people lived in the farmhouse before Heaney's death.

83. Marty Paul, "Toehold on the Land—#1," *The Catholic Worker* 14 (September 1947): 3; Larry Heaney, "Toehold on the Land," *The Catholic Worker* 14 (January 1948): 5; Paul, "Diary of a Romantic Agrarian," 327. Cf. Heaney, "Toehold on the Land," *The Catholic Worker* 15 (July–August 1948): 4; Paul, "Holy Trinity Farm," *The Catholic Worker* 16 (February 1949): 7; and "Holy Family Farm," *The Catholic Worker* 16 (June 1949): 5.

84. Paul, "Diary of a Romantic Agrarian," 327–28; Ruth Ann Heaney, interview with Troester, 33. Ironically, Patrick Quinlan's *Standing on Both Feet,* a postwar NCRLC pamphlet that extolled rural homesteads, included the following in its "Practical Points for Homesteaders": "Let no man tempt you to go into the chicken business unless you have had much experience. Inexperienced chicken farmers often lose small fortunes which have been acquired throughout the greater part of a life time." The insights of Raymond Thomas (1932–1998), who operated a chicken farm for more than twenty years in south-central Maine, proved immeasurably helpful with this particular problem facing Holy Family farm.

85. Paul, "Diary of a Romantic Agrarian," 328; Ruth Ann Heaney, interview with Troester, 30.

86. Paul, "Diary of a Romantic Agrarian," 328.

87. Day, "Death of an Apostle," 6; Ruth Ann Heaney, interview with Troester; Marty Paul, interview with Deanne Mowrer, 1968, MUA, DD-CW, W-9, box 1; William and Dorothy Gauchat, interview with Miller. By comparison, Paul simply remarked, "Larry died shortly after we got started there." Paul, interview with Francis Sicius, 17 June 1976, Boyne City, Mich., 4, MUA, DD-CW, W-9, box 1.

88. Paul, "Diary of a Romantic Agrarian," 328; Day, "Death of an Apostle," 6.

89. Ruth Ann Heaney, interview with Troester, 30; Paul, "Diary of a Romantic Agrarian," 327; John Magee to Dorothy Day, 4 August 1940, MUA, DD-CW, W-4, box 2.

90. Fisher, *Catholic Counterculture,* 43. In 1973 Veysey, in *The Communal Experience,* 39, noted that of the approximately twenty-five farms founded by the Catholic Workers during the 1930s, only one remained forty years later.

91. The Maryfarm visitor's book is in MUA, DD-CW, W-4.2, box 1.

92. Ruth Ann Heaney, interview with Troester, 15; Louis and Justine Murphy, in-

terview with Deanne Mowrer, 2 June 1968, 22, MUA, DD-CW, W-9, box 2. Correspondence between Maryfarm and the Philadelphia chancery is in MUA, DD-CW, W-4.2, box 1. See also John Hugo, *Weapons of the Spirit: Living a Holy Life in Unholy Times—Selected Writings of Father John Hugo,* ed. David Scott and Mike Aquilina (Huntingdon, Ind.: Our Sunday Visitor, 1997).

93. Piehl, *Breaking Bread,* 131, 156–57. Maryfarm was the center for a national Catholic Worker retreat in 1941. Day and Chicago Catholic Worker John Cogley met then to discuss their differences concerning military conscription (which Day opposed), but Cogley left the movement soon afterward.

94. Fisher, *Catholic Counterculture,* 54–56.

95. Bovée, "The Church and the Land," 246, 343–52; "Ed. S.J.", "Granger Subsistence Homesteads," 306; Skillin, "Granger Homesteads," 96. After World War II, the NCRLC endorsed land settlement for veterans and displaced persons. One colony founded was in York County, South Carolina. Bovée, "The Church and the Land," 246.

96. Skillin, "Granger Homesteads," 96; Eileen O'Hara, "Maryfarm," *The Catholic Worker* 15 (September 1948): 4.

97. Harry Donaghy and Kate Donaghy, "Adjusting to Life in the Country," *Integrity* 7 (January 1953): 5.

98. Ibid., 9.

99. Resolution V.1, National Catholic Rural Life Conference, *Proceedings of the Eleventh Annual Convention,* 84.

100. Mario Carota, "Toehold on the Land," *The Catholic Worker* 15 (April 1949): 4; Ruth Ann Heaney, interview with Troester, 30–31, 27.

101. Bovée, "The Church and the Land," 346; Roger S. Lorenz, "Outstretched Hand," *The Catholic Worker* 20 (June 1953): 5; Rollande Potvin, "Summer at Maryfarm," *The Catholic Worker* 20 (October 1953): 8. MUA, DD-CW, W-4, box 1, includes a file of letters to *The Catholic Worker* dating from 1947 to 1955 and including descriptions of farms in Missouri, New York, and Pennsylvania and of the Grail's farm near Loveland, Ohio.

102. Fisher, *Catholic Counterculture,* 125–29, makes the same point about the Marycrest community near West Nyack, New York.

103. Ahlstrom, *A Religious History of the American People,* 491; Bennett M. Berger, *The Survival of a Counterculture: Ideological Work and Everyday Life among Rural Communards* (Berkeley: University of California Press, 1981), 91–126. Berger writes (p. 96): "The pastoral myth—the vision of a simple and self-sufficient rural life in harmony with nature—connects the rural communards of the counterculture with the suburbanites of the 1950s and with the more distant American past."

104. Ahlstrom, *A Religious History of the American People,* 491; Fisher, *Catholic Counterculture,* 71, 110–25.

105. Paul, "Diary of a Romantic Agrarian," 330. On the same page, Paul remarks, "Now, after five years, I feel that I actually know something about farming."

106. Huff, *Allen Tate and the Catholic Revival,* 87; H[einrich] A. Reinhold, "Back to . . . What?" *Worship* 26 (April 1952): 254. Cf. Jay P. Corrin, "H. A. Reinhold: Liturgical Pioneer and Anti-Fascist," *Catholic Historical Review* 82 (1996): 436–58.

Chapter 3: Part of the Scenery

1. Luigi Ligutti, "The Monsignor Says," *The Christian Farmer* 1 (October 1947): 1, 2.

2. Eugene Geissler, "The Proposed Catholic Rural Life Monthly," attached to letter from Geissler to William Griffin, 14 January 1946, MUA, NCRLC, series 8/1, box 4,

folder 33; NCRLC correspondence, MUA, NCRLC, series 1/1, box 1; Bovée, "The Church and the Land," 315. Frederick Kenkel had called for a similar publication as early as 1936, and Ligutti originally intended *Land and Home* to become such a one after he became its editor in 1942 (Bovée, "The Church and the Land," 312).

3. The 1940 convention in St. Cloud, Minnesota, had eighteen thousand attendees. The 1948 convention in La Crosse, Wisconsin, brought in thirty thousand; no other convention, before or since, drew nearly as many.

4. J. E. Biehler, *One Hundred Years in Rock Creek Valley: A History of the St. Joseph Parish at Flush, Kansas* (Topeka, Kans.: Central Press, 1954), 19. Bovée, "The Church and the Land," 20–25. See Nathan O. Hatch, *The Democratization of American Christianity* (New Haven, Conn.: Yale University Press, 1989) for American Protestant revivalism's growth over the opposition of established church leaders along the eastern seaboard. See Laurie Maffly-Kipp, "Eastward Ho! American Religion from the Perspective of the Pacific Rim," in *Retelling U.S. Religious History,* ed. Thomas A. Tweed (Berkeley: University of California Press, 1996), 127–48, for an interesting revision of the assumed westward expansion narrative in American religious history.

5. Lyman Beecher quoted in Bovée, "The Church and the Land," 27. Henry Ward Beecher, Lyman's son, later supported Irish Catholic frontier colonization along with his better-known support of abolitionism. See Ahlstrom, *A Religious History of the American People,* 658, 739. See Fitzgerald, *Ghost Towns of Kansas,* 102–8, for a description of the Congregationalist "The Beecher Bible and Rifle Church" in Wabaunsee, Kansas.

6. Henthorne, *Irish Catholic Colonization Association,* 34, 103–88; Hennesey, *American Catholics,* 112. Yda Schreuder, *Dutch Catholic Immigrant Settlement in Wisconsin, 1850–1905* (New York: Garland, 1989), 3–5; Casper, *Catholic Chapters in Nebraska Immigration,* 148;

7. Joseph Kundek to the Leopoldine Society of Austria, 23 December 1844, quoted in Albert Kleber, O.S.B., *Ferdinand, Indiana, 1840–1940: A Bit of Cultural History* (St. Meinrad, Ind.: n.p., 1940), 64.

8. Maureen A. Harp, "The Leopoldine Foundation, Slovene Missionaries, and Catholic Rural Migration," *Mid-America* 75 (January 1993): 23–43; Stearns County's status as "most rural Catholic county" appears on Shannon, *Catholic Colonization,* 42; and Schmiedeler, *A Better Rural Life,* 69.

9. Mary Kelly, *Catholic Immigrant Colonization Projects,* 4, 132–39, 230–37.

10. "New Germania" was the name given to the Missouri River valley west of St. Louis by Gottfried Duden in 1829. A land rush by the German middle class soon took place in the area. Adolf E. Schroeder, introduction to Jette Bruns, *Hold Dear, As Always: Jette, a German Immigrant Life in Letters,* trans. Adolf E. Schroeder, ed. Adolf E. Schroeder and Carla Schulz-Geisberg (Columbia: University of Missouri Press, 1988), 2–3.

11. Jette Bruns to Heinrich [Geisburg, her brother], August 1839, in *Hold Dear, As Always,* 98; Mary Kelly, *Catholic Immigrant Colonization Projects,* 116–18; Gordon Isenmenter, "The McIntosh German-Russians: The First Fifty Years," *North Dakota History* 51 (1984): 4–11; Thomas W. Spalding, C.F.X., "German Parishes East and West," *U.S. Catholic Historian* 14 (1996): 44–51. See Colman Barry, O.S.B., *The Catholic Church and German Americans* (Milwaukee, Wis.: Bruce, 1953).

12. Mary Kelly, *Catholic Immigrant Colonization Projects,* 65, 152; *St. Joseph's Sesquicentennial: Westphalia, Missouri, 1836–1986* (Westphalia, Mo.: n.p., 1985), 4; *Sacred Heart Jubilee: Calumet, Michigan, 1868–1918,* CCUA, drawer 28, reel 7.

13. Bovée, "The Church and the Land," 13 (quote), 21; Mary Kelly, *Catholic Immigrant Colonization Projects,* 15. With these diocesan and parish histories, I am following the "hermeneutics of suspicion," discussed by feminist biblical scholar Elisabeth

Schüssler Fiorenza, to seek out the unregulated Catholic settlers amid all the narratives covering colonization projects. "Rather than understand the text as an adequate reflection of the reality about which it speaks, we must search for clues and allusions that indicate the reality about which the text is silent." Schüssler Fiorenza, *In Memory of Her: A Feminist Theological Reconstruction of Christian Origins* (New York: Crossroad, 1983), 41.

14. Timothy Dolan, *Some Seed Fell on Good Ground,* 2–3; Shannon, *Catholic Colonization on the Western Frontier,* 51, 98–99 (Ireland quote). St. Kilian, a German colony founded in 1887, was established independently of Bishop Ireland's projects.

15. Crozier, *Gathering a People,* 64–65. By contrast, Schreuder remarks that Dutch Catholics settled entirely by clerical direction; she reports no examples of Dutch Catholic rural "accretion." Schreuder, *Dutch Catholic Immigrant Settlement in Wisconsin,* 77.

16. Philip Vogt, O.S.B., to James O'Gorman, 24 August 1860, quoted in Casper, *The Church on the Northern Plains,* 130; Finke and Stark, *The Churching of America,* 141. On Trecy's 1856 mission trip, see Casper, *The Church on the Northern Plains,* 83.

17. Joseph F. McNamee, *Sketches of the Pioneer Priests* (Pacific, Mo.: Plowman Press, 1928), 3.

18. Jeane Gilmore, *The Legacy: The History of the St. Joseph Catholic Church, Edina, Missouri* (Quincy, Ill.: Jost & Kiefer, 1974), 9–13; Fitzgerald, *Ghost Towns of Kansas,* 184; Henthorne, *Irish Catholic Colonization Association,* 123–24;

19. Casper, *Catholic Chapters in Nebraska Immigration,* 81, 146.

20. Casper, *The Church on the Northern Plains,* 180–81, (Daxacher & McCall), 202, (Gutzon Borglum); See Hogan, *On the Mission in Missouri,* passim; Biehler, *One Hundred Years in Rock Creek Valley,* 2–38; Gilmore, *The Legacy,* 9–13; William Graves, Gilbert Garraghan, S.J., and George Towle, *Kickapoo Mission and Parish: The First Catholic Church in Kansas* (St. Paul, Kans.: The Journal Press, 1938), 77–78.

21. Henry Casper also comments negatively on the lay initiative in parish matters. This Nebraska version of trusteeism appears as "another of those incidents so common in the history of the American Church during the nineteenth century when one of the laity attempted to lift himself into a position of church proprietor." Casper, *Catholic Chapters in Nebraska Immigration,* 102-8, 170 [quoted]. Spalding, "German Parishes East & West," 50-51. On trusteeism conflicts in New York, see Patrick Carey, *Priests, Prelates, and Laypeople: Ecclesiastical Democracy and the Tensions of Trusteeism* (Notre Dame, Ind.: University of Notre Dame Press, 1987).

22. Ahlstrom, *A Religious History of the American People,* 754–62; Schreuder, *Dutch Catholic Immigrant Settlement,* 135. See John Ilmari Kolehmainen and George W. Hill, *A Haven in the Woods: The Finns of Northern Wisconsin,* 2d ed. (Madison: State Historical Society of Wisconsin, 1965); Carol Coburn, *Life at Four Corners: Religion, Gender, and Education in a German-Lutheran Community, 1868–1945* (Lawrence: University Press of Kansas, 1992); Rob Kroes, *The Persistence of Ethnicity: Dutch Calvinist Pioneers in Amsterdam, Montana* (Urbana: University of Illinois Press, 1992).

23. Shannon, *Catholic Colonization on the Western Frontier,* 53.

24. Maureen Harp argues that the regional identity of certain areas in the United States—for example, the northern Great Lakes, where many Slovenian Catholics settled—was shaped precisely by the influence of immigrant Catholics. Harp, "The Leopoldine Foundation," 27. Nicole Etcheson describes how a new "western" or "midwestern" identity was formed by the influx of both northern and southern Americans into Indiana, Illinois, Ohio, and Michigan. Etcheson, *The Emerging Midwest: Upland Southerners and the Political Culture of the Old Northwest, 1787–1861* (Bloomington: Indiana University Press, 1996), passim. Historian Dorothy Schwieder

writes that "Iowa's earliest religious institutions were dominated by the Roman Catholics and the Methodists." *Iowa: The Middle Land* (Ames: Iowa State University Press, 1996), 110.

25. Martin Towey, "Kerry Patch Revisited: Irish Americans in St. Louis in the Turn of the Century Era," in *From Paddy to Studs: Irish-American Communities in the Turn of the Century Era, 1880–1920,* ed. Timothy J. Meagher (New York: Greenwood, 1986), 141; Gerlach, *Immigrants in the Ozarks,* 33. For the etymology of *redneck, cracker, hoosier,* and other derogatory names, see David Hackett Fischer, *Albion's Seed: Four British Folkways in America* (New York: Oxford University Press, 1989), 756–58.

26. William A. Settle, *Jesse James Was His Name; or, Fact and Fiction concerning the Careers of the Notorious James Brothers of Missouri* (Columbia: University of Missouri Press, 1966); R. Douglas Hurt, *Agriculture and Slavery in Missouri's Little Dixie* (Columbia: University of Missouri Press, 1992), 201. See Stafford Poole, C.M., and Douglas Slawson, C.M., *Church and Slave: Perry County, Missouri, 1818–1865* (Lewiston, N.Y.: Edwin Mellen Press, 1986).

27. Hogan, *On the Mission in Missouri,* 133; W. M. Leftwich, *Martyrs in Missouri* (Chicago: n.p., 1868).

28. Bovée, "The Church and the Land", 27–30. Louisiana's rural Catholic population was approximately 300,000. New Mexico's small-town and rural Catholics constituted approximately 66 percent of the state's population (143,009 of 216,328). Bovée remarks that German Americans "were undoubtedly the most numerous ethnic group in Catholic rural America," being "particularly concentrated" in the Midwest, which he labels "the Catholic rural heartland" (33). He includes statistics for every state in 1900 on the basis of census reports for that year.

29. Finke and Stark, in *The Churching of America,* 143, observe: "In the final analysis, the Catholic Church succeeded in America because it too was an upstart sect. It offered an intense faith with a vivid sense of otherworldliness—Catholic evangelists could depict the fires of hell as graphically as any Baptist or Methodist. Like the Protestant upstart sects, moreover, the Catholic Church made serious emotional, material, and social demands on its adherents."

30. Catherine McNicol Stock, *Main Street in Crisis: The Great Depression and the Old Middle Class on the Northern Plains* (Chapel Hill: University of North Carolina Press, 1992), 18–30.

31. Pamela Riney-Kehrberg, *Rooted in Dust: Surviving Drought and Depression in Southwestern Kansas* (Lawrence: University Press of Kansas, 1994), passim. For Winkelmann's move, see chapter 1.

32. On Oklahoma's cultural marginality between the Midwest, the Great Plains, and the South, see James R. Shortridge, *The Middle West: Its Meaning in American Culture* (Lawrence: University Press of Kansas, 1989), 38–41.

33. Ronald E. Seavoy, "Portraits of Twentieth-Century American Peasants: Subsistence Social Values Recorded in *All God's Dangers* and *Let Us Now Praise Famous Men,*" *Agricultural History* 68 (1994): 217. Seavoy relies as well on Erskine Caldwell's *You Have Seen Their Faces.* John Egerton briefly discusses James Agee's and Erskine Caldwell's ambiguous role as native critics of Southern culture in *Speak Now against the Day,* 144–46.

34. Jane Adams, *The Transformation of Rural Life: Southern Illinois, 1890–1990* (Chapel Hill: University of North Carolina Press, 1994), 22–24, 109–12. Danbom, *The Resisted Revolution,* 135.

35. On the permanence of migrant and tenant farming, see Michael Harrington, *The Other America: Poverty in the United States* (1962, reprint, Baltimore: Penguin Books, 1965), 51–62.

36. Riney-Kehrberg, *Rooted in Dust,* passim; Stock, *Main Street in Crisis,* passim. Davidson, *Our Jewish Farmers,* 166–75, described some examples of Jewish farmers' success in, among other things, dairy and poultry production.

37. Danbom, *The Resisted Revolution,* 4–6; Carmen Delores Welch, "From an Illinois Farm," MUA, DD-CW, W-4, box 1, Nazareth House folder; James Agee with Walker Evans, *Let Us Now Praise Famous Men* (1941; reprint, Boston: Houghton Mifflin, 1980), 322.

38. Shapiro, "Catholic Agrarian Thought and the New Deal," 592–95; Shapiro, "The Catholic Rural Life Movement and the New Deal Farm Program," 324–31; Carmen Delores Welch, "From an Illinois Farm, Part 2," MUA, DD-CW, W-4, box 1, Nazareth House folder; Danbom, *Born in the Country,* 213–16.

39. Wolf, "I Left College to Become a Farmer," 3–4; Olin E. Hughes, "An Analysis of Farm Building Costs" (M.A. thesis, University of Missouri at Columbia, 1932), 25–27, 130–31. Hughes conducted part of his research in Linn County, Missouri, which was home to a Benedictine monastery. Linn County's Catholics also received praise from Father Joseph Hogan (quoted earlier).

40. Egerton, *Speak Now against the Day,* 205–6; Danbom, *The Resisted Revolution,* 133–34.

41. Harvey Green, *The Uncertainty of Everyday Life, 1915–1945* (New York: HarperCollins, 1992), 61–65, 101–2; Hildner, *One Hundred Years for God and Country,* 66.

42. Adams, *The Transformation of Rural Life,* 210; Skillin, "Granger Homesteads," 95.

43. Shortridge, *The Middle West,* 39; Sinclair Lewis, *Main Street* (New York: New American Library, 1961), 153; Anthony Channell Hilfer, *The Revolt from the Village, 1915–1930* (Chapel Hill: University of North Carolina Press, 1969), 159–67.

44. Robert S. Lynd and Helen Merrell Lynd, *Middletown: A Study in Modern American Culture* (San Diego, Calif.: Harcourt, Brace & Company, 1957), 322, 371.

45. Shortridge, *The Middle West,* 41, 52; Danbom, *Born in the Country,* 226–27.

46. Carey, "Presidential Address," 3; Edgar Lee Masters, *Spoon River Anthology* (New York: Macmillan, 1962), 254.

47. Susman, *Culture as History,* 109–11.

48. Green, *The Uncertainty of Everyday Life,* 36.

49. Ruth Ann Heaney, interview with Rosalie Riegle Troester, MUA, DD-CW, W-9, box 4; David M. Chalmers, *Hooded Americanism: The History of the Ku Klux Klan* (New York: New Viewpoints, 1965; Franklin Watt, 1981), 34, 109–10. Kenneth Jackson's *The Ku Klux Klan in the City, 1915–1930* (1967; reprint, New York: Elephant, Basic, 1992) makes a stronger case for the structurally urban character of the Klan's membership and leadership. Jackson admits (p. 195) that most of the members were not too far removed from the rural areas surrounding the rapidly growing industrial cities in which the Klan experienced the most growth, such as Indianapolis, Indiana, Youngstown, Ohio, and Denver, Colorado. On the Women of the Ku Klux Klan (WKKK), see Kathleen M. Blee, *Women of the Klan: Racism and Gender in the 1920s* (Berkeley: University of California Press, 1991).

50. Chalmers, *Hooded Americanism,* 4; Leonard J. Moore, *Citizen Klansmen: The Ku Klux Klan in Indiana, 1921–1928* (Chapel Hill: University of North Carolina Press, 1991), 11, 185. Chalmers, *Hooded Americanism,* 171–72, and Jackson, *The Ku Klux Klan in the City,* 90, describe the scandal surrounding the immensely popular Indiana Klansman David C. Stephenson. Besides pilfering state Klan donations, Stephenson was convicted of the rape and murder of his secretary Madge Oberholtzer. Subsequent investigations uncovered widespread corruption among Indiana Klansmen holding state offices. Moore's claim about Klan "ordinariness" also applied to the Klan in Grand Forks, North Dakota, where most members were business owners, not disaffected rural

Protestants. William L. Harwood, "The Ku Klux Klan in North Dakota," *South Dakota History* 4 (1971): 312.

51. Blee, *Women of the Klan,* 149; Chalmers, *Hooded Americanism,* 165, 167. William D. Jenkins, *Steel Valley Klan: The Ku Klux Klan in Ohio's Mahoning Valley* (Kent, Ohio: Kent State University Press, 1990), describes a similar altercation in Niles, Ohio, in which immigrant Catholic steelworkers organized to beat back a planned Klan march.

52. Chalmers, *Hooded Americanism,* 292; Coburn, *Life at Four Corners,* 63; Leonard Moore, *Citizen Klansman,* 11.

53. Christopher J. Kauffman, *Faith and Fraternalism: The History of the Knights of Columbus, 1882–1982* (New York: Harper & Row, 1982), 1–9. R. Laurence Moore, *Selling God,* 173–75, describes how the Catholic Church's opposition to the Knights of Labor stemmed from its opposition to secret societies, as well as from American culture's difficulty in combining religious practice and labor concerns. The Knights of Columbus reaped the rewards of this prohibition, as relatively few Catholics joined the labor organization.

54. Kauffman, *Faith and Fraternalism,* 10–17, 71; Jay Dolan, *The American Catholic Experience,* 257–58; Biehler, *One Hundred Years in Rock Creek Valley,* 125; Spalding, "German Parishes East and West," 51.

55. "President of Catholic Extension Society Says Rome 'Is in Politics,'" *The Menace,* no. 301 (1 November 1917): 4; Gilbert O. Nations and Billy Parker, "Popery, the World Crisis, and *The New Menace,"* *The New Menace* 3 (8 May 1920): 1, both on microfilm at CCUA, publications collection, drawer 11, reels 1, 2; Timothy Dolan, *Some Seed Fell on Good Ground,* 41–43, 45; Kauffman, *Faith and Fraternalism,* 281; Witte, *Twenty-five Years of Crusading,* 64, 68; Eckard V. Toy, "Robe and Gown: The Ku Klux Klan in Eugene, Oregon," in *The Invisible Empire in the West: Toward a New Historical Appraisal of the Ku Klux Klan of the 1920s,* ed. Shawn Lay (Urbana: University of Illinois Press, 1992), 171–74. Hennesey, *American Catholics,* 222, mentions *The Menace* and the "Loyalty Oath," which had previously been labeled the "Jesuit oath." For a study of how the national Catholic newspaper *Our Sunday Visitor* waged a similar battle against *The Menace* and other anti-Catholic publications, see Leon Hutton, "Catholicity and Civility: John Francis Noll and the Origins of *Our Sunday Visitor,"* *U.S. Catholic Historian* 16 (spring 1998): 1–22.

56. Jay Dolan, *The American Catholic Experience,* 326; Hayne, "Westphalia: Pattern and Promise," 19; Anderson, Indiana, *Herald,* quoted in *Catholic Rural Life* 5 (November 1926): 7. Community morals enforcement could still be a highly individual affair. When asked about his choice of wine instead of grape juice at a Holiness Church when celebrating communion, an Alabama man remarked that "drinking unfermented grape juice . . . would be like taking up a nonpoisonous snake." Dennis Covington, *Salvation on Sand Mountain: Snake Handling and Redemption in Southern Appalachia* (New York: Penguin Books, 1995), 116–17.

57. V. F. Mikolasek, "Bohemian Catholic Rural Activities," *Catholic Rural Life* 3 (July 1925): 6; "Notes and Comments: Catholic Farmers' Conference," *Catholic Rural Life Bulletin* 3 (November 1940): 15; Witte, *Twenty-five Years of Crusading,* 33; August Brockland, "The Catholic Union of Missouri," *St. Isidore's Plow* 2 (October 1923): 4.

58. Quoted in Biehler, *One Hundred Years in Rock Creek Valley,* 126; Catherine Albanese, "Exchanging Souls, Exchanging Selves: Contact, Combination, and American Religious History," in *Retelling U.S. Religious History,* ed. Thomas A. Tweed (Berkeley: University of California Press, 1996), 203.

59. Lynd and Lynd, *Middletown,* 333.

60. Hildner, *One Hundred Years for God and Country,* 67.

61. James T. Meehan, S.J., "Catholic Oberlin," *Land and Home* 6 (March 1943): 23.

62. *St. Martin's Parish, Caldwell, Kansas, Golden Jubilee: 1888–1938,* CCUA, drawer 28, reel 19.

63. Riney-Kehrberg, *Rooted in Dust,* 35; Hayne, "Westphalia: Pattern and Promise," 18.

64. Witte, *Twenty-five Years of Crusading,* 216.

65. Hayne, "Westphalia: Pattern and Promise," 18.

66. Vincent McNabb, O.P., "Women and the Land," pamphlet in MUA, NCRLC, series 3, box 17.

67. Alphonse H. Clemens, *Marriage and the Family: An Integrated Approach for Catholics* (Englewood Cliffs, N.J.: Prentice-Hall, 1957), 81–84, 89–100; George A. Kelly, *The Catholic Family Handbook* (New York: Random House, 1959), 130–39; Edgar Schmiedeler, O.S.B., *Marriage and the Family* (New York: McGraw-Hill, 1946), 170–89; Susan Frawley Eisele, "My Fair Lady," *The Christian Farmer* 1 (October 1947): 6. According to Eisele, the corners of square pot holders were apt to stick in freshly baked pies and cakes. Applesauce cake apparently was more economical "with the drive on for saving food."

68. "Cracked Corn: No Ration Points," *Land and Home* 7 (June 1944): 47. The article concluded: "Only the tender young leaves of plants should be selected for eating. Young crisp leaves are nice for salad, but these wild greens can also be cooked and served like spinach or chard with butter or a sauce."

69. Owen, "Kill . . . and Cure," 53.

70. Welch, "From an Illinois Farm," 7; Owen, "Kill . . . and Cure," 52.

71. *St. Martin's Parish, Caldwell, Kansas;* Gilmore, *The Legacy,* 74–75.

72. G. Edward White, *Creating the National Pastime: Baseball Transforms Itself, 1903–1953* (Princeton, N.J.: Princeton University Press, 1996), 5, 7.

73. *St. Mary's Parish, Westphalia, Michigan: 1836–1936* (Westphalia, Mich.: n.p., n.d.), 125, CCUA, drawer 28; Hayne, "Westphalia: Pattern and Promise," 19; "Activities of a Rural Community," *Catholic Rural Life* 3 (May 1925): 7.

74. Luigi Ligutti, "Religious Vacation Schools," *Catholic Rural Life* 4 (April 1926): 3; Biehler, *One Hundred Years in Rock Creek Valley,* 125; Gilmore, *The Legacy,* 79; "Activities of a Rural Community," 7.

75. Green, *The Uncertainty of Everyday Life,* 190; Carmen Welch to Dorothy Day, undated, MUA, DD-CW, W-4, box 1, Nazareth House folder.

76. Ray Wortmann, "Coughlin in the Countryside: Father Charles Coughlin and the National Farmers Union," *U.S. Catholic Historian* 13 (1995): 97–120; Alan Brinkley, *Voices of Protest: Huey Long, Father Coughlin, and the Great Depression* (New York: Knopf, 1982), 111–12, 124–25, 152–53, 254–61; David H. Bennett, *Demagogues in the Depression: American Radicals and the Union Party, 1932–1936* (New Brunswick, N.J.: Rutgers University Press, 1969), 44–45, 66, 88–89, 207, 269–72; Philip Jenkins, *Hoods and Shirts: The Extreme Right in Pennsylvania, 1925–1950* (Chapel Hill: University of North Carolina Press, 1997), 165–91. Fears of farm "collectivism" continued to characterize Coughlin's attitude after the election. Cf. Joseph P. Wright, "The Farmer Goose Steps," *Social Justice,* new series, 1A (7 March 1938): 5, 18.

77. Edgar Schmiedeler, O.S.B., "Trailing the Trailer Chapels," *Homiletic and Pastoral Review* 42 (1942): 244–45; Green, *The Uncertainty of Everyday Life,* 191.

78. Robert Stuhr to Luigi Ligutti, 11 October 1937; Mrs. Jessie T. Dutton to Luigi Ligutti, 31 October 1937; Howard M. Smith to "Rev. L. G. LaGoodie," 15 December 1937; A. A. Walch to "Father L. G. Liguddi," 18 December 1937, all in MUA, LGL, box C-1, Radio Address folder.

79. Schmiedeler, "Trailing the Trailer Chapels," 245; Edgar Schmiedeler, O.S.B., "Motor Missions, 1940," *Homiletic and Pastoral Review* 41 (1941): 399–400; Curtis W.

Ellison, *Country Music Culture: From Hard Times to Heaven* (Jackson: University Press of Mississippi, 1995), 20; David Fillingim, "The Gospel Songs and the Cheatin' Songs: Redneck Theological Discourse and the Problem of Suffering," *Studies in Popular Culture* 19 (October 1996): 185–95; Fillingim, "Redneck Liberation: Country Music as Theology" (paper presented at the American Academy of Religion convention, San Francisco, November 1997). The diocesan see in Concordia, Kansas, moved to Salina in December 1944.

80. Fabry, "The Surplus Farm Population," 28–30; Carmen Delores Welch to Dorothy [Day] and Ade [Bethune], undated, MUA, DD-CW, W-4, box 1, Nazareth House folder.

81. J. Jehowski to Dorothy Day, 7 October 1940, MUA, DD-CW, W-4, box 1, Nazareth House folder. Additional, undated letters from Welch thank Day for clarifying the matter.

82. Yzermans, *The People I Love,* 61; Alban J. Dachauer, S.J., ed., *The Rural Life Prayerbook* (Des Moines: National Catholic Rural Life Conference, 1956), 56–59, 130, passim.

83. Witte, *Twenty-five Years of Crusading,* 212–15; St. Isidore prayer card, undated, MUA, NCRLC, series 1, boxes 10, 11; Robert F. Jardes, undated memo on national shrine to St. Isidore, MUA, NCRLC, series 1/1, box 11. Jardes suggested that an advertising campaign for the DesMoines shrine begin in the dioceses of La Crosse, Wisconsin, and St. Cloud, Minnesota.

84. Company of St. Isidore folders; Edna Barrett to Michael Dineen, 4 December 1957; "The Company of St. Isidore, List #3," all in MUA, NCRLC, series 1, box 10; outdoor shrine advertisement, MUA, NCRLC, series 5/1, box 8; National Catholic Rural Life Conference, *St. Isidore, Patron of the Farmer* (Des Moines: NCRLC, n.d.), 18; Bovée, "The Church and the Land," 329–30. On Our Lady of the Fields, see Mary Jean Dorcy, *Our Lady of the Fields,* Land and Home Booklets (Des Moines: National Catholic Rural Life Conference, 1957).

85. Bovée, "The Church and the Land," 331; Hudnut-Beumler, *Looking for God in the Suburbs,* 177. Jay Dolan, *The American Catholic Experience,* 429–33, discusses the postconciliar development of devotional "rearguard actions" and "liturgically advanced" parishes.

86. Gilmore, *The Legacy,* 84–85; St. Andrew's parish report to NCRLC, 19 August 1953, MUA, NCRLC, series 1/1, box 3; Cf. National Catholic Rural Life Conference, *A Manual of Ceremonies for the Parish Observance of the Rogation Days* (Des Moines: NCRLC, 1953). Orsi, *The Madonna of 115th Street,* 223–31, makes a similar argument about liturgically created communities concerning the procession of the Virgin during the festival of Our Lady of Mt. Carmel.

87. Edwin O'Hara to William D. O'Brien, 13 July 1945, Loyola University of Chicago Archives, Catholic Church Extension Society papers, D/D3D, box 1, folder 1–5.

88. John E. McNamara, "Religious Difficulties among Catholic Farmers," *Catholic Rural Life Bulletin* 1 (May 1938): 21; the contest announcement appeared in *Catholic Rural Life* 4 (August 1926). Hill's and Iffrig's essays were published in November, while Umschied's and Greiner's appeared in December. Stock, *Main Street in Crisis,* 148–69, discusses the transformation of women's identity due to class changes resulting from the Depression in the Dakotas. Cf. Fink, *Agrarian Women,* 131–88.

89. McNamara, "Religious Difficulties among Catholic Farmers," 22.

90. Thomas and McShane, "Farmers Must Reform Methods of Farming," 100–102; Danbom, *The Resisted Revolution,* 138–42.

91. Luigi Ligutti, quoted in Yzermans, *The People I Love,* 106; Susman, *Culture as History,* xx, 211–29.

92. Parlette, "The Cities Do Not Make Their Own Steam," 6; Quinlan, *Standing on Both Feet.*

93. Luigi Ligutti, quoted in Yzermans, *The People I Love,* 84.

94. Joseph Finan to David F. Dunn, 20 August 1953, MUA, NCRLC, series 1/1, box 3.

95. H. L. Mencken, *A Mencken Chrestomathy* (New York: Knopf, 1949; reprint, New York: Vintage, Doubleday, 1982), 394–98. My use of Mencken follows that by David Edwin Harrell Jr. in "Religious Pluralism: Catholics, Jews, and Sectarians," in *Religion in the South: Essays,* ed. Charles Reagan Wilson (Jackson: University Press of Mississippi, 1985), 76–77.

96. Andrew Greeley, *The Church and the Suburbs* (New York: Sheed & Ward, 1959; rev. ed., Red Bank, N.J.: Deus Books, Paulist Press, 1963), 58.

Chapter 4: Muddy Roads and Rolling Stones

1. Flannery O'Connor, *Wise Blood,* 2d ed. (New York: Farrar, Straus & Giroux, 1962), 105, 109.

2. Schmiedeler, "Motor Missions," *Homiletic and Pastoral Review* 38 (1938): 578.

3. Walter Burke, C.S.P., "Rectory on Wheels," *American Ecclesiastical Review* 112 (1945): 95.

4. Edward L. Stephens, "The Motor Chapel in a Diocesan Mission Program," in *Proceedings of the National Catechetical Congress of the Confraternity of Christian Doctrine, 1939* (Paterson, N.J.: St. Anthony Guild, 1940), 324; R. Laurence Moore, *Selling God,* 10–11; Hatch, *The Democratization of American Christianity,* 30–34; Slawson, "Thirty Years of Street Preaching."

5. Kelley, *The Story of Extension,* 69–70, 90–110, passim; Loyola University of Chicago Archives, Catholic Church Extension Society collection, series X-1, box 1, Motor Chapel file, Chapel Car report binder. Cf. Salvatore Mondello, "Baptist Railroad Churches in the American West, 1890–1946," in *Religion and Society in the American West: Historical Essays,* ed. Carl Guarneri and David Alvarez, 105–27 (Lanham, Md.: University Press of America, 1987); Wilma Rugh Taylor and Norman Thomas Taylor, *This Train Is Bound for Glory: The Story of America's Chapel Cars* (Valley Forge, Pa.: Judson Press, 1999).

6. Conleth Overman, C.P., "The American Street-Preaching Movement," *Homiletic and Pastoral Review* 42 (1942): 432; Edgar Schmiedeler, O.S.B., to Luigi Ligutti, 11 August and 16 September 1937, MUA, NCRLC, series 13, box 1, folder 33; Schedule for the Nineteenth Annual Convention of the NCRLC (at Jefferson City, Missouri), MUA, NCRLC, series 13, box 1, folder 21, p. 13; John Heinz to Diocesan Directors, December 1948, MUA, NCRLC, series 13, box 1, folder 33.

7. Slawson, "Thirty Years of Street Preaching," 63. Cf. Stephen Leven, *Go Tell It in the Streets: The Autobiography of Stephen Leven* (Edmund, Okla.: n.p., 1984); Chalmers, *Hooded Americanism,* 49–56.

8. Slawson, "Thirty Years of Street Preaching," 64; "Catholic Motor Missions in America," photocopy in DeAndreis-Rosati Memorial Archives (DRMA), Perryville, Missouri, II-D-1, box 3; Schmiedeler, "Motor Missions, 1940," 388.

9. Schmiedeler, "Motor Missions, 1940," 391, 397–98; Edgar Schmiedeler, O.S.B., "Little Motor Mission Rationing," *Homiletic and Pastoral Review* 43 (1943): 516; Slawson, "Thirty Years of Street Preaching," 80. Schmiedeler's list does not include the diocese of Buffalo, New York, which he mentioned might be starting a similar ministry.

10. Stephen A. Leven, "Can Street Preaching Help?" *Homiletic and Pastoral Review* 37 (1937): 692; St. Martin's Parish, Caldwell, Kansas, CCUA, box 28, reel 19.

11. "St. Teresa's Village Is Run on Principles of Democracy," 9–10; Stephens, "The Motor Chapel in a Diocesan Mission Program." Terminiello delivered two papers about his work at the Catholic Conference of the South in 1941 and 1942. Andrew Moore covers the Alabama street-preaching apostolate in "Catholics in the Modern South: The Transformation of a Religion and a Region, 1945–1975" (Ph.D. diss., University of Florida, 2000). Stephens's legal background is mentioned in Schmiedeler, "Little Motor Mission Rationing," 509.

12. "Winchester's Paulists Have Made History," *Tennessee Register,* 5 April 1942, sec. 2, p. 2, copy in Diocesan Archives of Nashville, Tennessee. On Hecker and the Paulists, see Jay Dolan, *Catholic Revivalism: The American Experience, 1830–1900* (Notre Dame, Ind.: University of Notre Dame Press, 1978); and David O'Brien, *Isaac Hecker: An American Catholic* (New York: Paulist Press, 1992), 166–338. On Bishop and the Glenmarians, see Kauffman, *Mission to Rural America,* 160–85; and the correspondence in the Glenmary Home Missioners of America archives (GHMA), Cincinnati, Ohio.

13. On the Redemptorists, see Schmiedeler, "Trailing the Trailer Chapels," 238–40. On the Oblates of Mary Immaculate, see Edgar Schmiedeler, O.S.B., "Churches on Wheels," *Homiletic and Pastoral Review* 40 (January 1940): 366–68; and Marian DiMaggio, "Third National Street Preaching Institute for Priests, Carthage, Missouri, July 7–11, 1947," *Catholic Action* 29 (August 1947): 13. Schmiedeler lists the Benedictines, Capuchins, and Jesuits all in the Leavenworth diocese for 1941, in "Trailing the Trailer Chapels," 244–47.

14. Schmiedeler, "Little Motor Mission Rationing," 512; Hugo Hahn, C.Ss.R., "Motor-Mission Front," *Catholic Digest* 7 (December 1942): 25–26. Examples of lay assistance are in C. Richard Ginder, "Mass at Your Doorstep," *The Columbia* 17 (November 1937): 10, 21; and Henry Lexau, "Preaching on Ozark Trails," *Catholic Digest* 14 (January 1950): 62–63.

See Paul Dearing, "What Madding Crowd?" *The Sign* 25 (September 1945): 11–12; Mary Virginia Doyle, "Stumping for God," *America* 72 (3 March 1945): 426–27; Mary Ann Lund, "Girls in Oklahoma," *Catholic Digest* 5 (January 1941): 72–74; John E. McAniff, "The Catholic Evidence Guild on the Street Corner," *The Catholic Mind* 38 (8 February 1940): 53–60; John A. O'Brien, "Street Preaching among the Tarheels," *Ave Maria* 66 (4 October 1947): 423–26; and Marian Rauth, "Apostolate in the Mountains," *The Catholic World* 166 (December 1947): 259–62.

Debra Campbell has produced the best studies of the lay street-preaching apostolate: "David Goldstein and the Lay Catholic Street Apostolate, 1917–1941" (Ph.D. diss., Boston University, 1982); "The Catholic Evidence Guild: Towards a History of the Laity," *Heythrop Journal* 30 (1989): 306–24; "A Catholic Salvation Army: David Goldstein, Pioneer Lay Evangelist," *Church History* 52 (1983): 322–32; "Part-Time Female Evangelists of the Thirties and Forties: The Rosary College Catholic Evidence Guild," *U.S. Catholic Historian* 5 (1986): 371–83; and "The Rise of the Lay Catholic Evangelist in England and America," *Harvard Theological Review* 79 (1986): 413–37.

15. Quoted in Edward A. Freking, "Catholic Action through Mission Action," *Catholic Action* 19 (1937): 13.

16. Francis Wuest, "The Apostleship of Speech," *The Challenge* 5 (spring 1942): 8.

17. Rev. Ralph Egan to Bishop Louis B. Kucera, 10 February 1936, Diocesan Archives of Lincoln; GHMA, W. Howard Bishop Correspondence, 25626, 25621, 25619.

18. GHMA, Bishop Correspondence, 25616–17, 25626. The Vincentians' correspondence course apostolate is described in Schmiedeler, "Motor Missions" (1938): 582. Clemens Borchers, the Glenmary novice visiting the Vincentians, wrote Glenmary superior W. Howard Bishop that this was not an effective "follow-up" method. GHMA, Bishop Correspondence, 25621.

19. GHMA, Bishop Correspondence, 25617; Schmiedeler, "Trailing the Trailer Chapels," 240. Compared with the uproar over the 1952 publication of the Revised Standard Version (RSV) Bible, the motor missioners enjoyed relative peace. See Peter J. Thuesen, *In Discordance with the Scriptures: American Protestant Battles over Translating the Bible* (New York: Oxford University Press, 1999), especially 67–119.

20. Frank Sheed, "Street Corner Apologetic," *American Ecclesiastical Review* 90 (1934): 52; Lexau, "Preaching on Ozark Trails," 60, 63; Slawson, "Thirty Years of Street Preaching," 73.

21. *Manual for Street Preachers* (Denver: St. Thomas Seminary, 1941), 9, 10, 15–16, mimeograph copy in DRMA, II-D-1, box 3.

22. Leven, "Can Street-Preaching Help?" 694–96; Francis P. Broome, C.S.P., "The St. Lucy Catholic Trailer Chapel of Tennessee," in *Proceedings of the National Catechetical Congress of the Confraternity of Christian Doctrine, 1939*, 333.

23. R. Laurence Moore, *Selling God*, 146–71; *Manual for Street Preachers*, DRMA, II-D-1, box 3, contains fliers and bundles of handwritten questions.

24. Leven, "Can Street-Preaching Help?" 691; *Manual for Street Preachers*, DRMA, II-D-1, box 3.

25. North comment appears in DRMA, II-D-1, box 2, Riverton (Missouri) file; DRMA, I-D-1, box 3, Publicity file, 1939–1943. See also Hahn, "Motor Mission Front," 23; Broome, "St. Lucy Catholic Trailer Chapel," 333; Stephens, "The Motor Chapel," 327; "Catholic Motor Missions in America"; and Burke, "Rectory on Wheels," 96.

26. Ginder, "Mass at Your Doorstep," 10; Mary Perkins, "Heaven on Wheels," *The Sign* 22 (September 1942): 78.

27. Broome, "The St. Lucy Catholic Trailer Chapel," 332; "'Ceiling Zero' Does Not Befog Street Preachers' Clarity," *Denver Catholic Register*, 24 July 1952, 9, copy in Archdiocesan Archives of Denver; Burke, "Rectory on Wheels," 97, 98. Other estimates of trailer-chapel sound levels varied. According to Schmiedeler, the motor missions in Caldwell, Kansas, carried "four blocks away." "Motor Missions" (1938): 585. Apparently, a sound system was not a requirement for some missioners; Schmiedeler reported in "Trailing the Trailer Chapels," 245, that the Capuchin motor missions in the Concordia, Kansas, diocese began using a sound system only in 1941.

28. *Father Terminiello's 25th Anniversary*; Broome, "The St. Lucy Catholic Trailer Chapel," 338.

29. Broome, "The St. Lucy Catholic Trailer Chapel," 333; Richard Walsh, C.S.P., "Here Is Great Adventure," *The Sign* 25 (August 1945): 24.

30. Broome, "The St. Lucy Catholic Trailer Chapel," 335.

31. Hahn, "Motor Mission Front," 26; Slawson, "Thirty Years of Street Preaching," 68; Schmiedeler, "Churches on Wheels," 363 (quote), 364. The Vincentians recorded every mission's questions verbatim. The mission report for Piedmont, Missouri, 11 July 1937, includes the question about the priest's involvement with marriage consummation. DRMA, II-D-1, boxes 1, 2.

32. Edgar Schmiedeler, O.S.B., "Motor Missions," *American Ecclesiastical Review* 100 (February 1939): 140; Doyle, "Stumping for God," 426; Schmiedeler, "Motor Missions, 1940," 395, 392.

33. Kauffman, *Mission to Rural America*, 174; W. Howard Bishop, "On the 'Firing Line,'" *The Challenge* 5 (spring 1942): 4; Schmiedeler, "Little Motor Mission Rationing," 512; "Trailer Struck by Two 'Bombs' in Evensville," *Tennessee Register*, 27 September 1942, 1, 2, copy in Diocesan Archives of Nashville; Schmiedeler, "Motor Missions" (1938): 587.

34. DRMA, II-D-1, box 1; Slawson, "Thirty Years of Street Preaching," 68; "Work of Motor Chapel Described in Article," *The Register*, 4 October 1942, 1, 2, photocopy

in Diocesan Archives of Nashville; "Trailer Struck by Two 'Bombs' in Evensville," 2; Leven, "Can Street Preaching Help?" 695; Schmiedeler, "Churches on Wheels," 364–66; Burke, "Rectory on Wheels," 95.

35. Schmiedeler, "Churches on Wheels," 363, 366.

36. John A. O'Brien, "Methods of Reaching Converts," in *The White Harvest: A Symposium on Methods of Convert Making*, ed. John A. O'Brien (New York: Longmans, Green, 1930), 262; David Goldstein, "Lay Street Preaching," in O'Brien, *The White Harvest*, 209.

37. See Campbell, "A Catholic Salvation Army," 330; Campbell, "Part-Time Female Evangelists," 372, 377–82.

38. Rauth, "Apostolate in the Mountains," 259.

39. The last two quotes come from Perkins, "Heaven on Wheels," 77.

40. Stephens, "The Motor Chapel in a Diocesan Mission Program," 324–25.

41. *Manual for Street Preachers*, 2, DRMA, II-D-1, box 3; Dearing, "What Madding Crowd?" 11.

42. *Father Terminiello's 25th Anniversary*, 7; Lexau, "Preaching on Ozark Trails," 61; press release, 26 June 1936, Diocese of Lincoln, Diocesan Archives of Lincoln. Cf. Mark S. Massa, *Catholics and American Culture: Fulton Sheen, Dorothy Day, and the Notre Dame Football Team* (New York: Crossroad, 1999), 82–101.

43. "Right to be Unruly: The Terminiello Free Speech Case," *America* 81 (11 June 1949); 334

44. The story of Terminiello's speech is told in Ribuffo, *The Old Christian Right*, 216–18, 221–23. Terminiello was suspended from his priestly duties during the trial but was reinstated later. The laity's financial backing was just as influential as Sheed's theorizing. The Kuntz family of Dayton, Ohio, provided the funds for the Glenmarians' Chapel of the North American Martyrs and continued to donate Mass intentions throughout the 1940s. Some of the letters related to the Kuntzes' contributions are in the W. Howard Bishop correspondence, GHMA. Other orders benefited from lay support as well; the Vincentians compiled photos of their St. Anthony trailer chapel into a Christmas gift to the Vatterot family of St. Louis as a token of appreciation. Mention of Terminiello's troubles did not appear in the Vincentians' motor mission correspondence in DRMA, II-D-1, boxes 5 (photo album) and 6 (correspondence).

45. Schmiedeler, *Catholic Rural Life* (Washington, D.C.: National Council of Catholic Men, 1932), 10; Schmiedeler, "Motor Missions" (1938): 588. The program for the 1941 NCRLC convention is in MUA, series 8/1, box 4, file 21. Although he was not associated with that convention, Schmiedeler apparently had been considering something like it. A letter he wrote to Luigi Ligutti on 16 September 1937 mentioned the sessions for an upcoming Rural Life Diocesan Directors' meeting. The afternoon session included presentations on mission work by Father Stephens of Virginia and Father Terminiello of Alabama, with Schmiedeler presiding. MUA, NCRLC, series 13, box 1.

46. Walsh, "Here Is Great Adventure," 25; Broome, "The St. Lucy Catholic Trailer Chapel," 337.

47. "Six Week Tour Is Reported Successful by Father Kane," Diocesan Archives of Lincoln; Slawson, "Thirty Years of Street Preaching," 71 n. 29; Schmiedeler, "Churches on Wheels," 373; Ginder, "Mass at Your Doorstep," 10, 21. The Vincentians' motor mission reports alone, stretching from 1935 to 1964, take up three boxes in DRMA. On Father Ryan, "the poet priest of the Lost Cause," see Charles Reagan Wilson, *Baptized in Blood: The Religion of the Lost Cause, 1865–1920* (Athens: University of Georgia Press, 1980), 58–61.

48. McAniff, "The Catholic Evidence Guild," 58; GHMA, Bishop correspondence, 25624–25; Dearing, "What Madding Crowd?" 11; Burke, "Rectory on Wheels,"

102; Broome, "The St. Lucy Catholic Trailer Chapel," 339.

49. Ginder, "Mass at Your Doorstep," 21; DRMA, II-D-1, box 3, Publicity 1939–1943 file; Donald Barry to W. Howard Bishop, 21 September 1936, GHMA, Bishop correspondence, 13436.

50. Timothy D. Uhl discusses how St. Louis's Catholic population participated in this phenomenon in "The Naming of Catholic Parishes in St. Louis" (Ph.D. diss., Saint Louis University, 1997). Ann Taves describes the link between Marian piety and Catholic triumphalism in *The Household of Faith: Roman Catholic Devotions in Mid-Nineteenth-Century America* (Notre Dame, Ind.: University of Notre Dame Press, 1986), 106–11.

In 1938 Schmiedeler credited Terminiello with being the first priest "to undertake work by auto van in the South." Schmiedeler, "Motor Missions" (1938): 586. Terminiello is mentioned in all but the last of Schmiedeler's articles on motor missions, "Little Motor Mission Rationing." The Paulists' St. Lucy trailer chapel appears in them all; Father Broome's talk before the National Catechetical Congress of the Confraternity of Christian Doctrine also discusses the St. Lucy trailer. St. Rita appears in "Motor Missions, 1940," 388, and the rest of Schmiedeler's articles. The Vincentians' St. Anthony chapel, which was also the name of the first train-car chapel used by the Extension Society, is not mentioned at all by Schmiedeler, but is by Francis Massarella in his written reflections for W. Howard Bishop (GHMA, Bishop correspondence, 25622); according to Kauffman, *Mission to Rural America,* 147, Massarella's report would have been written after the summer of 1941. The North American Martyrs chapel received its first mention by Schmiedeler in "Trailing the Trailer Chapels," 247; Kauffman discusses it in *Mission to Rural America,* 145, 170. Hahn's article "Motor Mission Front" describes a day and a night with the Redemptorists' trailer chapel. Schmiedeler devotes significant attention to the Redemptorists in "Trailing the Trailer Chapels," 238–40; and "Little Motor Mission Rationing," 507–9.

The Dominicans' work in South Carolina came ten years after Schmiedeler's publications, but their trailer chapels were not mentioned in the postwar literature, either. A letter by Orville T. Carl, O.P., to Orliss North, 21 September 1949, enclosed a postcard of the Christ the King trailer chapel (DRMA, II-D-1, box 7). Although they are not mentioned in Carl's letter, a photograph in MUA, NCRLC, series 7/1, box 9, shows two trailer chapels—Holy Family and Christ the King. The handwritten caption on the back is dated 1950 and lists Rev. Orville Carl, O.P., and Patrick Walsh, O.P. Both vehicles were the auto-chapel type, converted from school buses or delivery trucks.

51. Taves, *The Household of Faith,* 128–33.

52. Ibid., 36–39; Colleen McDannell, *Material Christianity: Religion and Popular Culture in America* (New Haven, Conn.: Yale University Press, 1995), 132–60; Campbell, "A Catholic Salvation Army," 323; John O'Brien, "Methods of Reaching Converts," 263. Thomas A. Kselman and Steven Avella discuss the antitriumphalism in mid-twentieth-century Marian piety in "Marian Piety and the Cold War in the United States," *Catholic Historical Review* 72 (July 1986): 407–9, 420.

53. Halsey, *The Survival of American Innocence,* 138–53; on Native Americans, see Jay Dolan, *The American Catholic Experience,* 284–86; on Mexican Americans, see pp. 372–77; on African Americans, see pp. 365–71; Davis, *The History of Black Catholics,* passim. Steven M. Avella describes the convert work among African Americans directed by Archbishop Samuel Stritch, who also supported the NCRLC. Avella, *This Confident Church: Catholic Leadership and Life in Chicago, 1940–1965* (Notre Dame, Ind.: University of Notre Dame Press, 1992), 281–88.

54. Schmiedeler, "Motor Missions" (1939): 141; "Motor Missions, 1940," 397; "Motor Missions" (1938): passim.

55. Kauffman, *Mission to Rural America*, 180–81, 230–31; Arthur W. Terminiello, "The Catholic Settlement," in *Proceedings of the Second Annual Meeting of the Catholic Conference of the South* (Richmond, Va.: n.p., 1942), 65. The quotation about Tullahoma appears in Schmiedeler, "Churches on Wheels," 369.

56. Terminiello, "Discussion of James Cunningham's Report," in *Proceedings of the First Annual Meeting of the Catholic Conference of the South* (Richmond, Va.: n.p., 1941), 70. The Catholic rural life movement exhibited a general interest in the missionary significance of rural African Americans. Joseph Matt, editor of *The Wanderer* in St. Paul, Minnesota, delivered a paper at the 1937 NCRLC convention on Catholic rural life and black Americans. Later, in the 1960s, at least two African American priests participated in the motor missions themselves. See "Meet Madonna of the Highways," *Extension* 56 (August 1961): 20–24.

57. Robert Wuthnow, *The Restructuring of American Religion* (Princeton, N.J.: Princeton University Press, 1988), 156; "A One Night Stand for the Negroes . . .," DRMA, II-D-1, box 3, "Catholic Motor Mission Publicity, 1939–1943," 3; Schmiedeler, "Motor Missions," *American Ecclesiastical Review*, 142; Schmiedeler, "Churches on Wheels," 366–67. In "Trailing the Trailer Chapels," 245, Schmiedeler mentions in passing Benedictines from Atchison working in the Kickapoo Indian Reservation. See also James Cone, *Speaking the Truth: Ecumenism, Liberation, and Black Theology* (1986; reprint, Grand Rapids, Mich.: Wm. B. Eerdmans, 1990), 57.

58. Schmiedeler, "Churches on Wheels," 367; Schmiedeler, "Motor Missions, 1940," 398.

59. Schmiedeler, "Motor Missions," *American Ecclesiastical Review*, 142; Schmiedeler, "Motor Missions, 1940," 398; On the Missionary Catechists, see Schmiedeler, "Little Motor Mission Rationing," 510–11. On the Extension Society's efforts to support and strengthen the Church in Mexico and among Mexican immigrants in the United States (primarily the Southwest), see Jay Dolan, *The American Catholic Experience*, 377–78; and Kelley, *The Story of Extension*, 186–87, 238–39. In "Churches on Wheels," 362, Schmiedeler includes the following: "This summer [1942] . . . the trailer chapel [St. Rita] was used by the Missionary Catechists in their work of instructing Mexican children and adults of the diocese." This does not seem to suggest that the trailer served any liturgical function, as it did with the Paulist fathers. The Catechists usually sang hymns in Spanish. This use of a language other than English was not unique: at least one motor mission team in the Wichita, Kansas, diocese needed a priest fluent in Bohemian, and an interpreter apparently accompanied a mission team around Thoreau, New Mexico. Schmiedeler, "Motor Missions, 1940," 396, 398. "St. Benedict's Jubilee," CCUA, drawer 28, reel 16; Fathers Haverkamp, Spiegelhalter, and Hall are mentioned by Schmiedeler in "Trailing the Trailer Chapels," 245. "St. Patrick's Fiftieth Anniversary," CCUA, drawer 28, reel 17.

60. Schmiedeler, "Motor Missions," *American Ecclesiastical Review*, 139; "Vast Areas of Nation Priestless," *The Challenge* 1 (1938): 1. Kauffman explains "No Priest Land" in *Mission to Rural America*, 145–47.

61. Burke, "Rectory on Wheels," 102; Raphael Sourd, "Echoes from the Mission Front," *The Challenge* 6, no. 2 (summer 1943): 4. Coupal's observations on Marquette and Menominee are in DRMA, II-D-1, box 5, Michigan file.

62. Although all of Schmiedeler's articles contain statistics on the scarcity of rural Catholics, the "100-mile-wide parish" reference comes from "Trailing the Trailer Chapels," 242; the comparison between South Carolina and Mongolia, made by Maurice Fitzgerald, C.S.P., is on p. 244.

63. W. Howard Bishop, "A Plan for Mission Work in the Hinterlands," in Na-

tional Catholic Rural Life Conference, *NCRLC Proposals, 1937* (St. Paul, Minn.: NCRLC, 1938), 170; Bishop, "Invading No-Priest Land on Wheels," *The Challenge* 4, no. 3 (Christmas 1941): 5; Burke, "Rectory on Wheels," 95; Schmiedeler, "Motor Missions, 1940," 392.

64. McDannell, *Material Christianity,* 133.

65. Schmiedeler, "Churches on Wheels," 361; Walsh, "Here Is Great Adventure," 24.

66. Schmiedeler, "Motor Missions, 1940," 391; Walsh, "Here Is Great Adventure," 24.

67. Chalmers, *Hooded Americanism,* 317. Renehan quoted in Schmiedeler, "Little Motor Mission Rationing," 509; Lexau, "Preaching on Ozark Trails," 60–62.

68. Walsh, "Here Is Great Adventure," 24; Broome, "The St. Lucy Catholic Trailer Chapel," 338.

69. Eoin McKiernan, "Horse and Buggy Church," *The Catholic World* 155 (July 1942): 475; John Marquardt, "Sorghum Stir-Off," *Mission Digest* 9 (October 1951): 35. Ted Ownby, *Subduing Satan: Religion, Recreation, and Manhood in the Rural South, 1865–1920* (Chapel Hill: University of North Carolina Press, 1990), 167–93, describes how county fairs and traveling circuses helped relieve rural isolation in the South by offering entertaining breaks from the monotony of rural life. Traveling demonstrations had a history outside the South as well; an example from the late nineteenth century that promoted white racism and resettlement in Alabama is studied by Katharine M. Pruett and John D. Fair in "Promoting a New South: Immigration, Racism, and 'Alabama on Wheels,'" *Agricultural History* 66 (1992): 19–41.

70. Danbom, *The Resisted Revolution,* 87–94; Broome, "The St. Lucy Catholic Trailer Chapel," 338.

71. Ownby, *Subduing Satan,* 194–203, describes the impact of automobiles and American mass culture on Southern evangelicals. See also Virginia Scharff, *Taking the Wheel: Women and the Coming of the Motor Age* (New York: Free Press, 1991), 135–75. The emergence of the Book-of-the-Month Club serves as another example of the early-twentieth-century interconnection between cultural merchandise and the new freedoms American women could enjoy. Janice Radway, "On the Gender of the Middlebrow Consumer and the Threat of the Culturally Fraudulent Female," *South Atlantic Quarterly* 93 (fall 1994): 883.

72. "Mission Trailer: Paulist Fathers, Tennessee," *Liturgical Arts* 6 (second quarter 1937): 68–69; "St. Mary of the Highways Trailer Chapel," *Liturgical Arts* 7 (February 1939): 27. McDannell, *Material Christianity,* 163–97, discusses the role of *Liturgical Arts* in the growing condemnation of devotional Catholic "kitsch" throughout the 1940s, 1950s, and 1960s. Cf. McCarraher, "American Gothic," 7–8.

73. Schmiedeler, "Motor Missions," *American Ecclesiastical Review,* 138; Walsh, "Here Is Great Adventure," 24. A photograph of the cinema experiment is in DRMA, II-D-1, box 5. On the back is a handwritten description of the project; it ends, "Not Successful." Despite the praise showered on DeMille by Schmiedeler and the other motor mission priests, he was not the reigning moralist of Hollywood. R. Laurence Moore, in *Selling God,* 224, reveals that DeMille's successful religious films were his only such "moral" works. In fact, many liberal Protestants who were forming the industry's first censorship board found DeMille far too tolerant of adultery and other moral failings on the screen.

74. DiMaggio, "Third National Street Preaching Institute"; Archdiocesan Archives of St. Louis, motor mission file; Slawson, "Thirty Years of Street Preaching," 60–61. Herman W. Santen, *Father Bishop, Founder of the Glenmary Home Missioners*

(Milwaukee, Wis.: Bruce, 1961), after p. 18, includes a photograph of the North American Martyrs chapel; the caption states that the chapel "brought the first glimpse of a Catholic Church to thousands in the southern Appalachian mountains between 1940 and 1946. It was abandoned in favor of street preaching." A handwritten, undated manuscript entitled "Our Mission Movement" in the W. Howard Bishop collection at GHMA begins, "Our movement is *not* an 'outdoor preaching' or 'motor mission' movement. It is a missionary movement in a very thorough sense. It uses not only preaching as a means of making converts, but *life among the people to be converted*. . . . Our missioners give not certain times but their entire careers to the work." Copies of the pamphlet advertising Christ Week are in GHMA, "Resource and Development— Mission Education," box 3.

75. O'Connor, *Wise Blood,* 113; Brian Abel Ragen, *A Wreck on the Road to Damascus: Innocence, Guilt, and Conversion in Flannery O'Connor* (Chicago: Loyola University Press, 1989), 121.

76. Walsh, "Here Is Great Adventure," 25; Hahn, "Motor Mission Front," 27.

Conclusion: The Wheat and Chaff of Catholic Agrarianism

1. James Kenney to "Miss Naughton," 16 June 1948, MUA, DD-CW, W-6.1, box 1; Ruth Ann Heaney, interview with Troester, 42.

2. Yzermans, *The People I Love,* 39.

3. Dorman, *The Revolt of the Provinces,* 247; Allitt, *Catholic Converts,* 16.

4. For remarks about Masses celebrated in the barn at Maryfarm, see Joseph and Alice Zarrella, interview with William D. Miller, 10 July 1967, MUA, DD-CW, W-4 box 1. Fisher, *Catholic Counterculture,* 250, wrote: "None of the liturgical experimentation of the postconciliar period struck the older personalists as particularly innovative, especially compared to the rites performed at the Catholic Worker farms in the 1940s." Thomas Day's *Why Catholics Can't Sing: The Culture of Catholicism and the Triumph of Bad Taste* (New York: Crossroad, 1990), especially p. 6, offers a stinging indictment of the liturgical "rubricism" before the Council and the self-congratulatory "folk Mass" after it.

5. Shi, *The Simple Life,* 260; Donald E. Pitzer, "America's Communal Utopias Founded by 1965," in *America's Communal Utopias,* ed. Donald E. Pitzer (Chapel Hill: University of North Carolina Press, 1997), 456.

6. Bill Devall and George Sessions, "Deep Ecology," reprinted in *Earth Ethics: Environmental Ethics, Animal Rights, and Practical Applications,* ed. James P. Sterba (Englewood Cliffs, N.J.: Prentice Hall, 1995), 159–60; Martha F. Lee, *Earth First! Environmental Apocalypse* (Syracuse, N.Y.: Syracuse University Press, 1995), 26–27, 53–57, 85–86. On Thomas Berry, C.P., see Bery, *The Dream of the Earth* (San Francisco: Sierra Club Books, 1988); see also Sarah McFarland Taylor, "From the American Dream to the Dream of the Earth: Remapping Religion and Culture at Genesis Farm" (paper presented at the annual conference of the Society for the Scientific Study of Religion, San Diego, Calif., 9 November 1997).

7. Rupert Sheldrake, *The Rebirth of Nature: The Greening of Science and God* (Rochester, Vt.: Park Street Press, 1994), 190; Gary Snyder, quoted in Charles R. Strain, "The Pacific Buddha's Wild Practice: Gary Snyder's Environmental Ethic," in *American Buddhism: Recent Understandings and Scholarship,* ed. Duncan Ryuken Williams and Stephen S. Queen (Richmond, U.K.: Curzon, 1999), 148–49.

8. Albanese, *America: Religions and Religion,* 482–96; Roger Gottlieb, "The Transcendence of Justice and the Justice of Transcendence: Mysticism, Deep Ecology, and Political Life," *Journal of the American Academy of Religion* 67 (March 1999): 155.

9. H. Paul Santmire, *The Travail of Nature: The Ambiguous Ecological Promise of Christian Theology* (Philadelphia: Fortress Press, 1985), 9–10, 19–23, 189–218. Cf. Sallie McFague, *Models of God: Theology for Ecological, Nuclear Age* (Philadelphia: Fortress Press, 1987), 60–63, 69–78, 93–95; Laura Hobgood-Oster, "Stories Told through Animal Saints" (paper presented at the American Society of Environmental History convention, Tacoma, Wash., 18 March 2000).

10. Matthew Fox, *Original Blessing: A Primer in Creation Spirituality* (Santa Fe, N.M.: Bear & Company, 1983) (the date of 19,996,000,000 years is from p. 46); Fox, *Sheer Joy: Conversations with Thomas Aquinas on Creation Spirituality* (San Francisco: HarperSanFrancisco, 1992); Rosemary Radford Ruether, *Gaia and God: An Ecofeminist Theology of Earth Healing* (San Francisco: HarperSanFrancisco, 1992); Sheldrake, *The Rebirth of Nature*, 223. Cf. Max Oelschlaeger, *Caring for Creation: An Ecumenical Approach to the Environmental Crisis* (New Haven, Conn.: Yale University Press, 1994).

11. Mary Daly, *Gyn/Ecology: The Metaethics of Radical Feminism*, rev. ed. (Boston: Beacon, 1990), 20, 79–81, 313–424; Daly, *Outercourse: The Be-Dazzling Voyage* (San Francisco: HarperSanFrancisco, 1992), 195–239.

12. Fisher, *Catholic Counterculture*, 250; John Kennedy Toole, *A Confederacy of Dunces* (New York: Grove, 1980), 40–42, 402ff.; Martin Cruz Smith, *Gorky Park* (New York: Ballantine Books, 1981), 209–10.

13. Pope Paul VI, "Humanae Vitae," in *The Papal Encyclicals*, vol. 5, *1958–1981*, trans. Claudia Carlen (New York: McGrath, Consortium Books, 1981), 226; Mary Jo Weaver, "Resisting Catholic Sexual Teaching: Pro-Choice Advocacy and Homosexual Support Groups," in *What's Left? Liberal American Catholics*, ed. Mary Jo Weaver (Bloomington: Indiana University Press, 1999), 90; See also Gene Burns, "Abandoning Suspicion: The Catholic Left and Sexuality," in Weaver, *What's Left?* 74–80.

14. Cuneo, *The Smoke of Satan*, 81–119.

15. James Ridgeway, *Blood in the Face: The Ku Klux Klan, Aryan Nations, Nazi Skinheads, and the Rise of a New White Culture*, rev. ed. (New York: Thunder's Mouth Press, 1995), 65–72, 115 (quotation from Mathews), 150–59; Michael Barkun, *Religion and the Racist Right: The Origins of the Christian Identity Movement*, rev. ed. (Chapel Hill: University of North Carolina Press, 1997), 54–61, 228–31.

16. Cross, "The Changing Image of the City," 39. Cf. Eugene McCarraher, "The Saint in the Gray Flannel Suit: The Professional-Managerial Class, 'The Layman,' and American-Catholic-Religious Culture, 1945–1965," *U.S. Catholic Historian* 16 (spring 1998): 99–118.

17. Cross, "The Changing Image of the City," 33, 47, 52; Harvey Cox, *The Secular City: Secularization and Urbanization in Theological Perspective* (New York: Macmillan, 1965), especially 44–58.

18. Cecelia Tichi, *High Lonesome: The American Culture of Country Music* (Chapel Hill: University of North Carolina Press, 1994), 102.

19. Ibid., 42–48; Tex Sample, *White Soul: Country Music, the Church, and Working Americans* (Nashville, Tenn.: Abingdon Press, 1996), 110–20, 142–46.

20. Sample, *White Soul*, 69–78, 100–101, 163–75; Fillingim, "Redneck Liberation"; Schmiedeler, "Motor Missions, 1940," 399–400.

21. Carolyn Chute, *Letourneau's Used Auto Parts* (New York: Ticknor & Fields, 1988); Chute, *The Beans of Egypt, Maine* (New York: Ticknor & Fields, 1985); Chute, *Merry Men* (New York: Harcourt Brace, 1994); Ana Castillo, *So Far from God* (New York: Plume, 1994).

22. Christy Cousino, "'Almost as Good as Clancy but Catholic': Action-Adventure Goes to the Marian Millennium" (paper presented at the American Academy of Religion

convention, Orlando, Florida, 23 November 1998); Castillo, *So Far from God,* 191. Cousino refers to Bud Macfarlane, *Pierced by a Sword* (Fairview Park, Ohio: St. Jude Media, 1995).

23. Belden Lane, *The Solace of Fierce Landscapes: Exploring Desert and Mountain Spirituality* (New York: Oxford University Press, 1998). On Genesis Farm, see Taylor, "From the American Dream to the Dream of the Earth."

24. William Least Heat Moon [William Trogdon], *Blue Highways: A Journey into America* (Boston: Atlantic–Little, Brown, 1982), 62. Michael G. Dalecki and C. Milton Coughenour, "Agrarianism in American Society," *Rural Sociology* 57 (1992): 48–64; Shortridge, *The Middle West,* 10, 82–96; Claims for "the most Midwestern state" appear throughout James Madison, ed., *Heartland: Comparative Histories of the Midwestern States* (Bloomington: Indiana University Press, 1988).

25. Dawn Gibeau, "What Is Most Exalted about Life in America Is Still Most Likely to Be Found on the Land," *National Catholic Reporter* 30, no. 3 (5 November 1993): 5–9; Mary Ann Hinsdale, Helen M. Lewis, and S. Maxine Walker, *It Comes from the People: Community Development and Local Theology* (Philadelphia: Temple University Press, 1995), 251, 315–26; Goad, *The Redneck Manifesto,* 255.

26. Anthony DeCurtis, "Introduction: The Sanctioned Power of Rock & Roll," *South Atlantic Quarterly* 90 (fall 1991): 646; Peter L. Berger, *A Rumor of Angels* (New York: Doubleday & Company, Anchor Books, 1970), 18; David Danbom, "Romantic Agrarianism in Twentieth-Century America," *Agricultural History* 65 (fall 1991): 1–12.

Bibliography

Archives

Archdiocesan Archives of Denver, Colorado
Copies of *Denver Catholic Register*
Motor missions materials

Archdiocesan Archives of Mobile, Alabama
Arthur Terminiello materials

Archdiocesan Archives of St. Louis, Missouri
Donald F. Molitor papers
Motor mission file

Catholic Central Union of America archives (CCUA), St. Louis, Missouri
Catholic publications files
Microfilmed holdings

DeAndreis-Rosati Memorial Archives (DRMA), Perryville, Missouri
Vincentian Motor Missions files

Diocesan Archives of Lincoln, Nebraska
Motor missions materials

Diocesan Archives of Nashville, Tennessee
Copies of *Tennessee Register*

Glenmary Home Missioners of America archives (GHMA), Cincinnati, Ohio
W. Howard Bishop correspondence
Copies of *The Challenge*

Loyola University of Chicago Archives, Chicago, Illinois
Catholic Church Extension Society Collection

Marquette University Archives (MUA), Milwaukee, Wisconsin
Dorothy Day–Catholic Worker movement collection (DD-CW)
Luigi G. Ligutti collection (LGL)
National Catholic Rural Life Conference collection (NCRLC)

Saint Louis University Archives, St. Louis, Missouri

Printed Sources

Abbey, Edward. *Desert Solitaire: A Season in the Wilderness*. 1973. Rev. ed., New York: Bantam Books, 1990.

"Activities of a Rural Community." *Catholic Rural Life* 3 (May 1925): 7.

Adams, Jane. *The Transformation of Rural Life: Southern Illinois, 1890–1990*. Chapel Hill: University of North Carolina Press, 1994.

Agee, James, with Walker Evans. *Let Us Now Praise Famous Men*. 1941. Reprint, Boston: Houghton Mifflin, 1980.

Ahlstrom, Sydney. *A Religious History of the American People*. New Haven, Conn.: Yale University Press, 1972.

Albanese, Catherine. *America: Religions and Religion*. 3d ed. Berkeley, Calif.: Wadsworth, 1999.

———. "Exchanging Souls, Exchanging Selves: Contact, Combination, and American Religious History." In *Retelling U.S. Religious History*, edited by Thomas A. Tweed, 200–226. Berkeley: University of California Press, 1996.

Allitt, Patrick. *Catholic Converts: British and American Intellectuals Turn to Rome*. Ithaca, N.Y.: Cornell University Press, 1997.

"'Apostle of Rural Life' Dies at 88." *National Catholic Reporter* 20 (13 January 1984): 25.

Avella, Steven. "Sanctity in the Era of Catholic Action: The Case of Pius X." *U.S. Catholic Historian* 15 (1997): 57–80.

———. *This Confident Church: Catholic Leadership and Life in Chicago, 1940–1965*. Notre Dame, Ind.: University of Notre Dame, 1992.

"Back to the Country." *America* 48 (12 November 1932): 127.

"Back to the Farm." *America* 47 (23 July 1932): 368.

Baer, Urban. *Farmers of Tomorrow*. Sparta, Wis.: Monroe Publishing Company, 1939.

Barkun, Michael. *Religion and the Racist Right: The Origins of the Christian Identity Movement*. Rev. ed. Chapel Hill: University of North Carolina Press, 1997.

Barry, Colman, O.S.B. *The Catholic Church and German Americans*. Milwaukee, Wis.: Bruce, 1953.

Bartelt, Pearl W. "American Jewish Agricultural Colonies." In *America's Communal Utopias*, edited by Donald E. Pitzer, 352–74. Chapel Hill: University of North Carolina Press, 1997.

Baruch, Bernard M. "Solution to Rural Credits." *St. Isidore's Plow* 1 (March 1923): 1.

Baum, Gregory. *Catholics and Canadian Socialism: Political Thought in the Thirties and Forties*. New York: Paulist Press, 1980.

Bennett, David H. *Demagogues in the Depression: American Radicals and the Union Party, 1932–1936*. New Brunswick, N.J.: Rutgers University Press, 1969.

Berger, Bennett M. *The Survival of a Counterculture: Ideological Work and Everyday Life among Rural Communards*. Berkeley: University of California Press, 1981.

Berger, Peter L. *A Rumor of Angels*. New York: Doubleday & Co., Anchor Books, 1970.

Berry, Thomas. *The Dream of the Earth*. San Francisco: Sierra Club Books, 1988.

Bible. Douay-Rheims English Translation. New York: P. J. Kenedy and Sons, 1914.

Biehler, J. E. *One Hundred Years in Rock Creek Valley: A History of the St. Joseph Parish at Flush, Kansas*. Topeka, Kans.: Central Press, 1954.

Bishop, W. Howard. "Invading No-Priest Land on Wheels." *The Challenge* 4, no. 3 (Christmas 1941): 5.

———. "On the 'Firing Line.'" *The Challenge* 5 (spring 1942): 4, 8.

———. "A Plan for Mission Work in the Hinterlands." In National Catholic Rural Life Conference, *NCRLC Proposals, 1937*. St. Paul, Minn.: NCRLC, 1938.

———. "Presidential Address." In National Catholic Rural Life Conference, *Proceedings of the Eleventh Annual Convention, 1933,* 10–15. Washington, D.C.: National Catholic Welfare Council, Rural Life Bureau, n.d.

———. "A Step toward Rural Colonization." *Catholic Action* 14 (September 1932): 19.

Blee, Kathleen M. *Women of the Klan: Racism and Gender in the 1920s.* Berkeley: University of California Press, 1991.

Boorstin, Daniel J. *The Americans: The National Experience.* New York: Vintage Books, Random House, 1967.

Borsodi, Ralph. *Flight from the City.* New York: Harper and brothers, 1933.

———. *This Ugly Civilization.* New York: Simon, 1929.

Bovée, David S. "The Church and the Land: The National Catholic Rural Life Conference and American Society, 1923–1985." Ph.D. diss., University of Chicago, 1986.

Brinkley, Alan. *Voices of Protest: Huey Long, Father Coughlin, and the Great Depression.* New York: Knopf, 1982.

Brockland, August. "The Catholic Union of Missouri." *St. Isidore's Plow* 2 (October 1923): 4.

Bromfield, Louis. *Pleasant Valley.* New York: Harper & Brothers Publishers, 1945.

Broome, Francis P., C.S.P. "The St. Lucy Catholic Trailer Chapel of Tennessee." In *Proceedings of the National Catechetical Congress of the Confraternity of Christian Doctrine, 1939,* 331–39. Paterson, N.J.: St. Anthony Guild, 1940.

Brown, Alden. *The Grail Movement and American Catholicism, 1940–1975.* Notre Dame, Ind.: University of Notre Dame Press, 1989.

Bruns, Jette. *Hold Dear, As Always: Jette, a German Immigrant Life in Letters.* Translated by Adolf E. Schroeder, edited by Adolf E. Schroeder and Carla Schulz-Geisberg. Columbia: University of Missouri Press, 1988.

Burke, Walter, C.S.P. "Rectory on Wheels." *American Ecclesiastical Review* 112 (1945): 95–102.

Burns, Gene. "Abandoning Suspicion: The Catholic Left and Sexuality." In *What's Left? Liberal American Catholics,* edited by Mary Jo Weaver, 67–87. Bloomington: Indiana University Press, 1999.

Burns, Jeffrey M. *American Catholics and the Family Crisis, 1930–1962: The Ideological and Organizational Response.* New York: Garland Press, 1988.

Campbell, Debra. "The Catholic Evidence Guild: Towards a History of the Laity." *Heythrop Journal* 30 (1989): 306–24.

———. "A Catholic Salvation Army: David Goldstein, Pioneer Lay Evangelist." *Church History* 52 (1983): 322–32.

———. "David Goldstein and the Lay Catholic Street Apostolate, 1917–1941." Ph.D. diss., Boston University, 1982.

———. "Part-Time Female Evangelists of the Thirties and Forties: The Rosary College Catholic Evidence Guild." *U.S. Catholic Historian* 5 (1986): 371–83.

———. "The Rise of the Lay Catholic Evangelist in England and America." *Harvard Theological Review* 79 (1986): 413–37.

Campbell, J[oseph] M. "Credit Unions." In National Catholic Rural Life Conference, *Proceedings of the Eleventh Annual Convention, 1933,* 27–28. Washington, D.C.: National Catholic Welfare Conference, Rural Life Bureau, n.d.

Carey, Thomas. "Presidential Address." *Catholic Rural Life* 3 (November 1925): 3.

Carey, Patrick W. *Priests, Prelates, and Laypeople: Ecclesiastical Democracy and the Tensions of Trusteeism.* Notre Dame, Ind.: University of Notre Dame Press, 1987.

———. *The Roman Catholics.* Denominations in America, no. 6. Westport, Conn.: Greenwood Press, 1993.

Carota, Estelle and Mario. *We Shall Raise Our Voice Again: The Conflict between Doctrine and Canon Law.* Santa Cruz, Calif.: Christian Economic Networks, n.d.

Carota, Mario. "Toehold on the Land." *The Catholic Worker* 15 (April 1949): 4.

Carter, Lee. "Sharecroppers Homeless; Seek Free Land." *The Catholic Worker* 6 (March 1939): 1, 2.

Casper, Henry W., S.J. *Catholic Chapters in Nebraska Immigration, 1870–1900.* Vol. 3 of *The History of the Catholic Church in Nebraska.* Milwaukee, Wis.: Bruce, 1966.

———. *The Church on the Northern Plains.* Vol. 1 of *The History of the Catholic Church in Nebraska.* Milwaukee, Wis.: Bruce, 1960.

Castillo, Ana. *So Far from God.* New York: Plume, 1994.

Catholic Cooperative Committee. *Catholic Churchmen and Cooperatives.* Huntington, Ind.: Our Sunday Visitor, 1944.

"Catholic Worker Cells." *The Catholic Worker* 6 (September 1938): 7.

Chalmers, David M. *Hooded Americanism: The History of the Ku Klux Klan.* New York: New Viewpoints, 1965; Franklin Watt, 1981.

Chute, Carolyn. *The Beans of Egypt, Maine.* New York: Ticknor & Fields, 1985.

———. *Letourneau's Used Auto Parts.* New York: Ticknor & Fields, 1988.

———. *Merry Men.* New York: Harcourt Brace, 1994.

Clark, Henry W. "Resettlement on the Last Frontier." *Commonweal* 28 (1 July 1938): 266–68.

Clemens, Alphonse H. *Marriage and the Family: An Integrated Approach for Catholics.* Englewood Cliffs, N.J.: Prentice-Hall, 1957.

Coady, M. M. "Cooperation in Nova Scotia." In National Catholic Rural Life Conference, *Proceedings of the Twelfth Convention, 1934.* Washington, D.C.: National Catholic Welfare Conference, Rural Life Bureau, n.d.

———. *Masters of Their Own Destiny: The Story of the Antigonish Movement of Adult Education through Economic Cooperation.* New York: Harper, 1939.

Coburn, Carol. *Life at Four Corners: Religion, Gender, and Education in a German-Lutheran Community, 1868–1945.* Lawrence: University Press of Kansas, 1992.

Cone, James. *Speaking the Truth: Ecumenism, Liberation, and Black Theology.* 1986. Reprint, Grand Rapids, Mich.: Wm. B. Eerdmans, 1990.

Confrey, Burton. "Apostolate of the Spoken Word." *The Ave Maria* 53 (1 March 1941): 263–67.

Conkin, Paul. *Tomorrow a New World: The New Deal Community Program.* Ithaca, N.Y.: Cornell University Press for the American Historical Association, 1959.

Corrin, Jay P. *G. K. Chesterton and Hilaire Belloc: The Battle against Modernity.* Athens: Ohio University Press, 1981.

———. "H. A. Reinhold: Liturgical Pioneer and Anti-Fascist." *Catholic Historical Review* 82 (1996): 436–58.

Cousino, Christy. "'Almost as Good as Clancy but Catholic': Action-Adventure Goes to the Marian Millennium." Paper presented at the American Academy of Religion convention, Boston, Massachusetts, 22 November 1999.

Couture, C. E. "Colonization in Quebec." *Land and Home* 9 (June 1946): 48–49.

Covington, Dennis. *Salvation on Sand Mountain: Snake Handling and Redemption in Southern Appalachia.* New York: Penguin Books, 1995.

Cox, Harvey. *The Secular City: Secularization and Urbanization in Theological Perspective.* New York: Macmillan, 1965.

"Cracked Corn: No Ration Points." *Land and Home* 7 (June 1944): 47.

"Cracked Corn: Part-Time Farming Works." *Land and Home* 8 (March 1945): 20–21.

Cross, Robert D. "The Changing Image of the City among American Catholics." *Catholic Historical Review* 48 (1962): 33–52.

Crozier, William I. *Gathering a People: A History of the Diocese of Winona.* Winona, Minn.: Diocese of Winona, 1989.

Cuneo, Michael W. *The Smoke of Satan: Conservative and Traditionalist Dissent in Contemporary American Catholicism.* New York: Oxford University Press, 1997.

Dachauer, Alban J., S.J., ed. *The Rural Life Prayerbook.* Des Moines: National Catholic Rural Life Conference, 1956.

Dalecki, Michael G., and C. Milton Coughenour. "Agrarianism in American Society." *Rural Sociology* 57 (1992): 48–64.

Daly, Mary. *Gyn/Ecology: The Metaethics of Radical Feminism.* Rev. ed. Boston: Beacon, 1990.

———. *Outercourse: The Be-Dazzling Voyage.* San Francisco: HarperSanFrancisco, 1992.

Daly, Mildred. "Youth Seeks Quality in Choosing Spouse." *Catholic Rural Life Bulletin* 4 (February 1941): 13.

Danbom, David. *Born in the Country: A History of Rural America.* Baltimore: Johns Hopkins University Press, 1995.

———. *The Resisted Revolution: Urban America and the Industrialization of Agriculture, 1900–1930.* Ames: Iowa State University Press, 1979.

———. "Romantic Agrarianism in Twentieth-Century America." *Agricultural History* 65 (fall 1991): 1–12.

Davidson, Gabriel. *Our Jewish Farmers and the Story of the Jewish Agricultural Society.* New York: L. B. Fischer, 1943.

Davidson, James. *Courtesans and Fishcakes: The Consuming Passions of Classical Athens.* New York: St. Martin's Press, 1998.

Davis, Cyprian, O.S.B. *The History of Black Catholics in the United States.* New York: Crossroad, 1990.

Dawber, Mark A. *Rebuilding Rural America.* New York: Friendship Press, 1937.

Day, Dorothy. "Death of an Apostle." *The Catholic Worker* 16 (June 1949): 1, 6.

———. "Idea for a Farm Commune." *The Catholic Worker* 5 (January 1938): 8.

———. *Loaves and Fishes.* New York: Harper, 1963.

———. *The Long Loneliness: The Autobiography of Dorothy Day.* Rev. ed. New York: Harper & Row, 1981.

———. "Priest Starts Farm Co-op." *The Catholic Worker* 5 (January 1938): 1, 7.

Day, Thomas. *Why Catholics Can't Sing: The Culture of Catholicism and the Triumph of Bad Taste.* New York: Crossroad, 1990.

Day, Victor. "The Correspondence Course in Christian Doctrine." *St. Isidore's Plow* 2 (January 1924): 2.

Dearing, Paul. "What Madding Crowd?" *The Sign* 25 (September 1945): 11–12.

DeCurtis, Anthony. "Introduction: The Sanctioned Power of Rock & Roll." *South Atlantic Quarterly* 90 (fall 1991): 635–47.

Devall, Bill, and George Sessions. "Deep Ecology." Reprinted in *Earth Ethics: Environmental Ethics, Animal Rights, and Practical Applications,* edited by James P. Sterba, 157–65. Englewood Cliffs, N.J.: Prentice Hall, 1995.

DiMaggio, Marian. "Third National Street Preaching Institute for Priests, Carthage, Missouri, July 7–11, 1947." *Catholic Action* 29 (August 1947): 12–13.

Dolan, Jay P. *The American Catholic Experience: A History from Colonial Times to the Present.* Rev. ed. Notre Dame, Ind.: University of Notre Dame Press, 1992.

———. *Catholic Revivalism: The American Experience, 1830–1900.* Notre Dame, Ind.: University of Notre Dame Press, 1978.

Dolan, Timothy M. *Some Seed Fell on Good Ground: The Life of Edwin V. O'Hara*. Washington, D.C.: Catholic University of America Press, 1992.

Donaghy, Harry, and Kate Donaghy. "Adjusting to Life in the Country." *Integrity* 7 (January 1953): 3–9.

Dorcy, Mary Jean. *Our Lady of the Fields*. Land and Home Booklets. Des Moines: National Catholic Rural Life Conference, 1957.

Dorman, Robert L. *The Revolt of the Provinces: The Regionalist Movement in America, 1920–1945*. Chapel Hill: University of North Carolina Press, 1993.

Dorn, Jacob H. "The Rural Ideal and Agrarian Realities: Arthur E. Holt and the Vision of a Decentralized America in the Interwar Years." *Church History* 52 (1983): 49–65.

Doyle, Mary Virginia. "Stumping for God." *America* 72 (3 March 1945): 426–27.

"The Drift from the Farm." *America* 45 (19 September 1931): 558.

"Editor of *Social Justice*" [Frederick P. Kenkel]. "Granger Subsistence Homesteads." *Central-Blatt and Social Justice* 29 (January 1936): 305–6.

Egerton, John. *Speak Now against the Day: The Generation before the Civil Rights Movement in the South*. Chapel Hill: University of North Carolina Press, 1994.

Eisele, Susan Frawley. "My Fair Lady." *The Christian Farmer* 1 (October 1947): 6.

Eisenberg, Ellen. *Jewish Agricultural Colonies in New Jersey, 1882–1920*. Syracuse, N.Y.: Syracuse University Press, 1995.

Ellison, Curtis W. *Country Music Culture: From Hard Times to Heaven*. Jackson: University Press of Mississippi, 1995.

Ellwood, Robert S., and Harry B. Partin. *Religious and Spiritual Groups in Modern America*. 2d ed. Englewood Cliffs, N.J.: Prentice Hall, 1988.

Esser, Ignatius, O.S.B. "Significant Chapters in Benedictine History." *Catholic Rural Life Bulletin* 1 (November 1938): 21.

Etcheson, Nicole. *The Emerging Midwest: Upland Southerners and the Political Culture of the Old Northwest, 1787–1861*. Bloomington: Indiana University Press, 1996.

Fabry, Judith K. "The Surplus Farm Population: Agricultural Policy-Makers and the Program for Older Rural Youth, 1935–1940." *Journal of the West* 31 (October 1992): 26–32.

Faulkner, Edward H. *Plowman's Folly*. 1943. Reprint, Covelo, Calif.: Island Press, 1987.

Fillingim, David. "The Gospel Songs and the Cheatin' Songs: Redneck Theological Discourse and the Problem of Suffering." *Studies in Popular Culture* 19 (October 1996): 185–95.

———. "Redneck Liberation: Country Music as Theology." Paper presented at the American Academy of Religion convention, San Francisco, November 1997.

Fink, Deborah. *Agrarian Women: Wives and Mothers in Rural Nebraska, 1880–1940*. Chapel Hill: University of North Carolina Press, 1992.

Finke, Roger, and Rodney Stark. *The Churching of America, 1776–1990: Winners and Losers in Our Religious Economy*. New Brunswick, N.J.: Rutgers University Press, 1992.

Fischer, David Hackett. *Albion's Seed: Four British Folkways in America*. New York: Oxford University Press, 1989.

Fisher, James Terence. *The Catholic Counterculture in America, 1933–1962*. Chapel Hill: University of North Carolina Press, 1989.

———. *Dr. America: The Lives of Thomas A. Dooley, 1927–1961*. Amherst: University of Massachusetts Press, 1997.

Fitzgerald, Daniel. *Ghost Towns of Kansas: A Traveler's Guide*. Lawrence: University Press of Kansas, 1988.

Flynn, Kevin, and Gary Gerhardt. *The Silent Brotherhood: The Chilling Inside Story of America's Violent Anti-government Militia Movement.* New York: Signet, Penguin, 1995.

Foucault, Michel. *The Archeology of Knowledge.* Translated by A. M. Sheridan Smith. New York: Pantheon, 1972.

Fox, Matthew. *Original Blessing: A Primer in Creation Spirituality.* Santa Fe, N.M.: Bear & Company, 1983.

———. *Sheer Joy: Conversations with Thomas Aquinas on Creation Spirituality.* San Francisco: HarperSanFrancisco, 1992.

France, Albert L. C. "Economics and Authority." *Commonweal* 14 (14 October 1931): 581.

Freking, Edward A. "Catholic Action through Mission Action." *Catholic Action* 19 (1937): 13–14.

Gaffey, James P. *Francis Clement Kelley and the American Catholic Dream.* 2 vols. Bensenville, Ill.: Heritage Foundation, 1980.

Garraghan, Gilbert J. *The Jesuits of the Middle United States.* 3 vols. New York: America Press, 1938.

Gauchat, William. "Cult, Culture, and Cultivation." *Catholic Rural Life Bulletin* 4 (August 1941): 64–66.

———. "Our Lady of the Wayside Farm." *The Catholic Worker* 16 (June 1949): 5.

———. "Reflections on the Green Revolution." *The Catholic Worker* 20 (May 1953): 5.

Geissler, Eugene S. "Family Acres." Parts 1, 2. *New Heaven/New Earth,* 1984, 9–10; January 1985, 4, 10.

———. "Shaw, Chesterton, and the Country Boy." *Catholic Rural Life Bulletin* 3 (November 1940): 24–25.

Gerlach, Russell. *Immigrants in the Ozarks: A Study in Ethnic Geography.* Columbia: University of Missouri Press, 1975.

Gibeau, Dawn. "What Is Most Exalted about Life in America Is Still Most Likely to Be Found on the Land." *National Catholic Reporter* 30, no. 3 (5 November 1993): 5–9.

Gilmore, Jeane. *The Legacy: The History of the St. Joseph Catholic Church, Edina, Missouri.* Quincy, Ill.: Jost & Kiefer, 1974.

Ginder, C. Richard. "Mass at Your Doorstep." *The Columbia* 17 (November 1937): 10, 21.

Gleason, Philip. *The Conservative Reformers: German-American Catholics and the Social Order.* Notre Dame, Ind.: University of Notre Dame Press, 1968.

———. *Keeping the Faith: American Catholicism Past and Present.* Notre Dame, Ind.: University of Notre Dame Press, 1987.

Goad, Jim. *The Redneck Manifesto: How Hillbillies, Hicks, and White Trash Became America's Scapegoats.* New York: Simon & Schuster, Touchstone, 1997.

Goering, Violet, and Orlando J. Goering. "Jewish Farmers in South Dakota—The Am Olam." *South Dakota History* 12 (1982): 232–47.

Goldstein, David. "Lay Street Preaching." In *The White Harvest: A Symposium on Methods of Convert Making,* edited by John A. O'Brien, 209–38. New York: Longmans, Green, 1930.

Gottlieb, Roger. "The Transcendence of Justice and the Justice of Transcendence: Mysticism, Deep Ecology, and Political Life." *Journal of the American Academy of Religion* 67 (March 1999): 149–66.

Gould, Rebecca Kneale. "Getting (Not Too) Close to Nature: Modern Homesteading as Lived Religion in America." In *Lived Religion in America: Toward a History of Practice,* edited by David D. Hall, 217–42. Princeton, N.J.: Princeton University Press, 1997.

Grailville staff. *Restore the Sunday: The Christian Concept of the Sunday and Practical Suggestions for the Sanctification of the Sunday in Lay Life.* Loveland, Ohio: Grailville, 1949.

Graves, William, Gilbert Garraghan, S.J., and George Towle. *Kickapoo Mission and Parish: The First Catholic Church in Kansas.* St. Paul, Kans.: The Journal Press, 1938.

Greeley, Andrew. *The Church and the Suburbs.* New York: Sheed & Ward, 1959; rev. ed., Red Bank, N.J.: Deus Books, Paulist Press, 1963.

Green, Harvey. *The Uncertainty of Everyday Life, 1915–1945.* New York: HarperCollins, 1992.

Hahn, Hugo, C.Ss.R. "Motor-Mission Front." *Catholic Digest* 7 (December 1942): 23–27.

Hallett, Paul H. "Giuseppe Sarto's Boyhood." *Land and Home* 7 (1944): 50.

Halsey, William M. *The Survival of American Innocence: American Catholicism in an Era of Disillusionment, 1920–1940.* Notre Dame, Ind.: University of Notre Dame Press, 1980.

Harp, Maureen A. "The Leopoldine Foundation, Slovene Missionaries, and Catholic Rural Migration." *Mid-America* 75 (January 1993): 23–43.

Harrell, David Edwin, Jr. "Religious Pluralism: Catholics, Jews, and Sectarians." In *Religion in the South: Essays,* edited by Charles Reagan Wilson, 59–82. Jackson: University Press of Mississippi, 1985.

Harrington, Michael. *The Other America: Poverty in the United States.* 1962. Reprint, Penguin Books, 1965.

Harwood, William L. "The Ku Klux Klan in North Dakota." *South Dakota History* 4 (1971): 301–35.

Hatch, Nathan O. *The Democratization of American Christianity.* New Haven, Conn.: Yale University Press, 1989.

Hayne, Donald. "Westphalia: Pattern and Promise." *Catholic Rural Life Bulletin* 2 (August 1939): 18–19, 28.

Heaney, Larry. "Grow Your Own Food." *The Catholic Worker* 16 (June 1949): 4.

———. "Toehold on the Land." *The Catholic Worker* 14 (June 1947): 3.

———. "Toehold on the Land." *The Catholic Worker* 14 (January 1948): 5.

———. "Toehold on the Land." *The Catholic Worker* 15 (July–August 1948): 4.

———. "Work on the Land." *The Catholic Worker* 8 (September 1941): 8.

Heat Moon, William Least [William Trogdon]. *Blue Highways: A Journey into America.* Boston: Atlantic–Little, Brown, 1982.

Hennesey, James, S.J. *American Catholics: A History of the Roman Catholic Community in the United States.* New York: Oxford University Press, 1981.

Henthorne, Sister Mary Evangela, B.V.M. *The Irish Catholic Colonization Association of the United States.* Champaign, Ill.: Twin City, 1932.

Hermann, LaDonna. *Memories of "Isabelle": A 1929 Model A Ford Who Loved Life.* Privately published, 1991.

Hildner, George J. *One Hundred Years for God and Country: St. John's, the Church and the Community, 1839–1940.* Washington, Mo.: Washington Missourian, 1940.

Hilfer, Anthony Channell. *The Revolt from the Village, 1915–1930.* Chapel Hill: University of North Carolina Press, 1969.

Hinsdale, Mary Ann, Helen M. Lewis, and S. Maxine Walker. *It Comes from the People: Community Development and Local Theology.* Philadelphia: Temple University Press, 1995.

Hitchcock, James. "Postmortem on a Rebirth: The Catholic Intellectual Renaissance." *American Scholar* 49 (spring 1980): 211–25.

Hobgood-Oster, Laura. "Stories Told through Animal Saints." Paper presented at the American Society of Environmental History convention, Tacoma, Wash., 18 March 2000.

Hoehn, Matthew, O.S.B. *Catholic Authors: Contemporary Biographical Sketches, 1930–1947.* Newark, N.J.: St. Mary's Abbey, 1948.

Hogan, John J. *On the Mission in Missouri, 1857–1868.* 1892. Glorieta, N.M.: Rio Grande Press, 1976.

Howard, Thomas E. *Agricultural Handbook for Rural Pastors and Laymen: Religious, Economic, Social, and Cultural Implications of Rural Life.* Paterson, N.J.: St. Anthony's Guild, 1946.

Hudnut-Beumler, James. *Looking for God in the Suburbs: The Religion of the American Dream and Its Critics, 1945–1965.* New Brunswick, N.J.: Rutgers University Press, 1994.

Huff, Peter A. *Allen Tate and the Catholic Revival: Trace of the Fugitive Gods.* New York: Paulist Press, 1996.

Hughes, Olin E. "An Analysis of Farm Building Costs." M.A. thesis, University of Missouri at Columbia, 1932.

Hugo, John. *Weapons of the Spirit: Living a Holy Life in Unholy Times—Selected Writings of Father John Hugo.* Edited by David Scott and Mike Aquilina. Huntington, Ind.: Our Sunday Visitor, 1997.

Hurt, R. Douglas. *Agriculture and Slavery in Missouri's Little Dixie.* Columbia: University of Missouri Press, 1992.

Hutton, J. Gladden. "The Worn-out Farm." *Catholic Rural Life Bulletin* 2 (August 1939): 2.

Hutton, Leon. "Catholicity and Civility: John Francis Noll and the Origins of *Our Sunday Visitor.*" *U.S. Catholic Historian* 16 (spring 1998): 1–22.

Hynes, Emerson. "Consider the Person." *Catholic Rural Life Bulletin* 1 (May 1939): 7.

Isenmenter, Gordon. "The McIntosh German-Russians: The First Fifty Years." *North Dakota History* 51 (1984): 4–11.

Issel, William H. "Ralph Borsodi and the Agrarian Response to Modern America." *Agricultural History* 41 (April 1967): 155–66.

Jackson, Kenneth. *The Ku Klux Klan in the City, 1915–1930.* 1967. Reprint, New York: Elephant, Basic, 1992.

Jenkins, Philip. *Hoods and Shirts: The Extreme Right in Pennsylvania, 1925–1950.* Chapel Hill: University of North Carolina Press, 1997.

Jenkins, William D. *Steel Valley Klan: The Ku Klux Klan in Ohio's Mahoning Valley.* Kent, Ohio: Kent State University Press, 1990.

Jensen, Mildred. "Back to the Land." *The Catholic Woman's World* 3 (January 1941): 43, 48–49.

Kane, Paula M. *Separatism and Subculture: Boston Catholicism, 1900–1920.* Chapel Hill: University of North Carolina Press, 1995.

Kauffman, Christopher J. *Faith and Fraternalism: The History of the Knights of Columbus, 1882–1982.* New York: Harper & Row, 1982.

——. *Mission to Rural America: The Story of W. Howard Bishop, Founder of Glenmary.* New York: Paulist Press, 1991.

Kelley, Francis Clement. *The Story of Extension.* Chicago: Extension Press, 1922.

Kelly, George A. *The Catholic Family Handbook.* New York: Random House, 1959.

Kelly, Joseph. "What Does Youth Want?" *Catholic Rural Life Bulletin* 4 (February 1941): 12–13.

Kelly, Mary Gilbert, O.P. *Catholic Immigrant Colonization Projects in the United States, 1815–1860.* United States Catholic Historical Society Monograph Series, no. 17. New York: United States Catholic Historical Society, 1939.

Kerrigan, William. "The Trappists and the Prairie." *Land and Home* 7 (September 1944): 64–65.

Kleber, Albert, O.S.B. *Ferdinand, Indiana, 1840–1940: A Bit of Cultural History.* St. Meinrad, Ind.: n.p., 1940.

Kolehmainen, John Ilmari, and George W. Hill. *A Haven in the Woods: The Finns of Northern Wisconsin.* 2d ed. Madison: State Historical Society of Wisconsin, 1965.

Kroes, Rob. *The Persistence of Ethnicity: Dutch Calvinist Pioneers in Amsterdam, Montana.* Urbana: University of Illinois Press, 1992.

Kselman, Thomas A., and Steven Avella. "Marian Piety and the Cold War in the United States." *Catholic Historical Review* 72 (July 1986): 403–24.

La Farge, John, S.J. "Agriculture and Vocation." *Christian Rural Fellowship Bulletin* 34 (September 1938): 1–6.

———. "Catholic Agrarians Swing into Action." *America* 56 (14 November 1936): 129–30.

———. "Granger Prospers on an Iowa Prairie." *America* 68 (31 October 1942): 96–97.

———. "The Land: The Hope of the Future." In National Catholic Rural Life Conference, *Proceedings of the Eleventh Convention (1933),* 70–74. Washington, D.C.: National Catholic Welfare Conference, Rural Life Bureau, n.d.

———. *The Manner Is Ordinary.* New York: Harcourt, 1954.

———. "Unity of Mankind through Creation and Redemption, Basis of Interracial Justice." *The Queen's Work,* December 1934, 1, 7, 10.

———. "What May We Expect of the Landward Movement?" *Catholic Action* 14 (September 1932): 9–12.

Lane, Belden. *The Solace of Fierce Landscapes: Exploring Desert and Mountain Spirituality.* New York: Oxford University Press, 1998.

"Leaders Meet at Kansas Monastery." *Landward* 5 (spring 1937): 11.

Lears, T. J. Jackson. *No Place of Grace: Antimodernism and the Transformation of American Culture, 1889–1920.* New York: Pantheon, 1981.

Lee, Martha F. *Earth First! Environmental Apocalypse.* Syracuse, N.Y.: Syracuse University Press, 1995.

Leftwich, W. M. *Martyrs in Missouri.* Chicago: n.p., 1868.

Leopold, Aldo. *A Sand County Almanac.* London: Oxford University Press, 1949.

Lernoux, Penny. *Cry of the People: The Struggle for Human Rights in Latin America—The Catholic Church in Conflict with U.S. Policy.* Rev. ed. New York: Penguin Books, 1991.

Leven, Stephen A. "Can Street Preaching Help?" *Homiletic and Pastoral Review* 37 (1937): 691–97.

———. *Go Tell It in the Streets.* Edmund, Okla.: n.p., 1984.

———. "That There Be One Flock and One Shepherd." *Catholic Rural Life Bulletin* 1 (November 1938): 10–13, 16.

Lewis, Sinclair. *Main Street.* New York: New American Library, 1961.

Lexau, Henry. "Preaching on Ozark Trails." *Catholic Digest* 14 (January 1950): 59–63.

Ligutti, Luigi. "Cities Kill." *Commonweal* 32 (2 August 1940): 300–301.

———. "The Monsignor Says." *The Christian Farmer* 1 (October 1947): 1, 2.

———. "No Room for Others." *Land and Home* 8 (June 1945): 22–23.

———. "The Pope of Peace." *Catholic Rural Life* 7 (October 1958): 14.

———. "The Popes and Agriculture: A Brief Survey of Papal Documents Relating to the Soil and the Principles of Rural Life." *Commonweal* 31 (1 March 1940): 397–99.

———. "Religious Vacation Schools." *Catholic Rural Life* 4 (April 1926): 3.

———. "What's Wrong with Farmers?" *America* 69 (24 April 1943): 66–67.

Ligutti, Luigi, and John C. Rawe, S.J. *Rural Roads to Security: America's Third Struggle for Freedom.* Milwaukee, Wis.: Bruce, 1940.

Liph, Samson. "Jewish Farm Settlement." *Land and Home* 7 (September 1944): 62–64.

Longfield, Bradley J. *The Presbyterian Controversy: Fundamentalists, Modernists, and Moderates.* New York: Oxford University Press, 1994.

Lorenz, Roger S. "Outstretched Hand." *The Catholic Worker* 20 (June 1953): 5.

Lowdermilk, Walter C. "'Lebensraum'—Agrarianism vs. War." *Catholic Rural Life Bulletin* 3 (November 1940): 16–21.

Lucey, Lawrence. "A Cooperative Town: Resettlement Administration at Hightstown, New Jersey." *Commonweal* 25 (18 December 1936): 210–12.

Lund, Mary Ann. "Girls in Oklahoma." *Catholic Digest* 5 (January 1941): 72–74.

Lutzenberger, José, and Melissa Halloway. "The Absurdity of Modern Agriculture: From Chemical Fertilizers and Agropoisons to Biotechnology." In *The Meat Business: Devouring a Hungry Planet,* edited by Geoff Tansey and Joyce D'Silva. New York: St. Martin's Press, 1999.

Lynd, Robert S., and Helen Merrell Lynd. *Middletown: A Study in Modern American Culture.* San Diego, Calif.: Harcourt, Brace & Company, 1957.

Madison, James H. "Reformers and the Rural Church, 1900–1950." *Journal of American History* 81 (1987): 638–57.

———, ed. *Heartland: Comparative Histories of the Midwestern States.* Bloomington: Indiana University Press, 1988.

Maffly-Kipp, Laurie. "Eastward Ho! American Religion from the Perspective of the Pacific Rim." In *Retelling U.S. Religious History,* edited by Thomas A. Tweed, 127–48. Berkeley: University of California Press, 1996.

Marquardt, John. "Sorghum Stir-Off." *Mission Digest* 9 (October 1951): 34–36.

Marx, Paul B., O.S.B. *Virgil Michel and the Liturgical Movement.* Collegeville, Minn.: St. John's Abbey–Liturgical Press, 1957.

Marx, Walter J. "The Matanuska Colony." *Commonweal* 46 (23 May 1947): 139–41.

Massa, Mark S. *Catholics and American Culture: Fulton Sheen, Dorothy Day, and the Notre Dame Football Team.* New York: Crossroad, 1999.

Masters, Edgar Lee. *Spoon River Anthology.* New York: Macmillan, 1962.

Matt, Alphonse J. "The Family and Social Security." *Catholic Rural Life Bulletin* 2 (May 1939): 6–8.

Maurin, Peter. *The Green Revolution: Essays on Catholic Radicalism.* 1949. Chicago: Francis of Assisi House, 1976.

———. "Idle Hands and Idle Lands." *The Catholic Worker* 3 (February 1936): 1.

McAniff, John E. "The Catholic Evidence Guild on the Street Corner." *The Catholic Mind* 38 (8 February 1940): 53–60.

McCarraher, Eugene. "American Gothic: Sacramental Radicalism and the Neo-Medievalist Cultural Gospel, 1928–1948." *Records of the American Catholic Historical Society of Philadelphia* 106 (spring/summer 1995): 3–23.

———. "The Saint in the Gray Flannel Suit: The Professional-Managerial Class, 'The Layman,' and American-Catholic-Religious Culture, 1945–1965." *U.S. Catholic Historian* 16 (spring 1998): 99–118.

McCarron, Edward. "A Brave New World: The Irish Agrarian Colony of Benedicta, Maine in the 1830s and 1840s." *Records of the American Catholic Historical Society of Philadelphia* 105 (1994): 1–15.

McCarthy, Abigail Q. *Private Faces, Public Places.* Garden City, N.Y.: Doubleday, 1972.

McCool, Gerald, S.J. *Nineteenth-Century Scholasticism: The Quest for a Unitary Method.* Rev. ed. New York: Fordham University Press, 1989.

McCrank, Lawrence J. "Religious Orders and Monastic Communalism in America." In *America's Communal Utopias,* edited by Donald E. Pitzer, 204–52. Chapel Hill: University of North Carolina Press, 1997.

McDannell, Colleen. *Material Christianity: Religion and Popular Culture in America.* New Haven, Conn.: Yale University Press, 1995.

McDean, Harry. "Western Thought in Planning Rural America: The Subsistence Homesteads Program, 1933–1935." *Journal of the West* 31 (October 1992): 15–25.

McDonough, Peter. *Men Astutely Trained: A History of the Jesuits in the American Century.* New York: Free Press, 1992.

McFague, Sallie. *Models of God: Theology for Ecological, Nuclear Age.* Philadelphia: Fortress Press, 1987.

McGoey, Francis J. "The Canadian Landward Movement." In *Rural Catholic Action,* Diocesan Director's Series No. 1, 35–38. Washington, D.C.: National Catholic Welfare Conference, Rural Life Bureau, 1936.

McGreevy, John T. *Parish Boundaries: The Catholic Encounter with Race in the Twentieth-Century Urban North.* Chicago: University of Chicago Press, 1997.

McKiernan, Eoin. "Horse and Buggy Church." *The Catholic World* 155 (July 1942): 475–77.

McMahon, Dorothy. "Maryfarm." *The Catholic Worker* 19 (May 1953): 2.

McNamara, John E. "Religious Difficulties among Catholic Farmers." *Catholic Rural Life Bulletin* 1 (May 1938): 21–22.

McNamee, Joseph F. *Sketches of the Pioneer Priests.* Pacific, Mo.: Plowman Press, 1928.

McNicholas, John T. "Experiments in Solving Rural Catholic Problems." *St. Isidore's Plow* 2 (January 1924): 4.

McShane, James, S.J. "Sodality Activities in a Rural Parish." *Homiletic and Pastoral Review* 44 (December 1943): 185–89.

Meehan, James T., S.J. "Catholic Oberlin." *Land and Home* 6 (March 1943): 22–23.

"Meet Madonna of the Highways." *Extension* 56 (August 1961): 20–24.

Mellen, Francis. "A Farm Colonization Experiment." *Catholic Charities Review* 16 (1932): 288.

Mencken, H. L. *A Mencken Chrestomathy.* New York: Knopf, 1949; reprint, New York: Vintage, Doubleday, 1982.

Messmer, S[ebastian] G. "Some Moral Aspects of Country Life." *St. Isidore's Plow* 1 (March 1923): 2.

Michel, Virgil, O.S.B. "Agriculture and Reconstruction." *Commonweal* 29 (13 January 1939): 317–18.

———. "Christian Education for Rural Living." *Catholic Rural Life Bulletin* 1 (August 1938): 19–20.

———. "City or Farm?" *Orate Fratres* 12 (1938): 367–69.

———. Letter. *Catholic Rural Life Bulletin* 1 (August 1938): 3.

Mikolasek, V. F. "Bohemian Catholic Rural Activities." *Catholic Rural Life* 3 (July 1925): 6.

Miller, L[ouis] G., C.Ss.R. "Some Agrarian Beginnings." *Catholic Rural Life Bulletin* 3 (November 1940): 22–23.

Miller, Raymond W. *Monsignor Ligutti: The Pope's County Agent.* Washington, D.C.: University Press of America, 1981.

Millet, John H., S.J. "The Catholic Action Rural Movement." *American Ecclesiastical Review* 117 (November 1947): 348–60.

"Mission Trailer: Paulist Fathers, Tennessee." *Liturgical Arts* 6 (second quarter 1937): 68–69.

"Missionary Work in Rural Parishes." *Catholic Rural Life* 3 (May 1925): 5.

"Missouri Cooperative." *The Catholic Worker* 10 (March 1943): 8.

Molitor, Donald F. "The History of Glennonville and Adjacent Catholic Colonization Ventures in Southeastern Missouri: A Study in Changing Rural-Urban Patterns, 1905–1947." M.A. thesis, Saint Louis University, 1967.

Monahan, William. "Farm Demonstration as a Method of Extension Teaching." *St. Isidore's Plow* 1 (January 1923): 1.

Mondello, Salvatore. "Baptist Railroad Churches in the American West, 1890–1946." In *Religion and Society in the American West: Historical Essays,* edited by Carl Guarneri and David Alvarez, 105–27. Lanham, Md.: University Press of America, 1987.

Moore, Andrew. "Catholics in the Modern South: The Transformation of a Religion and a Region, 1945–1975." Ph.D. diss., University of Florida, 2000.

Moore, Leonard J. *Citizen Klansmen: The Ku Klux Klan in Indiana, 1921–1928.* Chapel Hill: University of North Carolina Press, 1991.

Moore, R. Laurence. *Religious Outsiders and the Making of Americans.* New York: Oxford University Press, 1986.

———. *Selling God: American Religion in the Marketplace of Culture.* New York: Oxford University Press, 1994.

Muench, Aloysius J. "Religion and Agrarianism." *The Catholic Mind* 38 (8 November 1940): 438–46.

National Catholic Rural Life Conference. *Catholic Rural Life Songs.* Des Moines: NCRLC, n.d.

———. *Manifesto on Rural Life.* Milwaukee, Wis.: Bruce, 1939.

———. *A Manual of Ceremonies for the Parish Observance of the Rogation Days.* Des Moines: NCRLC, 1953.

———. *NCRLC Proposals, 1937.* St. Paul, Minn.: NCRLC, 1938.

———. *1957: Serving Rural America 35 Years, National Catholic Rural Life Conference.* Des Moines: NCRLC, 1957.

———. *Proceedings of the Eleventh Annual Convention, 1933.* Washington, D.C.: National Catholic Welfare Conference, Rural Life Bureau, n.d.

———. *Proceedings of the Twelfth Annual Conference, 1934.* Washington, D.C.: National Catholic Welfare Conference, Rural Life Bureau, n.d.

———. "Rural Life in a Peaceful World." Statement of principles and methods adopted at the Wartime Meeting of the NCRLC executive committee and advisory board. Des Moines: NCRLC, 1944.

———. *St. Isidore, Patron of the Farmer.* Des Moines: NCRLC, n.d.

"The Negro." *The Catholic Worker* 15 (September 1948): 1, 4.

"Negro Agricultural School." *The Catholic Worker* 15 (September 1948): 1, 4.

"News from the Field." *Jesuit Educational Quarterly* 2 (March 1940): 207.

"News from the Field." *Jesuit Educational Quarterly* 3 (June 1940): 52–53.

Nietzsche, Friedrich. *Thus Spoke Zarathustra.* Translated by R. J. Hollingdale. New York: Penguin Books, 1969.

"Notes and Comments: Bishop Winkelmann." *Catholic Rural Life Bulletin* 3 (February 1940): 15.

"Notes and Comments: Catholic Farmers' Conference." *Catholic Rural Life Bulletin* 3 (November 1940): 15.

"Notes and Comments: Mr. and Mrs. R. B." *Catholic Rural Life Bulletin* 4 (May 1941): 45.

"Notes and Comments: The Papacy Forever!" *Catholic Rural Life Bulletin* 2 (May 1939): 14.

"Notes and Comments: The Popes and Agriculture." *Catholic Rural Life Bulletin* 4 (May 1941): 44.

"Notes and Comments: Songs and Singing." *Catholic Rural Life Bulletin* 2 (May 1939): 15.

Novitsky, Anthony. "The Ideological Development of Peter Maurin's Green Revolution." Ph.D. diss., State University of New York at Buffalo, 1977.

Nutting, Willis D. "The Catholic College and the Land." *Catholic Rural Life Bulletin* 1 (November 1938): 2–4, 22–24.

———. "What I Gained." In *The Road to Damascus: The Spiritual Pilgrimage of Fifteen Converts to Catholicism*, edited by John A. O'Brien, 153–67. Garden City, N.Y.: Image, Doubleday, 1955.

"N. Y. Milk Strikers Ask for Greater Share of Profits." *The Catholic Worker* 1 (September 1933): 1, 4.

O'Brien, C. M. "Economic and Sociological Aspects of the Columbia Basin Project." *Catholic Rural Life Bulletin* 2 (November 1939): 4–6, 28–29.

O'Brien, David. *American Catholics and Social Reform: The New Deal Years*. New York: Oxford University Press, 1968.

———. *Isaac Hecker: An American Catholic*. New York: Paulist Press, 1992.

O'Brien, John A. "Methods of Reaching Converts." In *The White Harvest: A Symposium on Methods of Convert Making*, edited by John A. O'Brien, 239–66. New York: Longmans, Green, 1930.

———. "Street Preaching among the Tarheels." *Ave Maria* 66 (4 October 1947): 423–26.

O'Connor, Flannery. *Wise Blood*. 2d ed. New York: Farrar, Straus & Giroux, 1962.

Oelschlaeger, Max. *Caring for Creation: An Ecumenical Approach to the Environmental Crisis*. New Haven, Conn.: Yale University Press, 1994.

O'Hara, Edwin V. "The Church and Rural Life." *St. Isidore's Plow* 1 (October 1922): 1.

———. *The Church and the Country Community*. New York: Macmillan, 1927.

———. "The Clergy and Rural Life." *St. Isidore's Plow* 2 (October 1923): 3.

O'Hara, Eileen. "Maryfarm." *The Catholic Worker* 15 (September 1948): 4.

Ong, Walter, S.J. *Frontiers of American Catholicism: Essays on Ideology and Culture*. New York: Macmillan, 1957.

Orsi, Robert A. *The Madonna of 115th Street: Faith and Community in Italian Harlem, 1880–1950*. New Haven, Conn.: Yale University Press, 1985.

O'Toole, James. *Militant and Triumphant: William Henry Cardinal O'Connell and the Catholic Church in Boston, 1859–1944*. Notre Dame, Ind.: University of Notre Dame Press, 1992.

Oved, Yaacov. *Two Hundred Years of American Communes*. New Brunswick, N.J.: Transaction Books, 1987.

Overman, Conleth, C.P. "The American Street-Preaching Movement." *Homiletic and Pastoral Review* 42 (1942): 432–37.

Owen, Louise. "Kill . . . and Cure." *Land and Home* 6 (June 1943): 52.

Ownby, Ted. *Subduing Satan: Religion, Recreation, and Manhood in the Rural South, 1865–1920*. Chapel Hill: University of North Carolina Press, 1990.

Parlette, Ralph. "The Cities Do Not Make Their Own Steam." *Catholic Rural Life* 3 (November 1925): 6.

Paul VI, Pope. "Humanae Vitae." In *The Papal Encyclicals*, vol. 5, *1958–1981*, translated by Claudia Carlen, 223–36. New York: McGrath, Consortium Books, 1981.

Paul, Marty. "Diary of a Romantic Agrarian." *Commonweal* 57 (2 January 1953): 327–30.

———. "Holy Family Farm." *The Catholic Worker* 16 (June 1949): 5.

———. "Holy Trinity Farm." *The Catholic Worker* 16 (February 1949): 7.

———. "Toehold on the Land—#1." *The Catholic Worker* 14 (September 1947): 3.

Perkins, Mary. "Heaven on Wheels." *The Sign* 22 (September 1942): 77–79.

Phillips, Carl. "Catechism Summer Schools." *St. Isidore's Plow* 1 (May 1923): 2.

Piehl, Mel. *Breaking Bread: The Catholic Worker and the Origin of Catholic Radicalism in America.* Philadelphia: Temple University Press, 1982.

Pitzer, Donald E. "America's Communal Utopias Founded by 1965." In *America's Communal Utopias,* edited by Donald E. Pitzer, 449–94. Chapel Hill: University of North Carolina Press, 1997.

———, ed. *America's Communal Utopias.* Chapel Hill: University of North Carolina Press, 1997.

Pius XII, Pope. "Address to the International Catholic Congress on Rural Problems, July 2, 1951." Reprinted as "Problems of Rural Life," *The Catholic Mind* 49 (October 1951): 708–11.

Placher, William C. *Unapologetic Theology: A Christian Voice in a Pluralistic Conversation.* Louisville, Ky.: Westminster/John Knox Press, 1989.

Pleasants, Julian. "Apologetics and Catholic Action." *The Notre Dame Scholastic,* 1940, 8.

———. "Basic Research to Save the Home." *America* (29 November 1947): 235–37.

———. "Four Acre Farming." *Interpreter,* March 1954, 17.

Poole, Stafford, C.M., and Douglas Slawson, C.M. *Church and Slave: Perry County, Missouri, 1818–1865.* Lewiston, N.Y.: Edwin Mellen Press, 1986.

Potvin, Rollande. "Summer at Maryfarm." *The Catholic Worker* 20 (October 1953): 8.

Prentiss, Craig R. "Taming Leviathan: The American Catholic Church and Economics, 1940–1960." Ph.D. diss., University of Chicago, 1997.

Proceedings of the National Catechetical Congress of the Confraternity of Christian Doctrine, 1939. Paterson, N.J.: St. Anthony Guild, 1940.

Pruett, Katharine M., and John D. Fair. "Promoting a New South: Immigration, Racism, and 'Alabama on Wheels.'" *Agricultural History* 66 (1992): 19–41.

Quinlan, Patrick T. "Catholic Social Teaching on Rural Life." *Catholic Mind* 43 (March 1945): 160–64.

———. *Standing on Both Feet: The Rural Homestead, a Necessity for an Era of Reconstruction.* Des Moines: National Catholic Rural Life Conference, n.d.

Radway, Janice. "On the Gender of the Middlebrow Consumer and the Threat of the Culturally Fraudulent Female." *South Atlantic Quarterly* 93 (fall 1994): 871–93.

Ragen, Brian Abel. *A Wreck on the Road to Damascus: Innocence, Guilt, and Conversion in Flannery O'Connor.* Chicago: Loyola University Press, 1989.

Rauth, Marian. "Apostolate in the Mountains." *The Catholic World* 166 (December 1947): 259–62.

Rawe, John C., S.J. "Biological Technology on the Land." *Catholic Rural Life Bulletin* 2 (August 1939): 1–3, 20–22.

———. "The Home on the Land." *Catholic Rural Life Bulletin* 2 (Feb. 1939): 24–25.

———. "Homesteading Solves the Problem of Farm Decline." *America* 60 (3 December 1938): 200–201.

———. "What, Where, and Why of Bio-Dynamics." *Land and Home* 6 (September 1943): 67–68.

Reinhold, H[einrich] A. "Back to . . . What?" *Worship* 26 (April 1952): 248–54.

Ribuffo, Leo. *The Old Christian Right: The Protestant Far Right from the Great Depression to the Cold War.* Philadelphia: Temple University Press, 1983.

Ridgeway, James. *Blood in the Face: The Ku Klux Klan, Aryan Nations, Nazi Skinheads, and the Rise of a New White Culture.* Rev. ed. New York: Thunder's Mouth Press, 1995.

"Right to be Unruly: The Terminiello Free Speech Case." *America* 81 (11 June 1949): 334

Riney-Kehrberg, Pamela. *Rooted in Dust: Surviving Drought and Depression in Southwestern Kansas.* Lawrence: University Press of Kansas, 1994.

Robb, Dennis Michael. "Specialized Catholic Action in the United States, 1936–1949: Ideology, Leadership, and Organization." Ph.D. diss., University of Minnesota, 1973.

Ruether, Rosemary Radford. *Gaia and God: An Ecofeminist Theology of Earth Healing.* San Francisco: HarperSanFrancisco, 1992.

Rural Parish Workers of Christ the King Newsletter. Vols. 1 (November 1946), 2 (November 1947), 6 (November 1951).

"The Rural Pastor's Page: Priests and Seminarians." *Land and Home* 7 (June 1944): 46.

Said, Edward W. *Orientalism.* New York: Vintage, 1979.

St. Joseph's Sesquicentennial, 1835–1985, Westphalia, Missouri. Westphalia, Mo.: n.p., 1985.

"St. Mary of the Highways Trailer Chapel." *Liturgical Arts* 7 (February 1939): 27.

"St. Teresa's Village Is Run on Principles of Democracy." *Action: A Catholic Pictorial News Monthly* 1 (June 1938): 6–10.

Sample, Tex. *White Soul: Country Music, the Church, and Working Americans.* Nashville, Tenn.: Abingdon Press, 1996.

Santen, Herman W. *Father Bishop, Founder of the Glenmary Home Missioners.* Milwaukee, Wis.: Bruce, 1961.

Santmire, H. Paul. *The Travail of Nature: The Ambiguous Ecological Promise of Christian Theology.* Philadelphia: Fortress Press, 1985.

Scharff, Virginia. *Taking the Wheel: Women and the Coming of the Motor Age.* New York: Free Press, 1991.

Scheckel, Roger Joseph. "The Origins of the National Catholic Rural Life Conference: A Historical and Theological Analysis." M.A. thesis, Catholic University of America, 1984.

Schilthuis, Willy. *Biodynamic Agriculture.* Translated by Tony Langham and Plim Peters. Hudson, N.Y.: Anthroposophic Press, 1994.

Schmiedeler, Edgar, O.S.B. *A Better Rural Life.* New York: Wagner, 1938.

———. "Beyond the NRA." *Commonweal* 19 (22 September 1933): 485–87.

———. *Catholic Rural Life.* Washington, D. C.: National Council of Catholic Men, 1932.

———. "Churches on Wheels." *Homiletic and Pastoral Review* 40 (January 1940): 361–74.

———. "Little Motor Mission Rationing." *Homiletic and Pastoral Review* 43 (1943): 503–16.

———. *Marriage and the Family.* New York: McGraw-Hill, 1946.

———. "Motor Missions." *American Ecclesiastical Review* 100 (February 1939): 132–42.

———. "Motor Missions." *Homiletic and Pastoral Review* 38 (March 1938): 578–88.

———. "Motor Missions, 1940." *Homiletic and Pastoral Review* 41 (1941): 388–400.

———. *Rural Catholic Action.* Huntington, Ind.: National Council of Catholic Men; Our Sunday Visitor, 1932.

———. "Trailing the Trailer Chapels." *Homiletic and Pastoral Review* 42 (1942): 237–48.

———. "Why Rural Life?" In National Catholic Rural Life Conference, *Proceedings of the Eleventh Convention, 1933,* 5–9. Washington, D.C.: National Catholic Welfare Conference, Rural Life Bureau, n.d.

Schneider, Mary L. "Visions of Land and Farmer: American Civil Religion and the National Catholic Rural Life Conference." In *An American Church: Essays on the Americanization of the Catholic Church,* edited by David J. Alvarez, 99–112. Moraga, Calif.: St. Mary's College of California, 1979.

Schreuder, Yda. *Dutch Catholic Immigrant Settlement in Wisconsin, 1850–1905.* New York: Garland, 1989.

Schuck, Michael J. *That They Be One: The Social Teaching of the Papal Encyclicals, 1740–1989.* Washington, D.C.: Georgetown University Press, 1991.

Schuler, Rudolph B. "Cooperation in the St. Louis Archdiocese." *Catholic Rural Life Bulletin* 4 (August 1941): 67–70.

———. "The St. Louis Archdiocesan Program." In *Rural Catholic Action,* Diocesan Director's Series, 5–12. Washington, D.C.: National Catholic Welfare Conference Rural Life Bureau, 1936.

Schüssler Fiorenza, Elisabeth. *In Memory of Her: A Feminist Theological Reconstruction of Christian Origins.* New York: Crossroad, 1983.

Schwieder, Dorothy. *Iowa: The Middle Land.* Ames: Iowa State University Press, 1996.

Seavoy, Ronald E. "Portraits of Twentieth-Century American Peasants: Subsistence Social Values Recorded in *All God's Dangers* and *Let Us Now Praise Famous Men.*" *Agricultural History* 68 (1994): 195–219.

Settle, William A. *Jesse James Was His Name; or, Fact and Fiction concerning the Careers of the Notorious James Brothers of Missouri.* Columbia: University of Missouri Press, 1966.

Shannon, James P. *Catholic Colonization on the Western Frontier.* New Haven, Conn.: Yale University Press, 1957.

Shapiro, Edward S. "Catholic Agrarian Thought and the New Deal." *Catholic Historical Review* 65 (1979): 583–99.

———. "The Catholic Rural Life Movement and the New Deal Farm Program." *American Benedictine Review* 28 (1977): 307–32.

———. "Decentralist Intellectuals and the New Deal." *Journal of American History* 58 (March 1972): 938–57.

Sheed, Frank. "Street Corner Apologetic." *American Ecclesiastical Review* 90 (1934): 44–56.

Sheldrake, Rupert. *The Rebirth of Nature: The Greening of Science and God.* New York: Rochester, VT: Park Street Press, 1994.

Shi, David. *The Simple Life: Plain Living and High Thinking in American Culture.* New York: Oxford University Press, 1985.

Shortridge, James R. *The Middle West: Its Meaning in American Culture.* Lawrence: University Press of Kansas, 1989.

Skillin, Edward, Jr. "Armchair Husbandry." *Commonweal* 35 (27 March 1942): 554–57.

———. "Coop's End in Hightstown." *Commonweal* 32 (3 May 1940): 31.

———. "Decentralization and the Land." *Commonweal* 31 (19 May 1939): 88–89.

———. "Granger Homesteads." *Commonweal* 32 (24 May 1940): 93–96.

———. "Homework That Pays." *Commonweal* 34 (5 September 1941): 465–69.

Slawson, Douglas. "Thirty Years of Street Preaching: Vincentian Motor Missions, 1934–1965." *Church History* 62 (1993): 60–81.

Smith, Eva. "Farming Commune." *The Catholic Worker* 8 (September 1941): 8.

———. "Vision on the Farm." *Commonweal* 34 (27 June 1941): 228.

Smith, Martin Cruz. *Gorky Park.* New York: Ballantine Books, 1981.

Sorg, Rembert, O.S.B. *Towards a Benedictine Theology of Manual Labor.* Lisle, Ill.: Benedictine Orient, 1951.

Sourd, Raphael. "Echoes from the Mission Front." *The Challenge* 6, no. 2 (summer 1943): 4.

Spalding, Thomas W., C.F.X. "German Parishes East and West." *U.S. Catholic Historian* 14 (1996): 37–52.

Sparr, Arnold. *To Promote, Defend, and Redeem: The Catholic Literary Revival and the Cultural Transformation of American Catholicism, 1920–1960.* New York: Greenwood, 1990.

Steinbeck, John. *The Grapes of Wrath*. New York: Viking, 1939.

Stephens, Edward L. "The Motor Chapel in a Diocesan Mission Program." In *Proceedings of the National Catechetical Congress of the Confraternity of Christian Doctrine, 1939*, 324–30. Paterson, N.J.: St. Anthony Guild, 1940.

Stock, Catherine McNicol. *Main Street in Crisis: The Great Depression and the Old Middle Class on the Northern Plains*. Chapel Hill: University of North Carolina Press, 1992.

Strain, Charles R. "The Pacific Buddha's Wild Practice: Gary Snyder's Environmental Ethic." In *American Buddhism: Recent Understandings and Scholarship*, edited by Duncan Ryuken Williams and Stephen S. Queen, 143–67. Richmond, U.K.: Curzon, 1999.

Stricklin, David. *A Genealogy of Dissent: The Culture of Progressive Protest in Southern Baptist Life, 1920–1995*. Lexington: University Press of Kentucky, 1999.

"Subsistence Homesteads of Earlier Days: Austria in the Eighteenth Century." *Central-Blatt and Social Justice* 29 (November 1936): 235–36.

"Superior School of Agriculture, Ste. Anne-de-la-Pocatière, Quebec." *Commonweal* 30 (15 September 1939): 484.

Susman, Warren I. *Culture as History: The Transformation of American Society in the Twentieth Century*. New York: Pantheon, 1984.

Swanson, Merwin. "The American Country Life Movement, 1900–1940." Ph.D. diss., University of Minnesota, 1972.

———. "The 'Country Life Movement' and the American Churches." *Church History* 45 (1977): 358–73.

Swierenga, Robert P. "Theoretical Perspectives on the New Rural History: From Environmentalism to Modernization." *Agricultural History* 56 (1982): 495–502.

Taves, Ann. *The Household of Faith: Roman Catholic Devotions in Mid-Nineteenth-Century America*. Notre Dame, Ind.: University of Notre Dame Press, 1986.

Taylor, Sarah McFarland. "From the American Dream to the Dream of the Earth: Remapping Religion and Culture at Genesis Farm." Paper presented at the annual conference of the Society for the Scientific Study of Religion, San Diego, Calif., 9 November 1997.

Taylor, Wilma Rugh, and Norman Thomas Taylor. *This Train Is Bound for Glory: The Story of America's Chapel Cars*. Valley Forge, Pa.: Judson Press, 1999.

Tentler, Leslie Woodcock. "'A Model Rural Parish': Priests and People in the Michigan 'Thumb,' 1923–1928." *Catholic Historical Review* 78 (1992): 413–30.

———. "On the Margins: The State of American Catholic History." *American Quarterly* 45 (March 1993): 104–27.

Terminiello, Arthur W. "The Catholic Settlement." In *Proceedings of the Second Annual Meeting of the Catholic Conference of the South*, 65–67. Richmond, Va.: n.p., 1942.

———. "Discussion of James Cunningham's Report." In *Proceedings of the First Annual Meeting of the Catholic Conference of the South*, 68–70. Richmond, Va.: n.p., 1941.

Thomas, John L., S.J. *The Catholic Viewpoint on Marriage and the Family*. Garden City, N.Y.: Hanover House, 1958.

Thomas, John, and James McShane. "Farmers Must Reform Methods of Farming." *Catholic Rural Life Bulletin* 4 (November 1941): 100–103, 106.

Thorman, Donald. "Experiment in Christian Living." *Voice of St. Jude*, November 1960, 20.

Thuesen, Peter J. *In Discordance with the Scriptures: American Protestant Battles over Translating the Bible*. New York: Oxford University Press, 1999.

Tichi, Cecelia. *High Lonesome: The American Culture of Country Music*. Chapel Hill: University of North Carolina Press, 1994.

Toole, John Kennedy. *A Confederacy of Dunces*. New York: Grove, 1980.

Towey, Martin. "Kerry Patch Revisted: Irish Americans in St. Louis in the Turn of the Century Era." In *From Paddy to Studs: Irish-American Communities in the Turn of the Century Era, 1880–1920*, edited by Timothy J. Meagher, 139–59. New York: Greenwood, 1986.

Toy, Eckard V. "Robe and Gown: The Ku Klux Klan in Eugene, Oregon." In *The Invisible Empire in the West: Toward a New Historical Appraisal of the Ku Klux Klan of the 1920s*, edited by Shawn Lay, 153–84. Urbana: University of Illinois Press, 1992.

Tracy, David. *The Analogical Imagination: Christian Theology and the Culture of Pluralism*. New York: Crossroad, 1981.

Tweed, Thomas A., ed. *Retelling U.S. Religious History*. Berkeley: University of California Press, 1996.

"Two Rural Life Conferences." *St. Isidore's Plow* 2 (October 1923): 2.

Uhl, Timothy D. "The Naming of Catholic Parishes in St. Louis." Ph.D. diss., Saint Louis University, 1997.

Urbain, Joseph V. "Educating Rural Youth for Home Life." *Family Digest* 1 (February 1946): 41–42.

"Vast Areas of Nation Priestless." *The Challenge* 1 (1938): 1.

Veysey, Laurence. *The Communal Experience: Anarchist and Mystical Counter-Cultures in America*. New York: Harper & Row, 1973.

Villmer, Natalie. *History of the Old Mines Area, Washington County, Missouri*. Old Mines, Mo.: Old Mines Area Historical Society, 1973.

Wachsmuth, Guenther. *The Life and Work of Rudolf Steiner from the Turn of the Century to His Death*. 2d ed. Translated by Olin D. Wannamaker and Reginald E. Raab. Blauvelt, N.Y.: Garber Communications, 1955.

Walker, Williston, et al. *A History of the Christian Church*. 4th ed. New York: Charles Scribner's Sons, 1985.

Walsh, James J. *The Thirteenth, the Greatest of Centuries*. New York: Catholic Summer School Press, 1907.

Walsh, Richard, C.S.P. "Here Is Great Adventure." *The Sign* 25 (August 1945): 23–25.

Ward, Leo R., C.S.C. "The Land and Human Values." *Catholic Rural Life Bulletin* 1 (August 1938): 2–4, 18.

Weaver, Mary Jo. "Resisting Catholic Sexual Teaching: Pro-Choice Advocacy and Homosexual Support Groups." In *What's Left? Liberal American Catholics*, edited by Mary Jo Weaver, 88–108. Bloomington: Indiana University Press, 1999.

———, ed. *What's Left? Liberal American Catholics*. Bloomington: Indiana University Press, 1999.

Westfall, William. "Voices from the Attic: The Canadian Border and the Writing of American Religious History." In *Retelling U.S. Religious History*, edited by Thomas A. Tweed, 181–99. Berkeley: University of California Press, 1996.

White, G. Edward. *Creating the National Pastime: Baseball Transforms Itself, 1903–1953*. Princeton, N.J.: Princeton University Press, 1996.

Widmer, Alice, and LaDonna Hermann. *Bits of History*. N.p., 1992.

Williamson, J. W. *Hillbillyland: What the Movies Did to the Mountains and What the Mountains Did to the Movies*. Chapel Hill: University of North Carolina Press, 1995.

Wilson, Charles Morrow. "American Peasants." *Commonweal* 20 (8 December 1933): 147–49.

Wilson, Charles Reagan. *Baptized in Blood: The Religion of the Lost Cause, 1865–1920*. Athens: University of Georgia Press, 1980.

Winkelmann, Christian H. "The City Church Helps the Country Church." In *Rural Catholic Action,* Diocesan Director's Series, 53–56. Washington, D.C.: National Catholic Welfare Conference Rural Life Bureau, 1936.

Witte, Raymond, S.M. *Twenty-five Years of Crusading: A History of the National Catholic Rural Life Conference.* Des Moines: National Catholic Rural Life Conference, 1948.

Wolf, C. E[dward]. "Granger's Fifth Birthday." *Commonweal* 34 (24 January 1941): 348–49.

———. "I Left College to Become a Farmer." *Catholic Rural Life Bulletin* 4 (February 1941): 1–4.

Wortmann, Ray. "Coughlin in the Countryside: Father Charles Coughlin and the National Farmers Union." *U.S. Catholic Historian* 13 (1995): 97–120.

Wright, Joseph P. "The Farmer Goose Steps." *Social Justice,* new series, 1A (7 March 1938): 5, 18.

Wuest, Francis. "The Apostleship of Speech." *The Challenge* 5 (spring 1942): 8.

Wuthnow, Robert. *The Restructuring of American Religion.* Princeton, N.J.: Princeton University Press, 1988.

"A Year with the Rural Parish Workers." *Review for Religious* 12 (September 1953): 242–48.

Yzermans, Vincent A. *The People I Love: A Biography of Luigi G. Ligutti.* Collegeville, Minn.: Liturgical Press, 1976.

Index